D1548315

Anthropology of Tourism in Central and Eastern Europe

Anthropology of Tourism:
Heritage, Mobility, and Society

Series Editors

Michael A. Di Giovine (West Chester University of Pennsylvania),
Noel B. Salazar (University of Leuven)

Mission Statement

The Anthropology of Tourism: Heritage, Mobility, and Society series provides anthropologists and others in the social sciences and humanities with cutting-edge and engaging research on the culture(s) of tourism. This series embraces anthropology's holistic and comprehensive approach to scholarship, and is sensitive to the complex diversity of human expression. Books in this series particularly examine tourism's relationship with cultural heritage and mobility and its impact on society. Contributions are transdisciplinary in nature, and either look at a particular country, region, or population, or take a more global approach. Including monographs and edited collections, this series is a valuable resource to scholars and students alike who are interested in the various manifestations of tourism and its role as the world's largest and fastest-growing source of socio-cultural and economic activity.

Advisory Board Members

Quetzil Castañeda, Saskia Cousin, Jackie Feldman, Nelson H. H. Graburn, Jafar Jafari, Tom Selwyn, Valene Smith, Amanda Stronza, Hazel Tucker, and Shinji Yamashita

Books in Series

Alternative Tourism in Budapest: Class, Culture, and Identity in a Postsocialist City, by Susan E. Hill
Tourism and Prosperity in Miao Land: Power and Inequality in Rural Ethnic China, by Xianghong Feng
Tourism and Language in Vieques: An Ethnography of the Post-Navy Period, by Luis Galanes Valldejuli
Cosmopolitanism and Tourism: Rethinking Theory and Practice, edited by Robert Shepherd
Apprenticeship Pilgrimage: Developing Expertise through Travel and Training, by Lauren M. Griffith and Jonathan S. Marion
Anthropology of Tourism in Central and Eastern Europe: Bridging Worlds, edited by Sabina Owsianowska and Magdalena Banaszkiewicz

Anthropology of Tourism in Central and Eastern Europe

Bridging Worlds

Edited by
Sabina Owsianowska
and Magdalena Banaszkiewicz

Foreword by
Michał Buchowski

LEXINGTON BOOKS
Lanham • Boulder • New York • London

Published by Lexington Books
An imprint of The Rowman & Littlefield Publishing Group, Inc.
4501 Forbes Boulevard, Suite 200, Lanham, Maryland 20706
www.rowman.com

Unit A, Whitacre Mews, 26-34 Stannary Street, London SE11 4AB

British Library Cataloguing in Publication Information Available

Library of Congress Cataloging-in-Publication Data Is Available

ISBN 978-1-4985-4381-1 (cloth: alk. paper)
ISBN 978-1-4985-4382-8 (electronic)

∞™ The paper used in this publication meets the minimum requirements of American National Standard for Information Sciences—Permanence of Paper for Printed Library Materials, ANSI/NISO Z39.48-1992.

Printed in the United States of America

Contents

Acknowledgments

The book that we place in your hands is a special creation—it is the result of the involvement of many people who challenged each other to "bridge worlds."

Looking for a handy metaphor that would portray the essence of tourism anthropology, we can use the image of a meeting on a road. Both the physical (when the anthropologist goes out to meet people and the phenomena that he/she will investigate) and intellectual (when confronted with his/her ideas in dialogue with other research proposals). In both senses, there is an encounter, opening wider horizons and revealing new paths. This unique meeting, which inspired the creation of this volume, was the international conference "Anthropology of Tourism—Heritage and Perspectives" held on June 1–2, 2015 in Kraków. Most of the authors of this book took part in this conference, as well as a vast number of others, who for various reasons could not participate in this publication.

Therefore, we would first like to thank all participants and conference organizers, especially the outstanding keynote speakers: Prof. Anna Wieczorkiewicz, Prof. Cara Aitchison, Prof. Nelson Graburn, and Prof. Tom Selwyn. Their enthusiasm for building bridges has become the foundation for this project. We are very grateful to Prof. Michał Buchowski, who saw the potential in our initiative and enriched the book with his introduction. We also thank Naomi Leite for her commitment, despite all the difficulties. Obviously, we are inexpressibly thankful to all authors, whose commitment firmly exceeded our expectations.

We would like to show our gratitude to the Lexington Books editors who gave us confidence and support at every stage of our work. First of all, Michael di Giovine and Noel Salazar, whose openness for dialogue was fundamental in coming into terms with all the cultural and linguistic nuances and the reviewers whose constructive comments helped us to enhance significantly the book. Furthermore, we thank Kasey Beduhn for motivating and supporting us by her encouraging correspondence.

We would like to especially thank our loved ones, who stayed by us all this time, generously sharing their advice and empowering us to achieve our goals.

Lastly, thanks to all who accompanied us on this journey in any way, without whom we would not have been able to reach our destination.

Foreword

Michał Buchowski

As the editors of this book write, studies on tourism in Central and Eastern Europe (CEE) were established a long time ago, in some countries already in the 1950s, in others, later.[1] For instance, the first academic chair focusing explicitly on this topic in Poland was established in Poznań in 1975. It is true that freedom of movement in the communist bloc was much more restricted than in the so-called West, but that does not mean tourism did not exist there or even thrive. The internal tourist industry, often organized and subsidized by the state, was very popular among ordinary people and millions of them spent holidays at the seaside, by lakes, and in the mountains using public—subsidized by the state or state-owned companies—tourist infrastructure. In the 1970s, cross-border tourism became quite common and, even though the communist system was famous for controlling access to passports that enabled travel to noncommunist countries (although, in general, this policy was liberal in Yugoslavia, and was steadily liberalized in Poland and Hungary since the beginning of the 1970s), tourists could quite easily go for holidays within the socialist camp borders by simply using their ordinary identity cards. Such a massive and popular phenomenon attracted the attention of scholars and, therefore, research institutions focused on tourism was the obvious outcome. However, it means that studies on tourism are not a total novelty in CEE.

Yet another issue is the anthropology of tourism which, as such, was not practiced in CEE. There were two major reasons for this state of affairs. First, ethnology under socialist regimes was based on continental models of *Volkskunde* and *Völkerkunde*. In the late socialist period, between the early 1970s and the collapse of the Berlin Wall in 1989, in some of the most liberal communist countries, Anglo-American sociocultural anthropology ideas began to be imported on an unprecedented scale up to that time. Ultimately, it led to the creation of a hybrid model of a discipline, which takes its inspiration from both continental ethnology and anthropology. However, back then, the anthropology of tourism as it is understood today, could simply not exist, although a historically ethnographic description of any region was part and parcel of *krajoznawstwo*, or *Landeskunde* in German, which included information relevant for touristic purposes and for all those who show their love for a country, *Landesliebe*. The boom in internal tourism in the communist era was followed by several studies concerned with relations between local populations and visitors. These studies paid attention to the effects tourism and tourist-designated souvenir production had on the transformations of local traditions, especially "traditional handicrafts" and the standardization of artistic styles. One could compare these efforts to the mode of analysis carried out by Theron A. Nuñez,[2] in which tourism was interpreted in traditional disciplinary paradigms. In today's vocabulary, these kinds of endeavors would be described as "tourism and cultural heritage studies." Within this framework, changes in local population lifestyles and modes of subsistence were also addressed. Secondly, one should also keep in mind that "anthropology of tourism" itself is a young subdiscipline. As Georgette L. Burns writes, although anthropological articles on tourism in specialized journals appeared in the 1970s, first such texts in anthropological journals were published only a decade ago and, later, Dennison Nash's article,[3] published in the globally circulated *Current Anthropology*, stands as a milestone in the publication record of the anthropology of tourism. For a long time, interest in the topic was not considered a serious academic undertaking in anthropological circles.

It is a pleasure to write a few introductory words to this book edited by Magdalena Banaszkiewicz and Sabina Owsianowska. It represents the CEE anthropologists' reaction to the increased tourist mobility in the region and beyond. This mobility is different than that witnessed in the socialist past in its form and meaning and, therefore, researching it is a timely and adequate scholarly response to new social practices. Also, the conceptual tools used to interpret these events and trends are distinct from past ones, arising from novel anthropological findings produced all around the world, and, additionally, from an application of original analytical tools enabling the interpretation of specific local phenomena.

This book, *Anthropology of Tourism in Central and Eastern Europe: Bridging Worlds*, is yet another in a series of works demonstrating that anthropology in the region has been doing well for a long time and has gained pace in the last three decades. Arguments feeding the image of the theoretically backward and thematically retarded academics in CEE can merely uphold unfounded stereotypes. These unsubstantiated claims tend to reproduce existing hierarchies of knowledge according to which academic centers, practically all of them placed in Western academia, and most of them in English-speaking countries, are foundries of avant-garde ideas that should be emulated elsewhere.[4] In the globalized academia, this image can no longer be sustained, although existing differences in economic and symbolic capitals do not help to advance appeals for equality based on quality espoused by the "world anthropologies movement."[5] The point is not to blindly copy models imposed by privileged knowledge producers of entrenched power relations but to advance multidirectional flow of knowledge leaning on exchange of concepts and understandings derived from diverse sources. This is a quest for a cosmopolitan and decentralized knowledge which, at the same time, is embedded in local contexts.

The best way to implement these ideas, laudable and profitable for advancement of knowledge, is to conduct research and share the results in an innovative, justifiable, and convincing manner for other researchers. This book represents all those virtues. It proves that the skillful combination of local traditions and imported ideas brings results which are communicable worldwide, shedding new light on important social phenomena and enriching their general erudition. It also confirms that the demise of the Iron Curtain does not involve a change of perspective only in the former socialist countries, but it forces scholars in the West and elsewhere to change theirs.

NOTES

1. I have written this text as a visiting overseas professor at the National Museum of Ethnology in Osaka, Japan, in the 2016–2017 academic year. I thank my hosts for their support for my research.

2. Theron A. Nuñez, "Tourism, Tradition and Acculturation: Weekendismo in a Mexican Village," *Ethnology* 2 (1963): 347–52.

3. Georgetta A. Burns, "Anthropology and Tourism: Past Contributions and Future Theoretical Challenges," *Anthropological Forum* 14 (2004): 5–22.

4. Michał Buchowski, "Intricate Relations between Western Anthropologists and Eastern Ethnologists," *Focaal: Journal of Global and Historical Anthropology* 63 (2012): 20–38.

5. Cf. Gustavo Lins Ribeiro, "World Anthropologies: Anthropological Cosmopolitanism and Cosmopolitics," *Annual Review of Anthropology* 43 (2014): 483–98.

REFERENCES

Buchowski, Michał. "Intricate Relations between Western Anthropologists and Eastern Ethnologists." *Focaal: Journal of Global and Historical Anthropology* 63 (2012): 20–38.

Burns, Georgetta A. "Anthropology and Tourism: Past Contributions and Future Theoretical Challenges." *Anthropological Forum* 14 (2004): 5–22.

Nash, Dennison. "Tourism as an Anthropological Subject." *Current Anthropology* 22 (1981): 461–81.

Nuñez, Theron A. "Tourism, Tradition and Acculturation: Weekendismo in a Mexican Village." *Ethnology* 2 (1963): 347–52.

Ribeiro, Gustavo Lins. "World Anthropologies: Anthropological Cosmopolitanism and Cosmopolitics." *Annual Review of Anthropology* 43 (2014): 483–98.

Introduction

Anthropological Studies on Tourism in Central and Eastern Europe

Magdalena Banaszkiewicz and
Sabina Owsianowska

Anthropology of Tourism in Central and Eastern Europe: Bridging Worlds
aims to dispose of limitations on the anthropological study of tourism, which
stem from both the domination of researchers from Western Europe, the
United States, Australia, and New Zealand and the specific situation of studies on tourism in Central and Eastern Europe (CEE). The long-lasting political separation of the region after the Second World War meant that scientists
typically did not enjoy easy access to the latest trends of anthropological
research, the opportunity for a direct exchange of experiences, and a chance
to take part in international projects. After the political transformation of
Eastern Bloc states, started in 1989, many of those limitations disappeared,
but the geographic, economic, and linguistic roadblocks still play a part
and mean that the academic achievements of researchers from Central and
Eastern Europe are not known well enough in the international environment.
It is worth distinguishing that scholars from CEE work both in the region and
out of the region, since one of the characteristic consequences of the transi-
tional processes is a brain drain—an outflow of highly qualified scholars who
search for more pleasant environments. The specific historical, social, and
political situation creates barriers that limit the influence of the researchers
who work in the region on the developing anthropology of travel and tourism.

The main subjects of this book concern the anthropological background
of tourism studies and inspirations that cultural and social anthropologists
can find for their research in analyses of past and contemporary travels. In
this introduction, we will try to outline the determinants of our conception of
this book, the meeting of different academic traditions that is reflected by the

metaphor of the bridge. The debate over the title was an excellent opportunity to confront research perspectives, verify intellectual roots, and negotiate stylistic traits. Tourism, predicated on Otherness,[1] provides an exceptional occasion for examining this diversity and facilitates the kinds of dialogues we feel are important in the inter- and intra-disciplinary pursuit of knowledge.

CENTRAL AND EASTERN EUROPE

First of all, we would like to strongly highlight the use of the term "Central and Eastern Europe" instead of the wider-known "Eastern Europe." It has always been problematic to define precisely the boundaries of Western and Eastern Europe, since this attempt was basically conceptual and, as such, it referred to various, equivocal indicators (historical, geographical, cultural, political). Moreover, as long as the Iron Curtain covered up the heterogeneity of Eastern Europe, it was not so debatable in general, Western discourse. However, after the fall of communism, the fragmentation of this part of the continent became more visible.

We refer, thus, to a term that may raise questions: firstly, why the term "Central and Eastern Europe" should be used; secondly, whether it is possible to clearly distinguish the two parts; and thirdly, what countries each of the territories includes. The division of Europe into Western and Eastern, established after the Second World War, unveiled differences between the parts that were relatively easy to point out: the Iron Curtain separated the zones of influence of the victorious powers, as well as set different directions for development. From the *westerners'* perspective, all postsocialist countries were referred to as "Eastern Europe," regardless of intraregional, historical, cultural, and social as well as economic diversification. However, the sense of continual belonging to Europe and Western civilization among the inhabitants of countries between East and West has been a source of resistance in such unequivocal situations. It is noteworthy that such a clash of viewpoints is the essence of the debate on Central Europe, on the concepts underlying the idea, the criteria for defining the region, and the attempts to demarcate its geographical boundaries.[2]

The changes initiated in 1989 made the term "Eastern Europe" a simplification too far-reaching and detached from reality. Discussions were triggered on identity and belonging to Europe (implicitly, Western Europe, and institutionally also to the European Union); borders, borderlands, and territorial reconfigurations; and memory of the former multicultural and multiethnic character of the areas, which was forgotten for decades and restored after the collapse of communism. The process of EU enlargement significantly proved that Eastern Europe is not a homogeneous monolith—some countries from the early 1990s strived for accession (e.g., Poland). Others, preoccupied with domestic problems, could not (e.g., Croatia). Some were more hesitant about this perspective (Ukraine) or even openly rejected this idea (Belarus).

Particularly for postsocialist countries, membership in the European Union has symbolically impersonated belonging to Europe "as Europe" and has opened a new chapter in a discussion about globalization/regionalism, identity, and values. Initially, the German concept of *Mitteleuropa* was strictly geopolitical. Since the 1970s the term "Central Europe" has come to be used as the emancipatory tool for determining a region's mental and cultural membership to the Western European tradition fixed by currents like the Renaissance or Enlightenment. For Central Europe, conceptualized as the West "kidnapped" by the "barbaric, Asiatic East,"[3] it was highly important to go back to its European roots and outline its own unique identity after 1989. Therefore, we adhere to the distinction between Central-Eastern Europe (e.g., Poland, Slovakia, Czech Republic, Austria, the Baltic States) and Eastern Europe (e.g., Ukraine, Belarus, Russia) and propose that this intentionally exclusive perspective can be argued with reference to tradition in scholarship among others.

To summarize, Central Europe is a historical-geopolitical concept and a symbolic construction that appeared in response to identity dilemmas and that definitely extends beyond the boundaries of any territory within the wider area of Eastern Europe. This determines the inclusion of authors representing countries closely related to the region's past; for example, ones that were not under Soviet dominance but had a significant role in previous centuries (e.g., Austria), as well as those that culturally and mentally might seem closer to Northern Europe and Scandinavia yet are part of the former communist system (e.g., Estonia). By taking into account various points of view we have tried to embrace the complexity, ambiguity, and interconnectedness of issues and case studies analyzed in our book.

BRIDGING WORLDS

This book reflects on the condition of the regional scholarship attempting to become visible and audible in the global academic world. In Cold War discourse, the division of the states of Earth into three broad categories—the first world (the Western countries), the second world (the Eastern Bloc), and the third world (all countries that remained nonaligned with either NATO or the Communist Bloc)—has been a quite powerful geopolitical concept. After 1989 it ceased to be functional in the political sense, but the impact of the different historical paths has still been noticeable. The symbol of the bridge gives us a very simple but strong image that helps to anchor reflection on the meeting(s) between intellectual traditions, alliances of research, or stages of scholarship development. In that sense, our book contributes to the wider discussion concerning the geopolitics of knowledge.[4] The spatial disproportion of the impact of various intellectual traditions, with the predominance of Anglophone discourse, is deeply rooted in the past and can be recognized as one of the symptoms of the division into the center and the peripheries. The Western expansion was not limited only to the economy and politics, but spread into educational and intellectual matters. Therefore, as Ribeiro and Escobar claim: "We can understand the dominance of some styles of anthropology only if we relate them to unequal power relations."[5] While in other regions this remark refers to the postcolonial condition, in Central and Eastern Europe we may relate it to postsocialism.[6] Over the last quarter of a century, we notice a considerable increase in the international exchange of knowledge. Yet the process of "giving voice" to minorities marginalized in the dominant Anglophone discourse is difficult because of the deep asymmetries in relations, of which the language barrier seems to be the most obvious example. The problem of linguistic hegemony of international anthropological scholarship that many of us face is simple: publish in English or perish.[7] On one hand, its consequence is "metropolitan provincialism," which is the "Western" ignorance of knowledge production of practitioners on non-hegemonic sites. "Metropolitan provincialism" is contradicted by "provincial cosmopolitanism."[8] Scholars from non-hegemonic sites often have exhaustive knowledge of the production of hegemonic centers, but they lack discernment of their own "academic yard," because it is regarded as weaker. Stanislav Ivanov, a Bulgarian tourism scholar and editor-in-chief of the *European Journal of Tourism Research*, considering the small representation of scientists from CEE on the scientific boards of fifty major magazines in the field of tourism, notes: "The Iron Curtain towards former communist countries in Central and Eastern Europe in the field of tourism/hospitality studies has not fallen yet!"[9]

While working on this book, we had to face the fact that information flow is rather limited when it comes to the state-of-the-art of scholarship in native languages other than English. The growing popularity of Internet-based initiatives that support the exchange of knowledge plays an invaluable role in facilitating such contact, but we must frankly admit that scholars even from one region often get to know each other's achievements only after they start to circulate within the Anglophone environment. Therefore, even though the dominance of English as the modern *lingua franca* evokes much hesitation, the only possible way to establish some balance in global knowledge production is to strongly support every initiative that presents achievements of periphery scholarship in English (one among the significant examples of fruitful East-West dialogue was MESS—Mediterranean Ethnological Summer School—carried out between 1994 and 2010). This book is one project of that kind, the work of many people who have initiated a dialogue across boundaries. The conference "Anthropology of tourism—heritage and perspectives," held in Kraków in 2015, which gathered almost a hundred scientists, many of whom came from abroad,[10] became a stimulus for the book. It showed that in CEE, research in tourism is being carried out in the anthropological perspective, and that at the same time some scholars among the Anglophone scientists' circle are keenly interested in exchanging ideas and experiences with representatives of the "periphery," as well as strongly supporting the process of giving voice to minorities.

ANTHROPOLOGY OF TOURISM IN CENTRAL AND EASTERN EUROPE

Another important record of the existence of geopolitics of knowledge is the terminological diversity connected with the roots and traditions of the scholarship of anthropology of tourism in particular and anthropology in general. We would like to outline the specifics of the Central and Eastern European tradition, which though strongly anchored in global scholarship, has its own unique features.[11]

Historically speaking, the main difference lies in the close ties of Western anthropology to colonialism.[12] While anthropologists from the colonial states concentrated mostly on the "noble savage" of the periphery, the tradition of those countries that did not conquer overseas regions is different. Instead of searching for "primitive Others," who live in very distant regions, local researchers limited their interest mostly to the native country people who were considered to be the "local alterity."[13] It has been particularly significant for those nations in CEE (e.g., Poles, Latvians, Czechs) that, in the nineteenth century, had to sustain/create their identity without political sovereignty—the intellectuals strived to find in their own "primitive Others" an embodiment of the authentic spirit of national culture.[14] Collecting old songs, tales, and descriptions of rituals became for the first ethnographers like Oskar Kolberg[15] in Poland or Ilmari Manninen[16] in Estonia the basis for expressing national identity and solidarity. Peasants' culture was considered to be archaic and untouched by civilization, which should have enabled the first generations of scholars to track in the country life a linkage to the past and roots of the national culture. The study of folklore in this part of Europe was, however, different in comparison to the situation in the regions colonialized by the Western empires. Here, it was conducted by local scholars who did the fieldwork mostly personally, contrary to the colonial collectors who represented the conquerors and aimed to publish the material in their own countries and languages. What is more, ethnographic research in CEE was closely related to history, contrary to American tradition where anthropology developed rather as part of the social sciences.[17] The tradition of studying alterity "at home" was reinforced in the Soviet era. Firstly, because of restrictions in the study of exotic cultures overseas, the characteristic lack of mobility outside the Eastern Bloc made impossible any distant fieldwork. Secondly, research on one's own vanishing folk groups was a handy solution to escape the ideological pressure of Marxist-Leninist doctrine.[18] This ethnographic tradition of exploring alterity at home seems to be one of the most significant if not the most significant feature determining the identity of ethnology/anthropology of CEE and is probably the most important contribution of CEE scholarship to world anthropology. However, starting in the 1970s and 1980s, the previous historical orientation as well as the empiricism of ethnography was replaced by a much stronger concentration on modern culture and the search for the new paradigms inspired by increasing contacts with Western scholarship.

Interest in one's own region has borne fruit in the shape of extended anthropological research in the transition and post-transition period. The focus on comparative analysis of the process in different countries with particular attention to changing lifestyles and everyday *milieu* was reflected in the cooperation between regional researchers who more or less simultaneously have been recently trying to tackle the issues of borderlands and transcultural relations, mobility and identity, memory and heritage.[19.]Another important path of inquiry for the past three decades has been meta-reflection on the awkward condition of regional scholarship, shifting between social and cultural anthropology, ethnography/ethnology, and cultural studies.[20]

This leads us to the role of tourism as a specific topic explored from an anthropological perspective within the framework of multidisciplinary tourism studies in Central and Eastern Europe. Because for many decades tourism as a typically modern phenomenon had not been a matter of interest to anthropologists/ethnologists,[21] similarly to Western scholarship, research on tourism development in Central and Eastern Europe was not initially connected with the humanities. In Poland for instance, there were geographers who first created an institutional unit called the Study of Tourism in the 1930s, whose activity was disturbed by the outbreak of the Second World War.[22] The Study was established in 1936 as a result of previous educational and scientific initiatives, dating back to the nineteenth century. The program of teaching included interdisciplinary knowledge, with specific attention given to geography as a comprehensive examination of the natural and sociocultural environment.

After 1945, both in the Soviet Union and in the states that were under its more-or-less direct control, the characteristic feature of tourism research was its orientation in physical culture and sport, and thus the scholarship was more concentrated on health-oriented and leisure functions of tourism, while its important economic and cultural dimensions were underestimated. The development of tourism in the socialist countries was centrally controlled by the state; however, it should be remembered that the period between 1945 and 1990 may be divided into several stages, with different degrees of restriction in mobility.[23] With tourism's popularization not only as a leisure activity, but also as an important sector of the economy, as well as a significant cultural-social phenomenon, new research inspirations, problems, and challenges emerged.[24] Changes in leisure patterns and choices of new travel destinations, both by local residents and visitors from other countries, stimulated initiatives for education and research on tourism, such as the first scientific journals (e.g., *Turizam/Tourism: An International, Interdisciplinary Journal*, issued by Institut za Turizam in Croatia, started in 1953) or faculties of tourism and leisure (e.g., at Polish universities of physical education in Poznań in 1975 and Kraków in 1976).[25]

The political transformation after 1989 brought, among other things, increased mobility of the inhabitants of states previously separated by the Iron Curtain. Tourism dynamically developed and modern infrastructure was created—for example, travel agencies, hotels, and tourist information centers. Gradually, new solutions proven in the Western European countries were implemented, such as construction of the national tourist administration (NTA) and national tourist organizations (NTO). Following the enlargement of the European Union at the beginning of the twenty-first century, tourist development of postsocialist countries was stimulated by support from EU funds. With criteria for awarding grants to specific projects, the EU programs directed further strategic actions of initiators, e.g., taking into account the principles of sustainable tourism development or the multicultural traditions of the region.[26]

In the initial, formational period of the theory of tourism, as mentioned, issues related to the health-oriented significance of tourist activity (including spa tourism), social tourism, ecology, and space planning were dominant. Development of the tourist industry in the postsocialist countries justified the dominance of research from a business perspective (which undoubtedly has become the most powerful orientation in Russian tourism studies). However, since the 1980s, the anthropological dimension of the phenomenon has also been appreciated, continued in times of economic and political transfor-mation in the coming decades. Researchers explored issues such as travel experience; the relationship between guests and hosts; importance of cultural heritage; similarities between postsocialism and postcolonialism; globaliza-tion; sustainability; and the ethics of tourism. Since the 2000s, tourism stud-ies embrace two fundamental areas of research: the first—which is definitely more popular—concerns mainly market issues and the question of manage-ment, while the second goes beyond business and economics and concentrates on the critical study of the phenomenon. One of the first prominent promoters of humanistic reflection on tourism in CEE was Professor Krzysztof Przecławski (1927–2014).[27] In his publications and teaching, he referred to the most important anthropological and sociological concepts, paid attention to ethical issues, analyzed the positive and negative aspects of tourism development, and emphasized its educational role. It is significant that as early as the 1970s, he was actively involved in an international community of tourism researchers; belonged to organizations such as International Academy for the Study of Tourism (IAST) and International Association of Scientific Experts in Tourism (AIEST); and was a member of the editorial board of *Annals of Tourism Research*, invited by its first chief editor, the anthropologist Jafar Jafari. In the 1990s Prof. Przecławski made efforts to create an intercollegiate Department of Tourism on the basis of the University of Physical Education, the University of Economics, and the Jagiellonian University in Kraków, but this proved impossible to achieve.

Despite the fact that the activities of persons interested in anthropological research of tourism are dispersed among various institutions, successful attempts have been made to establish contact and cooperation. Some of them are possible within Erasmus and other EU programs,[28] and some are supported by governmental or nongovernmental bodies. On one hand, new institutes and universities were being established, and scholars—from different basic disciplines—took up topics connected with tourism and the current sociocultural and economic situation. They referred to their native traditions and drew on the experience of scholars from the West. The challenges they faced resulted from regional characteristics and concerned universal dilemmas accompanying the expansion of tourism, such as the commercialization of heritage, the destruction of nature, and interpersonal relationships. The progressive specialization and fragmentation of research on specific topics with the use of tools developed in the basic disciplines, was accompanied by efforts that would lead to the autonomy of the "science(s) of tourism." The accumulated body of knowledge, terminology, and methodology were to form the basis for the separation of that discipline, but the objective has not been achieved until now. On the other hand, the (controversial) tourist industry increasingly attracted the attention of representatives of the humanities and social sciences. Tourism ceased to be regarded as too "trivial" a research issue—as was also the case in Western countries—and it was recognized to be an important phenomenon of cultural and social nature, which was worth analyzing not only in itself, but was "a handy metaphor" used in the description of a (post)modern society.[29]

In fact, it is exceptionally hard to outline the unique contribution of CEE scholarship to global tourism studies. First and foremost, as we have already pointed out, local ideas are not widely recognized. One of the only eagerly cited academics, Zygmunt Bauman, who uses tourism as a metaphorical tool to characterize the condition of consumerist society,[30] arguably represents regional scholarship. Probably the situation would look better if the development of anthropologically oriented tourism studies at a research center did not depend only on the interests of the scholars employed there, but also on such factors as university policy; favor with the department's authorities; the possibility of winning grants; funding participation in conferences and internships abroad; institutional support in translation of texts into English; purchasing books; access to international databases; etc. The fact that drew the attention of the above-cited Ivanov[31] applies not only to the composition of the scientific councils of the fifty most important international journals, but also to the under-representation of papers published by authors from CEE, which, to a great extent, is determined by the indicated factors.

Higher education and research on tourism in CEE function in different fields of knowledge. In the well-known database of Centre d'International de Recherches et d'Études Touristiques (CIRET), composed of approximately fifty institutions, the vast majority of research is associated with the universities or faculties of economics and management, followed by geography and environmental sciences.[32] Such a situation affects the development of anthropologically oriented research on contemporary travel and its place within the framework of interdisciplinary tourism studies and/or other sciences. Noteworthy is the collaboration of research centers on regional and international levels, dealing with different aspects of contemporary travel and the tourist industry, also analyzed anthropologically. In Poland the activity of researchers focused on cultural heritage tourism,[33] including series of monographs or edited volumes (e.g., *Tourism in the humanistic perspectives*); journals (e.g., *Turystyka Kulturowa/Cultural Tourism*); seminars; or conferences should be underlined. In Slovenia, the Faculty of Tourism Studies Turistica has played a very special role in stimulating international and interdisciplinary projects, such as the biennial conference "Encuentros" or summer/winter schools within Erasmus Programme.[34] Even though management and innovation issues are significant in most cases, the organizers do not forget that tourism education cannot be conducted only in the field of vocational training; the liberal, philosophic background of teaching and learning is also important to enhance critical thinking skills, improve ability to analyze and interpret information, and draw conclusions based on overall knowledge.[35] To conclude, there is growing awareness that a solid knowledge of ethnology/cultural anthropology allows better preparation of professionals in tourism.

Although anthropological research on tourism in the CEE is still relatively nascent, several achievements are appreciated, at least at the regional level. They concern both ethnologists/anthropologists examining tourism and tourism researchers referring to anthropological theories and methods. Publications such as Anna Wieczorkiewicz's "Apetyt turysty. O doświadczaniu świata w podróży/A tourist's appetite. The experience of world in travel"[36] or the monographic bilingual edition of the journal *Folia Turistica* titled "The Master Classes"[37] are of particular importance since they provide an overview of many concepts delimiting the directions of anthropological and sociological reflection on tourism.[38] Similarly to initiatives oriented in the cooperation of regional anthropologists in general, there have been a few attempts recently to establish such a regional network among anthropologists who specialize in tourism. The heterogeneity of topics as well as the variety of the authors' academic provenance is remarkably represented by special issues of scientific journals dedicated to anthropology in CEE.[39]

Worth noticing is the fact that topics that particularly attract the attention of scholars from CEE—especially the younger generations—continue the trajectories of regional anthropology, but gain new momentum when implemented to tourism. Below we evoke some researchers who might represent this trend.[40] Modern mobility, migration and tourism, and particularly tourism imaginaries and experience in the context of postcolonial critics are the main area of research of Natalia Bloch. Her study proves a strong linkage to the burgeoning international scholarship on tourism mobilities and tourism imaginaries.[41] As long as Bloch conducted her fieldwork mostly in India, the postcolonial perspective adopted by Anna Horolets, and to a lesser extent by Agata Bachórz,[42] was a tool to explore travel experience in the postsocialist countries and Russia. Both of the authors recognize the importance of historical and cultural background in tourist encounters. One of the willingly undertaken topics is also various effluences of heritage and the challenges connected with its utilization in tourism. Magdalena Banaszkiewicz has recently explored postsocialist heritage that becomes a tourist attraction and—in consequence—a source of dissonances in interpretations and narratives. Sabina Owsianowska, whose earlier research concentrated on semiotics and tourism discourse, has recently examined the Polish borderlands' difficult heritage, its new images, and historical narratives created for tourism purposes, to reveal forgotten pasts of different ethnic and national groups. Juraj Buzalka has also investigated the questions of multiculturalism and ethnicity in the context of globalization and "Europeanization" of heritage in Slovakia, South-East Poland, and Western Ukraine. Ester Bardone has been highly commended for her research on rural tourism and small-scale rural entrepreneurship, which contributes to heritage production in Estonia. Hana Horáková's projects concern the host-guest relationship and the transformation of local communities in the Czech Republic within the European Union, as well as the anthropology of tourism in general. In Slovenia, Irena Weber's works are devoted to such topics as heritage narratives of the Istrian coast or women traveling.

The most encouraging initiatives are those that allow all marginalized participants of scientific debate to be heard, which is the sine que non condition to engage in dialogue. This is one of the reasons why this book, in its theme and structure, is unique. This is the first study that gives voice to a wide range of research from scholars hailing from Central and Eastern Europe. Interestingly, the second part of the book presents in particular their recent research and fieldwork. But it doesn't simply outline their work inside Central and Eastern Europe; rather, some of the case studies were specifically chosen to highlight their work outside of Europe. The book thus emphasizes that these scholars, like their Western, Anglophone colleagues, work across the world/worlds, but they provide unique perspectives in their analysis of global tourism. Thanks to representatives of the world of anthropology accepting the invitation to participate in our project, we have an innovative perspective on many issues so far discussed from the point of view of either Western scholars or researchers from Central and Eastern Europe.

THE BOOK

The following section, titled "Bridging Academic Worlds: An Insider-Outsider's Perspective," aims to provide a more holistic look at the development of the anthropology of tourism in Central and Eastern Europe. It is shaped as the dialogue of two texts. The introduction shows the inner perspective of scholars from CEE. The chapter "Inside and Outside the Anglophone Snake—Alterities and Opportunities," written by Nelson Graburn, represents an Anglophone scholar's perspective that is consistent with the introduction. The choice of the author is not accidental. Graburn belongs to an influential circle of prominent scholars whose role can be labeled as mentors and promoters of researchers from Asia, CEE, and other marginalized areas. For a few decades, he has been one of the major researchers in tourist studies; therefore, his personal comments concerning the development of anthropological research on tourism from the 1970s in the context of the relationship between world anthropology and the emerging anthropologies of tourism from the marginalized regions are invaluable. Graburn's close involvement in the global spread of academic, particularly anthropological, scholarship in tourism (with a special focus on Japan and China) provides a helpful, holistic context to the book, notwithstanding the fact that he is an outsider in the Eastern European anthropological movement. The introduction and chapter 1 frame the whole book by highlighting that the symbolical "bridging worlds" is a long-term process based on good will and strenuous efforts of many parties.

The second part of the book focuses on describing the peculiarity of the anthropology of tourism in the broader context of tourism studies. These articles are more theoretical and ethno-historical in nature, which solidifies the rationale of the book and makes it reflexive. The aim of this part of the book is to give commentaries that helpfully historicize or problematize the uniqueness of the perspectives and anthropological work done in the "second world" region in the past and especially during the last twenty-six years.

The first chapter of part II introduces the Anglophone scholarship perspective. Tom Selwyn examines the conditions of theory and ethnography in the anthropology of tourism. The ethnographic background is the city of Sarajevo in Bosnia-Herzegovina. In its author's opinion, the specific manner in which ethnographers study the surrounding reality seems to be one of the most promising paths to understanding how complex the relationships between humans and culture are in the context of modern mobility. Maarja Kaaristo's chapter points out the particular aspects of the methodology of Central and Eastern European anthropology, which is far more rooted in ethnology and has a more intimate relationship with history than is common for the Western anthropology. The study written by Anna Wieczorkiewicz sheds light on the nature of travel by analyzing the significant role maps play in the travel experience. Wieczorkiewicz shows how perception of the landscape depends on the visual imagination and depicts the perceived consequences of this to a tourist or a traveler. In the fourth contribution to this part, Maria Zowisło aims to provide a more holistic understanding of the tourist experience with reference to the tradition of philosophical reflection on travel. Magdalena Banaszkiewicz gives a historical background for the recent trends in the Russian tourist market. She points out that the specificity of tourism development in Russia can be perceived from the perspective of the tension between domestic tourism preferred by the national authorities and outbound tourism, which in some periods was regarded as a potential threat to a state's social and political order. Finally, Sabina Owsianowska describes the ways Central and Eastern Europe has been portrayed in tourism discourse, especially after 1989. The author examines narrative strategies, creating images of people and places and mediating tourist encounters.

Part III consists of eight chapters and opts to present recent anthropological research on tourism through the lens of case studies by Central and Eastern European scholars. This section highlights some of the interesting work being done both inside and outside of Europe. In the first set of contributions the subject of host-and-guest relationships is raised. The authors of the presented case studies contribute to the anthropological understanding of tourism because they work in a particular perspective anchored in the intellectual tradition of the region, as well as in other historical, political, and sociocultural contexts than Western scholars. Moreover, they incorporate in their projects the achievements of Central and Eastern European anthropologists and tourism researchers whose works are not known in the West. In chapter 8, Carla Bethmann focuses on alcotourism as a barbarian invasion in Golden Sands, Bulgaria. She argues that alcotourism was co-constructed and the tourism industry and resort workers actively contributed to its growth, both out of sheer necessity ("alcotourism is better than no tourism") and a desire for individual financial gain. However, the trend toward alcotourism was also challenged by tourism workers because it had become a symbol of decline, namely, the decline of their country, of their resort, and of resort workers individually and as a social group. Natalia Bloch examines the complex power relations between residents, local elites, and tourists in Hampi, the Indian UNESCO World Heritage Site and holy Hindu pilgrimage site. Her chapter is based on ethnographic fieldwork, and the author discusses the topic from the postcolonial perspective. This is an interesting case in which postcolonial perspective is utilized by an anthropologist who comes from the region that is also researched through this lens. This experience provides a unique insight into the processes of power-knowledge relations.

The next contribution emphasizes the importance of taste in constructing symbolic geography. Agata Bachórz investigates the relationships between sensual experiences of tourists in Russia and cultural discourses by highlighting the role of cuisine in perceiving the local heritage. Apart from its concentration on the tourists and hosts who experience the local cuisine differently, this chapter introduces the theme of heritage interpretation. The next chapters draw our attention to the issue of heritage and how it is used, created, and interpreted in the tourism industry. The authors' attention is not limited to the physical sphere, but—contrarily—it mainly indicates different kinds of intangible features of heritage. Anna Sznajder and Katarzyna Kosmala investigate the links between tourism development and women's innovative working strategies in lacemaking entrepreneurs from Bobowa, Southern Poland, by applying the concept of creative tourism. Armin Mikos von Rohrscheidt raises the question of how professional guides interpret heritage, which is, as he demonstrates, mediated and inter-subjectively constructed. Focusing on Polish "urbex" teams and individuals, Małgorzata Nieszczerzewska pays particular attention to urban exploration as an "interior tourism" in the context of abandoned places as a tourism destination *à rebours*. Michael Zinganel presents a slightly different aspect of abandoned places. He concentrates on spectacular monuments of the socialist and modernist period in different successor states of the former Yugoslavia in order to illustrate an obvious desire for revisiting, re-appropriating, and re-evaluating these politically highly contested ruins of the bygone period. On the basis of the analysis of online photoblogs of highly educated, creative hipsters, he points out a rather ambiguous search for identity between serious commemoration of historic events and hedonistic emotional and aesthetic excitement, applying a rather free interpretation to the sites. The book closes with a historical study. Małgorzata

Radkiewicz, similarly to Michael Zinganel, also employs photography as a medium helpful in the interpretation of tourism culture. Her chapter shows the growing presence of women in public spaces in Polish Galicia, which is a testimony to their emancipation and changing cultural patterns of travel at the beginning of the twentieth century.

In the conclusion, the editors present final remarks and prospects for further development and dialogue between researchers from different cultural backgrounds. It opens up space for discussion and sets new paths of inquiry.

OUR PERSPECTIVE—GLOBAL PERSPECTIVE

Initiatives such as our book serve as one of the strongest proofs that plenty of bridges help scholars to set up an enlightening dialogue. Although the bridge is only a symbol playing on the imagination, it helps to emphasize that mobility of knowledge also exists. Previously limited, it has become more and more intensive and hopefully less asymmetric. Each conference or project like this acts as original evidence of this mobility, similar to statistics of flights that could be used for characterizing tourist flows. What makes the book unique is the fact that this is the first study that presents a wide range of research of scholars from Central and Eastern Europe. Therefore, this publication may be considered an attempt to fill the gap in tourism studies and beyond, and it is an opportunity to make the academic achievements of the Central and Eastern European researchers part of the world's record.

Certainly, the importance of tourist studies as a key to better understanding economic and above all, cultural processes, is obvious for scholars who specialize in the topic of modern travel. This book exemplifies that the range of issues that could be researched from the perspective of anthropology of tourism is surprisingly wide: identity, gender, visuality, memory, heritage, intercultural relationships, and globalization. Still, this list might include many others. Therefore, we would like to stress that acknowledging scholarship of tourism studies is highly advisable for those who might still not be aware of or who might underestimate the role of tourism in modern culture. The goal that we wanted to achieve was also to show that present tourism development in Central and Eastern Europe can be and should be studied with a strong linkage to historical background as a very recent phenomenon characteristic of the global culture. It is not enough to interpret everything by using the "post-transitory" key. The analysis of the particular case studies, which are rooted in locality, introduces some universal issues that undoubtedly might find supplementation in the research of other regions. We, as scholars who regard themselves as a part of the global community of scholarship, present here our findings, strongly convinced that it is not a marginal, peripheral output, but is equal to those who represent other parts of the world. The dialogue that is vital for all scholarship feeds on the mobility of ideas. We would like to invite you to accompany us in this travel by reading our book.

NOTES

1. Michael di Giovine and David Picard, eds., *Tourism and the Power of Otherness: Seductions of Difference* (Bristol: Channel View Publications, 2014).
2. Timothy G. Ash, "Does Central Europe Exist?" in *The Uses of Adversity: Essays on the Fate of Central Europe* (New York: Random House, 1989); Jacques Attali, *Europe(s)* (Paris: Fayard, 1994); Michał Buchowski and Izabela Kolbon, "Od 'Mitteleuropy' do Europy Środkowej. Zarys dziejów idei," *Sprawy Narodowościowe. Seria Nowa,* 19, 2001; Gerard Delanty, "Peripheries and Borders in a Post-Western Europe," *Eurozine* (August 27, 2007), accessed August 27, 2017, http://www.euro-zine.com/peripheries-and-borders-in-a-post-western-europe/; Lonnie Johnson, *Central Europe: Enemies, Neighbours, Friends* (Oxford: Oxford University Press, 2002); Catherine Lee and Robert Bideleux, "East, West, and the Return of 'Central'," in *The Oxford Handbook of Postwar European History,* ed. Dan Stone (Oxford: Oxford University Press, 2014): 79–97; Andrzej Stasiuk and Jurij Andruchowycz, *Moja Europa. Dwa eseje o Europie zwanej Środkową* (Czarne: Wołowiec, 2007); Piotr Wandycz, *The Price of Freedom: A History of East Central Europe from the Middle Ages to the Present* (London: Routledge, 2001); Larry Wolff, *Inventing Eastern Europe: The Map of the Civilization on the Mind of the Enlightenment* (Stanford, CA: Stanford University Press, 1994). See also chapter 7 in this book.
3. Milan Kundera, "The Tragedy of Central Europe," *The New York Review of Books,* 26 April 1984. The evolution implementations are plainly described by Michal Buchowski and Hana Cervinkowa. See: Michal Buchowski and Hana Cervinkova, "On Rethinking Ethnography in Central Europe: Toward the Cosmopolitan Anthropologies in the 'Peripheries'," in *Rethinking Ethnography in Central Europe,* ed. Michał Buchowski, Hana Cervinkova, and Zdenek Uherek (New York: Palgrave Macmillan, 2015), 1–20.
4. Walter Mignolo, *Local Histories/Global Designs: Coloniality, Subaltern Knowledge, and Border Thinking* (Princeton, NJ: Princeton University Press, 2000).
5. Gustavo Lins Ribeiro and Arturo Escobar, "World Anthropologies: Disciplinary Transformations within Systems of Power," in *World Anthropologies: Disciplinary Transformations within Systems of Power,* ed. Gustavo Lins Ribeiro and Arturo Escobar (Oxford: Berg, 2006): 2.
6. There is a well-established scholarship critically analyzing the possibilities of examining postsocialism by means of postcolonialism. See for instance: Hana Cervinkova, "Postcolonialism, Postsocialism and the Anthropology of East-Central Europe," *Journal of Postcolonial Writing* 48 (2012): 155–63; Sharad Chari and Katherine Verdery, "Thinking Between the Posts: Postcolonialism, Postsocialism, and Ethnography after the Cold War," *Comparative Studies in Society and History* 51, no. 1 (2009): 6–34.

7. László Kürti and Peter Skalnik, "Introduction," 17.

8. Gustavo Lins Ribeiro and Arturo Escobar, *World Anthropologies*, 13.

9. Stanislav Ivanov, from discussion on TriNet, 3 October 2016, 15:43.

10. Although most participants of the conference came from Poland and the neighboring countries (e.g., the Czech Republic or Lithuania), other regions of the world were also represented by scholars from Belgium, Bulgaria, Chile, Cypr, France, Hong-Kong, Italy, Japan, Malta, Mexico, UEA, the United Kingdom, and the United States.

11. Starting from the terminology which generally distinguishes the European tradition of ethnology/ethnography from the Anglophone tradition of cultural/social anthropology.

12. Nelson Graburn, "The Anthropology of Tourism," *Annals of Tourism Research* 10, no. 1 (1983): 9–33; Edward Bruner, *Culture on Tour: Ethnographies of Travel* (Chicago: University of Chicago Press, 2005).

13. Such tradition of research existed also in the Western scholarship, but was carried under the umbrella of discipline known as folklore studies or ethnology.

14. See further: Janusz Barański, "On Contemporary European and Polish Anthropology," *Our Europe. Ethnography—Ethnology—Anthropology of Culture* 1 (2012): 5–18. http://www.ptpn.poznan.pl/Wydawnictwo/czasopisma/our/our_europe_2012. html, accessed November 7, 2016.

15. Between 1869–1890 Oskar Kolberg publishes 33 volumes of regional monographs which describe the Polish folk culture of the nineteenth century. This gigantic project, titled "The People: Their Customs, Way of Life, Language, Folktales, Proverbs, Rites, Witchcraft, Games, Songs, Music and Dances," is considered to be the most complex study of the intangible heritage of folk culture of Poland. See more: The Institute of Oskar Kolberg, http://www.oskarkolberg.pl/en-US/Page/500, accessed November 2016.

16. Ülo Valk, "Establishment of the Estonian Folkore Collections and the Concept of Authenticity," in *Volkskundliche Großprojekte*, ed. Christoph Schmitt (Münster: Waxmann Verlag, 2005), 33–38.

17. A discipline comparable with Eastern European ethnography were in the American tradition folk studies. See further: Regina Bendix, *In Search of Authenticity: The Formation of Folklore Studies* (Madison: University of Wisconsin Press, 1997).

18. See further: Chris Hann, Mihály Sárkány, and Peter Skalnik, eds., *Studying Peoples in the People's Democracies: Socialist Ear Anthropology in East-Central Europe* (Münster: LIT Verlag, 2005); Nikolai Vahtin, "Transformation in Siberian Anthropology," in *World Anthropologies: Disciplinary Transformations within Systems of Power*, ed. Gustavo Lins Ribeiro and Arturo Escobar (Oxford: Berg, 2006), 49–68; Zbigniew Jasiewicz, "The Beginnings of Ethnology/Anthropology in Poland: The Search for the Names of Research Interests and the Emerging Discipline," in *The Anthropologist to the Present*, ed. Anna Malewska-Szałygin, Magdalena Radkowska-Walkowicz (Warsaw: University of Warsaw Press, 2010), 36–51; Zbigniew Jasiewicz, "Etnologia polska. Między etnografią a antropologią kulturową" [Polish Ethnology: Between Ethnography and Cultural Anthropology], *Nauka* 2 (2006): 65–80; Ants Viires, "The Development of Estonian Ethnography during the 20th Century," *Journal*

of Baltic Studies 22 (1999): 123–32; Valery Tishkov, "The Crisis in Soviet Ethnography," *Current Anthropology* 33 (1992): 371–94.

19. For the synthetic analysis of state-of-the-art see: Michał Buchowski, "Anthropology in Postsocialist Europe," in *A Companion to the Anthropology of Europe*, ed. Ullrich Kockel, Máiréad Nic Craith, and Jonas Frykman (London: Wiley & Blackwell, 2015), 68–87. Further: László Kürti and Peter Skalnik, eds., *Postsocialist Europe: Anthropological Perspectives from Home* (Oxford: Berghahn Books, 2009); Michał Buchowski, Hana Cervinkova, and Zdenek Uherek, eds., *Rethinking Ethnography in Central Europe* (New York: Palgrave Macmillan, 2015); Waldemar Kuligowski and Richárd Papp, eds., *Sterile and Isolated? An Anthropology Today in Hungary and Poland* (Poznań: TIPI, 2015).

20. Michał Buchowski, "Hierarchies of Knowledge in Central-Eastern European Anthropology," *Anthropology of East Europe Review* 22 (2004): 5–14; Aleksander Posern-Zieliński, ed., *Etnologia polska między ludoznawstwem a antropologią* (Poznań: Drawa, 1995); Janusz Barański, *Etnologia i okolice. Eseje antyperyferyjne* (Krakow: Wydawnictwo Uniwersytetu Jagiellońskiego, 2010); Waldemar Kuligowski, *Antropologia współczesności. Wiele światów, jedno miejsce* (Krakow: Universitas, 2007). See also the discussion on the shape of European anthropology/ ethnology conducted in the pages of the journal of the European Association of Social Anthropologists, *Social Anthropology/Anthropologie Sociale* 23 (3) and 23 (4), 2015.

21. Until 1980s the discipline in Poland was called "ethnology." About European ethnology and difference with social and cultural anthropology see further: Regina Bendix, "Translating between European Ethnologies," in *The Times, Places, Passages: Ethnological Approaches in the New Millennium, 7th SIEF Conference*, ed. Attila Paládi (Budapest: Akadémiai Kiadó, 2004), 371–80.

22. Teofila Jarowiecka, "Początki działalności dydaktycznej i naukowo-badawczej w zakresie turystyki i rekreacji w Akademii Wychowania Fizycznego w Krakowie (do 1975 r.)" [The Beginnings of Didactic and Research Activity in the Field of Tourism and Leisure in AWF in Kraków (till 1975)], in *Antropologia turystyki [Anthropology of Tourism]*, ed. Sabina Owsianowska and Ryszard Winiarski (Kraków: University of Physical Education in Kraków Press, 2017), 13–38. See also the first works on tourism education in general and in CEE: Jafar Jafari and J. R. B. Ritchie, "Towards a Framework for Tourism Education," *Annals of Tourism Research* 8 (1981): 14–34; Greg Richards, ed., *Tourism in Central and Eastern Europe: Educating for Quality* (Tilberg: Tilberg University Press, 1995).

23. Magdalena Banaszkiewicz, Nelson Graburn, and Sabina Owsianowska, "Tourism in (Post)socialist Eastern Europe," *Journal of Tourism and Cultural Change* 15 (2017): 109–21.

24. Ryszard Winiarski and Wiesław Alejziak, "Perspektywy rozwoju nauk o turystyce/Prospects for the Development of Tourism Studies," in *Nauki o turystyce/ Tourism Sciences*, Vol. 1, ed. Ryszard Winiarski (Kraków: Studia i Monografie AWF Kraków, 2003), 157–66.

25. Teofila Jarowiecka, "Początki działalności dydaktycznej i naukowo-badawczej"; Ryszard Winiarski, "Scientific and Educational Achievements in

Tourism at the Academy of Physical Education in Kraków," in *Tourism in Scientific Research in Poland and Worldwide*, ed. Wiesław Alejziak and Ryszard Winiarski (Rzeszow: WSiZ Press, 2006), 279–89.

26. Sabina Owsianowska, "Multiculturality and Lifelong Learning: A Polish Case," in *Lifelong Learning for Tourism: Concepts, Policy and Implementation*, ed. Violet Cuffy, David Airey, and Georgios Papageorgiou (London: Routledge, 2018), 127–42; Magdalena Banaszkiewicz et al., "Tourism in (Post)socialist Eastern Europe."

27. Krzysztof Przecławski, *Socjologiczne problemy turystyki* (Warszawa: Instytut Wydawniczy CRZZ, 1979); *Człowiek a turystyka. Zarys socjologii turystyki* (Kraków: Albis, 1996); *Profesor Krzysztof Przecławski: doktor honoris causa Akademii Wychowania Fizycznego w Krakowie* (Kraków: University of Physical Education in Kraków Press, 2006); Wiesław Alejziak, "Życie ludzkie jest wędrowaniem— wspomnienie o Profesorze Krzysztofie Przecławskim (1927–2014)," *Folia Turistica* 36 (2015): 201–14.

28. LLP Erasmus—a lifelong learning program established in 1987 which enabled student and scholar exchanges, replaced in 2014 by Erasmus+, a program of the European Union in the domain of education, trainings, youth and sport, addressed, for example, to students and academic teachers.

29. Anna Wieczorkiewicz and Blanka Brzozowska, "Wyobraźnia turystyczna. Wprowadzenie," *Kultura Współczesna. Teoria, intepretacje, krytyka* 3 (2010): 5–7; Sabina Owsianowska, "W poszukiwaniu nowych metafor podróży," in *Góry— człowiek—turystyka. Księga Jubileuszowa dedykowana A. Matuszykowi*, ed. Piotr Cybula, Marek Czyż, and Sabina Owsianowska (Sucha Beskidzka: WSTiE-Proksenia, 2011), 391–98.

30. Zygmunt Bauman, "From Pilgrim to Tourist – or a Short History of Identity," in *Questions of Cultural Identity*, ed. Stuart Hall and Paul Du Gay (London: SAGE, 1996), 18–36.

31. Stanislav Ivanov, from discussion on TriNet, October 3, 2016, 15:43. See further Jana Kučerová and Harald Pechlaner, eds. "Tourism Research and Education in Central and Eastern Europe—History and Contemporary Issues," *European Journal of Tourism Research* 17 (2017).

32. http://www.ciret-tourism.com/encyclopaedia/list_of_centers_a.html, accessed November 16, 2016.

33. Armin Mikos von Rohrscheidt, "Scientific Centers and Researchers of Cultural Tourism in Poland," *Turystyka Kulturowa* 10 (2014): 123–40. http://turystykakulturowa.org/ojs/index.php/tk/article/view/523/524; "Tourism from the Humanistic Perspective" includes a series of monographs edited by Marek Kazimierczak and published by University of Physical Educations in Poznan, that is, *Turystyka w humanistycznej perspektywie/Tourism from the Humanistic Perspective* (2004); *Współczesne podróże kulturowe/Contemporary Cultural Travels* (2010); Karolina Buczkowska, "Studia turystyki kulturowej na polskich uczelniach w latach 2002–2015," *Turystyka Kulturowa* 8 (2015): 122–5, http://turystykakulturowa.org/ojs/index.php/tk/article/view/650/592; Elżbieta Puchnarewicz, ed., *Wielokulturowość w turystyce* (Warszawa: WSTiJO Press, 2010); Elżbieta Puchnarewicz, ed. *Dziedzictwo*

kulturowe regionów świata i ich znaczenie w turystyce (Warszawa: WSTiJO Press, 2011); Zbigniew Krawczyk, Ewa Lewandowska-Tarasiuk, and Jan Wiktor Sienkiewicz edited three monographs (published by DrukTur ALMAMER WSE Press in Warsaw): *Turystyka jako dialog kultur/Tourism as a Dialogue of Cultures* (2005); *Bariery kulturowe w turystyce/Cultural Barriers in Tourism* (2007) and *Człowiek w podróży/Man in Travel* (2009).

34. http://en.turistica.si/research, accessed November 16, 2016.

35. John Tribe, "The Indiscipline of Tourism," *Annals of Tourism Research* 24 (1997): 638–57; Diane Dredge, David Airey, and Michael Gross, eds., *The Routledge Handbook of Tourism and Hospitality Education* (London: Routledge, 2015).

36. Anna Wieczorkiewicz, *Apetyt turysty. O doświadczaniu świata w podróży* [A Tourist's Appetite: The Experience of the World in Travel] (Krakow: Universitas, 2008). See also: "Wyobraźnia turystyczna," ed. Anna Wieczorkiewicz and Blanka Brzozowska, special issue of *Kultura Współczesna* 3 (2010).

37. *Folia Turistica*, ed. Wiesław Alejziak, 25, no. 1–2 (2011).

38. See also: Krzysztof Podemski, *Socjologia podróży* (Poznań: Wydawnictwo UAM, 2005); Magdalena Banaszkiewicz et al. "Tourism in (Post)socialist Eastern Europe."

39. Magdalena Banaszkiewicz and Sabina Owsianowska, eds., "The Anthropology of Tourism," *Folia Turistica* 37 (2015); Magdalena Banaszkiewicz et al., "Tourism in (Post)socialist Eastern Europe."

40. See e.g.: Natalia Bloch, "Kolonizatorzy, turyści, antropolodzy. Dziedzictwo kolonialne w turystyce i kolonialna nostalgia w antropologii," *Konteksty* (2014): 187–95; Anna Horolets, *Konformizm, bunt, nostalgia. Turystyka niszowa z Polski do krajów byłego ZSRR* (Universitas, Kraków: 2013); Agata Bachórz, *Rosja w tekście i doświadczeniu. Analiza współczesnych relacji z podróży* (NOMOS, Kraków: 2013); Magdalena Banaszkiewicz, *Dialog międzykulturowy w turystyce. Przypadek polsko-rosyjski* (Kraków: Jagiellonian University Press, 2013); Sabina Owsianowska, "Tourist Narratives about the Dissonant Heritage of the Borderlands: The Case of South-Eastern Poland," *Journal of Tourism and Cultural Change* 15 (2017): 167–84; Juraj Buzalka, "Scale and Ethnicity in Southeast Poland: Tourism in the European Periphery," *Etnográfica* 13 (2009): 373–93; Ester Bardone, *My Farm is my Stage: A Performance Perspective on Rural Tourism and Hospitality Services in Estonia*, Humaniora (Tartu: University of Tartu Press, 2013); Hana Horáková, "Post-Communist Transformation of Tourism in Czech Rural Areas: New Dilemmas," *Anthropological Notebooks* 16 (2010): 59–77; Irena Weber, "Heritage Narratives on the Slovenian Coast: The Lion and the Attic," in *Cultural Heritages as Reflexive Traditions*, ed. Ulrich Kockel and Máiréad Nic Craiht (London: Palgrave Macmillan, 2007): 158–70.

41. See further: Noel Salazar and Nelson Graburn, eds., *Tourism Imaginaries: Anthropological Approaches* (Oxford: Berghahn Books, 2014); Maria Gravari-Barbas and Nelson Graburn, eds., *Tourism Imaginaries at the Disciplinary Crossroads: Place, Practice, Media* (London: Routledge, 2016).

42. Agata Bachórz, *Rosja w tekście i doświadczeniu.*

REFERENCES

Alejziak, Wiesław, ed. "The Master Classes." *Folia Turistica* 25, no. 1–2 (2011).

Alejziak, Wiesław. "Życie ludzkie jest wędrowaniem—wspomnienie o Profesorze Krzysztofie Przecławskim (1927–2014)." *Folia Turistica* 36 (2015): 201–14.

Ash, Timothy G. "Does Central Europe Exist?" In *The Uses of Adversity: Essays on the Fate of Central Europe.* New York: Random House, 1989.

Attali, Jacques. *Europe(s).* Paris: Fayard, 1994.

Bachórz, Agata. *Rosja w tekście i doświadczeniu. Analiza współczesnych relacji z podróży.* Kraków: NOMOS, 2013.

Banaszkiewicz, Magdalena. *Dialog międzykulturowy w turystyce. Przypadek polsko-rosyjski.* Kraków: Jagiellonian University Press, 2013.

Banaszkiewicz, Magdalena, and Sabina Owsianowska, eds. From the Editors. "The Anthropology of Tourism." *Folia Turistica* 37 (2015).

Banaszkiewicz, Magdalena, Nelson Graburn, and Sabina Owsianowska, "Tourism in (Post)socialist Eastern Europe," *Journal of Tourism and Cultural Change* 15 (2017): 109–21.

Barański, Janusz. *Etnologia i okolice. Eseje antyperyferyjne.* Kraków: Wydawnictwo Uniwersytetu Jagiellońskiego, 2010.

Barański, Janusz. "On Contemporary European and Polish Anthropology." *Our Europe. Ethnography—Ethnology—Anthropology of Culture* 1 (2012): 5–18. http://www.ptpn.poznan.pl/Wydawnictwo/czasopisma/our/our_europe_2012.html, accessed November 7, 2016.

Bardone, Ester. *My Farm is my Stage: A Performance Perspective on Rural Tourism and Hospitality Services in Estonia.* Humaniora. Tartu: University of Tartu Press, 2013.

Bauman, Zygmunt. "From Pilgrim to Tourist – or a Short History of Identity." In *Questions of Cultural Identity*, edited by Stuart Hall and Paul Du Gay, 18–36. London: SAGE, 1996.

Bendix, Regina. *In Search of Authenticity: The Formation of Folklore Studies.* Madison: University of Wisconsin Press, 1997.

Bendix, Regina. "Translating between European Ethnologies." In *The Times, Places, Passages: Ethnological Approaches in the New Millennium, 7th SIEF Conference,* edited by Attila Paládi, 371–80. Budapest: Akadémiai Kiadó, 2004.

Bloch, Natalia. "Kolonizatorzy, turyści, antropolodzy. Dziedzictwo kolonialne w turystyce i kolonialna nostalgia w antropologii." *Konteksty* (2014): 187–95.

Bruner, Edward. *Culture on Tour: Ethnographies of Travel.* Chicago: University of Chicago Press, 2005.

Buchowski, Michał. "Hierarchies of Knowledge in Central-Eastern European Anthropology." *Anthropology of East Europe Review* 22 (2004): 5–14.

Buchowski, Michał. "Anthropology in Postsocialist Europe." In *A Companion to the Anthropology of Europe*, edited by Ullrich Kockel, Máiréad Nic Craith, and Jonas Frykman, 68–87. London: Wiley & Blackwell, 2015.

Buchowski, Michał, and Hana Cervinkova. "On Rethinking Ethnography in Central Europe: Toward the Cosmopolitan Anthropologies in the 'Peripheries'."

In *Rethinking Ethnography in Central Europe,* edited by Michał Buchowski, Hana Cervinkova, and Zdenek Uherek, 1–20. New York: Palgrave Macmillan, 2015.

Buchowski, Michał, and Izabela Kolbon. "Od 'Mitteleuropy' do Europy Środkowej. Zarys dziejów idei." *Sprawy Narodowościowe. Seria Nowa* 19, 2001.

Buchowski, Michał, Hana Cervinkova, and Zdenek Uherek, eds. *Rethinking Ethnography in Central Europe.* New York: Palgrave Macmillan, 2015.

Buczkowska, Karolina. "Studia turystyki kulturowej na polskich uczelniach w latach 2002–2015." *Turystyka Kulturowa* 8 (2015).

Buzalka, Juraj. "Scale and Ethnicity in Southeast Poland: Tourism in the European Periphery." *Etnográfica* 13 (2009): 373–93.

Cervinkova, Hana. "Postcolonialism, Postsocialism and the Anthropology of East-Central Europe." *Journal of Postcolonial Writing* 48 (2012): 155–63.

Chari, Sharad, and Katherine Verdery. "Thinking Between the Posts: Postcolonialism, Postsocialism, and Ethnography after the Cold War." *Comparative Studies in Society and History* 51 (2009): 6–34.

Delanty, Gerard. "Peripheries and Borders in a Post-Western Europe." *Eurozine* (August 27, 2007). http://www.eurozine.com/peripheries-and-borders-in-a-post-western-europe, accessed August 27, 2017.

di Giovine, Michael, and David Picard. *Tourism and the Power of Otherness: Seductions of Difference.* Bristol: Channel View Publications, 2014.

Dredge, Diane, David Airey, and Michael Gross, eds. *The Routledge Handbook of Tourism and Hospitality Education.* London: Routledge, 2015.

Graburn, Nelson. "The Anthropology of Tourism." *Annals of Tourism Research* 10 (1983): 9–33.

Gravari-Barbas, Maria, and Nelson Graburn. *Tourism Imaginaries at the Disciplinary Crossroads: Place, Practice, Media.* London: Routledge, 2016.

Hann, Chris, Mihály Sárkány, and Peter Skalnik, eds. *Studying Peoples in the People's Democracies: Socialist Ear Anthropology in East-Central Europe.* Münster: LIT Verlag, 2005.

Horáková, Hana. "Post-Communist Transformation of Tourism in Czech Rural Areas: New Dilemmas." *Anthropological Notebooks* 16 (2010): 59–77.

Horolets, Anna. *Konformizm, bunt, nostalgia. Turystyka niszowa z Polski do krajów byłego ZSRR.* Kraków: Universitas, 2013.

Jafari, Jafar, and J. R. B. Ritchie. "Towards a Framework for Tourism Education." *Annals of Tourism Research* 8 (1981): 14–34.

Jarowiecka, Teofila. "Początki działalności dydaktycznej i naukowo-badawczej w zakresie turystyki i rekreacji w Akademii Wychowania Fizycznego w Krakowie (do 1975 r.)." In *Antrologia turystyki,* edited by Sabina Owsianowska and Ryszard Winiarski, 13–38. Kraków: University of Physical Education Press, 2017.

Jasiewicz, Zbigniew. "Etnologia polska. Między etnografią a antropologią kulturową" [Polish Ethnology: Between Ethnography and Cultural Anthropology]. *Nauka* 2 (2006): 65–80.

Jasiewicz, Zbigniew. "The Beginnings of Ethnology/Anthropology in Poland: The Search for the Names of Research Interests and the Emerging Discipline." In *The*

Anthropologist to the Present, edited by Anna Malewska-Szałygin and Magdalena Radkowska-Walkowicz, 36–51. Warsaw: University of Warsaw Press, 2010.

Johnson, Lonnie. *Central Europe: Enemies, Neighbours, Friends.* Oxford: Oxford University Press, 2002.

Kazimierczak, Marek, ed. *Turystyka w humanistycznej perspektywie.* Poznan: University of Physical Education in Poznan, 2004.

Kazimierczak, Marek, ed. *Współczesne podróże kulturowe.* Poznan: University of Physical Education in Poznan, 2010.

Krawczyk, Zbigniew, Ewa Lewandowska-Tarasiuk, and Jan Wiktor Sienkiewicz, eds. *Turystyka jako dialog kultur.* Warszawa: DrukTur ALMAMER WSE Press, 2005.

Krawczyk, Zbigniew, Ewa Lewandowska-Tarasiuk, and Jan Wiktor Sienkiewicz, eds. *Bariery kulturowe w turystyce.* Warszawa: DrukTur ALMAMER WSE Press, 2007.

Krawczyk, Zbigniew, Ewa Lewandowska-Tarasiuk, and Jan Wiktor Sienkiewicz, eds. *Człowiek w podróży.* Warszawa: DrukTur ALMAMER WSE Press, 2009.

Kučerová, Jana, and Harald Pechlaner, eds. "Tourism Research and Education in Central and Eastern Europe—History and Contemporary Issues." *European Journal of Tourism Research* 17 (2017).

Kuligowski, Waldemar. *Antropologia współczesności. Wiele światów, jedno miejsce.* Kraków: Universitas, 2007.

Kuligowski, Waldemar, and Richárd Papp, eds. *Sterile and Isolated? An Anthropology Today in Hungary and Poland.* Poznań: TIPI, 2015.

Kundera, Milan. "The Tragedy of Central Europe." *The New York Review of Books,* 26 April 1984.

Kürti, László, and Peter Skalnik, eds. *Postsocialist Europe: Anthropological Perspectives from Home.* Oxford: Berghahn Books, 2009.

Kürti, László, and Peter Skalnik. "Introduction: Postsocialist Europe and the Anthropological Perspectives from Home." In *Postsocialist Europe: Anthropological Perspectives from Home,* edited by László Kürti and Peter Skalnik. Oxford: Berghahn Books, 2009.

Lee, Catherine, and Robert Bideleux, "East, West, and the Return of 'Central'." In *The Oxford Handbook of Postwar European History,* edited by Dan Stone, 79–97. Oxford: Oxford University Press, 2014.

Lins Ribeiro, Gustavo, and Arturo Escobar. "World Anthropologies: Disciplinary Transformations within Systems of Power." In *World Anthropologies: Disciplinary Transformations within Systems of Power,* edited by Gustavo Lins Ribeiro and Arturo Escobar. Oxford: Berg, 2006.

Mignolo, Walter. *Local Histories/Global Designs: Coloniality, Subaltern Knowledge, and Border Thinking.* Princeton, NJ: Princeton University Press, 2000.

Mikos von Rohrscheidt, Armin. "Scientific Centers and Researchers of Cultural Tourism in Poland." *Turystyka Kulturowa* 10 (2014).

Owsianowska, Sabina. "W poszukiwaniu nowych metafor podróży." In *Góry—człowiek—turystyka. Księga Jubileuszowa dedykowana A. Matuszykowi,* edited by Piotr Cybula, Marek Czyż, and Sabina Owsianowska, 391–98. Sucha Beskidzka: WSTiE-Proksenia, 2011.

Owsianowska, Sabina. "Multiculturality and Lifelong Learning: A Polish Case." In *Lifelong Learning for Tourism: Concepts, Policy and Implementation*, edited by Violet Cuffy, David Airey, and Georgios Papageorgiou, 127–42. London: Routledge, 2018.

Owsianowska, Sabina. "Tourist Narratives about the Dissonant Heritage of the Borderlands: The Case of South-Eastern Poland." *Journal of Tourism and Cultural Change* 15 (2017): 167–84.

Podemski, Krzysztof. *Socjologia podróży.* Poznań: Wydawnictwo UAM, 2005.

Posern-Zieliński, Aleksander, ed. *Etnologia polska między ludoznawstwem a antropologią.* Poznań: Drawa, 1995.

Profesor Krzysztof Przecławski: doktor honoris causa Akademii Wychowania Fizycznego w Krakowie. Kraków: University of Physical Education in Kraków Press, 2006.

Przecławski, Krzysztof. *Socjologiczne problemy turystyki.* Warszawa: Instytut Wydawniczy CRZZ, 1979.

Przecławski, Krzysztof. *Człowiek a turystyka. Zarys socjologii turystyki.* Kraków: Albis, 1996.

Puchnarewicz, Elżbieta, ed. *Wielokulturowość w turystyce.* Warszawa: WSTiJO Press, 2010.

Puchnarewicz, Elżbieta, ed. *Dziedzictwo kulturowe regionów świata i ich znaczenie w turystyce.* Warszawa: WSTiJO Press, 2011.

Richards, Greg, ed. *Tourism in Central and Eastern Europe: Educating for Quality.* Tilberg: Tilberg University Press, 1995.

Salazar, Noel, and Nelson Graburn. *Tourism Imaginaries: Anthropological Approaches.* Oxford: Berghahn Books, 2014.

Social Anthropology/Anthropologie Sociale 23 and 23 (2015).

Stasiuk, Andrzej, and Jurij Andruchowycz. *Moja Europa. Dwa eseje o Europie zwanej Środkową.* Czarne: Wołowiec, 2007.

Stone, Dan, ed. *The Oxford Handbook of Postwar European History.* Oxford: Oxford University Press.

Tishkov, Valery. "The Crisis in Soviet Ethnography." *Current Anthropology* 33 (1992): 371–94.

Tribe, John. "The Indiscipline of Tourism." *Annals of Tourism Research* 24 (1997): 638–57.

Vahtin, Nikolai. "Transformation in Siberian Anthropology." In *World Anthropologies: Disciplinary Transformations Within Systems of Power,* edited by Gustavo Lins Ribeiro and Arturo Escobar, 49–68. Oxford: Berg, 2006.

Valk, Ülo. "Establishment of the Estonian Folkore Collections and the Concept of Authenticity." In *Volkskundliche Großprojekte,* edited by Christoph Schmitt. Münster: Waxmann Verlag, 2005.

Viires, Ants. "The Development of Estonian Ethnography during the 20th Century." *Journal of Baltic Studies* 22 (1999): 123–32.

Wandycz, Piotr. *The Price of Freedom: A History of East Central Europe from the Middle Ages to the Present.* London: Routledge, 2001.

Weber, Irena. "Heritage Narratives on the Slovenian Coast: The Lion and the Attic." In *Cultural Heritages as Reflexive Traditions,* edited by Ulrich Kockel and Máiréad Nic Craiht, 158–70. London: Palgrave Macmillan, 2007.

Wieczorkiewicz, Anna. *Apetyt turysty. O doświadczaniu świata w podróży.* Kraków: Universitas, 2008.

Wieczorkiewicz, Anna, and Blanka Brzozowska, eds. "Wyobraźnia turystyczna." *Kultura Współczesna* 3 (2010).

Winiarski, Ryszard. "Scientific and Educational Achievements in Tourism at the Academy of Physical Education in Kraków." In *Tourism in Scientific Research in Poland and Worldwide,* edited by Wiesław Alejziak and Ryszard Winiarski, 279–89. Rzeszow: WSiZ Press, 2006.

Winiarski, Ryszard, and Wiesław Alejziak. "Perspektywy rozwoju nauk o turystce." In *Nauki o turystyce* (vol. 1) edited by Ryszard Winiarski, 157–66. Studia i Monografie AWF Kraków, 2003.

Wolff, Larry. *Inventing Eastern Europe: The Map of the Civilization on the Mind of the Enlightenment.* Stanford, CA: Stanford University Press, 1994.

Part I

BRIDGING ACADEMIC WORLDS

An Insider-Outsider's Perspective

Chapter 1

Inside and Outside the Anglophone Snake

Alterities and Opportunities

Nelson Graburn

This short chapter[1] will introduce and explore the personal and academic history of my recent relationship with Polish scholars Magdalena Banaszkiewicz and Sabina Owsianowska through the anthropology of tourism. Though raised in the Anglophone establishment of Kings Canterbury, Cambridge, McGill, and the University of Chicago, through close family relationships in Malaya, Singapore, Ceylon [Sri Lanka], and Sicily, I was exposed to and identified with "alterity," impelling me, many have said, toward anthropology, after a successful scholastic career in the natural sciences. While these family bonds did not include Central and Eastern Europe, at primary and secondary (boarding) schools[2] I had important friends from Poland and Russia, and later my work on Inuit and circumpolar peoples (e.g., Graburn and Strong 1973) put me in touch with anthropologists such as Sergei Arutiunov, Igor Krupnik, Krzysztof Przeclawski, Nikolay Vakhtin, and others with whom I stayed and worked both before and after the fall of the Soviet Union. Though I have had strong links with Japanese anthropologists since 1978, and with Chinese since 1989, the opportunity to work with Central and Eastern European anthropologists, especially the editors of this book, did not come "out of the blue."

The international conference upon which this book is based, organized in Kraków in 2015, was an extraordinarily rich occasion,[3] which had a special meaning for me. The last time I had been in the beautiful city of Kraków was in 1989, as part of the first meeting of the International Academy for the Study of Tourism, which met in Warsaw, Zakopane, and Kraków. Although our nominal leader was the Academy founder Jafar Jafari, the leader of this conference in Poland was the late Krzysztof Przeclawski, the famous Polish sociologist, founder of tourism studies and editor of the respected journal *Problemy Turystyki*. 2015 was also the centennial of the year that Jagiellonian

University graduate, Bronisław Malinowski[4], went to carry out his long-term field research in the Trobriand Islands of New Guinea. We can say that his landmark book *Argonauts of the Western Pacific* (1922) was an exemplary initial study in the anthropology of mobility and tourism. This was a study of the Kula Ring, a periodic travel from their home islands to other islands nearby, to meet friends, exchange gifts, and carry on trade. Thus, today we could say that the Kula was a form of VFR (Visiting Friends and Relatives), business travel, and the grand tour, with a touch of pilgrimage. It was the ideal situation for anthropological research. Malinowski knew the travelers well after living in their home communities and experiencing the exciting anticipation of the voyage. He traveled with them as a participant observer, and accompanied them back home. He witnessed their reintegration and listened to the post-tour narratives and saw the bragging and the distribution of the souvenirs from the trip.

In the next sections, I want to briefly cover three sequential topics: the origins and growth of tourism studies, which brought forth major problem areas and concepts, to consider which of those original problems and concepts are still central and contested, and, lastly, to consider the globalization of studies of tourism in the meeting of "world" (cosmopolitan) and "peripheral" networks and academic communities. In the past fifty years of tourism research, opinions and depictions of tourists and tourism have varied widely. Some have insulted and ridiculed them[5]—while others have acknowledged or respected their values.[6] These approaches have been elaborated by middle-level theorizing aimed at more elaborate classifications and understandings.[7] But all of these generalizing schemes have been called into question by the more recent plethora of excellent ethnographies, some of which have enlarged our understanding of particular types,[8] while others have emphasized the permeability of definitional and disciplinary boundaries, the pliability of tourists' feelings, and the ultimate connectivity between tourism and the rest of tourists' lives.

THEMES IN TOURISM RESEARCH

In our assessment of anthropological interventions in tourism research,[9] we spelled out the topics of the first thirty years,[10] and then Leite and Graburn briefly considered the newer, developing parts of the field. In this chapter, I briefly outline these topics and consider some of this book's contributions to these fields.[11] In the Anglophone social sciences, geography and economics were the first fields to focus on tourism. In the 1950s and 1960s, tourism was seen as a possible avenue for economic growth.[12] Tourism was a relatively low-cost industry in which workers could be employed with existing or easily learned skills, such as gardening, cleaning, cooking, serving, and an industry which could raise the "standard of living" and "modernize" undeveloped (rural, backward) regions in the developed "First World" or on the recently decolonized poor areas of the "Third World." Critiques of tourism development started as elitist complaints about the tourists themselves, especially when rising incomes and jet travel allowed mass tourists to "invade" previously "unspoiled" cultural and natural destinations. Works by Boorstin, Haden-Guest, and Turner and Ash[13] made fun of mass tourists or even condemned them morally for their crass pleasure-seeking behavior, a moralization that is still common in the tourism-research literature, even if it appears in new forms. In the 1960s, criticism of mass tourism came from a more serious direction: detailed economic analyses of the impacts of tourism, which was supposed to alleviate poverty through earning foreign exchange and the subsequent multiplier effect (the money earned would circulate and enrich the local community), showed that multipliers were sometimes negative and "leakage" was greater than income, owing interest on money borrowed for investment in infrastructures and tourism facilities, the salaries of expatriates at the upper levels, and the import of most of the consumables such as food, drink, fuel, and the like.[14]

Sociocultural Impact Studies

The anthropological beginnings of tourism studies[15] mainly came about by chance, or, shall we say, serendipity. Berkeley doctoral anthropology student Theron Nuñez found a novel topic in his research on cultural change in Morelos, Mexico, to present as a job talk—the urbanization caused by cosmopolitans from Mexico City, buying or renting peasant houses to visit on weekends and holidays. This was published as "Tourism, Tradition, and Acculturation: Weekendismo in a Mexican Village."[16] In 1953, geographer Valene Smith proposed tourism as a subject for a course. Later she visited Alaska and saw the impact of tourism on the Inupiat (North Alaskan Eskimos). She switched to anthropology for a PhD and worked with her mother as her travel agent, while her husband piloted their own plane[17]. Dennison Nash, trained as a sociologist, took a sabbatical in Barcelona where he ran across a temporary community of Americans living there "like tourists" and wrote "Community in Limbo."[18]

Similarly, my own "discovery" came in 1959. While pursuing my MA research among the Canadian Inuit of the Hudson Strait, I found and focused on their newly developed soapstone carvings which were exported by ship to southern Canada where they were sold as curios and souvenirs. Running across these export art forms elsewhere, I wrote "The Eskimos and Airport Art."[19] These works were mainly concerned with the sociocultural impacts of tourism, a topic that I came up with after I realized that economic impacts were not necessarily positive. In this vein were general works such as Young's "Tourism: Blessing or Blight"[20] and case studies such as Finney and Watson's "A New Kind of Sugar,"[21] which showed that tourism had overtaken sugar production as the leading industry in Hawaii, though remaining just as exploitative.

My own focus was on studying the effects of tourism and commoditization on the arts and crafts of minority people. I attempted to provide a comparative framework to my own ethnographic work. At the 1970 American Anthropological Association meeting, I convened a panel of anthropologists interested in contemporary traditional arts and acculturative change, which resulted in the book "Ethnic and Tourist Arts."[22] Valene Smith brought us all together when she convened a panel at the American Anthropological Association meetings in Mexico City in 1974, from which she edited "Hosts and Guests."[23] The majority of the chapters were case studies such as Smith's own "Eskimo Tourism: Micro-Models and Marginal Men" and Nash's more general theory "Tourism as a Form of Imperialism."[24] Nash saw tourism as a continuation of colonial-like influence in the postcolonial era, as reflected by some contributors in this book.

Tourism, Ritual, and Experience

Developing more slowly than impact studies was the study of tourists, their lived experience, and the exercise of tourism as a mobile practice, with origins and parallels in pilgrimages all around the world. After a sojourn in Paris witnessing the power of tourism exceeding the student movement and general strike of 1968, MacCannell developed the concept of "staged authenticity"[25] as a response to critics who assailed mass tourists for mindlessly enjoying the contrived and the fake. MacCannell, following Goffman's dramaturgical approach to social analysis,[26] claimed the contrary, that tourists, alienated from the shallowness of modern urban life, travel elsewhere in search of authenticity. In this radical modification of Marx's concept of alienation, tourists are said to seek wholeness and meaning in socially approved parts of nature, history, or the supposedly simpler lives of other people. In "The Tourist," he suggested that modern tourism is a secular pilgrimage from one marked (labeled) tourist attraction to the next.

The tourism industry knows this and "stages"—that is, creates, marks off, and advertises—tourist attractions, presenting tourists with things created expressly for them. Knowing that things "on stage" are put there as entertainment, tourists believe that the "real," authentic parts of the world may be found "backstage," or hidden from view. The tourism industry responds by making what is public and easily accessible look like something that is hidden, or by inviting tourists into what appears to be hidden from view, but is really something that is easily accessible. According to this model, tourists are doomed to fail in their search for authenticity. Almost simultaneously I suggested tourism as a secular pilgrimage, following the ritual theory of Leach and later of Turner,[27] wherein the tourist seeks an out of the ordinary, magic, or "sacred" experience by switching key variables such as climate, culture, language, sleep, drinking or sex patterns, and social milieu. I suggested the emphasis was on the change or alterity of the experience rather than its absolute qualities—think about the wealthy "slumming."[28]

Three challenges have been raised in response to MacCannell's argument: (1) Are all tourists really alienated and searching for authenticity? (2) Does involvement with the tourism industry necessarily render something "inauthentic"? And (3) what precisely is meant by the term "authenticity"? In relation to the first of these, Cohen[29] argues that tourists differ widely in their degree of alienation: some are satisfied with their home life, while others search for something "different" away from home but happily return, and the most alienated experiment with or even emigrate to adopt more "authentic" lifestyles elsewhere. He also argues that authenticity resides primarily in the minds of tourists,[30] and thus commodification for tourism does not automatically produce inauthenticity: objects, places, practices, and even peoples transformed for tourist consumption can themselves become accepted as "authentic" over time, in a process he calls *emergent authenticity*. In a penetrating analysis that makes liberal use of ethnographic examples, Wang summarizes the extensive debate prompted by MacCannell's model and suggests that we distinguish between three understandings of authenticity: (1) Objectivist, where something can be examined by an expert to determine its true nature, also called "museum authenticity"; (2) Constructivist, where authenticity is not an ontological condition, but a label or perceived status determined according to socially constructed criteria; and (3) Existential, where tourists focus on the "truth" of their inner and interpersonal feelings during the journey.[31]

Much ethnographic evidence has been marshaled to challenge and expand upon MacCannell's framework—for example, Bruner's work in relation to tourist destinations and performances.[32] Urry[33] showed that the majority of working-class English tourists were not alienated and preferred to travel in company of their own kind, as do most of the world's tourists, a form he named the "collective gaze" as opposed to the "MacCannellesque" more educated tourists who preferred to leave their own sociocultural "bubble" behind and alone, or with a few close mates, try to experience other societies and habitats, which Urry named the "Romantic Gaze." Following Feifer, he claimed that many English white-collar workers were savvy enough to know that most things were created expressly for tourists, but enjoyed them precisely for the aesthetic and humorous qualities of their "inauthenticity."

Labeled "post-tourists," these travelers are said to characterize postmodern tourism, which blurs the modernist distinction between real and fake.[34]

Gender and Tourism

Gender has entered into tourism studies in many ways, starting with impact studies in which the exploitation of women was frequently mentioned, often in association with sex tourism.[35] Though the early criticism of prostitution was heavily moral, more nuanced analyses emerged, when considering women tourists who sought or paid for sex. Wright's insightful ethnographic film, *The Toured: The Other Side of Barbados* (1992), left the viewer feeling no one was "guilty," and this became labeled "romance" tourism. Advances in ethnographic sensibilities have now allowed us to understand the detailed personal, moral, and financial negotiations on both sides of such encounters.[36]

In the chapters of this book on Central and Eastern European tourism, sexual exploitation is not brought up and gender makes a different entrance. Radkiewicz's historical study "Kodak Girls on a trip. Travelling Women from Polish Galicia in photographs of 1910–1930s photography" focuses on gendered aspects of tourist experience and shows the growing presence of women in public space in Polish Galicia, which is a testimony to their emancipation and changing cultural patterns of travel at the beginning of the twentieth century. In a similar vein, Sznajder and Kosmala's chapter, "'Let's Make Laces in the Garden': Creative Tourism in Rural Poland," emphasizes women's innovative working strategies. The authors apply the concept of creative tourism to the links between tourism development and heritage preservation/enhancement, taking us to the topic of the next section.

Heritage and Tourism

Heritage tourism is a global form of tourism at every level, directed locally, or "internally," at one's own heritage, in cultural, historical, and nature tourism, to "elsewhere," perhaps in search of MacCannell's "authenticity of alterity," but increasingly because of the expanding appropriation of the heritage of "others" as one's own, to the point where world heritage is deemed to "belong" to everyone, especially when labeled and sanctioned by powerful organizations such as UNESCO.[37] Heritage is the conscious selection, preservation, and, like MacCannell's tourist attractions, signification (marking), and often elevation of anything that survives from the past—material things such as buildings, artifacts, archaeologies, and landscapes, and immaterial (intangible) features such as languages, performances, technologies, histories, and memories, any of which can be featured, labeled, contextualized, presented, copied, and even sold. As Tunbridge and Ashworth[38] point out, someone makes these selections and modern societies have specialized professions whose job it is to select, conserve, name, evaluate, and present aspects of the past and, thereby, "deselect" other pasts, just as Nora[39] showed that experts such as historians decide what memories of the past are true and should be documented, museumized, and licensed as *lieux de mémoires*. The propagation of these official opinions has been called "authorized heritage discourse."[40] Not surprisingly in the light of recent and long-term political, ethnic, and national turmoil in Central and Eastern Europe, local researchers focus their attention on cases of emotionally loaded dissonant heritage. This widespread situation stems from either memories and features of the past of which people are not proud—crimes, repressions, civil wars, exploitation—or struggles over who has the right to authorize the heritage discourse and hence neglect or suppress other features of the past.

Heritage provides opportunities and attractions for tourism at every level, but the process is dialectical. Tourism provides motives, political and economic, for the "finding" and processing of heritage. Tourism may even provide the financial means for protection and presentation and may be "created" or enhanced in order to provide financial rewards from a flourishing tourism industry. This book provides nuanced examples of both political and economic mechanisms.

Photography, Media, and Tourism

There are striking similarities between anthropologists and tourists. Both are traveling seekers who try to explain alterity and bring back souvenirs and other "data."[41] Prime among both their activities since the 1850s has been taking photos and, more recently, making movies and videos.[42] For tourists, picture books and postcards have long been key features in constructing and spreading tourist imaginaries.[43]

Anthropologists commonly use their own photographs to both analyze and illustrate their research on tourism, itself a very visual phenomenon. They may also use documentary photographs and snapshots to analyze the past. Radkiewicz's chapter, "The 'Kodak Girl' on a Trip," demonstrates the presence and nature of women tourists in early twentieth-century Poland. Her title alone reminds us of the intimate relationship between tourists and snapshots, an inexpensive form of photography, and family memories, made possible by the Kodak Co. Anthropologists in turn used photography by teaching their hosts, often indigenous peoples, how to take photographs and make movies in order to further understand their "world view,"[44] and anthropologists studying tourism have done the same thing. For instance, Jenny Chio, studying ethnic tourism in minority minzu villages in China, lent her video cameras to the Miao villagers of Jidao to film themselves to show to other minorities in the more prosperous Zhuang village of Ping'An and later to show Ping'An tourism to their fellow Miao back home.[45]

More common is the analysis of tourists' photographs, commonly in albums[46] and slide shows[47] and more recently on the internet. The posting of vacation photographs, videos, and blogs has become so common that they are a major source of data for anthropologists and visual researchers. Zinganel's chapter, "Recalling the Ruins of Socialist Modernity," looks at the online foto-blogs of creative hipsters in their rather ambiguous search for identity somewhere between factual history and hedonistic, aesthetic excitement. Lo and McKercher did the same in looking at the post-vacation shifting personal relationships among young Chinese holiday makers.[48]

Tour Guides and Tourism Imaginaries

The role of tour guides has been a topic mentioned in tourism-research publications since the beginning—for instance, in many of the chapters of "Hosts and Guests," under the role of "mediator." In 1985 the *Annals of Tourism Research* devoted a special issue to the topic and Cohen's introduction was a masterly consideration of many of the facets of the topic. McDonnell pointed out that little was understood about the transfer of knowledge to visitors.[49] It is the work of Noel Salazar that focused more deeply on the role of the tour guide in the production of meaning (as well as self-identity) in tourist situations.[50] Mikos von Rohrscheidt's chapter raises the issue of how guides interpret the heritage and demonstrates that the notion of heritage and a kind of "destination imaginary" is mediated and intersubjectively constructed. Salazar, working with tourists and guides in both Indonesia and Tanzania, studied the images and ideas that the tourists carried to a destination were enhanced, modified, and negotiated by the local tour guides. These images and ideas that define the power of a place as a tourist destination, according to Rachid Amirou, have been called *tourist imaginaries*.[51]

Imaginaries overlap with older anthropological conceits such as culture, ideology, and collective representations, which are both shared collective beliefs and individual mental constructs. This concept conveys a visual approach of images and representations, but it overlaps with the concept of tourist "narratives,"[52] which emphasizes the stories the tourist has been told about the place, the tourist's own experiences, and the stories they retell (and continue to modify) after they get home.

Disciplinarity

A number of the chapters in this book, including this chapter, touch upon or bring to the surface questions of the nature of the anthropology of tourism and interdisciplinarity, and, indeed, the "disciplinary nature" of anthropology itself. This topic was first subject to major examination in the book edited by Graburn and Jafari,[53] in which we asked the editors of the ten disciplines of the *Annals of Tourism Research* to each demonstrate the strengths of their disciplines' contributions to tourism research and we, as editors, asked ourselves about cross-disciplinary or multidisciplinary contributions. We came to the preliminary conclusions that "adjacent" disciplines shared methods and cited each other only when focused on the same problems, but, as the world was converging and more of everyone's lives became globalized, this should happen increasingly frequently, leading to a reintegration of many disciplines. But we found there was a solid barrier between the quantitative and non-quantitative disciplines with few even reading each other's publications.[54]

John Tribe has long published on the nature of our tourism research noted on this growing interdisciplinarity.[55] In a recent reexamination of the academic disciplines that focus on tourism Graburn and Gravari-Barbas found more transdisciplinarity in the past twenty-five years with more researchers prepared to use multiple methodologies and to cite widely.[56] They found that the "meta-discipline" of cultural studies, with its focus on searching for (and assuming) political causalities and approaching the contemporary world with a critical stance, provides an underlying directional (and narrowing) unity to many of today's disciplinary practices, both academic and advisory.

CONCLUSIONS

Banaszkiewicz and Owsianowska point out that Central and Eastern European studies of tourism, like other regional research fields have been, for decades, "invisible" to the rest of the world. This is both because of (linguistic) isolation—their works have not been read—and geographical peculiarities—their long territorially fluid relationships to each other and with Russia and their recent post-socialist emergence are topics unfamiliar to much of the rest of the world. Furthermore, with some exceptions, few Polish and regional scholars have been trained or held positions in academia outside of their region. Bronisław Malinowski was a remarkable exception. He took the world by storm. A forceful plurilingual writer and speaker, he was known globally and influenced generations of academics.[57] Even before the collapse of the Soviet system, Polish-trained academics were beginning to work with the metropolitan academic world of tourism researchers. I have already mentioned Krzysztof Przecławski, a prominent sociologist who examined both the pragmatic and the spiritual aspects of the growth of tourism, and worked with Jafar Jafari and others in the International Academy for the Study of Tourism (IAST), most notably organizing their first international meeting in Warsaw, Zakopane, and Kraków in summer 1989. The organizers and contributors to this book are part of a new generation which has already made contacts within world anthropology and forged links which are bringing both their regionally and historically special ethnographic experience and their own ideas of interpretation to the wider academic world.[58]

The "critical turn" in the social sciences and tourism studies has identified the power differentials and structural marginalization of certain segments. Often these are non-English speaking, that is, outside the geographical "Anglophone snake"—Scotland, England, Canada, the United States, Hong Kong, Australia, New Zealand (and Israel[59]?), the non-Western (or non-European) educated, those trained outside the cosmopolitan educational systems, as well as the non-white, wrong class, gender,[60] the young, and sometimes the old or infirm.

The criticism of this world-order arrangement has brought forth countermovements centering on relations to "World Anthropology."[61] This is primarily a Third World[62] movement, but it is being taken very seriously through IUAES (International Union of Anthropological and Ethnological Sciences) and by the American Anthropological Association, which is sponsoring an issue with chapters each devoted to a regional/national "subaltern" anthropology in relation to world anthropology.[63] Let us examine for a moment what is meant by "World Anthropology" from which Eastern European and other regions have been excluded until recently. As suggested above, it is more of a network of knowledge and power based on close collegial and *deshi*[64] disciple-like relationships than any dominant scientific paradigm. Anthropology since its origins has combined scientific exploration with sociopolitical improvement of the human condition. However, since the rejection of unilinear bio-sociocultural evolutionism, and its uniformitarian twin diffusionism,[65] at the turn of the twentieth century (Boas, Kroeber, Westermarck, Malinowski), there have been competing paradigms: from the two forms of functionalism in between-the-wars British social anthropology, to culture and personality, interpretivism, structuralism, post-structuralism, postcolonialism, and so on, to say nothing of the regional and subject matter specialties. So-called world anthropology is more like a strongly-networked academic club to which admission by outsiders is rare, with exceptions such as Malinowski (Poland), Jomo Kenyatta (Kenya), Fei Xiaotong (China), M. N. Srinivas (India), and Koentjaraningrat (Indonesia).

Let me briefly expand upon my own excursions from "the Snake" to engage and mentor younger scholars in the far-flung world of anthropology and tourism studies. Like many English youth, I had a "double identity," thinking of myself as "British Malay" as nearly all my father's family and some of my mother's spent their adult lives in Malaya (and Amoy [China],

Hong Kong, Singapore, and Thailand[66]). My mother and father often spoke Malay at home and sometimes had to defend colonized peoples against the imaginaries of home-bound English. For example, "Tell me Henry, you've lived out there. Are the Chinese really human?" To which my father replied, "Yes, and they are real gentlemen if you treat them like one!" And my mother had to assure our neighbors that it was fine to let Natives[67] into the kitchen to handle and cook the family food. In addition, my aunt had married a brilliant law student from Ceylon (now Sri Lanka) who came to study in England in 1892 and who later worked as a civil servant for the Empire in Amoy, Singapore, and Malaya, where he eventually became chief justice. Later many equally dark-skinned members of his family came to England for their education and remained for very successful professional careers. As an only child, I spent my winter and summer holidays with these close "cousins," whom I loved and admired. So, from an early age I was exposed to and stimulated by learning about and from "alterity." And some of my frustrating experiences at a boy's boarding school made me want to teach for the sake of the pupils.

After fieldwork with the Canadian Inuit in 1959, 1960, and 1963–1964, I came to teach anthropology at Berkeley. Over the years I found I was advising a number of minority graduate students, both Black-Americans (Tony Johnson, Toby Coles, Nathan Oba Strong, Nell Gabiam, Mitzi Cater, Yvonne Daniel[68]) and Hispanics (Moira Perez, Robert Gonzales). A number of non-Anglophone European students gravitated my way, both regular Berkeley graduate students (Christiana Giordano, Alexei Gostev, Ieva Tretjuka) and international students (Steffan Appelgren, Tom Selanniemi, Hugo de Block, Lina Tegtmeyer, Katrin Einarsdottir, Noel Salazar, David Picard, Valerio Simoni). I have mentored Berkeley students from the Middle East and beyond, both in anthropology (Seteney Shami, Zeynep Gursel, Amal Sachadena) and in Architecture and Planning, with many of them being students of Nezar AlSayyad (Swetha Vijayakumar, Amna al Rueli, Shahrzad Shirvani, Amir Gohar), as well as Linda Boukhris and Madina Regnault, who came to Berkeley through my work with Maria Gravari-Barbas at the Sorbonne-Panthéon, Paris. From South Africa, Kathryn Mathers came to study with me at Berkeley and Thokozani Khuzwayu came as a visiting scholar. I also worked closely with a few Latin American students who came to Berkeley (Ivan Arenas, Pablo Seward, and Hernan Hernao—unfortunately murdered in his office after he returned to Colombia). Brazilian tourism anthropologist Dr. Rodrigo de Grunewald came to work with me for a year, and I was invited to teach at the Universidade Rio Grande del Sol, Porto Alegre, in 2007. There I taught a young scholar Luis Felipe Murillo, whom I encouraged to come to the United States for his doctorate, and he ended up going to UCLA for his PhD, with a postdoc at Harvard.

Relations with East Asian students and scholars have been somewhat different and more complex. Some came to Berkeley to study tourism and other topics (Jeehwan Park, Geon Soo Han, Sujin Eom, media-tourism specialist Yongmin Choe from Korea; Hideaki Matsuoka, Kensuke Sumii, Sawako Sonoyama, Maki Tanaka, Yuko Okubo from Japan; and Maggie Mosher, Yang Ying, Zhang Xiaoping, De Qing from China, and Shuwei Tsai from Taiwan). Others were immigrants or the immediate descendants of Chinese immigrants (Lindy Li Mark, Ling Liu, Jenny Leung, and tourism/media anthropologist Jenny Chio).

However, my visit to Kagoshima, Japan, with my Japanese-American wife and her mother in 1974 led to my later study and research in Japan (1978–1979, 1989–1990, 2005 etc.). My wife and I also visited China on a research trip with Yang Ying in 1991, the first of many studies, research, and lecturing trips from 1999 onward. So, I was not just teaching these Asian students about tourism and heritage but also researching their national cultures, which engaged them as partners and advisees from whom I could learn a great deal. In Japan I worked with then-junior scholars Ishimori Shuzo, Yamashita Shinji, and Ikeda Mitsuho (at the National Museum of Ethnology, Osaka), while Nakafuchi Yasuyuki, Wakamatsu Koji and Sekiya Toshiyuki visited Berkeley. More recently I worked (and published) with junior tourism scholars Shoiji Yuko and Doshita Megumi.

Senior Chinese scholars Zhang Xiaoping and Yang Hui of Kunming and Peng Zhaorong of Xiamen (where my uncle from Ceylon and my aunt had lived 1896–1900 when it was called Amoy!) visited Berkeley in the early 2000s, returned home and quickly wrote articles and books about Western tourism research often in relation to Chinese tourism research. They positioned themselves as my *deshi* and encouraged their students to spend a year or more with me in Berkeley, while inviting me to lecture and teach in China (at more than thirty universities). These three senior Chinese scholars (and later Zhang Xiaosong of Guiyang) recommended their current and ex-students to become visiting scholars at Berkeley (in chronological order: Zhang Ying, Hong Ying, Zhang Jinfu, Ma Congling, Li Chunxia, Zhou Xuefan, Ge Rongling, Jin Lu, He Jingming, Suo Nan Cuo [Tibetan, with whom I had toured her homelands], Gong Na, Zhong Jie, Li Fei, Zhao Hongmei, Zheng Xiangchun, Fang Fang, Sa Lusha). Others came through different networks (Yu Luo and Ge Jing as postdocs, Uighur folklorist Rehile Dawuti from Urumqi, Iris Sheungtung Lo from Hong Kong, and recently Duan Xialei and Wang Zhe from Hong Kong). Others I have met, mentored, and served on their committees or worked with outside of Berkeley (Wang Yu of Kunming, Hong Kong, and Duke University; Zhu Yujie of Lijiang, Heidelberg, and Australia; Yang Xiaoyi, an art historian of Beijing and Bard School NYU; Liu Zixian, Dai Gaizhen; and others). I have taught many of them in seminars but more importantly I have visited them at their field sites, helped them apply for jobs, write and give papers and edit articles, published their works in edited volumes, and, most importantly for me, many of them have translated my works for publication in Chinese, and I have co-authored and published works with at least five (so far) in both Chinese and English!

And so it was that when EASA (European Association of Social Anthropologists) announced the call for papers for the 2014 meeting in Tallinn, Estonia, I sent out a call for papers on the underresearched topic "Tourism in Postsocialist Eastern Europe" using my existing contacts in Russia, Eastern Europe, and the United Kingdom. I was delighted to work with enthusiastic younger scholars, especially Magda Banaszkiewicz and Sabina Owsianowska, in organizing the triple panel of twelve papers, whittled down from the seventeen offered (with discussant Dr. Svetlana Ryzhakova, Russian Academy of Sciences). We worked together on editing and publishing a book of these papers in the United Kingdom and planned to enlarge on this topic for the 2015 Kraków meeting which resulted in this collection.

This book shows how Central and Eastern European anthropologists and their colleagues inspired by anthropological perspectives on studying tourism have become familiar with mainstream Western tourism-research concepts and methods and are contributing to them. They are also *au courant* with more recent developments, which have become important in the last decade, and they are at the cutting edge with a number of research directions where they may be leading their peers elsewhere. The range of the papers shows that these social scientists no longer limit their focus to their own regional cultures; they also extend their gaze to places outside of Europe. This step from an internal or local focus and being subject to the anthropological gaze of others, to joining the "world anthropologies" with a global gaze, is an important mark not only of maturity but a purposive show of self-confidence.[69]

NOTES

1. "I have conceived of the Anglophone Snake," the remnants of Empire, as the academic network stretching through Scotland, England, Canada, United States, Hong Kong, Australia, New Zealand (and Israel?). It is a core versus the non-Anglophone, the non-establishment, the lower classes, and, some would say, the female and LGBT thought circles.

2. At which we were forced to learn Latin and Greek six days a week. As children of the Cold War, we thought it more useful if we had learned Russian and Chinese. But, in case of a Russian invasion, we were all taught to say "Zdytyia, zdytyia. Ya znayu fiziku!" ["Stop, don't shoot. I know physics!"]

3. The author wishes to thank Magdalena Banaszkiewicz and Sabina Owsianowska for organizing and inviting me to the 2015 conference in Kraków. I also want to

thank Noel Salazar, Naomi Leite, Valerio Simoni, Lina Tegtmeyer, Rodanthi Tzanelli, and Annelou Ypeij for their guidance and suggestions.

4. Bronisław Malinowski, D.Sc. London School of Economics 1916, Trobriand Is. Research 1915–1918. I want to assert that Malinowski was a Polish, not British, social scientist. After education in Poland and Germany, he went to Britain to implant a completely new approach to anthropology. He often contrasted his "warm Slavic" approach to ethnography and functionalist theory with Radcliffe-Brown's British "structural functionalist" approach.

5. Zygmunt Bauman, "From Pilgrim to Tourist—A Short History of Identity," in *Questions of Cultural Identity*, ed. Stuart Hall and Paul Du Gay (London: Sage, 1996), 18–37; Daniel Boorstin, *The Image: A Guide to Pseudo-Events in America* (New York: Atheneum, 1964).

6. Dean MacCannell, *The Tourist: a New Theory of the Leisure Class* (New York: Schocken, 1976); Nelson Graburn, "Tourism: The Sacred Journey," in *Hosts and Guests: The Anthropology of Tourism*, ed. Valene Smith (Philadelphia: University of Pennsylvania Press, 1977), 17–32.

7. Valene Smith, ed. *Hosts and Guests: The Anthropology of Tourism* (Philadelphia: University of Pennsylvania Press, 1977); Erik Cohen, "The Phenomenology of Tourist Experience," *Sociology* 13 (1979): 180–201; John Urry, *The Tourist Gaze* (London: Sage, 1990); John Urry, *Mobilities* (Cambridge: Polity, 2007).

8. Edward M. Bruner, *Culture on Tour: Ethnographies of Travel* (Chicago: The University of Chicago Press, 2005); Julia Harrison, *Being a Tourist: Finding Meaning in Pleasure Travel* (Vancouver: University of British Columbia Press, 2003); Naomi Leite, *Unorthodox Kin: Portuguese Marranos and the Global Search for Belonging* (Berkeley: University of California Press, 2017).

9. Naomi Leite and Nelson Graburn, "Anthropological Interventions in Tourism Studies," in *Handbook of Tourism Studies*, ed. Mike Robinson and Tazim Jamal (London: Sage, 2009), 35–64.

10. Since Valene Smith, ed. *Hosts and Guests: The Anthropology of Tourism* (Philadelphia: University of Pennsylvania Press, 1977).

11. Though I "assign" each chapter to a topic, most chapters contribute to or bridge more than one subject area. Indeed, the authors might even choose a different "first topic." I will also comment on some subjects which are current but do not appear in this book.

12. Emanuel De Kadt, ed. *Tourism: Passport to Development?* (Oxford: Oxford University Press, 1979).

13. Daniel Boorstin, *The Image*; Anthony Haden-Guest, *Down the Programmed Rabbit Hole* (New York: HarperCollins, 1972); Louis Turner and John Ash, *The Golden Hordes: Tourism and the Pleasure Periphery* (London: Constable, 1975).

14. John Bryden, *Tourism and Development: A Case Study of the Commonwealth Caribbean* (New York: Cambridge University Press, 1973); George Young, *Tourism: Blessing or Blight?* (Harmondsworth, UK: Penguin, 1973).

15. Earlier social science works underlay the analyses of tourism. Particularly cogent were: Redfield, Linton, and Herskovits in "Memorandum on Acculturation," see: Robert Redfield, Ralph Linton, and Melville Herskovits, "Memorandum for

the Study of Acculturation," *Man* 35 (1935): 145–48. [Also in *American Anthropologist* 38, no. 1 (1936): 149–52]; Huizinga, *Homo Ludens*—about groups who travel together to play sports as a basis for studies of traveling collectivities, with anticipation, effervescence, bonding, and lasting memories, see: Johann Huizinga, *Homo Ludens* (London: Routledge, 1944). Later Edmund Leach on masking and festivals, see: Edmund Leach, "Time and False Noses," in *Rethinking Anthropology*, ed. Edmund Leach (London: Athlone Press, 1961) and Victor Turner on ritual and pilgrimage, see: Victor Turner, *The Ritual Process: Structure and Anti-Structure* (Chicago: Aldine, 1967); Victor Turner and Edith Turner, *Image and Pilgrimage in Christian Culture* (New York: Columbia University Press, 1983).

16. Theron Nuñez, "Tourism, Tradition, and Acculturation: Weekendismo in a Mexican Village," Ethnology 2 (1963): 347–52.

17. Valene Smith, *Stereopticon: Entry to a Life of Travel and Tourism Research* (New York: Cognizant Communication Corporation, 2015).

18. Dennison Nash, *A Community in Limbo: An Anthropological Study of an American Community Abroad* (Bloomington: Indiana University Press, 1970).

19. Nelson Graburn, "The Eskimos and 'Airport Art'," *Transaction* 4 (1967): 28–33.

20. George Young, *Tourism: Blessing or Blight* (London: Penguin, 1973).

21. Ben Finney and Karen Watson, *A New Kind of Sugar: Tourism in the Pacific* (Honolulu: East-West Center and Center for Pacific Studies, 1977).

22. Nelson Graburn, ed., *Ethnic and Tourist Arts: Cultural Expressions from the Fourth World* (Berkeley: University of California Press, 1976).

23. Valene Smith, *Hosts and Guests*.

24. Dennison Nash, "Tourism as a Form of Imperialism," in *Hosts and Guests: The Anthropology of Tourism*, ed. Valene Smith (Philadelphia: University of Pennsylvania Press, 1977), 33–47.

25. Dean MacCannell, *The Tourist*.

26. Erving Goffman, *The Presentation of Self in Everyday Life* (New York: Anchor, 1959).

27. Nelson Graburn, "Tourism: The Sacred Journey," in *Hosts and Guests: The Anthropology of Tourism*, ed. Valene Smith (Philadelphia: University of Pennsylvania Press, 1977), 17–32; Edmund Leach, "Time and False Noses," in *Rethinking Anthropology*, ed. Edmund Leach (London: Athlone Press, 1961); Victor Turner, *The Ritual Process: Structure and Anti-Structure* (Chicago: Aldine, 1967).

28. Alma Gottlieb, "Americans' Vacations," *Annals of Tourism Research* 9 (1982): 165–87.

29. Erik Cohen, "The Phenomenology of Tourist Experience," *Sociology* 13, no. 2 (1979): 180–201.

30. Erik Cohen, "Authenticity and Commoditization in Tourism," *Annals of Tourism Research* 15 (1988): 371–86.

31. Ning Wang, "Rethinking Authenticity in Tourism Experience." *Annals of Tourism Research* 26 (1999): 349–70.

32. Edward M. Bruner, *Culture on Tour*.

33. John Urry, *The Tourist Gaze* (London: Sage, 1990).

34. Maxine Feifer, *Going Places: The Ways of the Tourist from Imperial Rome to the Present Day* (London: Macmillan, 1985).

35. Nelson Graburn, "Tourism and Prostitution: A Review Article," *Annals of Tourism Research* 10 (1983): 437–56; Margaret B. Swain and Janet Momsen, eds. *Tourism/Gender/Fun(?)* (New York: Cognizant Communications, 2002).

36. Valerio Simoni, *Tourism and Informal Encounters in Cuba* (Oxford: Berghahn, 2016).

37. David Lowenthal, *The Past is a Foreign Country* (Cambridge: Cambridge University Press, 1985); David Lowenthal, *The Past is a Foreign Country—Revisited* (Cambridge: Cambridge University Press, 2015).

38. John Tunbridge and Gregory Ashworth, *Dissonant Heritage: The Management of the Past as a Resource in Conflict* (New York: Wiley, 1996).

39. Pierre Nora, "Between Memory and History. Les Lieux de Mémoire," *Representations* 26 (1989): 7–24.

40. Laurajane Smith, *Uses of Heritage* (London: Routledge, 2006).

41. Georges van den Abeele, "Sightseers."

42. Jenny Chio, "Fieldwork, Film, and the Tourist Gaze: Making 农家乐 Peasant Family Happiness," *Visual Anthropology Review* 30 (2014): 62–72.

43. Noel Salazar and Nelson Graburn, *Tourism Imaginaries*. In Europe, see: Estelle Sohier, "From the Invention of an Imaginary to the Promotion of Tourism: Greece through the Lens of the Photographer F. Boissonnas (1903–1930)," in *Tourism Imaginaries at the Disciplinary Crossroads: Places, Practices, Media*, eds. Maria Gravari-Barbas and Nelson Graburn (London: Routledge, 2016), 210–32; in Asia, see: Sidney C. H. Cheung, "Men, Women and 'Japanese' as Outsiders: A Case Study of Postcards with Ainu Images," *Visual Anthropology* 13 (2010): 227–55.

44. Sol Worth and John Adair, *Through Navajo Eyes* (Bloomington: Indiana University Press, 1972).

45. Jenny Chio, 农家乐 *Peasant Family Happiness*. Video, 70 mins.: Berkeley Media, 2013; Jenny Chio, *A Landscape of Travel: The Work of Tourism in Rural Ethnic China* (Seattle: University of Washington Press, 2014).

46. Tom Selanniemi, *Matka ikuiseen kesaan: Kulttuuriantropologinen nakokulma suomalaisten etelanmatkailuun* [A Journey to Eternal Summer: an Anthropological Perspective on Finnish Sunlust Tourism] (Helsinki: Suomalaisen Kirjallisuuden Seura, 1996).

47. Julia Harrison, *Being a Tourist*.

48. Iris S-T Lo and Bob McKercher, "Beyond Imaginary of Place: Performing, Imagining, and Deceiving Self through Online Tourist Photography," in *Tourism Imaginaries at the Disciplinary Crossroads: Places, Practices, Media*, ed. Maria Gravari-Barbas and Nelson Graburn (London: Routledge, 2016), 233–45.

49. Ian McDonnell, "The Role of the Tour Guide in Transferring Cultural Understanding," Working Paper No. 3, School of Leisure, Sport and Tourism, University of Technology, Sydney, 2001.

50. Noel Salazar, "Tourism and Glocalization: 'Local' Tour Guiding," *Annals of Tourism Research* 32 (2005): 628–46.

51. Rachid Amirou, *Imaginaire touristique et sociabilités du voyage* (Paris: Presses Universitaires de France, 1995).

52. Edward M. Bruner, *Culture on Tour.*
53. Nelson Graburn and Jafar Jafari, eds. *Tourism Social Sciences*, Special issue of *Annals of Tourism Research* 18 (1991).
54. We also found a similar language barrier with few people, especially Anglophones, reading outside of their own literature. More non-Anglophones were likely to cite English literature and, within Western Europe, often each other's works. Most Asian scholars read English and more rarely other Asian languages. One effort to overcome Anglophone isolation was Dann and Parrinello's book, see Graham Dann and Giuli Liebman Parrinello, eds. *The Sociology of Tourism: European Origins and Developments* (Bingley: Emerald, 2009). On the other hand, the e-journal *Via@ Tourism Review* (http://viatourismreview.com/) accepts papers in any of seven European languages and translates them into two or three others to be published in the same issue.
55. John Tribe, "The Indiscipline of Tourism," *Annals of Tourism Research* 24 (1997): 638–57; John Tribe, *Philosophical Issues in Tourism* (Bristol: Channel View, 2009). The Statement of Purpose of Berkeley's Tourism Studies Working Group, founded in 2003 says "The Tourism Studies Working Group provides a forum in which faculty and graduate students from a wide range of disciplines can exchange ideas, circulate and/or informally present works in progress, hear from visiting scholars, and receive feedback on their research. Rather than a discipline in its own right, we see tourism studies as a node at which numerous disciplines intersect and cross-fertilize" (www.tourismstudies.org). The same interdisciplinary approach characterizes EIREST *(Équipe Interdisciplinaire de Recherche sûr le Tourisme)*, founded in 2008 at Paris 1 University.
56. Nelson Graburn and Maria Gravari-Barbas, "Introduction: Tourism Imaginaries at the Disciplinary Crossroads," in *Tourism Imaginaries at the Disciplinary Crossroads: Places, Practices, Media*, eds. Maria Gravari-Barbas and Nelson Graburn (London: Routledge, 2016), 1–31.
57. One might be tempted to put Zygmunt Bauman into this category, for he has made contributions to tourism and mobility theory (Zygmunt Bauman, "From pilgrim to Tourist—a short history of identity") and had a position in the center of the cosmopolitan world of academia. Given his early escape and his immersion in the Russian (Soviet) system, it would be more difficult to claim him geographically.
58. Magdalena Banaszkiewicz, Nelson Graburn, and Sabina Owsianowska, eds. *Tourism in Post-Socialist Eastern Europe*. Special Issue of *Journal of Tourism and Cultural Change* 15 (2017); Sabina Owsianowska and Ryszard Winiarski, eds. *Antropologia turystyki/Anthropology of Tourism* (Kraków: University of Physical Education in Kraków Press, 2017).
59. One could suggest that the international Jewish network contributes to the expansion of the academic network; it is one of the few which has consistently crossed linguistic boundaries especially in Europe and North America.
60. Irena Ateljevic, Annette Pritchard, and Nigel Morgan, eds. *The Critical Turn in Tourism Studies: Innovative Research Methods* (London: Routledge, 2007). To this day there are also worldwide accusations that women, though not barred from entry into the field of tourism studies, are rarely allowed to occupy positions of leadership, as keynote speakers, or decision-making, as journal editors.

61. Gustavo Lins Ribeiro and Arturo Escobar, eds. *World Anthropologies. Disciplinary Transformations within Systems of Power* (Oxford: Berg, 2006).

62. Previously known as the Developing World, but the concept of "development" itself has also come under severe criticism, see: Arturo Escobar, *Encountering Development: The Making and Unmaking of the Third World* (Princeton, NJ: Princeton University Press, 1995), recently North and South have become the relevant adjectives.

63. Noel Salazar, ed., "World Anthropologies of Tourism," Special issue of *American Anthropologist* 119 (2017).

64. I use the Japanese word for student and follower which expresses the lifelong relationship engendered by training and lasts even at great geographical distances. And in a sense, I am bringing a concept from a marginalized, certainly non-Anglo-European into that very circuit, much as we bring a "regional" anthropology into the Anglophone world.

65. Through the later nineteenth-century Central and Northern European (and Japanese) anthropologies, often under the name of ethnology or folklore, were inward looking, focused on revealing the true cultural origins of emergent nations.

66. Nelson Graburn, "Tourism through the Looking Glass," in *Tourism Study: Anthropological and Sociological Beginnings*, ed. Dennison Nash (London: Pergamon Press, 2007), 93–107.

67. Referring to the non-English inhabitants of the colonies. As a boy, I was proud to be compared with Natives who could run fast, climb trees, and see great distances, though they were subject to accusations about drink and womanizing.

68. I have served as chief adviser for nearly sixty anthropology graduate students at Berkeley, and I have served on the doctoral committees of at least that number of other students within anthropology and other disciplines. This chapter also mentions on whose committees I have served outside the United States.

69. The symbolic importance of "overseas ethnography" (*haiwai minzuzhi*) for Chinese, see further: Yujie Zhu, Lu Jin, and Nelson Graburn. "Domesticating Tourism Anthropology in China," *American Anthropologist* 119, no. 4 (2017).

REFERENCES

Amirou, Rachid. *Imaginaire touristique et sociabilités du voyage*. Paris: Presses Universitaires de France, 1995.

Ateljevic, Irena, Annette Pritchard, and Nigel Morgan, eds. *The Critical Turn in Tourism Studies: Innovative Research Methods*. London: Routledge, 2007.

Banaszkiewicz, Magdalena. "The 'Embodiments' of Stalin in the Tourism Landscape of Moscow." *International Journal of Tourism Anthropology* 5 (2016): 221–34.

———. "A Dissonant Heritage Site Revisited—The Case of Nowa Huta in Krakow." *Journal of Tourism and Cultural Change* 15 (2017): 185–97.

Banaszkiewicz, Magdalena, Nelson Graburn, and Sabina Owsianowska, eds. "Tourism in (Post-Socialist) Eastern Europe". Special Issue of *Journal of Tourism and Cultural Change* 15 (2017): 109–21.

Bauman, Zygmunt. "From Pilgrim to Tourist—A Short History of Identity." In *Questions of Cultural Identity*, edited by Stuart Hall and Paul du Gay, 18–37. London: Sage, 1996.

Boorstin, Daniel. *The Image: A Guide to Pseudo-Events in America*. New York: Atheneum, 1964.

Bruner, Edward M. *Culture on Tour: Ethnographies of Travel*. Chicago: The University of Chicago Press, 2005.

Bryden, John. *Tourism and Development: A Case Study of the Commonwealth Caribbean*. New York: Cambridge University Press, 1973.

Cheung, Sidney C. H. "Men, Women and 'Japanese' as Outsiders: A Case Study of Postcards with Ainu Images." *Visual Anthropology* 13 (2010): 227–55.

———. 农家乐 *Peasant Family Happiness*. Video, 70 mins.: Berkeley Media, 2013.

Chio, Jenny. "Fieldwork, Film, and the Tourist Gaze: Making 农家乐 Peasant Family Happiness." *Visual Anthropology Review* 30 (2014): 62–72.

———. *A Landscape of Travel: The Work of Tourism in Rural Ethnic China*. Seattle: University of Washington Press, 2014.

Cohen, Erik. "The Phenomenology of Tourist Experience." *Sociology* 13, no. 2 (1979): 180–201.

———. "The Tourist Guide: The Origins, Structure and Dynamics of a Role." *Annals of Tourism Research* 12, no. 1 (1985): 5–29.

———. "Authenticity and Commoditization in Tourism." *Annals of Tourism Research* 15 (1988): 371–86.

Dann, Graham, and Giuli Liebman Parrinello, eds. *The Sociology of Tourism: European Origins and Developments*. Bingley: Emerald, 2009.

de Kadt, Emanuel, ed. *Tourism: Passport to Development?* Oxford: Oxford University Press, 1979.

Escobar, Arturo. *Encountering Development: The Making and Unmaking of the Third World*. Princeton, NJ: Princeton University Press, 1995.

Feifer, Maxine. *Going Places: The Ways of the Tourist from Imperial Rome to the Present Day*. London: Macmillan, 1985.

Finney, Ben, and Karen Watson. *A New Kind of Sugar: Tourism in the Pacific*. Honolulu: East-West Center and Center for Pacific Studies, 1977.

Goffman, Erving. *The Presentation of Self in Everyday Life*. New York: Doubleday Anchor, 1959.

Gottlieb, Alma. "Americans' Vacations." *Annals of Tourism Research* 9 (1982): 165–87.

Graburn, Nelson. "The Eskimos and 'Airport Art'." *Transaction* 4 (1967): 28–33.

———, ed. *Ethnic and Tourist Arts: Cultural Expressions from the Fourth World*. Berkeley: University of California Press, 1976.

———. "Tourism: The Sacred Journey." In *Hosts and Guests: The Anthropology of Tourism*, edited by Valene Smith, 17–32. Philadelphia: University of Pennsylvania Press, 1977.

———, ed. *The Anthropology of Tourism*. Special Issue of *Annals of Tourism Research* 10, no. 1 (1983).

———. "Tourism and Prostitution: A Review Article." *Annals of Tourism Research* 10 (1983): 437–56.

————. "The Ethnographic Tourist." In *The Tourist as a Metaphor of the Social World*, edited by Graham Dann, 19–39. Wallingford: CAB International, 2002.

————. "Tourism through the Looking Glass." In *Tourism Study: Anthropological and Sociological Beginnings*, edited by Dennison Nash, 93–107. London: Pergamon Press, 2007.

————. "The Dark is on the Inside: The *Honne* of Japanese Exploratory Tourists." In *Emotion in Motion: Tourism, Affect and Transformation*, edited by David Picard and Mike Robinson, 49–71. Farnham: Ashgate, 2012.

————. "The Tourist." In *Key Figures of Human Mobility*. Special issue of *Social Anthropology/Anthropologie Sociale*, edited by Noel B. Salazar and James Coates 25, no. 1 (2017): 83–92.

Graburn, Nelson, and Maria Gravari-Barbas, eds. *Imagined Landscapes of Tourism*. Special issue of *Journal of Tourism and Cultural Change* 9, no. 3 (2011).

————. "Introduction: Tourism Imaginaries at the Disciplinary Crossroads." In *Tourism Imaginaries at the Disciplinary Crossroads: Places, Practices, Media*, edited by Maria Gravari-Barbas and Nelson Graburn, 1–31. London: Routledge, 2016.

Graburn, Nelson, and Jafar Jafari, eds. *Tourism Social Sciences*. Special issue of *Annals of Tourism Research* 18, no. 1 (1991).

Haden-Guest, Anthony. *Down the Programmed Rabbit Hole*. New York: HarperCollins, 1972.

Harrison, Julia. *Being a Tourist: Finding Meaning in Pleasure Travel*. Vancouver: University of British Columbia Press, 2003.

Huizinga, Johann. *Homo ludens*. London: Routledge, 1944.

Leach, Edmund. "Time and False Noses." In *Rethinking Anthropology*, edited by Edmund Leach. London: Athlone Press, 1961.

Leite, Naomi. *Unorthodox Kin: Portuguese Marranos and the Global Search for Belonging*. Berkeley: University of California Press, 2017.

Leite, Naomi, and Nelson Graburn. "Anthropological Interventions in Tourism Studies." In *Handbook of Tourism Studies*, edited by Mike Robinson and Tazim Jamal, 35–64. London: Sage, 2009.

Lo, Iris S-T, and Bob McKercher. "Beyond Imaginary of Place: Performing, Imagining and Deceiving Self through Online Tourist Photography." In *Tourism Imaginaries at the Disciplinary Crossroads: Places, Practices, Media*, edited by Maria Gravari-Barbas and Nelson Graburn, 233–45. London: Routledge, 2016.

Lowenthal, David. *The Past is a Foreign Country*. Cambridge: Cambridge University Press, 1985.

————. *The Past is a Foreign Country-Revisited*. Cambridge: Cambridge University Press, 2015.

MacCannell, Dean. *The Tourist: A New Theory of the Leisure Class*. New York: Schocken, 1976.

Malinowski, Bronisław. *Argonauts of the Western Pacific: An Account of Native Enterprize and Adventures in the Archipelagoes of Melanesian New Guinea*. London: Routledge, 1922.

McDonnell, Ian. "The Role of the Tour Guide in Transferring Cultural Understanding." Working Paper No. 3, School of Leisure, Sport and Tourism, University of Technology, Sydney, 2001.

Nash, Dennison. *A Community in Limbo: An Anthropological Study of an American Community Abroad.* Bloomington: Indiana University Press, 1970.

————. "Tourism as a Form of Imperialism." In *Hosts and Guests: The Anthropology of Tourism*, edited by Valene Smith, 33–47. Philadelphia: University of Pennsylvania Press, 1977.

Nora, Pierre. "Between Memory and History. Les Lieux de Mémoire." *Representations* 26 (1989): 7–24.

Nuñez, Theron. "Tourism, Tradition, and Acculturation: Weekendismo in a Mexican Village." *Ethnology* 2 (1963): 347–52.

Owsianowska, Sabina. "Tourist Narratives about the Dissonant Heritage of the Borderlands: The Case of South-eastern Poland." *Journal of Tourism and Cultural Change* 15 (2017): 167–84.

Owsianowska, Sabina, and Ryszard Winiarski, eds. *Antropologia turystyki/ Anthropology of Tourism.* Kraków: University of Physical Education in Kraków Press, 2017.

Picard, David, and Mike Robinson, eds. *Emotion in Motion: Tourism, Affect and Transformation.* Farnham: Ashgate, 2012.

Przecławski, Krzysztof. *Człowiek a turystyka. Zarys socjologii turystyki* [*Man and Tourism. An Outline of Sociology of Tourism*]. Kraków: Albis, 1996.

Redfield, Robert, Ralph Linton, and Melville Herskovits. "Memorandum for the Study of Acculturation." *Man* 35 (1935): 145–48. [Also in *American Anthropologist* 38, no. 1 (1936): 149–52.]

Ribeiro, Gustavo Lins, and Arturo Escobar, eds. *World Anthropologies. Disciplinary Transformations within Systems of Power.* Oxford: Berg, 2006.

Salazar, Noel. "Tourism and Glocalization: 'Local' Tour Guiding." *Annals of Tourism Research* 32 (2005): 628–46.

————. *Envisioning Eden: Mobilizing Imaginaries in Tourism and Beyond.* Oxford: Berghahn, 2010.

————, ed. *World Anthropologies: The Local and the Global.* Special Issue of *American Anthropologist* 119, no. 4 (2017).

Salazar, Noel, and Nelson Graburn, eds. *Tourism Imaginaries: Anthropological Approaches.* London: Berghahn, 2014.

Selanniemi, Tom. *Matka ikuiseen kesaan: Kulttuuriantropologinen nakokulma suomalaisten etelanmatkailuun* [A Journey to Eternal Summer: An Anthropological Perspective on Finnish Sunlust Tourism]. Helsinki: Suomalaisen Kirjallisuuden Seura, 1996.

Simoni, Valerio. *Tourism and Informal Encounters in Cuba.* Oxford: Berghahn, 2016.

Smith, Laurajane. *Uses of Heritage.* London: Routledge, 2006.

Smith, Valene, ed. *Hosts and Guests: The Anthropology of Tourism.* Philadelphia: University of Pennsylvania Press, 1977.

48 *Nelson Graburn*

————. "Eskimo Tourism: Micro-Models and Marginal Men." In *Hosts and Guests: The Anthropology of Tourism*, edited by Valene Smith, 51–70. Philadelphia: University of Pennsylvania Press, 1977.

————. *Stereopticon: Entry to a Life of Travel and Tourism Research*. New York: Cognizant Communication Corporation, 2015.

Sohier, Estelle. "From the Invention of an Imaginary to the Promotion of Tourism: Greece through the Lens of the Photographer F. Boissonnas (1903–1930)." In *Tourism Imaginaries at the Disciplinary Crossroads: Places, Practices, Media*, edited by Maria Gravari-Barbas and Nelson Graburn, 210–32. London: Routledge, 2016.

Swain, Margaret B., and Janet Momsen, eds. *Tourism/Gender/Fun(?)* New York: Cognizant Communications, 2002.

Tribe, John. "The Indiscipline of Tourism." *Annals of Tourism Research* 24 (1997): 638–57.

————. *Philosophical Issues in Tourism*. Bristol: Channel View, 2009.

Tunbridge, John, and Gregory Ashworth. *Dissonant Heritage: The Management of the Past as a Resource in Conflict*. New York: Wiley, 1996.

Turner, Louis, and John Ash. *The Golden Hordes: Tourism and the Pleasure Periphery*. London: Constable, 1975.

Turner, Victor. *The Ritual Process: Structure and Anti-Structure*. Chicago: Aldine, 1967.

Turner, Victor, and Edith Turner. *Image and Pilgrimage in Christian Culture*. New York: Columbia University Press, 1983.

Urry, John. *The Tourist Gaze*. London: Sage, 1990.

————. *Mobilities*. Cambridge: Polity, 2007.

van den Abeele, George. "Sightseers: The Tourist as Theorist." *Diacritics* 10 (1980): 3–14.

Wang, Ning. "Rethinking Authenticity in Tourism Experience." *Annals of Tourism Research* 26, no. 2 (1999): 349–70.

Worth, Sol, and John Adair. *Through Navajo Eyes*. Bloomington: Indiana University Press, 1972.

Young, George. *Tourism: Blessing or Blight?* Harmondsworth, UK: Penguin, 1973.

Zhu, Yujie, Lu Jin, and Nelson Graburn. "Domesticating Tourism Anthropology in China." *American Anthropologist* 119, no. 4 (2017): 730–35.

Part II

ANTHROPOLOGY AND TOURISM

Relationships in Theory and Practice

Chapter 2

The Sarajevo Library, the Mostar Bridge, and Anthropology of Travel, Tourism, and Pilgrimage

Tom Selwyn

This chapter uses the case of a research and development project focusing on tourism, pilgrimage, and the cultural industries in Bosnia-Herzegovina (hereafter BiH), which ran from 2001 to 2004 and was funded and managed by the European Commission (EC) to make a contribution to the aims of this book, namely to discuss the anthropology of travel, tourism, and pilgrimage (hereafter ATTP) from a Central and Eastern European point of view.

The slightly longer title for the field, incorporating as it does pilgrimage and travel, is arguably preferable to the shorter "Anthropology of Tourism" for three reasons. First, the boundaries between tourism and pilgrimage are fluid and mutually reinforcing. This makes full discussions of the former dependent on the latter. Second, in the case of BiH, pilgrimage, as well as cultural events of many kinds, constitute a major part of the Bosnian tourism offer: the Christian and Muslim pilgrimage sites of Medjugorje and Ajvatovica respectively receive large numbers of visitors, the former effectively qualifying as a mass tourism destination. Third, both tourism and pilgrimage are clearly embedded within the long history of travel and travelers—any reflection of contemporary tourism and pilgrimage accordingly needs historical contextualization.

It is worth stressing that the subfield within anthropology devoted to the study of tourism is, effectively, a part of a scholarly tradition of work by social thinkers—from (at least) classical Greek and Roman times onward—concerned with the relation between travel and social thought. This interest is, as Judith Adler[1] has emphasized, rooted within the nature of travel itself, founded as this is on a variety of fundamental human needs: among other things, trade and the need for diplomatic relations with others, quests for spiritual enlightenment through pilgrimage, and a basic desire to know the world and the nature of others in order to better understand oneself. We will bear this in mind as we proceed.

As noted above, the present chapter uses an example of an exercise in "engaged anthropology,"[2] or applied anthropology, to generate insights into the nature of the field of ATTP. The project described here was part of the EC's TEMPUS (Trans-European Mobility Program for University Studies). The aim of this TEMPUS Institution Building (TIB) project, the first of its kind in BiH, was to create a program of research, education, and training in the tourism and cultural industries in BiH with a view to advancing the field of TTP as a medium for development in the country. The project partners came from five European universities: Sarajevo and Banja-Luka in BiH, Bologna in Italy, and University College London (UCL) and London Metropolitan University (LMU) in London. Starting as it did six years after the signing of the 1995 Dayton Agreement, which brought the three-and-a-half year civil war to an end, its overall aim was to contribute to the building of peace and reconciliation in the region through interuniversity cooperation in the field of TTP. Members of the project management team (university faculty from the five universities) included colleagues from several disciplinary backgrounds, including anthropology, Balkan studies, architecture, archaeology, development planning, economics, and tourism management. The overall project was designed and directed by anthropologists.

This chapter is organized into four main sections. The first explores how and why the EC is set up by the TEMPUS Institution Building projects in the first place and what the commission's objectives were in so doing. The second describes how a team of university academics set out to respond to the EC's challenge, outlining what its own particular aims were (one of the requirements laid out by the EC for TEMPUS projects was that each individual project should have a measure of independence from the wider and overall objectives of the EC itself). The main aim of the project was to put together a master's degree for students in the two Bosnian universities addressing the topics of travel, tourism, pilgrimage, and cultural heritage. The third reports on aspects of the master's degree: the subjects of the teaching modules, the students' MA dissertations, the project's design, and publication of a strategy for tourism development in BiH. The fourth section reflects on how the first three sections help us understand the theory and practice of ATTP. There is also a brief conclusion.

TEMPUS INSTITUTION BUILDING (TIB) PROJECTS AND TEMPUS BIH

The aim of the EC's TIB projects in the late 1990s and early 2000s was to incorporate universities in the so-called CE-10 countries (Bulgaria, the Czech

Republic, Estonia, Hungary, Latvia, Lithuania, Poland, Romania, Slovakia, and Slovenia) along with partner universities in member states into the process of accession into the European Union. Specifically, TEMPUS projects were (as they still are, in relation to countries on the European Union's southern borders) designed to make a contribution, through the work of universities, to three characteristics required of candidate countries to join the European Union: (i) that they possess stable institutions guaranteeing democracy, the rule of law, human rights, and respect for and protection of minorities; (ii) that there is a functioning market economy in the country; and (iii) that the country is fit and able to take on all the obligations of membership of the European Union.

TIB projects followed long-established ideas and practices of the United Nations Development Program (UNDP). These included the commitment for projects to work across public, private, and voluntary sectors, ensuring the well-being of each, ensuring participation in development by universities, and meeting the fundamental need for TIB projects to have a degree of independence and autonomy from the program overseers in the EC.

The project discussed here resolved to proceed by setting up a master's course in TTP as described above. The MA recruited twenty postgraduate students and consisted of nine individual course units each lasting ten days. Teaching took place, more or less in rotation, at the campuses of the five project member universities. The project as a whole was founded on the principle of decentralized cooperation, with its primary engagement being not so much with the state but rather with representative institutions under the level of the state. The project was designed to encourage institutions, at various levels of civil society supported by national and international administration, to work effectively and cooperatively in the field of travel, tourism, pilgrimage, and the cultural industries in BiH.

Icons of the Project

The project's first public engagement was held in London at the time of the first of our nine course units. Our event took place in Westminster Hall, opposite the British Houses of Parliament, with Paddy (now Lord) Ashdown (later to become High Representative in BiH) and Mladan Ivanic (then prime minister of Republika Srpska [RS], later BiH foreign minister, and presently member of the Presidency of Bosnia and Herzegovina) present. This was the occasion at which we, as a newly formed project group of twenty Bosnian students and half a dozen staff (from both BiH and the United Kingdom), carefully chose two icons to symbolically represent our project.

THE SARAJEVO LIBRARY

The National and University Library of Bosnia-Herzegovina, to give it its full title, has been one of the defining buildings of the city since it was built, originally as the Sarajevo City Hall, in 1896 by the Austro-Hungarian authorities. It was built in what is now termed "pseudo-Moorish" style following two visits by its architect to Cairo while drawing up the plans. Between 1910 and 1914, it housed the Bosnian parliament. It was first established as a library in 1945 and became part of the university in 1957.

In August 1992 most of its collection of books, archival material, and periodicals, together with the library catalog, was destroyed in the siege of Sarajevo. After many years during which the building remained in its postwar bombed-out state, it has recently been rebuilt. It has been widely agreed that the bombing of the library was an act designed physically to attack and metaphorically to destroy the cosmopolitanism of the city and BiH as a whole.

Its former director Enes Kujundic[3] has described the library's collection in terms of its Bosniak, Croatian, Muslim, Serbian, and Jewish provenance, recording that the library held works in Latin, English, German, Italian, French, Turkish, Persian, Hebrew, and Arabic, among other languages, and written in various scripts including Latin, Cyrillic, Old Bosnian, Glagolithic, Church Slavonic, and Hebrew.

Kujundzic argued that this linguistic diversity reflects the country's multicultural character. In this he followed the work of Jasna Samic (1966) in her *Bosnie: Pont des Deux Mondes*. Samic describes how in the Ottoman period some literature by Bosniaks was written, using Bosnian words, in Turkish, Arabic, and Persian. She also describes how the particular (poetic) genre of Alhamijado literature was written by Bosnian Muslims using Arabic script and by Bosnian Jews using Hebrew script. She further describes the similarities between popular Bosnian Muslim and Christian literary styles.

After the bombing, and in its reduced state, the library moved to temporary accommodation elsewhere in the city and resumed its role as center for regional professional solidarity by taking part in the regular meetings of the six central libraries of the now independent states of the former Yugoslavia. It is also the focus for wider regional networks of libraries. Recent links have been established with the Alexandrina, the newly built library in Alexandria, thus reaffirming its relations with Egypt. A link with the British library, established shortly after the most recent wars, is set to develop further in the near future.

THE BRIDGE AT MOSTAR

Many people in Northern and Western Europe are aware that the famous sixteenth-century Ottoman bridge over the Neretva river in Mostar was destroyed in November 1993 and most of those would agree with Misha Glenny's[4] observation that the single act of its destruction "seemed to represent the utter senselessness and misery of the entire conflict." Far fewer people outside BiH may know much about the bridge's history—or the fact that the motif of this bridge and bridges in general are ubiquitous symbols in the imagining of BiH by citizens and visitors alike.

The aim of the present chapter is to use the bridge (and everything that surrounds it) as a guiding symbol in our thinking about tourism and the reconstruction of civil society in BiH. Here are two quotations, one from the distinguished Sarajevan painter Afan Ramic[5] and the second from Alija lzetbegovic, erstwhile Bosnian president. This will lead to a brief report on a set of ongoing plans for postwar reconstruction in Mostar which, in turn, will serve as a way of extending the bridge metaphor into some thoughts about issues having to do with tourism and the cultural industries on a wider geographical level.

Following its destruction, Ramic addressed an assembly of people from Mostar with the following words about the bridge:

> Besides its architectural beauty, the Mostar bridge linked not only two river banks but two civilizations that intertwine at precisely the point where the cultures of East and West have been destined to permeate each other for centuries. That mutual permeation of cultures embodies the dignity of the peoples who know Bosnia and Herzegovina as their only shared country. . . . The bridge is in and of itself the link between everything that exists between these two cultures.

In a similar vein, Alija lzetbegovic, president of BiH from 1992 until 1996 and part of the Presidency of BiH until 2000, addressed a meeting of planners in Mostar. He started his speech by suggesting that there was no sense in speaking of social or cultural divisions in Bosnia.

> There is only one division which does make sense . . . a division which . . . will remain. . . . It is the division between the people who destroy bridges and the ones who build them.

Our project was founded upon an association with the latter sentiment.

THE TEMPUS PROJECT

The three-year course of the TEMPUS MA in tourism and the cultural industries in BiH has been described more fully elsewhere.[6] In the present chapter the focus is primarily on dissertation work by a select number of MA students and the ways that these led to the composition by all students and staff, overseen toward the climax of this effort by the late and distinguished anthropologist Jeremy Boissevain, erstwhile professor of anthropology at the University of Amsterdam, of *The Strategy for Tourism and the Cultural Industries in BiH* (hereafter *The Strategy*).

The MA Teaching Modules

The master's degree initiated under the aegis of the TEMPUS program was taught over two years in the campuses of the five project partners. It consisted of nine modules. Module one, held in London, discussed the shape and content of the project to come, exploring, inter alia, the appropriateness of our two icons to represent one of our determining ideological foundations, namely cosmopolitanism and religious pluralism and the rationale for building a program of tourism and cultural industries in the country on these principles. The second module, held in Sarajevo, identified the BiH "tourism offer." The third module, held at Banja-Luka, discussed relations between tourism and the natural environment. We visited national parks and raised a variety of issues (including environmental pollution and waste, logging, and lack of protective environmental planning). The fourth module was held at the Ancona campus of Bologna University and discussed Italian leisure and "cultural industries" (from ceramics to spas and theatres). The fifth, held in Bologna and neighboring towns, was concerned with museums, souvenirs, and designs. The sixth, held at University College London, focused on tourism planning. The seventh consisted of a mobile module with parts being taught in Mostar, Neum (on the Bosnian coast), and Trebinje. In the last-named town, located in the RS just north of Dubrovnic, we visited both Bogomil monuments and a damaged mosque being rebuilt by UNESCO.

At the conclusion of each module, students submitted essays and at the conclusion of the course they prepared a final dissertation. It is to a selection of these that we now turn.

DISSERTATIONS

Parks and Cities

Two dissertations discussed natural and built aspects of the material world. One consisted of a detailed account of the history and present organization of Sutjeska National Park, stressing its significance as one of the principal representatives of the wealth of natural attractions in the country. Emphasis was given to the memorial to Tito and the partisans situated in the center of the park. The second analyzed the ubiquity in BiH tourist brochures and other media of the image of Sarajevo as one of the great cosmopolitan cities of Europe. Images of Sarajevo routinely display photographic collages of synagogues, cathedrals, and mosques as well as parts of the Old City with its Ottoman buildings and the newer part of the city with architecture derived from traditions of the Austro-Hungarian period.

Tourism Organization

Several dissertations were concerned with the governance of tourism and the cultural industries in BiH. The central feature of tourism organization in the country was (as it remains) today that there was no statewide policy, planning, strategy, or governance. Instead there was (and is) a complex structure fragmented along ethnic and "entity" (the colloquialism given to the geographic and "ethnically" defined territories agreed at the Dayton Agreement) lines. Thus, in the Federation of BiH (i.e., the part of BiH associated in shorthand manner with mainly Muslim Bosniaks) a "Tourism Community of BiH" answered to cantonal ministries of tourism which, in turn, answered to the Federation's Ministry of Trade, while a "Tourism Organization of the RS" answered to the Ministry of Trade and Tourism of Republika Srpska. A substantial part of Bosnian Croatian tourism was driven and underpinned from Croatia itself. (It would be surprising if this organizational structure were intelligible to any outside observer, let alone any insider).

A group of dissertations were preoccupied with the economic management of tourism in the country and the role of tourism in its economic development. One (whose author worked for a bank) consisted of a sophisticated discussion of micro-credit arrangements enabling small- and medium-sized enterprises to find the financial capital to start businesses. Another examined the complex relationships between the Bosnian tourism industry and donor agencies associated with foreign governments involved in Bosnian economic regeneration.

The Spiritual and Symbolic Worlds

At least three dissertations considered the role of religious and symbolic sites in the BiH tourism offer. One compared the enormous popularity and substantial infrastructural development of the Catholic pilgrimage site of Medjugorje with the popular but relatively less developed Muslim pilgrimage center of Ajvatovica. The argument was that the several million annual visitors to the former resulted in healthy profits for both the site itself and also Croatia, from where many pilgrims came. It was further argued that the enhancement of Ajvatovica would not only generate additional tourists in Bosnia in the shape of Islamic travelers from countries such as Iran, Indonesia, and Malaysia but also promote good relations between BiH and these and other countries with Muslim populations.

Another thesis examined the famous tombs of the Bogomils, found as these are all over the country. Already a tourist attraction of some note, it was argued that they could well become a much more potent tourist attraction. The writer, a student from Banja-Luka, pointed out that there was a degree of historical uncertainty about the Bogomils and that it was thought by some that certain classes of Bogomils had converted to Islam in the early Ottoman period: a thought that promoted questions not only about the tombs as tourist attractions but also as possible subjects to shape school history curricula based on cosmopolitan interpretations of Bosnian history and culture.

The most artistically talented of the group produced a thesis examining the extent to which the design of certain fashions had been influenced by traditional Islamic imagery.

Identities

In some senses all the theses produced by members of the TEMPUS group were concerned with questions of self and identity. We need to keep in mind that the course was offered in the two universities, one in the Federation of BiH, the other in the RS (as well as additional universities in European member states), necessarily raising all sorts of questions about "ethnic" loyalties and affiliations. Additionally, the breakup of a former socialist republic and the emergence of new state setting itself toward a European market economy raised questions about both ethnicity and economics. In this landscape of jagged ethnic, economic, political, organizational, and cultural differences more or less *every* consideration concerning tourism, pilgrimage, and cultural heritage (i.e., from religious issues to questions of micro-credit) also raised profound questions about the natures of identity, selves, and others. Furthermore, all of this led directly and inevitably toward questions of historical truth and the nature of knowledge.

Knowledge in the Tourism Domain

One of the more striking dissertations, written by a student from Banja-Luka, proposed that a new curriculum for tour guides in BiH should be composed. The aim was to write a national curriculum and initiate a tour guiding school in two locations, Sarajevo and Banja-Luka. Guides would receive identical narratives to present to tourists. Once again the purpose was to find a way to promote the notion of a unified cosmopolitan Bosnia with a plurality of cultural and religious traditions.

Following this idea, a dissertation written by a student from Sarajevo (the deputy director of the National and University Library) discussed the future of the library, arguing for a return to its symbolic and architectural dominance of the city's urban fabric and skyline as well as its position as *the* center for local and tourist activity alike.

Dissertations as a Whole

The value of the theses, considered collectively, was that they combined considerations of the governance of tourism and heritage, with a realistic and detailed appreciation of what constitutes cultural and environmental capital. They also mined the past for inspiration about the possibilities for future initiatives in the field (the text on design being a particularly effective example of this) and followed this up into the field of history and education. While all of them explicitly and implicitly spoke about the uses of their work in economic development, all approached this subject with an awareness of the social and cultural context under which such development should proceed. Their general cultural aim was to prepare the ground for the new independent tourists toward whom Bosnian tourism markets looked with growing anticipation.

BIH TOURISM STRATEGY

One lasting achievement of the project was the production of what is still, up to the time of writing this chapter, the only state wide, comprehensive, tourism strategy for BiH. The six-chapter, ninety-page, document was produced by teams of the project participants. Each team consisted of members from all parts of BiH. The production was supervised by two anthropologists (the present writer and the late Jeremy Boissevain from the University of Amsterdam) together with other members of staff in the project team. The point of emphasis here is that this was a strategy designed in its entirety by Bosnian graduates from disparate parts of the country, working as they were through the universities of Sarajevo and Banja-Luka. The following is a select commentary, with quotations, from the chapters of *The Strategy*.

Chapter 1 ("Tourism Offer") was composed by Esma Kreso, Dunja Pejic-Hadzie, Lejla Baljevic, and Tatjana Spasojevic. The authors began with the claim that, though a relatively small country, BiH had great tourism potential with a mix of Eastern and Western civilizations and cultures. They followed this by suggesting that the cooperation, participation, and support of the community was a prerequisite in creating and developing a successful tourism offer. They further pointed to the large number of "transit tourists" on their way from further east to the mainly Croatian coast.

At the center of their chapter the authors emphasized the

> multifaceted spiritual and cultural practices of the country making it one of the
> most naturally and culturally diversified countries in Europe. Throughout the
> generations of Illyrian, Byzantian, Western European, Romanesque, and Otto-
> man influences, the Slavic tribes of Bosnia and Herzegovina have harvested a
> resounding pride in the many ethnic backgrounds that dominate present day BiH.

In addition to the three monotheistic religions the authors highlighted the
presence of the

> heretic Bosnian Church of the Bogumils, while the ancient heretic beliefs of
> Mithraism are still present in the caves and catacombs of Jajce, and a number of
> monasteries and Moslem dervish houses (tekija).

Chapter 2 ("Geographic and Environmental Aspects") was written by
Biljana Josic, Amela Gacanovic-Tutnjevic, Esma Kreso, and Fuad Kozadra
and examined the geography of BiH focusing on the country's mountains,
rivers, springs, and caves. The tourism potential of each of these aspects
was discussed with regard to the possibilities they held for nature reserves
and national parks. It was pointed out that some mountains had already been
developed as tourism centers while others remained in a pristine state. Each
of these mountains was described in terms of climate, transport, forests, and
the natural products found in them.

The authors suggested that the mountains leaned themselves to different
types of tourism inter alia:

> Sportsmen, ramblers and walkers interested in gathering and picking forest
> fruits and/or medicinal herbs or picnicking beside the mountain spring, skiers
> and hikers. There are numerous trails marked and maintained by mountaineer-
> ing clubs from the region. There are spaces for recreation, alpinism, hunting and
> for simple nature lovers.

The authors further remind us that Jahorina, Bjelašnica, Igman, and
Trebević hosted the 1984 Winter Olympic Games and that caves and their
surroundings in Bosnia and Herzegovina provide excellent conditions for
alpinism, speleology, mushroom picking, and medicinal herb picking.

However, if the first half of the chapter had a lyrical character to it the
authors were highly critical of aspects of environmental governance in the
country, claiming that environmental protection and management in the
country were lamentable. Rivers with solid waste abounded, pollution was
present in many forms, and there were no policies or institutions to deal with

these issues. They concluded that "environmental protection, post war, has been a low-priority, and the devastation of the environment continues, not supported by legislation that would protect nature and natural resources."

The third chapter ("Economic Aspects of Tourism in BiH") was written by Aleksandar Ljuboja, Valentina Zmaric, Vanesa Murvat, and Igor Dodig and consisted of reflections about privatization, tourism growth, fiscal policies in the tourism sector, and issues of investment. They observed that BiH was undergoing painful transition, arguing that privatization processes occurring in BiH shared the difficulties experienced by other former Eastern bloc countries but also has specific difficulties caused by war and the 5–7 years postponement of the economic transition process. They further emphasized that privatization in the RS, on the one hand, the Federation of Bosnia and Herzegovina, on the other, are totally separate processes based on quite different models. They further argued that privatization will change the whole culture of doing business.

> The main problem for BiH is that the part of capital that is still state-owned and scheduled to have been privatized has had difficulties in finding buyers. Currently, the state still owns the greater part of the larger companies such as (the Pension Fund and Restitution Fund), and no one has currently expressed interest to invest money in these companies under the privatization process.
>
> Furthermore almost every company that is involved in the privatization process has a burden of debts. Additionally almost every company is over-employed, that is it has too many workers on its books. Under the socialist system and in the years afterwards, these companies played a social role in society.

The fourth chapter ("Institutional Aspects of Tourism and Pilgrimage Organization in BiH") was written by Jadranka Stojanovic, Mirsada Buric, Azemina Njuhovic, and Katerina Peros described the byzantine (lower case b) structures of existing institutional arrangements and to suggest a more rational structure. They suggested that

> the state government of BiH should declare tourism a strategic branch of the economy and then establish an appropriate institutional structure in the form of a state-level ministry or office whose main task will be the development of tourism in BiH. A new tourism development strategy should be composed and adopted, government support should be given to stakeholders to develop tourism products by supporting and developing different programs of revitalization for the tourism industry. Encourage local and foreign credit institutions and funds to introduce regional programs for financing investments and micro-credits. Ensure the preservation of tourist resources by carrying out environmental impact assessments prior to any site development.

The authors described the present fragmented administrative structures associated with tourism, noting that there were few, if any, professional associations at the state level. The second half of the chapter set out in very considerable detail the institutional shortcomings of the present organizational arrangements, emphasizing (above all) the absence of state oversight, lack of coordination, the failure of the authorities to improve the image of the country, and to harness civil society in BiH in pursuit of an effective tourism strategy. They produced a very lengthy and comprehensive list of reforms and initiatives that needed to be put into action, concluding with the submission that there was a lack of long-term vision about potential investments in the tourist sector, insufficient level of competence and poor organization of the current institutions in charge of tourism development, ending with the comment that "sustainable tourism development needs to be urgently adopted in order to restore the image of country as a peaceful and safe destination."

The fifth chapter, written by Kenan Zekic, Almedina Causevic-Esko, and Alexander Sukalo concerned the marketing of tourism and pilgrimage. The authors considered domestic, regional, and international tourism. They adopted five main objectives: the targeting of independent tourists (rather than group tourists and pilgrims), the encouragement of repeat visitors, product development, tourism awareness, and a sophisticated program of branding. Heritage tourism was singled out for some emphasis. Domestic tourism, they argued, could include segments such as business, visiting friends and relatives, and holiday tourists (spa tourists, families, and winter sports for example) while regional international tourism should encourage citizens of neighboring countries visiting BiH, specifically Croatia, Montenegro, and Serbia in segments such as business, visiting friends and relatives, transit and holiday tourists (spa tourists, families, and winter sports for example). International tourism should be aimed at high-yielding segments such as meetings and conventions, heritage and cultural tourists, backpackers, study tourists, international diaspora, adventure tourists, and ecotourists.

The authors drew attention to one of the emerging contemporary trends in global tourism, namely the emergence of the independent tourism sector, one of the highest-yielding segments within this market being the backpacker segment: young well-educated Western travelers who desire to make the majority of their own travel decisions with little reliance on existing travel agencies. Typically, using existing transport and accommodation infrastructure and relying heavily on guidebooks to direct their travel patterns, they are focused on experiential tourism and desire to see a country in its natural state interacting with the local population as much as they can. They call themselves travelers rather than tourists. They argued that BiH was currently well set up to attract this high-yielding market to travel throughout the country in combination with other destinations.

The sixth and final chapter ("Social, Religious, and Symbolic Aspects of Tourism") was written by Aleksandra Isrvanic, Dijana Lajic, Edin Smajic, and Majda Fetahagic.

The authors began by observing that

> the two most important aspects of the society as segment of tourism are religious communities and civil society. Although religious communities are considered as part of the civil society, the role of these communities in BiH makes it important to discuss them separately. Traditionally religious communities have played a pro-active role in the daily lives of the people from this region and despite the fact that the scope of operation of these communities was very limited during the communist era people trusted and relied on them.

They went on to report that after the fall of communism, religious communities revived many of their activities and that they helped people during the war with whatever limited sources they had. The revival continued after the war when the major religious communities—Islamic, Orthodox, and Catholic Churches, and Jewish—established an NGO named the "Inter-religious Council." This became a platform for the exchange of ideas and for dialogue and discussion and as well as a base for solution-seeking. The NGO declared that "religious communities could play a valuable role in the development of tourism, culture, and related industries in tourism awareness building, moral and ethics awareness, religious festivals and holy days, pilgrimage sites, and inter-religious dialogue and cooperation."

The chapter continued with a detailed consideration of the role of civil society in tourism development and organization. Tasks to which civil society organizations could be dedicated included auditing tourist sites, research, adult education, networking locally, regionally, and internationally, engaging in media output, and cross border initiatives.

LESSONS FROM TEMPUS FOR ATTP

How does this particular project, carried out by postgraduate Bosnian students, help us identify the contours of ATTP?

If we look at the TEMPUS dissertations and relate these to the Tourism Strategy, we may see five themes at work. The placing of these themes alongside the wider context of international work by anthropologists working in the field of tourism, pilgrimage, and the cultural industries helps point us toward the theoretical and practical architecture of ATTP itself.

The first theme concerns the material world: land, mountains, rivers, and the streets and buildings (including the library in Sarajevo) of cities in BiH.

Two chapters of the Strategy followed suit in the wider field of ethnographic writing on ATTP. The material world, defined as above, has been the starting point of all ethnographies in field. For example, David Picard's[7] study of tourism in the Indian Ocean island of La Réunion stresses the abundant flora (carefully tended as these are by the tourism authorities) in the island while Hazel Tucker's[8] ethnography of rural Cappadocia introduces us to the famous rock cones of Goreme. Natasha Rogelja and Alenka Spreizer[9] look at tourism along the coast of Slovenia through the lens of the sea and its fish while Hazel Andrews's[10] portrait of the mass tourism resort of Magaluf is written from the point of view of its hotels, streets, souvenir shops, cafés, and other buildings. Accounts of tourism and pilgrimage in Palestine/Israel[11] start with the centrality of Palestinian land and its cities.

The second theme concerns governance. As noted above, most theses rehearsed the shortcomings of tourism organization and administration in the country. The TEMPUS Strategy addressed the consequences of this failure. Thus, a state-level institutional structure was drawn up, initiatives about micro-credit assistance to civil society organizations were proposed, and coherent laws were outlined.

This work from BiH fits into the wider ATTP field, especially, since the pioneering work of de Kadt[12] on the role of tourism in economic development. Much ethnographic work has followed in the same vein. Yiota Kululas and Michel Awad report that the fairly recent reestablishment of Abraham's Path[13] from the north to the south of Palestine encourages walkers and hikers to use home-stay accommodation in villages along the way. The route is designed to link municipalities of towns and villages together and thus to encourage coherent policy coordination and tourism governance. Picard describes government policies toward setting up and managing ecologically friendly tourism in La Réunion while Tucker addresses the role of public policy and planning, including the various cooperative ventures between government and such international agencies as UNESCO. Rogelja and Spreizer examine the economics of the fishing economy along the Slovenian coast, showing how life and work there are set within complex policies and activities of local, regional (including the European Union), and national government, associations of fishing boat owners, unions, and various types of visitors who are taking part in the building of a fishing/tourist economy.

The third theme concerns spiritual and symbolic features of tourism in BiH. Several dissertations referred variously to Medjugorje, Ajvatovica, Bogomil graves, Ottoman mosques, Orthodox monasteries, churches, and synagogues in Sarajevo. The Strategy pointed up the salience of the symbolic world in a wider sense, including work in such fields as tourism marketing and design.

Interest in the spiritual and the symbolic have been prominent features of ATTP since the 1970s. Dean MacCannell[14] followed Roland Barthes's[15] work on cultural imagery, symbolism, and mythology while Picard likens projects in La Réunion to conserve the island's coral reefs to liturgical rituals. Tucker's interlocutors—residents and visitors alike—emphasize the symbolic associations between the enchanted landscapes around Goreme with romantic human entanglements. Studies in ATTP focusing on tourist-related symbolism remind us of the artistic and aesthetic foundations of the field.

The fourth theme, apparent in both dissertations and *The Strategy*, consists of issues of identity and the natures of selves and others. We may keep in mind that the course was offered in the two universities, one in the Federation of BiH (i.e., the predominantly Muslim part of the country) the other in the RS (the predominantly Christian Orthodox part), necessarily drawing attention to questions about the primacy or otherwise of "ethnic" territories and histories. Additionally, the breakup of Yugoslavia and the emergence of BiH raise questions about both ethnicity and economics. This is a landscape of jagged ethnic, economic, political, organizational, and cultural differences. In such a context more or less *every* consideration of tourism, pilgrimage, and cultural heritage involves both religious and economic issues (which are generally intertwined).

From the publication of Valene Smith's "Hosts and Guests" (1977) onward, ATTP has been concerned with identity and relations of self to other. More recently, Rogelja and Spreitzer report that Slovenians find themselves poised between two contrasting fish and their symbolic associations. The Adriatic mullet is always on the move, engaged daily in swimming across national maritime boundaries while the sea bass is farmed in Slovenian fishponds. A clearer pair of allegories of Slovenian historic attachment to the former Yugoslavia (and wider world), on the one hand, and contemporary independence and self-sufficiency, on the other, would be hard to find. Picard's entire book is designed to place issues of self and other within a symbolic universe in which the islanders of La Réunion are rendered not just protectors of the island's flora and fauna but as an integral part of that natural world. For observers in the wider ("Western") world this global garden state is thus incorporated into a symbolic repertoire of nostalgic colonialism behind which global economic liberalism may operate, as it were, behind the garden fence. Tucker reports from Goreme that her young male interlocutors describe their romantic attachments with foreign girls in terms of their (i.e., the boys') newly found capacity to move from the confining contours of parental and kinship relationships to less constraining contexts in which, as seemingly free individuals, they feel able to be themselves.

The fifth and final theme concerns the role of knowledge production and consumption in, among other spheres, tourism-related activities, thus involving consideration of institutions designed for learning and knowledge gathering, such as libraries and museums. This was a theme that reoccurred throughout dissertations and *The Strategy*—ranging as it did from the emphasis on the central place in BiH of the National Library to the uniquely innovative notion of a state-level (rather than "entity"-level) curriculum for guides.

Ethnographic work throughout ATTP, as studied globally, has consistently been concerned with knowledge and its uses (and abuses) in tourism-related institutions. Ethnographic work on museums is now well established, Jane Nadel-Klein, David Clark, and Julie Scott[16] and others having made notable contributions to the field. Additionally, all the work on tourist guides and tourism brochures[17] are examples of explorations about the kind of knowledge that tourists receive about people and places.

CONCLUSION

Our Bosnian TEMPUS graduates teach us that ATTP is built on five theoretical and practical pillars or domains: the material world; issues of governance and administration, the symbolic and connotative structures of the field, issues of identity, including questions about the nature of self and other, and questions of tourism-related knowledge.

Building on these insights, the field is seen to consist, firstly, of the identification of persons and objects belonging to each of the five domains and, secondly, analysis of the relationships between the domains. In this light ATTP appears in large measure as the political economy of cultural production and consumption.

Following this line of thought, we may draw this chapter to an end by returning to our project icons. We may then see the Mostar bridge materially reassembled stone by stone, administratively brought into the center of tourism itineraries as a symbol of the link between continents, potentially subverting both the city's sharp "ethnic" divisions and forms of knowledge that speak of the inevitability of social and cultural separation. As for the library, we may see it reemerging as *the* material object dominating the skyline of Sarajevo and, moreover, like the bridge, occupying a central place in tourism organization, in the process appearing as a symbol of cosmopolitanism rather than one of narrow nationalism. If the aim of bombing it was to snuff such knowledge out, the aim of repairing it was to resurrect cosmopolitan visions after the war and thus invite everyone (both residents and visitors) to share and find pleasure (a prime motivational force behind tourism) in them.

The skills to join and dynamically relate the five domains—material, organizational, symbolic, psycho-cultural, ideological—to each other are clearly exhibited by the ethnographers we have quoted here. What we have additionally attempted is to show how a network of Bosnian postgraduate students have carried the theoretical insights of international contemporary scholars in ATTP into the realms of policy and practice. By so doing they have moved us decisively forward into a world in which travel, social thought, and politics recover their close kinship.

NOTES

1. Judith Adler, "The Origins of Sightseeing," *Annals of Tourism Research* 16 (1989): 7–29.

2. Cf Simone Abram, "Anthropology, Tourism, and Intervention?" in *Thinking Through Tourism*, ed. Julie Scott and Tom Selwyn (Oxford: Berg, 2010), 231–53.

3. Enes Kujundzic, "The National and University Library of Bosnia and Herzegovina in Sarajevo" (Address at Library, Sarajevo, 2002).

4. Misha Glenny, *The Balkans 1804–1999: Nationalism, War and the Great Powers* (London: Granta, 1999), 646.

5. Afan Ramic, "Uniting a Nation with Bridge and Brochure" (Times Higher Education, 1994, Supplement, January 18th), 22.

6. Tom Selwyn and Jonathan Karkut, "The Politics of European Co-operation: An Account of an EC TEMPUS Project in Bosnia-Herzegovina," in *Tourism and Politics: Global Frameworks, Local Realities*, ed. Peter Burns and Marina Novelli (London: Elsevier, 2007), 123–46.

7. David Picard, *Tourism, Magic and Modernity: Cultivating the Human Garden* (New York: Berghahn, 2011).

8. Hazel Tucker, *Living with Tourism: Negotiating Identities in a Turkish Village* (London: Routledge, 2003).

9. Natasha Rogelja and Alenka Janko Spreizer, *Fish on the Move: Fishing between Borders and Discourses in the Northern Adriatic* (New York: Springer, 2017).

10. Hazel Andrews, *The British on Holiday* (Bristol: Channel View Publications, 2014).

11. Tom Selwyn, "Tourism, Sight Prevention, and Cultural Shutdown: Symbolic Violence in Fragmented Landscapes," in *Tourism and Violence*, ed. Hazel Andrews (Farnham: Ashgate, 2014); Isaac Rami, C. Michael Hall, and Freya Higgins-Desbiolles, eds. *The Politics and Power of Tourism in Palestine* (London: Routledge, 2015).

12. Emanuel de Kadt, ed. *Tourism: Passport to Development?: Perspectives on the Social and Cultural Effects of Tourism in Developing Countries (A Joint World Bank–Unesco Study)* (Oxford: Oxford University Press, 1979).

13. Yiota Kutulas and Michael Awad, "Bike and Hike in Palestine," in *The Politics and Power of Tourism in Palestine*, eds. Isaac Rami et al. (London: Routledge, 2016), 53–63.

14. Dean MacCannell, *The Tourist. A New Theory of the Leisure Class* (New York: Schocken, 1976).

15. Roland Barthes, *Mythologies*, trans. Annette Lavers (London: Paladin, 1973).

16. Jane Nadel-Klein, *Fishing for Heritage: Modernity and Loss along the Scottish Coast* (Oxford: Berg, 2003); David Clark, "Jewish Museum: Performing the Present

through Narrating the Past," *Jewish Cultural Studies* 4 (2010): 271–92; Julie Scott, "Mapping the Past: Turkish Cypriot Narratives of Time and Place in the Canbulat Museum, Northern Cyprus," *History and Anthropology* 13 (2002): 217–30.

17. Graham Dann, *The Language of Tourism. A Sociolonguistic Perspective* (Wallingford, UK: CABI, 1996) and Erik Cohen, "The Tourist Guide: The Origins, Structure and Dynamics of a Role," *Annals of Tourism Research* 12, no. 1 (1985): 5–29.

REFERENCES

Abram, Simone. "Anthropology, Tourism, and Intervention?" In *Thinking through Tourism*, edited by Julie Scott and Tom Selwyn, 231–53. Oxford: Berg, 2010.

Adler, Judith. "The Origins of Sightseeing." *Annals of Tourism Research* 16 (1989): 7–29.

Andrews, Hazel. *The British on Holiday*. Bristol: Channel View Publications, 2011.

Barthes, Roland. *Mythologies*. Translated by Annette Lavers. London: Paladin, 1973.

Clark, David. "Jewish Museum. Performing the Present through Narrating the Past." *Jewish Cultural Studies* 4 (2010): 271–92.

Crick, Malcolm. "Representations of International Tourism in the Social Sciences: Sun, Sex, Sights, Savings and Servility." *Annual Reviews of Anthropology* 18 (1989): 307–44.

Cohen, Erik. "The Tourist Guide: The Origins, Structure and Dynamics of a Role." *Annals of Tourism Research* 12 (1985): 5–29.

Dann, Graham. *The Language of Tourism: A Sociolinguistic Perspective*. Wallingford, UK: CABI, 1996.

Franklin, Adrian, and Mike Crang. "The Trouble with Tourism and Travel Theory?" *Tourist Studies* 1, no. 1 (2001): 5–22.

Gellner, Ernest. *Legitimation of Belief*. Cambridge: Cambridge University Press, 1974.

Glenny, Misha. *The Balkans 1804–1999: Nationalism, War and the Great Powers*. London: Granta, 1999.

de Kadt, Emanuel, ed. *Tourism: Passport to Development?: Perspectives on the Social and Cultural Effects of Tourism in Developing Countries (A Joint World Bank–UNESCO Study)*. Oxford: Oxford University Press, 1979.

———. "Making the Alternative Sustainable: Lessons from Development for Tourism." Working Paper Institute of Development Studies. Brighton: University of Sussex, 1990.

Kujundzic, Enes. "The National and University Library of Bosnia and Herzegovina in Sarajevo." Address at Library, Sarajevo, 2002.

Kutulas, Yiota, and Michael Awad. "Bike and Hike in Palestine." In *The Politics and Power of Tourism in Palestine*, edited by Isaac Rami, C. Michael Hall, and Freya Higgins-Desbiolles, 53–63. London: Routledge, 2016.

MacCannell, Dean. *The Tourist: A New Theory of the Leisure Class*. New York: Schocken, 1976.

Meethan, Kevin, Alison Anderson, and Steve Miles, eds. *Tourism, Consumption, and Representation: Narratives of Place and Self.* Oxford: CABI, 2006.

Nadel-Klein, Jane. *Fishing for Heritage: Modernity and Loss along the Scottish Coast.* Oxford: Berg, 2003.

Picard, David. *Tourism, Magic and Modernity: Cultivating the Human Garden.* New York: Berghahn, 2011.

Pocock, David. *Understanding Social Anthropology.* London: Hodder and Stoughton, 1975.

Rami, Isaac. Michael C. Hall, and Freya Higgins-Desbiolles, eds. *The Politics and Power of Tourism in Palestine.* London: Routledge, 2015.

Ramic, Afan. "Uniting a Nation with Bridge and Brochure." *Times Higher Education,* 1994, Supplement, January 18th.

Rogelja, Nataša, and Alenka Janko Spreizer. *Fish on the Move: Fishing Between Borders and Discourses in the Northern Adriatic.* New York: Springer, 2017.

Šamić, Jasna. *Bosnie Pont des Deux Mondes,* Istanbul: Isis, 1996.

Scott, Julie. "Mapping the Past: Turkish Cypriot Narratives of Time and Place in the Canbulat Museum, Northern Cyprus." *History and Anthropology* 13 (2002): 217–30.

Selwyn, Tom. "Tourism, Sight Prevention, and Cultural Shutdown: Symbolic Violence in Fragmented Landscapes." In *Tourism and Violence,* edited by Hazel Andrews. Farnham: Ashgate, 2014.

———. "Tourism, Travel, and Pilgrimage: Anthropological Approaches." In *Encyclopedia of Anthropology,* edited by Hillary Callan. Chichester: Wiley, 2018.

Selwyn, Tom, and Jonathan Karkut. "The Politics of European Co-operation: An Account of an EC TEMPUS Project in Bosnia-Herzegovina." In *Tourism and Politics: Global Frameworks, Local Realities,* edited by Peter Burns and Marina Novelli, 123–46. London: Elsevier, 2007.

Smith, Valene. *Hosts and Guests: The Anthropology of Tourism.* Philadelphia: University of Pennsylvania Press, 1977.

Tucker, Hazel. *Living with Tourism: Negotiating Identities in a Turkish Village.* London: Routledge, 2003.

Chapter 3

Engaging with the Hosts and Guests

Some Methodological Reflections on the Anthropology of Tourism

Maarja Kaaristo

INTRODUCTION: TOURISM AND ANTHROPOLOGY

Anthropology has traditionally engaged in studying various social and cultural phenomena, focusing on the individual as the active agent in their (re) creation[1]. The study of tourism would seem a naturally interesting topic in that regard; however, it is a relatively new subject area within the discipline. The first publication focusing exclusively on the subject dates back to 1963 when Nuñez published his paper "Weekendismo in a Mexican Village,"[2] a study of interaction between the residents of a fishing village with visiting affluent city dwellers in the framework of acculturation theory. The study of tourism as an anthropological subject matter gathered momentum slowly and steadily and, by 1974, there were enough anthropologists researching the topic for Valene Smith to organize the first American Anthropological Association tourism symposium. The papers presented there eventually became *Hosts and Guests: The Anthropology of Tourism*,[3] a seminal book and an important milestone in the development of the discipline.

The "discovery" of this topic took place rather late, especially when considering some sociologists were publishing on the subject in the first half of the twentieth century, most notably Durant's *The Problem of Leisure*.[4] The reason for that is what Burns[5] calls an "avoidance relationship," consisting of three main aspects. First, the academic study of tourism is quite often (outside of the dedicated tourism and tourism management departments) seen as something frivolous, a pursuit a "serious" scholar would not engage in. This attitude is probably most famously depicted in David Lodge's 1991 novel *Paradise News*,[6] featuring a hedonistic, pleasure-seeking anthropologist, conducting research on Hawaiian tourism. Secondly, the relationship between anthropology and tourism is somewhat too close and intermingled for anthropologists' liking, as studying tourism would inevitably bring forth an uncomfortable question of in what ways do a tourist and an anthropologist actually differ (at least in the first stages of fieldwork). In order to deal with these questions, the anthropologist would have had to turn their gaze on themselves as an important actor within the study and on the research field—and this self-reflexive position is something that was only fully internalized in the social sciences in the 1980s within the postmodernist frame of thinking.[7] The third reason for the avoidance of the topic was the general lack of attentiveness to, and awareness of, the significance of tourism as a social and cultural as well as historical phenomenon. Because of the above-mentioned motives, as well as anthropology's traditional disciplinary focus of studying non-Western cultures, anthropologists seem to have been under the impression that studying tourism would mean studying mainly tourism generating areas and (predominantly) Western tourists, which is therefore better left to the disciplines of economics and sociology.

The topics that were discussed in the anthropological study of tourism have thus far mainly focused on the questions of commodification and acculturation, involving an "investigation of change supposedly fostered by Western tourism in some society or sub-society on the Western periphery."[8] In her review of the main issues discussed in the anthropology of tourism, Stronza[9] identifies two key themes in the field: the tourism origins focusing on the tourists, and the tourism impacts focusing on the locals. She suggests that the factors explaining local involvement in host communities should be further studied, as well as the various effects traveling has on the tourists' attitudes, values, and behaviors. Stronza acknowledges that in her own research she too, like many anthropologists, focuses mainly on the socioeconomic inequalities and disparities created by international tourism. While a lot of valuable research has been produced in this frame of thinking, it has also been criticized for often reducing people living and working in tourist destination regions to passive recipients of the outside influences, and thus oftentimes creating simplified dualisms of an empowered guest versus a disempowered host.[10] Therefore, it is important to remember that the "centre-periphery tourism"[11] that has long preoccupied anthropologists is just one possible avenue of study. There is a need to turn the gaze back to tourism generating societies, to take the hosts' agency more into consideration, to study the influence the hosts have on the guests, as well as just focus more on the "centre-centre" tourism. Furthermore, this is also especially important since the binary opposition of host-guest has been contested for a while now as the concepts of local, tourist, migrant, visitor, etc. have become increasingly blurred and fluid in the "glocal" world. As Sherlock[12] noted in her 2001 study of an Australian tourism town, the "overlaps between host and guest, migration and tourism, were taken for granted by most participants yet appear to be largely unarticulated in the tourism literature." In the past 15 years, these overlaps have started receiving more and more attention and have resulted in more detailed analysis on changing tourism and mobilities related phenomena and have been labeled "niche tourism,"[13] "lifestyle tourism,"[14] "lifestyle migration,"[15] "residential tourism,"[16] "second home tourism,"[17] and, more coherently, bringing many of them together, "lifestyle mobilities."[18]

Leite and Graburn[19] do not regard the anthropology of tourism as a dedicated subdiscipline, and suggest that we instead talk about "anthropological interventions" in tourism research as, indeed, the anthropology of tourism does not (yet?) hold an established place within the discipline that for instance anthropology of religion or environmental anthropology do. There are currently no high-ranking journals focusing exclusively on the anthropology of tourism; however, anthropologists do publish prolifically in general tourism studies journals, such as *Annals of Tourism Research, Journal of Travel Research, Current Issues in Tourism, Tourist Studies, Journal of Tourism and Cultural Change*, and others. Yet this subfield is very active and growing, as there are international conferences held; numerous panels, sessions and workshops organized; books and PhD theses written; and more and more commonly, courses taught in higher learning institutions, including a specific program at the SOAS University of London. There is an Anthropology of Tourism Interest Group at the American Anthropological Association (AAA), and a Commission on the Anthropology of Tourism at the International Union of Anthropological and Ethnological Sciences (IUAES).

An anthropological approach to tourism means asking particular anthropologically guided research questions and gathering primary empirical data using a set of research methods characteristic to the discipline (such as participant observation). In regards of theories, there is a tendency toward interpretivist, rather than political and economic, paradigms.[20] Anthropologists have without doubt contributed significantly to the development of critical tourism theories—for example, studying tourism as a liminal stage and a secular ritual,[21] or a catalyst for cultural commodification.[22] They have studied tourism imaginaries[23] and interrogated different approaches pertaining to the idea of "authenticity."[24][25] There is, however, definitely a need for more theorizing in the field, in order for it to be fully realized as a subdiscipline.

These anthropological investigations into tourism are also part of a larger, and more loosely defined discipline (or indiscipline[26]) of tourism studies: a multi-, inter- and transdisciplinary project comprising of various disciplines in social sciences and humanities such as geography, sociology, business and management, anthropology, cultural studies, development studies, psychology, history, political science, and others.[27] Yet, despite of this wide variety of disciplines, and by extension the potential methodologies associated with them, positivist and post-positivist research philosophies and quantitative methods have mostly dominated this emergent field until the end of the twentieth century. This means that qualitative methods and other epistemological approaches, such as those grounded in critical theory, social constructivism, postmodernism, and phenomenology, have been mostly marginalized.[28] The existing qualitative studies in tourism also tended to take more of an industry and policy-making orientated view on the subject, treating the tourist as primarily a consumer, and focusing mainly on potential applications in business, management, and marketing.[29] This marginalization is well exemplified in Tribe's overview of the field that divides tourism research into two main areas: "tourism business studies" and "non-business tourism studies,"[30] essentially defining studying the social and cultural topics in tourism by negation.

In tourism business studies, qualitative approaches, even when applied, remain mainly a set of data collection methods and the opportunities to utilize them for critical thinking and analyzing different ways of knowing and being in regard to tourism, have often not been taken.[31] Jamal and Hollinshead[32] have called for moving toward more interpretive qualitative tourism research and for departing from the above-mentioned static and largely (post)positivist means of knowledge production. In the past 15 years, these calls have been indeed answered by sociology, anthropology, human geography, and related disciplines providing more and more individual-centered critical research grounded in empirical data but also highly theorized.[33] Furthermore, as a discipline, anthropology is uniquely equipped for these endeavors by using unique methodological approaches and by asking research questions that other disciplines might not. This chapter is therefore looking at ways how to better utilize classical anthropological and ethnological methodology, namely that of ethnography, for tourism research. I will argue that anthropological methods applied in combination of the practices of (Eastern) European ethnology, and in the framework of the new mobilities paradigm, would give especially fruitful results in understanding the contemporary phenomenon of tourism.

REFLEXIVE ETHNOGRAPHY AND TOURISM RESEARCH

Nash suggests ethnography, "small, first-hand, intensive, exploratory study of people in the field" as a useful approach for researching tourism.[34] Ethnography, well-known and well used in anthropology, is a methodology where the operational and theoretical parts of the study are interconnected, incorporating critical social and cultural theory as well as a method for documenting and studying the phenomenon at hand.[35] As such, it is especially well suited for the task of qualitative tourism research to "understand the human dimensions of society, which in tourism include its social and cultural implications."[36]

In terms of the methods of data collection, ethnographical research is participatory, bringing together the perspective of the research participants, researcher, and the wider theoretical considerations informing the work and growing out from it. The ethnographer is the main catalyst of creating and constructing data, usually in the form of field notes and qualitative interviews. Any aspect of tourism can, and should be, ethnographically studied, including but not limited to its main and defining characteristics, causes, effects, and various processes involved. Such research would typically be small-scale, empirically-driven with original primary data, reflexive, present the *emic* insider's view of the studied phenomena, analytical as well as theoretically focused.

The main method used in ethnographic research is participant observation, pioneered by anthropologists in the beginning of the twentieth century and most explicitly described and explained first by Malinowski.[37] Participant observation means immersing yourself deliberately and totally into the studied phenomena with the intention of acquiring knowledge from the point of view of the studied group and thus obtaining first-hand knowledge of their lifeworlds. It is "a method in which a researcher takes part in the daily activities, rituals, interactions, and events of a group of people as one of the means of learning both the explicit and tacit aspects of their life routines and culture."[38] The method, therefore, requires a conscious and ongoing, processual introspection and self-examination on the researcher's part—both in relation to the studied topic as well as research participants. In contemporary anthropology, the participant observation is usually characterized by living in the researched location for a longer time period (ideally at least a year); acquiring the local language for communication with the studied group; actively participating in the everyday lives of the studied people; using (informal) interviews for data collection; engaging in informal observing in various situations; gathering data in the form of field notes, photos and videos; and using both implicit as well as explicit information in the analysis.[39]

All researchers, but especially anthropologists and ethnologists, are closely connected to and therefore influence their research objects, subjects, participants, and environments in varied ways and degrees. Thus, it is common practice for them to consider, trace and discuss the ways in which they affect their research from initial selection of topic to the published (or, in case of visual anthropology, exhibited or screened) result. This means taking painstaking care in being aware of their influence on producing the data as well as how their presence in the field affects their ways of knowledge construction. Both the relationship with the research participants as well as the researcher's own subjective values and identities have to be taken into account.[40] When engaging in what Davies calls reflexive ethnography, the ethnographer therefore is constantly in the process in developing suitable forms of study "that fully acknowledge and utilize subjective experience and reflection on it as an intrinsic part of research."[41]

Hall[42] criticizes large parts of tourism research for its lack of reflexivity, which he regards "critical to all tourism research practice, even if it is not as well acknowledged as it should be." Employing reflexive ethnography, where the researcher's personal connection to the research participants forms an important basis for the analysis of the gathered data as well as subsequent theorizing is a fruitful way for moving toward more interpretive and theoretically grounded tourism research. Reflexivity, an endeavor to look at one's own research activities from data collection to writing in a critical, insightful, and analytical manner, should be one of the main features of contemporary tourism ethnography.

What then could be the best ways of applying ethnographic methodology to various tourism related phenomena and retain the integrity and quality of the data necessary for engaging with the methods associated with it? When studying tourism, specific issues arising from the nature of the field(s) and the inherently temporal qualities of the phenomenon must be taken into consideration. I suggest that turning our focus to European ethnology with its tradition of shorter term fieldworks and combine it with various mobile methods might give good results.

BACK AND FORTH ON THE MOBILE FIELD OF TOURISM

Participant observation, a trademark ethnographic research method, has also proved to be extremely popular outside of the discipline and has been utilized by virtually all other fields practicing qualitative research; one can find studies using (or claiming to use) it, ranging from nursing to education to marketing. However, Ingold criticizes this development, arguing that in many cases the concept of ethnography is used as a substitute to other forms of qualitative research which therefore dilutes the original idea:

How many research proposals have we read, coming from such fields as sociology, social policy, social psychology and education, in which the applicant explains that he or she will conduct "ethnographic interviews" with a sample of randomly selected informants, the data from which will then be processed by means of a recommended software package in order to yield "results"? Such a procedure, in which ethnographic appears to be a modish substitute for qualitative, offends every principle of proper, rigorous anthropological inquiry—including long-term and open-ended commitment, generous attentiveness, relational depth, and sensitivity to context—and we are right to protest against it.[43]

In tourism research, however, it is only possible to apply the classical, long-term participant observation to certain topics: mainly when studying the "hosts"—those living and working in tourist destinations. Studying the tourists with the same method is more difficult and complex for the temporal and mobile nature of tourism and tourist practices. This means that the anthropologists have had to and will have to adapt their research methods in order to capture the fleeting phenomenon, practice, and experience that is tourism.[44]

One of the solutions would be making use of other, equally participatory, ethnographical research methods, that have developed in parallel, but also in dialogue with sociocultural anthropology—namely those from (Eastern) European ethnology. The discipline of ethnology historically grew out of German *Volkskunde* (transl. the study of people), traditionally focused on one's own (folk) culture as opposed to *Völkerkunde* (transl. the study of the world's peoples), and now commonly associated with social and cultural anthropology. There have been many discussions (that still go on today) on the differences and similarities of the two disciplines. Arguments range from the histories of the two research traditions, their position in national academic hierarchies, as well as their positions in regards to their respective centers and peripheries (as ethnology is generally more associated with the Continental European academic perspective, and the anthropological center lies in the Anglo-American (or, if including France, "Franglus") sphere.[45] Another important point of discussion for the (dis-)similarities of the two academic traditions, and one that has been reflected on less in the literature, is the question of fieldwork methods.[46]

Both the traditions of ethnology and sociocultural anthropology are primarily qualitative endeavors, relying on ethnographical fieldwork, where the most common methods continue to be participant observation and ethnographic interviewing. However, there is a certain difference in executing the method historically: while in anthropology one of the most important requirements for fieldwork is long-term stay, ethnology has relied more on multiple short-term field-trips (usually to the researcher's own country of residence/origin), and uses more targeted interviews, with concentrated, intensive observations. Brković and Hodges[47] identify these contrasting two approaches to fieldwork as "extended stay" (that they categorize as "Anglo-Saxon" based) meaning spending at least a year in one location; and "back and forth," that they label as a "Balkan and Eastern European" approach, where researchers make short trips to the studied field, sometimes repeatedly over many years.

It has to be noted, however, that the whole discipline of Continental European ethnology, including Scandinavian culture analysis, actually have followed, or follow, this particular model. Löfgren[48] identifies four key aspects of European ethnology's research methodology. First, it was, and is, a discipline

dedicated to the study of the (seemingly) trivial and every day, putting painstaking efforts to record and document the minutest details. Secondly, it relies
on ethnographic fieldwork, a method that it shares with anthropology, but the
regularity and intensity of the participant observation differs depending upon
various circumstances. As traditionally ethnologists have studied their own
culture (or the ones that are rather similar to them), the questions of one's
relationship to the field are paramount—which puts a great importance on the
reflexive approach. Ethnology's third feature is its frequent use of historical
perspective and dimension (since ethnologists have often been trained in the
history departments.) Finally, its fourth characteristic is its flexibility, a great
sensitivity to use and combine various perspectives, theories, approaches, and
methodologies that could be used to research different phenomena.

When discussing the long- and short-term fieldwork models, Brković and
Hodges[49] define "movement" as one of the most important issues to consider: the epistemological movement of the researcher across various social
and cultural spaces as well as her movement between the "field" and the
"desk." Indeed, anthropological knowledge about certain phenomena, such
as tourism, can no longer be defined by utilizing just one particular kind
of research method such as long-term participant observation—it can and
should also be acquired by other means. Tourism is "no longer a specialist
consumer product or mode of consumption: [it] has broken away from its
beginnings as a relatively minor and ephemeral ritual of modern national life
to become a significant modality through which transnational modern
life is organized."[50] In the context of Eastern and Central European tourism anthropology, Banaszkiewicz, Graburn, and Owsianowska[51] identify
several important avenues for further research such as the individualization
of the tourism practices; the values and identities of the traveler; the relationship between tourism, recreation, and leisure; socialist and industrial
heritage; glocalization, and the often complicated relationship with history
and memory.

A fruitful way to study these themes would be to utilize "back and forth"
ethnography combined with the techniques of mobile methods developed in
recent years as part of the new mobilities paradigm. Theorizing in terms of
mobile practices started in the mid-2000s with Sheller and Urry arguing that
the issues of mobility had mostly been excluded from the thus far static and
"a-mobile" social sciences, failing to study "how the spatialities of social
life presuppose (and frequently involve conflict over) both the actual and the
imagined movement of people from place to place, person to person, event
to event."[52]

As a sociocultural phenomenon, tourism is not just a temporary form of
mobility, but also different mobilities influence, and are influenced by, tourism.[53] Analyzing tourism from the mobilities perspective brings attention to

various practices that are much more than linear movement, but are rather lived experiences where attention ought to be paid to the practices, materialities, technologies, and both the imagined and virtual mobilities. Tourist practices should be researched by "trying to move with, and to be moved by, the fleeting, distributed, multiple, non-casual, sensory, emotional and kinaesthetic."[54] This means doing ethnography while moving alongside the research participants, such as the tourists, tour guides, hotel workers, tour groups, employees of hotel chains, crews of airlines, etc. Mavric and Urry[55] point namely to ethnography as a starting point for mobile research techniques that can be used to study and conceptualize the world as a network of mobilities— but also immobilities. Mobile tourism ethnography can then be done in various (social, geographical, hierarchical, administrative, etc.) spaces and places simultaneously,[56] coupling participant observation with the use of "go-along" method,[57] netnography,[58] sensory ethnography,[59] participant diaries,[60] as well as utilizing visual and literary sources and archival material.

The combination of these various methods allows to study the complexity of contemporary tourism, where it is increasingly difficult to define what is "field," as well as where and when does it begin and end:

> My research experience was not marked solely by "leaving for the field" for an extended period of time. Mine was the experience of continually coming and going to and from the field, to the point where, at times, the field became indistinguishable from home. . . . Blurring field/home boundaries was further enhanced by technologies that facilitated these crossings by linking my field with home, home with other fields and my home with other homes. . . . At times, I did not need to physically travel to the field to be able to reach my "key" informants or for them to reach me. . . . Keeping the field and home conceptually separate and distinct in practice, a key marker of "real" fieldwork, was impossible for me.[61]

Caputo, quoted above, studied the gender performances of schoolchildren in Toronto, the city that she herself resided in. Indeed, when talking about "back and forth" research, the inevitable question arises: back and forth from where and to what?[62] The blurred (and further blurring) boundaries of "home" and "field," are extremely important in the qualitative study of tourism, which often needs to start with reconceptualizing two important aspects of the field: the place and the duration. Studying spatially fixed groups of people for longer or shorter periods of time can prove difficult in a tourism context, and so other methods would have to be chosen and adopted. For example, one could decide on studying a particular tourism space by staying for months in a specific tourist locale[63] or actively travel with the tourists, by becoming either a tourist oneself, or a tour guide.[64] Sometimes the studied group (the tourists) and the place (the tourist destinations) are not permanent and stable in any way, but temporary and mobile, as groups and individuals move about various destinations for differing periods of time. This means, that subscribing to the classical one-year extended stay may not be feasible, or even possible, as tourism in itself is a phenomenon mainly characterized by its temporal nature.

Therefore, following the ethnological back-and-forth short-term fieldwork model can provide better results, as long as the fieldworker subscribes to the "ontological commitment,"[65] a participant observation where the knowledge to the studied phenomena organically grows out of the lived experience and where knowing is not separated from being. The knowledge about the world thus obtained consists of skills of perceiving and decision capacities that develop during the sensory, and sensuous, direct engagements with the surrounding world. The "observation" in participant observation never takes a step back in trying to be distant or "objective"—it always includes being part of, and present in, the situation-specific network of phenomena, events, people, and ideas that is the studied field. The researcher has to constantly reflect on the processes of data generation and the ways of approaching it— since it will later reflect on the analysis of the data.

Participant observation, therefore, can only be successful if the researcher is able to immerse herself in the studied field, regardless of its temporal and spatial properties. The mere fact of being in the field (for however long) does not necessarily guarantee immersion, because it can only be achieved via the ethnographical practice of becoming part of certain social, cultural, and political relations. Immersing yourself in the field means being part of (an always incomplete) process of finding your conceptual place in changing networks of various social and cultural relations and, therefore, the temporal length of stay is less important than taking into account the particularities of certain research problems.[66] Studying tourism ethnographically would then mean producing mobile ethnographies, where the researcher traces the hosts and/or guests across and within their numerous activity sites, and where various places, spaces, sites, and people are linked more or less loosely together into a general touristscape.

CONCLUSION

After the initial academic avoidance, the subject of tourism has become an important part of the general discipline of anthropology, and it has a lot more to offer to it, from particular research questions to its research methodologies. Of those methodologies, ethnography especially has translated extremely well to tourism studies in particular but also to wider social sciences and humanities in general. Anthropology has traditionally focused on studying traditional, small-scale societies and communities (often in "exotic" locations) and when turning its focus to tourism, this empirical focus continued, as anthropologists mainly analyzed the influences of international tourism and the social and cultural change caused by it.

As traditionally practiced in anthropology however, the ethnographical method is temporally rather demanding, requiring an extensive stay at the field (usually at least a year). Yet in tourism research, this is not always feasible or possible, requiring certain modifications to the methodology. While anthropology's relationship with (Eastern) European ethnology has been well discussed from the perspective of disciplinary history, its specific fieldwork methods, namely short-term ethnography that is still grounded in the anthropological sensibilities, have received much less attention. This chapter is an attempt to bring the short-term field methods specific to European ethnology back into the dialogue with general anthropology, to employ them for studying tourism in the framework of mobilities studies.

Pursuing short-term ethnography in combination with the mobile methods as proposed here is a fruitful way of researching many forms and expressions of tourism that are otherwise difficult to capture due to their specific temporal and spatial qualities. This chapter has discussed these issues in a more general level; future studies, however, could provide a more detailed review on tourism studies conducted in the framework of (Eastern) European ethnology in regards to their methodologies. Further discussion on the new mobilities paradigm and its intersections with anthropology, as well as tourism studies, is also needed. Anthropological research on tourism has at last found its rightful place within tourism studies, and therefore there are many reasons to argue that it is gathering more and more momentum as a lively, and fruitful, area of study, hopefully in its way of becoming finally a more recognized and practiced subdiscipline of anthropology.

NOTES

1. The publication of this chapter has been supported by the institutional research funding IUT34-32 (*Cultural Heritage as a Socio-Cultural Resource and Contested Field*) of the Estonian Ministry of Education and Research.

2. Theron A. Nuñez, "Tourism, Tradition, and Acculturation: Weekendismo in a Mexican Village," *Ethnology* 2, no. 3 (1963): 347–352.

3. Valene L. Smith, ed., *Hosts and Guests: The Anthropology of Tourism* (Oxford: Basil Blackwell, 1977).

4. Henry Durant, *The Problem of Leisure* (London: George Routledge and Son, 1938).

5. Georgette Leah Burns, "Anthropology and Tourism: Past Contributions and Future Theoretical Challenges," *Anthropological Forum* 14, no. 1 (2004): 5–22.

6. David Lodge, *Paradise News: A Novel* (London: Secker & Warburg, 1991).

7. James Clifford and George Marcus, *Writing Culture: The Poetics and Politics of Ethnography* (Berkeley: University of California Press, 1986).

8. Dennison Nash, "New Wine in Old Bottles. An Adjustment of Priorities in the Anthropological Study of Tourism," in *Qualitative Research in Tourism: Ontologies, Epistemologies and Methodologies*, ed. Jenny Phillimore and Lisa Goodson (London: Routledge, 2004), 171.

9. Amanda Stronza, "Anthropology of Tourism: Forging New Ground for Ecotourism and Other Alternatives," *Annual Review of Anthropology* 30 (2001): 261–283.

10. Raoul V. Bianchi, "The 'Critical Turn' in Tourism Studies: A Radical Critique," *Tourism Geographies* 11, no. 4 (2009): 484–504.

11. Nash, "New Wine," 171.

12. Kirsty Sherlock, "Revisiting the Concept of Hosts and Guests," *Tourist Studies* 1, no. 3 (2001): 271.

13. Marina Novelli, ed., *Niche Tourism: Contemporary Issues, Trends and Cases* (Amsterdam: Elsevier, 2005).

14. Noel B. Salazar and Yang Zhang, "Seasonal Lifestyle Tourism: The Case of Chinese Elites," *Annals of Tourism Research* 43 (2013): 81–99.

15. Michaela Benson, *The British in Rural France: Lifestyle Migration and the Ongoing Quest for a Better Way of Life* (Manchester: Manchester University Press, 2011).

16. Mason R. McWatters, *Residential Tourism: (De)Constructing Paradise* (Bristol: Channel View Publications, 2008).

17. Zoran Roca, ed., *Second Home Tourism in Europe: Lifestyle Issues and Policy Responses* (London: Routledge, 2016).

18. Tara Duncan, Scott A. Cohen, and Maria Thulemark, eds., *Lifestyle Mobilities: Intersections of Travel, Leisure and Migration* (London: Routledge, 2016).

19. Naomi Leite and Nelson Graburn, "Anthropological Interventions in Tourism Studies," in *The SAGE Handbook of Tourism Studies*, ed. Tazim Jamal and Mike Robinson (Los Angeles: SAGE, 2009), 35–64.

20. Leite and Graburn, "Anthropological," 35–64.

21. Nelson Graburn, "Tourism: The Sacred Journey," in *Hosts and Guests: The Anthropology of Tourism*. Second edition, ed. Valene Smith (Philadelphia: University of Pennsylvania Press, 1989 [1977]), 17–32.

22. David J. Greenwood, "Culture by the Pound: An Anthropological Perspective on Tourism as Cultural Commoditization," in *Hosts and Guests*, 171–86.

23. Noel Salazar and Nelson Graburn, eds., *Tourism Imaginaries: Anthropological Approaches* (New York: Berghahn, 2014).

24. Tom Selwyn, ed., *The Tourist Image: Myths and Mythmaking in Tourism* (New York: Wiley, 1996).

25. For overviews on anthropological research in tourism done so far, see: Stronza, "Anthropology of Tourism: Forging New Ground for Ecotourism and Other Alternatives"; Burns, "Anthropology and Tourism: Past Contributions and Future Theoretical Challenges"; Leite and Graburn, "Anthropological Interventions in Tourism Studies."

26. John Tribe, "The Indiscipline of Tourism," *Annals of Tourism Research* 24, no. 3 (1997): 638–57.

27. Charlotte M. Echtner and Tazim B. Jamal, "The Disciplinary Dilemma of Tourism Studies," *Annals of Tourism Research* 24, no. 4 (1997): 868–83.

28. Gayle R. Jennings, "Methodologies and Methods," in *The SAGE Handbook of Tourism Studies*, ed. Tazim Jamal and Mike Robinson (Los Angeles: SAGE, 2009), 672–91.

29. Michael Hall, "Reflexivity and Tourism Research: Situating Myself and/ with Others," in *Qualitative Research in Tourism: Ontologies, Epistemologies and Methodologies*, ed. Jenny Phillimore and Lisa Goodson (London: Routledge, 2004), 137–55.

30. Tribe, "The Indiscipline of Tourism."

31. Jenny Phillimore and Lisa Goodson, "Progress in Qualitative Research in Tourism: Epistemology, Ontology and Methodology," in *Qualitative Research in Tourism: Ontologies, Epistemologies and Methodologies*, ed. Jenny Phillimore and Lisa Goodson (London: Routledge, 2004), 3–29.

32. Tazim B. Jamal and Keith Hollinshead, "Tourism and the Forbidden Zone: The Underserved Power of Qualitative Inquiry," *Tourism Management* 22, no. 1 (2001): 63–82.

33. For an overview, see Dennison Nash, ed., *The Study of Tourism: Anthropological and Sociological Beginnings* (Oxford: Elsevier, 2007).

34. Dennison Nash, "Ethnographic Windows on Tourism," *Tourism Recreation Research* 25, no. 3 (2000): 29.

35. Riall W. Nolan, *A Handbook of Practicing Anthropology* (Oxford: Wiley-Blackwell, 2013).

36. Phillimore and Goodson, "Progress," 4.

37. Bronislaw Malinowski, *Argonauts of the Western Pacific: Native Enterprise and Adventure in Melanesian New Guinea* (London: G. Routledge & Sons, 1922).

38. Kathleen Musante, "Participant Observation," in *Handbook of Methods in Cultural Anthropology*, ed. Russell H. Bernard, and Clarence C. Gravlee (London: Rowman & Littlefield, 2015), 251.

39. Kathleen M. DeWalt and Billie R. DeWalt, *Participant Observation: A Guide for Fieldworkers* (Lanham, MD: AltaMira Press, 2011).

40. Nazia Ali, "Researcher Reflexivity in Tourism Studies Research: Dynamical Dances with Emotions," in *Critical Turn in Tourism Studies: Creating an Academy of Hope*, ed. Irena Ateljevic, Nigel Morgan, and Annette Pritchard (London: Routledge, 2012), 13–26.

41. Charlotte Aull Davies, *Reflexive Ethnography: A Guide to Researching Selves and Others* (London: Routledge, 2012), 151.

42. Michael Hall, "Reflexivity and Tourism Research: Situating Myself and/with Others," in *Qualitative Research in Tourism: Ontologies, Epistemologies and Methodologies*, ed. Jenny Phillimore and Lisa Goodson (London: Routledge, 2004), 150.

43. Tim Ingold, "That's Enough about Ethnography," *HAU: Journal of Ethnographic Theory* 4, no. 1 (2014): 384.

44. Leite and Graburn, "Anthropological Interventions."

45. Chris Hann, "The Theft of Anthropology," *Theory, Culture & Society* 26, no. 7–8 (2009): 126–147; Chris Hann, "Rooted Anthropologies of East-Central Europe," in *Enduring Socialism: Explorations of Revolution and Transformation, Restoration*

and Continuation, ed. Harry West and Parvathi Raman (New York: Berghahn Books, 2009), 214–230; Ullrich Kockel, "European Ethnology, Europeanist Anthropology and Beyond," *Anthropological Journal of European Cultures* 21, no. 2 (2012): 1–4; Han F. Vermeulen and Arturo Álvarez Roldán, *Fieldwork and Footnotes: Studies in the History of European Anthropology*. European Association of Social Anthropologists (London: Routledge, 1995); Tamas Hofer, "Anthropologists and Native Ethnographers in Central European Villages: Comparative Notes on the Professional Personality of Two Disciplines," *Current Anthropology* 9, no. 4 (1968): 311–15.

46. Aet Annist and Maarja Kaaristo, "Studying Home Fields: Encounters of Ethnology and Anthropology in Estonia," *Journal of Baltic Studies* 44, no. 2 (2013): 121–51; Čarna Brković and Andrew Hodges, "Rethinking World Anthropologies through Fieldwork: Perspectives on 'Extended Stay' and 'Back-and-forth' Methodologies," *Anthropological Notebooks* 21, no. 1 (2015): 107–20.

47. Brković and Hodges, "Rethinking."

48. Orvar Löfgren, "When is Small Beautiful? The Transformations of Swedish Ethnology," in *Everyday Culture in Europe: Approaches and Methodologies*, ed. Máiréad Nic Craith, Ullrich Kockel, and Johrel Reinhard (Aldershot, UK: Ashgate, 2008), 119–32.

49. Brković and Hodges, "Rethinking."

50. Adrian Franklin and Mike Crang, "The Trouble with Tourism and Travel Theory?" *Tourist Studies* 1, no. 1 (2001): 6–7.

51. Magdalena Banaszkiewicz, Nelson Graburn, and Sabina Owsianowska, "Tourism in (Post)socialist Eastern Europe," *Journal of Tourism and Cultural Change* 15, no. 2 (2017): 109–21.

52. Mimi Sheller and John Urry, "The New Mobilities Paradigm," *Environment and Planning A* 38, no. 2 (2006): 208.

53. Kevin Hannam, Gareth Butler, and Cody Morris Paris, "Developments and Key Issues in Tourism Mobilities," *Annals of Tourism Research* 44, no. 1 (2014): 171–85.

54. Monika Büscher, John Urry, and Katian Witchger, *Mobile Methods* (Abingdon: Routledge, 2011), 1.

55. Mišela Mavric and John Urry, "Tourism Studies and the New Mobilities Paradigm," in *The SAGE Handbook of Tourism Studies*, ed. Tazim Jamal and Mike Robinson (Los Angeles: SAGE, 2009), 645–57.

56. George E. Marcus, "Ethnography in/of the World System: The Emergence of Multi-sited Ethnography," *Annual Review of Anthropology* 24 (1995): 95–117.

57. Margarethe Kusenbach, "Street Phenomenology: The Go-along as Ethnographic Research Tool," *Ethnography* 4, no. 3 (2003): 455–85.

58. Robert V. Kozinets, *Netnography: Doing Ethnographic Research Online* (Los Angeles: SAGE Publications, 2012).

59. Sarah Pink, *Doing Sensory Ethnography* (Los Angeles: SAGE, 2009).

60. Paula Meth, "Entries and Omissions: Using Solicited Diaries in Geographical Research," *Area* 35, no. 2 (2003): 195–205.

61. Virginia Caputo, "At 'Home' and 'Away': Reconfiguring the Field for Late Twentieth-century Anthropology," in *Constructing the Field: Ethnographic*

Fieldwork in the Contemporary Field, ed. Vered Amit (London: Routledge, 2000), 26.
62. Brković and Hodges, "Rethinking."
63. Tim Edensor, *Tourists at the Taj: Performance and Meaning at a Symbolic Site* (London: Routledge, 1998).
64. Edward M. Bruner, *Culture on Tour: Ethnographies of Travel* (Chicago: The University of Chicago Press, 2005).
65. Ingold, "That's Enough."
66. Brković and Hodges, "Rethinking."

REFERENCES

Ali, Nazia. "Researcher Reflexivity in Tourism Studies Research: Dynamical Dances with Emotions." In *Critical Turn in Tourism Studies: Creating an Academy of Hope,* edited by Irena Ateljevic, Nigel Morgan, and Annette Pritchard, 13–26. London: Routledge.

Annist, Aet, and Maarja Kaaristo. "Studying Home Fields: Encounters of Ethnology and Anthropology in Estonia." *Journal of Baltic Studies* 44 (2013): 121–51.

Banaszkiewicz, Magdalena, Nelson Graburn, and Sabina Owsianowska. "Tourism in (Post) Socialist Eastern Europe." *Journal of Tourism and Cultural Change* 15, no. 2 (2017): 109–21.

Benson, Michaela. *The British in Rural France: Lifestyle Migration and the Ongoing Quest for a Better Way of Life.*" Manchester: Manchester University Press, 2011.

Bianchi, Raoul V. "The 'Critical Turn' in Tourism Studies: A Radical Critique." *Tourism Geographies* 11 (2009): 484–504.

Brković, Čarna, and Andrew Hodges. "Rethinking World Anthropologies through Fieldwork: Perspectives on 'Extended Stay' and 'Back-and-forth' Methodologies." *Anthropological Notebooks* 21 (2015): 107–20.

Bruner, Edward. *Culture on Tour: Ethnographies of Travel.* Chicago: The University of Chicago Press, 2005.

Burns, Georgette L. "Anthropology and Tourism: Past Contributions and Future Theoretical Challenges." *Anthropological Forum* 14 (2004): 5–22.

Büscher, Monika, John Urry, and Katian Witchger. *Mobile Methods.* Abingdon: Routledge, 2011.

Caputo, Virginia. "At 'Home' and 'Away': Reconfiguring the Field for Late Twentieth-century Anthropology." In *Constructing the Field: Ethnographic Fieldwork in the Contemporary Field*, edited by Vered Amit, 19–31. London: Routledge, 1999.

Clifford, James, and George E. Marcus. *Writing Culture: The Poetics and Politics of Ethnography.* School of American Research advanced seminar series. Berkeley: University of California Press, 1986.

Davies, Charlotte. A. *Reflexive Ethnography: A Guide to Researching Selves and Others.* London: Routledge, 2012.

Duncan, Tara, Scott A. Cohen, and Maria Thulemark, eds. *Lifestyle Mobilities: Intersections of Travel, Leisure and Migration.* London: Routledge, 2016.

Durant, Henry. *The Problem of Leisure.* London: George Routledge and Son, 1938.

Echtner, Charlotte M., and Tazim B. Jamal. "The Disciplinary Dilemma of Tourism Studies." *Annals of Tourism Research* 24 (1997): 868–83.

Edensor, Tim. *Tourists at the Taj: Performance and Meaning at a Symbolic Site.* London: Routledge, 1998.

Franklin, Adrian, and Mike Crang. "The Trouble with Tourism and Travel Theory?" *Tourist Studies* 1 (2000): 5–22.

Graburn, Nelson. "Tourism: The Sacred Journey." In *Hosts and Guests: The Anthropology of Tourism.* Second edition, edited by Valene L. Smith, 17–32. Philadelphia: University of Pennsylvania Press, 1989 [1977].

Greenwood, D. J. "Culture by the Pound: An Anthropological Perspective on Tourism as Cultural Commoditization." In *Hosts and Guests: The Anthropology of Tourism.* Second edition, edited by Valene L. Smith, 171–86. Philadelphia: University of Pennsylvania Press, 1989 [1977].

Hall, Michael. "Reflexivity and Tourism Research: Situating Myself and/with Others." In *Qualitative Research In Tourism: Ontologies, Epistemologies and Methodologies,* edited by Jenny Phillimore and Lisa Goodson, 137–55. London: Routledge, 2004.

Hann, Chris. "The Theft of Anthropology." *Theory, Culture & Society* 26 (2009): 126–47.

———. "Rooted Anthropologies of East-Central Europe." In *Enduring Socialism: Explorations of Revolution and Transformation, Restoration and Continuation,* edited by Harry West and Parvathi Raman, 214–30. New York: Berghahn Books, 2009.

Hannam, Kevin, Gareth Butler, and Cody M. Paris. "Developments and Key Issues in Tourism Mobilities." *Annals of Tourism Research* 44 (2014): 171–85.

Hofer, Tamas. "Anthropologists and Native Ethnographers in Central European Villages: Comparative Notes on the Professional Personality of Two Disciplines." *Current Anthropology* 9 (1968): 311–15.

Ingold, Tim. "That's Enough about Ethnography." *HAU: Journal of Ethnographic Theory* 4 (2014): 383–95.

Jamal, Tazim, and Keith Hollinshead. "Tourism and the Forbidden Zone: The Underserved Power of Qualitative Inquiry." *Tourism Management* 22 (2001): 63–82.

Jennings, Gayle R. "Methodologies and Methods." In *The SAGE Handbook of Tourist Studies,* edited by Tazim Jamal and Mike Robinson, 672–91. Los Angeles: SAGE, 2009.

Kockel, Ulrich. "European Ethnology, Europeanist Anthropology and Beyond." *Anthropological Journal of European Cultures* 21 (2012): 1–4.

Kozinets, Robert V. *Netnography: Doing Ethnographic Research Online.* Los Angeles: SAGE, 2012.

Kusenbach, Margarethe. "Street Phenomenology: The Go-along as Ethnographic Research Tool." *Ethnography* 4 (2003): 455–85.

Leite, Noami, and Nelson Graburn. "Anthropological Interventions in Tourism Studies." In *The SAGE Handbook of Tourist Studies*, edited by Tazim Jamal and Mike Robinson, 35–64. Los Angeles: SAGE, 2009.

Lodge, David. *Paradise News: A Novel*. London: Secker & Warburg, 1991.

Löfgren, Orvar. "When is Small Beautiful? The Transformations of Swedish Ethnology." In *Everyday Culture in Europe: Approaches and Methodologies*, edited by Máiréad N. Craith and Ulrich Kockel, 119–32. Aldershot, UK: Ashgate, 2008.

Malinowski, Bronisław. *Argonauts of the Western Pacific: Native Enterprise and Adventure in Melanesian New Guinea*. London: G. Routledge & Sons, 1922.

Marcus, George E. "Ethnography in/of the World System: The Emergence of Multi-sited Ethnography." *Annual Review of Anthropology* 24 (1995): 95–117.

Mavric, Mišela, and John Urry. "Tourism Studies and the New Mobilities Paradigm." In *The SAGE Handbook of Tourist Studies*, edited by Tazim Jamal and Mike Robinson, 645–57. Los Angeles: SAGE, 2009.

McWatters, Mason R. *Residential Tourism: (De)Constructing Paradise*. Bristol: Channel View Publications, 2008.

Meth, Paula. "Entries and Omissions: Using Solicited Diaries in Geographical Research." *Area* 35 (2003): 195–205.

Musante, Katheen. "Participant Observation." In *Handbook of Methods in Cultural Anthropology*, edited by Russell H. Bernard and Clarence C. Gravlee, 251–92. London: Rowman & Littlefield, 2015.

Nash, Dennison. "Ethnographic Windows on Tourism." *Tourism Recreation Research* 25 (2000): 29–36.

———, ed. *The Study of Tourism: Anthropological and Sociological Beginnings*. Oxford: Elsevier, 2007.

———. "New Wine in Old Bottles: An Adjustment of Priorities in the Anthropological Study of Tourism." In *Qualitative Research in Tourism: Ontologies, Epistemologies and Methodologies*, edited by Jenny Phillimore and Lisa Goodson, 170–84. London: Routledge, 2009.

Nolan, Riall W. *A Handbook of Practicing Anthropology*. Oxford: Wiley-Blackwell, 2013.

Nuñez, Theron A. "Tourism, Tradition, and Acculturation: Weekendismo in a Mexican Village." *Ethnology* 2 (1963): 347–52.

Novelli, Marina, ed. *Niche Tourism: Contemporary Issues, Trends and Cases*. Amsterdam: Elsevier, 2005.

Phillimore, Jenny, and Lisa Goodson. "Progress in Qualitative Research in Tourism: Epistemology, Ontology and Methodology." In *Qualitative Research in Tourism: Ontologies, Epistemologies and Methodologies*, edited by Jenny Phillimore and Lisa Goodson, 3–29. London: Routledge, 2009.

Pink, Sarah. *Doing Sensory Ethnography*. Los Angeles: SAGE, 2009.

Roca, Zoran, ed. *Second Home Tourism in Europe: Lifestyle Issues and Policy Responses*. London: Routledge, 2016.

Salazar, Noel, and Nelson Graburn. *Tourism Imaginaries: Anthropological Approaches*. New York: Berghahn Books, 2014.

Salazar, Noel B., and Yang Zhang. "Seasonal Lifestyle Tourism: The Case of Chinese Elites." *Annals of Tourism Research* 43 (2013): 81–99.

Sheller, Mimi, and John Urry. "The New Mobilities Paradigm." *Environment and Planning* 38 (2006): 207–26.

Sherlock, Kirsty. "Revisiting the Concept of Hosts and Guests." *Tourist Studies* 1, no. 3 (2001): 271–95.

Selwyn, Tom, ed. *The Tourist Image: Myths and Mythmaking in Tourism.* New York: Wiley, 1996.

Smith, Valene L., ed. *Hosts and Guests: The Anthropology of Tourism.* Oxford: Basil Blackwell, 1989.

Stronza, Amanda. "Anthropology of Tourism: Forging New Ground for Ecotourism and Other Alternatives." *Annual Review of Anthropology* 30 (2001): 261–83.

Tribe, John. "The Indiscipline of Tourism." *Annals of Tourism Research* 24 (1997): 638–57.

Vermeulen, Han F., and Arturo Álvarez Roldán. *Fieldwork and Footnotes: Studies in the History of European Anthropology.* European Association of Social Anthropologists. London: Routledge, 1995.

Chapter 4

A Map or a Calendar?

Travelers' Imaginary and a Travel Framework (The Case of Poland Following the Economic and Political Transformation)

Anna Wieczorkiewicz

I shall begin this chapter with a discussion on two passages from books written by Polish authors. They describe traveling by plane before the world was colonized by Google Earth; at that time, the Earth as seen from the window of a plane implied a specific relationship between the viewer and this view. The first text was published in the 1980s, shortly after the journey took place; the second one was published many years later, at the beginning of the twenty-first century. The way the authors used the bird's-eye view motif is significant, whereas the way it was subsequently transformed and applied is symptomatic of broader processes that take place in the area of the travelers' imaginary and related practices.

In Poland, they are under dual influences: on the one hand, of global cultural processes; on the other, of changes in the mentality of Poles following the political transformation which changed the geopolitical characteristics of their country. These local examples are used to indicate the more general mechanism of how the imaginative framework for the travelers' experience is constructed. What I am interested in is how the travelers' imaginary operates within this framework, understood as a set of basic categories that are activated in determining a travel's conditioning. Travelers' projects are regarded as feasible if they can be settled within this framework.

The concept of "travelers' imaginary" that I use, refers to the socially generated mode of visualizing areas located outside of everyday life routine, to associating these images with certain sets of meanings and referring these entireties to one's own biography, that is, to the biography currently experienced, to the one that is gone, or the one that is being designed. In many respects, it coincides with the concept of tourist imaginary.[1] However, I am writing about the travelers' imaginary, since the term "traveler" connotes certain identity projects. The notions "traveler"/"tourist" were used as opposites in the data that I have examined and were evaluative in nature (the values were in accordance with how the traveler/tourist were pictured in the 1960s by Daniel Boorstin).[2] I assume that this juxtaposition is essential for conceptualizing various kinds of mobilities as opposed to practices of everyday life.

Travelers' imaginary immanently involves the totality of social life,[3] the more touristification of everyday life supplies a form for many mundane practices and also fuels various types of mobility experience.[4] The social space of everyday life is saturated with various "signs of exotic places" which invite people to exoticize their routine practices; the items which are used in these practices circulate within the processes of the global culture industry.[5] Therefore, in this context, imagination is a factor of culture, which is influenced by global flows, and, on the one hand, deterritorialized, and, on the other, associated with meanings which can be defined in terms of definite cultural spaces[6] and locally processed. What is extremely important when conducting studies on travelers' imaginary, is its performative aspect.[7]

The examples that I later refer to seem to be heterogeneous, as they are taken from travel literature, ethnographic interviews, internet travel forums, and travel blogs.[8] However, I regard these data as drawn from complementary sources; what I want to emphasize by referring to them is to indicate that the pieces of tourist knowledge circulate in various areas of socio-cultural life; in fact, excerpts taken from different sources use the same topoi (*loci communes*).[9]

A MAP AND A LANDSCAPE COMBINED IN EXPERIENCE

In the 1980s, in her book *Tam, gdzie bogowie są wiecznie młodzi* [Where the Gods Are Always Young], Monika Warneńska described her journey to Nepal.[10] At that time, the world behind the Iron Curtain was hard for Poles to reach. In fact, little by little, foreign tourism possibilities were becoming more and more available for Poles, especially to the countries of the socialist camp, but as far as long-distance travels were concerned, there were political and economic barriers.[11] Monika Warneńska, a reporter and, previously, a war correspondent in Vietnam, described the journey that could only be dreamed of by most Poles. To introduce the readers to how unusual the journey was, she wrote as follows:

> While flying to Kathmandu, I put the key information about the geography of Nepal in order in my memory. A country that with its shape resembles an elongated, non-regular rectangle, borders with India from the east, west and south. . . . I look at the map. The mountains cannot yet be seen.[12]

The knowledge of maps precedes the knowledge of terrains; it is also known that a map will clarify a terrain effectively. A territory is perceived as topography; little by little, it is saturated with information on the surface, bordering countries, natural and cultural peculiarity; only afterwards does the topography become transformed into landscape saturated in terms of aesthetics. Entering the journey involves updating the relationship between the map and the territory. As the map is referred to the view stretched in front of the traveler, the drawing gains concreteness:

> I clung to the airplane windows; the terrain below is waving and slight rises make it warped; the rises are still not very high yet.[13]

It seems that the contour is transferred from the map to the ground; respective names adhere to the mountain ranges, and eventually, topography becomes landscape:

> Deep down, silvery, tiny serpentine lines of rivers flicker that can barely be noticed. This part of the valley is called: the inner Terai. And then, the mountains commence. With patches of blue shades of violet, the steel-gray peaks are so high that they nearly seem to reach the wings of the airplane; they are stunning with how vast and close they are. They are perfectly visible: distinct contours of ravines, gullies, faults can be clearly seen in the sunshine; as well as valleys deeply stuck with shimmering streaks of rivers or waterfalls at the bottom or on the slopes. These are not the Himalayas yet; this is a range of slight rises called Mahabharat.[14]

This is how the narration follows the pace of travel and represents the mood of expectation. Of course, this does not mean that it is a mirrored reflection of reality; however, it is significant which motifs were chosen and exposed in the process of elaboration of the experience for literature, since it indicates a certain cognitive and, at the same time, travelers' project. By combining the map with the landscape, the travelers' experience described in this passage makes the map objectivize the landscape, and the landscape anesthetizes the map.

Map and landscape are associated with certain cultural practices. It is assumed that a map invites us to become part of the practical relation to space, whereas landscape representation invites us to become lined up opposite it and makes us adopt an aesthetic attitude.[15] However, the nature of connections between them varies throughout history. In medieval maps, representations were ordered in a spiritual and moral dimension; it referred to the sacred history. In the geographical discoveries of that age, we can see ships, characters, and animals that evoke tales about journeys, meetings, and adventures.[16] Before maps became abstract images, they were "a result of experience and a practical need of people from the Middle Ages, who began to travel more than ever before, rather than the result of absolute mathematical measurement."[17] It can also be regarded as a cultural and visual strategy, which, together with landscape, "reduce the complex multi-sensual experience to visually encoded features and then organize and synthetize these into a meaningful whole"[18] and, at the same time, they are tools for control and surveillance.[19]

In its basic meaning, a modern map is a reproduction of space according to certain rules, by means of conventional signs, usually in a map graticule. Warneńska's narrative directs attention to certain patterns of relationships between a map (understood this way) and travel practices by exposing, watching, and understanding, but it also shows how these types of representations are able to activate a travel experience.

The second excerpt was taken from the book of the widely-read Polish reporter Ryszard Kapuściński, entitled *Podróże z Herodotem* [Travels with Herodotus]. The book was published in 2004, after the political system transformation in Poland (this transformation is regarded to have taken place in 1989). In *Travels with Herodotus*, the author describes many of his journeys, but he starts with the one he calls his first travel abroad. It was a business trip to India, which he made in the 1950s as a young journalist employed by the newspaper called *Sztandar Młodych*. In fact, Kapuściński had previously been in Berlin; in 1951, he traveled to Berlin for an international youth festival.[20] However, in his story, it is the Indian journey that gained the status of an opening event; it appears as a turning point between two periods in his life.

Kapuściński had a flight to India with a connection in Rome. The description of air travel evokes peculiar meanings. The view as seen from above does not exist only in the order of representation; the narrative brings out the performative aspect. Traveling by plane is a bodily, sensual experience:

> We flew in the dark; even in the cabin, the light bulbs just barely glowed, when suddenly the tension that holds all the particles of the plane as the engines are in top gear, began to decrease, the sound of engines became more calm and relaxed which meant we were approaching our destination.[21]

The traveler's memory saved both the view of the plane—from the outside and from the inside ("It was an old, double-engine DC-3, battered in front-line flights, its wings were blackened by exhaust fumes and there were patches on the fuselage, but it was flying; it was flying almost empty, with only a few passengers, to Rome"[22]), and the view beheld and seen from the window, which was unusual since it was a novelty and its overview perspective was unique ("I was sitting by the window, concerned, keeping my eyes fixed on it because for the first time, I saw the world from high above, it was the first time I had a bird's-eye view of it; I have even never been in the mountains before, let alone such a sky-high situation. In front of us, multicolored chessboards, motley patchworks and gray-green carpets move slowly, all stretching away, spread out over the ground, as if it was supposed to dry out in the sun"[23]). The author presents a viewing experience that is interactive in nature: light is not so much seen as it enters the viewer's eyes; image pulsation and vibrations also embrace the viewer's body. It is an initiation into a new world—into a world that has just lighted up in front of the viewer, coming closer; the world into which he may finally enter:

> I looked at it and I was stunned. Below me, the entire length and width of the bottom of this darkness we were flying in, was filled with light. It was an intense light, beating one's eyes, quivering, shimmering. One may get the impression that down there, is a liquid matter that glows; its shiny coating pulsates with brightness, rises and falls, stretches and shrinks because this whole luminous image is a living thing, full of mobility, vibration, energy.[24]

The symbolic potential of this image was used to bring out the importance of opening up to the vast world. When looking down, the impact of political borders is symbolically eliminated; the traveler is above them in the literal and metaphorical sense. In the plan of the narrative, beauty of the image (experienced by the whole body) reveals a moment prior to interpretation so that, for a moment, it exists for itself, for autotelic aesthetic value—as if it was a pity to sentence it to the status of a designator designed to articulate certain meanings.

In the book by Warneńska, political and economic barriers and borders are hidden rather than exposed, but it is obvious to readers that they existed. The rhetorical work on shaping the imaginary consists here in blurring information on the real difficulties that the Poles were facing when dreaming of journeys to faraway countries by the narrative on how hard it was (and what fun it was) to get more and more information on different countries, their natures and cultures. The writer begins with emphasizing the contemplative aspect of viewing a map, which, if borders are closed, sometimes is a window on the world of dreams. While telling readers stories of how she left the country and traveled to a distant world, she, at the same time, excuses herself for this fact, referring to the mysterious figures of "gatekeepers":

> At this moment, I only sigh and keep staring at the map. Until at last, it turns out that some of the people have been fascinated with Asia for a long time, who had a "hellish" build-up of energy and curiosity about the world, settled in Kathmandu, the capital of Nepal, for several years. Then, slowly, everything becomes easier.[25]

The book *Podróże z Herodotem* [Travels with Herodotus], describing the journey that took place in the 1950s, even many years after it took place, emphasizes how important the (political and mental) borders are. At the same time, the author's past in the Polish People's Republic becomes exoticized. Long passages describe how the young reporter experienced the existence of physical borders when traveling around the country and how intense his desire was to cross these borders. He also recalls his conversation with the chief editor of the newspaper he worked for:

> I would like to go abroad someday very much.—Abroad?—she said, surprised and a bit frightened, because at the time, it was not a usual thing to go abroad.—Where? What for?—she asked.—I was thinking about Czechoslovakia—I said. Because it was not the point to go to Paris or London, no. I have not even tried to imagine these things and I was not even curious about them, I just wanted to cross the border to somewhere, no matter which one, because what was important to me was not a goal, not an end, not a finish line, but the almost mystical and transcendental act of crossing the border alone.[26]

Therefore, "abroad" was a very general concept, although the specific countries were more or less abroad. If Czechoslovakia seemed to be less foreign than London, then India reached the limits of what could have hardly been imagined. It was distant more because Poland was politically closed rather than because of its geographical location. What is more, because of politics, the directions of the world were shifting in terms of how they were imagined. Since the reporter was flying to Delhi via Rome, the trip took on a Western flavor. At this point, India has become more Western than oriental (in order to get there, it was necessary to "break through" the West). However, once the reporter arrived in India, it turned out India is close to Poland that in many respects. As the young traveler did not know English at that time, he was in the position comparable to that of the uneducated class. The view of barefoot people evoked in the travelers' imaginary wartime memories of childhood and dreaming of shoes: "Now, when I saw that in India millions cannot afford their shoes, I realized that deep inside I had the feeling of community, brotherhood with these people, and as the time passed, I was even seized with the mood that we feel when we return to our childhood home."[27] This feeling of "community of fate," which was recalled many years later, was based on the concept of some kind of lack, that is, India was becoming similar to Poland through its distance from the great (rich) world. However, this tale on being close was composed many years after the event; whereas, on an ongoing basis, in coverages prepared for the newspaper in 1956, the author presented this event in a different way. Poverty was depicted as what makes India distant from Poland:

India is so unlike Poland! The same concepts but they do not mean the same thing out there. "I have no home—my friend from Warsaw says—I live literally on the streets." But if the homeless Indian man gives me the address: "Mutra Street Roadway more or less between the bridge and the cinema," then I can easily look for him at this location: he will certainly "live" out there.[28]

Freedom, being part of this story by Kapuściński, is the freedom of space (although *Podróże z Herodotem* is intended to be a book about time and the specific meaning of history). The type of memory of how imagined border lines were marked is clearly emphasized here. The author wrote: "The desire to cross the border, to keep your eyes open on what is beyond, was always alive inside me."[29] When looking down, you were able to rise above the boundaries in space; this is why the view was so impressive. The viewer's view of the reality became wider; however, the viewer did not feel like the ruler of the world, but as one who would like to enter this world.

FROM FREEDOM OF SPACE TO FREEDOM OF TIME

In contemporary narratives about journeys, everything happens faster. Flight time seems to be "empty," the space traveled over during the flight seems to be deprived of views, and the routes of flights are model non-places[30] that allow different destinations to refer to each other. Google-Earth-ization of imaginary determines simulacric order: the view of blue oceans and green-brown lands was familiar to most travelers before, having seen it previously on screens of different devices, and the Earth reproduction that can be manipulated, are part of the everyday life. Quite often, travel narratives make sudden jumps to some "other places," and then they present attempts at feeling the very place, incorporating it through experience. The beginning of the book by a young Polish traveler, Marzena Filipczak, *Jadę sobie. Azja. Przewodnik dla podróżujących kobiet* [I Just Keep Going. Asia. A Guide for Women Travelers], published in 2009, is typical in this respect. The story begins at the airport; the woman traveler finds herself in the wild world of an Asian city:

It was three a.m., and I have just landed at the airport in Bangalore in the south of India. Without any reservations or any idea what next, being in Asia for the first time and for the first time, anywhere alone. . . . There were dozens of taxi drivers outside, but can I go with one of them to look for a hotel at night? And can I go out at all, if a policeman with a gun sits along the way? I walked out of the terminal, without walking away further than a few meters from the door, just in case.[31]

The structure of this book reflects two aspects of rhetoric that works toward constructing the traveler's imaginary; it is intended to alienate the space of travel, and, almost at the same time, it presents strategies to make it familiar. The first part (called "Jadę sobie" [Just Keep Going]) is based on a blog from journeys to several Southeast Asian countries. The author creates an image of a European woman breaking through the exotic world and overcoming a variety of adversities (fighting with cockroaches in an Indian bathroom, struggling with the local transportation, etc.). The second part, entitled "Jadę sama" [I Go Alone], gives instructions that make a foreign world easy to use. This is how the moments of experiencing and describing approach each other; as the author ends describing, she immediately tells you what to do to set off on a journey. "An instant project" is created that can be put into practice: in the real world or in the imaginary one.

The book by Marzena Filipczak is seemingly devoted to covering space; however, it in fact indicates the fight against time. For example, let us pay attention to this passage: "I spent a lot of time on the road travelling by local buses, trains, common Jeeps, taxi boats and a rented bike."[32] It is the time spent on the road rather than the space covered that gives you an idea of the hardships of a journey. We can see the itinerary on the map reproduced in the book. The map looks as if it was sketched with a child's hand. It depicts places typical of trips to India (including the package trips)—such as Delhi, Jaipur, Agra, Varanasi. Decisions on how to freely spend your time and free-dom of choice are supposed to be a rebellious part of the trip as compared to the pattern of package tourism:

> I did not make it a point of honor to see all the monuments and temples, to attend each safari, to walk each trekking expedition. I chose what I found most interesting. I spent the rest of my time hanging around at local pubs, laying by the river, staring at the mountains, roaming around the maze of narrow streets of Asian cities. I have travelled by the local trains, buses, Jeeps, boats, vans and rickshaws for hours.[33]

What is interesting, there is no map on the list of things that the author recommends to take with you on your journey. There is something else instead: an alarm clock. To her regret, the author did not have it with her on the journey since it happened that the battery of her mobile phone, which can be used to measure time, died. We can assume that the woman traveler "gets confused" regarding the time then. This does not mean that she does not know where she is or where she is heading; however, it appears that it is easier for her to manage space than to manage time when on a journey:

> Over the last *ten days* I covered so many kilometers that I do not know how to count them. Once again, I did not plan the journey the best I could have, and

when it came to confirm with the calendar *how much time is left until the end*, it turned out that it is *not enough* to get anywhere I wanted. I tried to trim the route using the "a little bit everywhere" method, but it was still far from enough. I made a deletion with a single resolute movement: further into the mountains.[34]

Space (distance) must be adapted to time (calendar) rather than *vice versa*. The pleasure of moving in space is obscured by the effort you put into the fight against time; incompatibility of timetables with the actual time of rides (or in general the absence of what a traveler considers to be a timetable), dates of visa validity and the return date that has already been fixed. Space seems to cause less difficulties; it is relatively easy to cover, whereas, usually, there are several modes to do it (associated with specific symbolic values). In other words, the spatial colonization of the world carried out using a vehicle of the traveler's imaginary does not seem to go hand in hand with temporal colonization.

Landscape (as an object of contemplation) gives way to landscape that absorbs the traveler, attacks him or her, stimulates the senses. The traveler gives it a quick look and immerses himself in experience. This does not mean that the gaze lacks concentration. Sometimes, it is similar to the one that is focused toward the water surface a moment before diving headfirst, when assessing distance, when transferring the view to the movement of the body that is about to feel water.

It can be argued that this is the inevitable result of the complex, interrelated phenomena synthetically referred to as time-space compression.[35] We find ourselves in the circumstances of progressive acceleration, when the phenomena that involve mobility increasingly attract attention,[36] causing the area of social sciences to become redefined both as far as selection of areas of research interest is concerned, and creation of the conceptual apparatus that allows to distance the researcher from sedentary thinking[37]).

And thus, what I am interested in are the strategies that are created in the traveler's imaginary that still uses the classic, largely colonial topoi (*loci communes*) of acquiring and mastering the world.[38] It seems that while practices of everyday life are involved in time, space is left to the creative imagination.

In the next part, I try to illustrate this phenomenon using ethnographic interviews and travel forums. I pose the question: what is perceived by today's travelers as a framework for organizing their journeys? Based on the above discussion, it may be suspected that time and space do not play the same role in constructing this frame. Literary texts present experience that is carefully processed, they indicate *the project* of traveler's imaginary, while travel forums give insight into the efforts made by travelers to produce this experience and shape it in a specific way (they often use the same set of *topoi* which is active in the process of elaborating the experience for literature). The ethnographic material which I discuss can give insight into the issues that travelers themselves perceive as problematic.

THE BUILDING BLOCKS OF TRAVEL FRAMEWORK

Having previously traveled both as part of organized tramping tours and as an individual traveler, the woman traveler talks about the inconveniences of traveling independently as follows:

> Trying to find accommodation . . . *takes a lot of time* here because you do not find the hotel that you would like, that is available at a good price right away, so you have to run around everywhere. . . . The same is true when it comes to looking for places to eat, or doing some shopping, buying some fruit, food and things like that. You have to take care of many things before you go. Visas—if you go with the travel office, then you send your passport and you don't give a rat's . . . about it at all, right? . . . But here, you have to go to the embassy by yourself, you have to complete all the formalities, and pay. *It takes time.* (22-W-ti,ttr; emphasis AW)[39]

The time motif also appeared in her conversation when she recalled participating in the organized tramping tour:

> A serious drawback of traveling in a group: *you always have to wait for someone.* This drove me crazy. *People are late,* they do not come to the pick-up point, you sit, you do not know. . . . *Waiting* for the rest of the group is terrible. There were 12 people and I was irritated; I prefer not to imagine what happens when there are 30. (22-W-ti,ttr; emphasis AW)

It seems that there will always be shortfalls; regardless of whether you are traveling with an organized tour or alone; there will always be a problem with time. Dates and timetables are issues extensively discussed on forums devoted to various forms of travel. It often comes down to "inserting" a given tour into a specified period of time. The following statement on a forum devoted to package tourism is typical in this respect:

> I, in turn, will probably leave between January and March, we'll see what comes of this. For the time being, we both, me and my husband, need to find out if we will be given holidays at such a time :). As far as the dates are concerned, everybody goes when they can or when the employer allows ;). Most of our trips to Asia were during the rainy season, because this is when were given holidays.[40]

If the favorable configuration includes the professional schedule of the woman tourist, and her husband's schedule (whereas both of them are dependent on employers' schedules), and the date of the tour, then the departure will take place. Somewhere in the background of expectations for this conjunction to happen, there is knowledge that the Earth turns around, and the seasons change according to a certain rhythm; however, you need to ignore this rhythm. The trip event will be fit into it when the said conjunction takes place.

My next illustration shows how the category of time is associated with other categories that are important when clarifying travel projects. In the section "Seeking a travel companion, seeking people for a journey" on the tourist portal called www.travelbit.pl, a woman traveler from Warsaw opened a topic thread called "India 2016" as follows:

> Hi there, I am going to travel to India and this time I want to focus on the northern part of the country. Two weeks as yet. The route is rather classic. "Going" from the north: Ladakh, Śrimagar, Amritsar/Atarii (Chandigarh and Rishkesh—alternatively), New Delhi, Agra, Jaipur (Udaipur—alternatively), Varanasi. Due to the temperature in the Himalayas and driving conditions, the best time is May–August. The exact date is subject to the price of the ticket. If you dream of northern India and are looking for a companion, write! Details always to be agreed on.[41]

Here is how the travel frame is created: first, the author of the post indicates *the destination* (India, the northern part of the country); immediately afterward, she gives information about *the time* of its duration (two weeks as yet), followed by alternated information on space with the information on time: sketch of the (classic) route and the date (optimal due to weather) are further clarified. The description of conditions is supplemented with the third factor: *the price* of the ticket. These three conditions: temporal, spatial, and economic—are not equally important. The route can be discussed (the author of the post points out that it is subject to modification); it seems much more difficult to discuss the other two types of conditions.

The same arrangement of items, that is, *space—time—price*, was used by the travelers that were the subject of our ethnographic research. Sometimes, the first item of the system, that is, destination, seemed to be the result of a configuration in which the other two were used, that is, time and price. A woman began the story about traveling to Goa as follows:

> We made this travel because of the price, of course. We took the tour which was not supposed to reach the first day of Christmas and Christmas Eve. (7-W-tz,ti)

The interlocutor dwelled on the time topic for a long period of time, talking about mistakes in interpreting the date. She explained that this was "a package tour, but an atypical one, because it was a very, very cheap trip." She quoted a quite precise amount, and then, she elaborated on this subject: "This is really amazing money as for India; when someone asked 'where have you been' and I went—'to India,' then, there were comments like: 'well, well, . . .' I came across bargains like this several times, perhaps because it was the holiday season and the tours were launched for only a moment. There were people in the same group of tourists who paid 5–6 thousand for this trip" (7-W-tm,ti).

In this statement, India (as a destination) remains somewhere in the background; it exists as a place that was encountered by purchasers of the recreational event as a result of the occasional configuration of time and price factors. Price serves as a gate opening up space to travelers, or creates barriers that cannot be overcome by them. Destinations are expressed in prices; transport routes are constructed of prices as well. A woman that took part in many organized tours presented it as follows:

> There are actually two restrictions like this. The first one is economic: at some point, destinations financially available are sold out, and what remains, is just those that are very high-end ones, which means they are so distant and so expensive that actually . . . well, at the moment, I cannot afford them. But there is also that stupid time barrier, which I happened to have. . . . I can only depart in August; I have no other dates for trips like this. (1-W-tm)

A person who chose an organized tramping tour told her story as follows: "I compared prices, I checked if they had any good reviews on forums, I called the office, I spoke with the staff of these offices, and all in all, I chose this office. Probably also because they had good dates that matched my dates and the price was relatively low" (22-W-ti, ttr).

The time factor seems to be a primary mode in the travel machinery; if your plan for it to operate is wrong, there will immediately be clashes. The time topic was taken up as a response to a previously quoted post of the traveler who was looking for a traveling companion. A forum member suggested that the presented plan cannot be implemented:

> I just wanted to suggest that your plan is too ambitious for a 16-day trip. It just cannot be accomplished in such a short time. Unless you treat it as a casual suggestion "to choose—to be agreed on."[42]

However, the author of the post does not get baffled. She argues by referring to her previous travel experience:

> I am absolutely aware of the fact that it is unrealistic to see all the places I named in 2 weeks. The "must see" list will be created collectively, if someone decides to join in. If I travel alone, it is possible that I will spend most of my time in the Himalayas. My experience in traveling around India is "so-so." I have been living in Hyderabad for 4.5 months and I was not able to see everything in the south of India. Therefore, I am aware that two weeks is a very short time.[43]

Here, it is not difficult to note the rhetoric of making the author's image part of the traveler identity project: *this time*, the traveler is planning to go (this means she has already traveled to India before); she is focused on selected areas, she has "so-so" experience in traveling; she emphasizes her detachment from this fact with a quotation, thereby suggesting that she is not going to boast, because she does not have to build up her position in this way; however, the readers should appreciate the fact that she *has been living* in Hyderabad (thus, her experience is certainly above average; surely, she is not a so-called tourist). Since she *has been living* in the south for four and a half months, she knows what it means to stay in the north for two weeks; she knows what will fit within this period.

Referring it to the rhetoric activated by the traveler's imaginary, it can be said that true freedom is expressed by indicating the traveler's independence from time constraints. Covering huge amounts of space will not be as impressive as treating time offhandedly. The longer the travel, the better; whereas the really free traveler is one who would go somewhere and stay there for a very long time. On travel forums, those who have been traveling for a couple of months used to emphasize this fact when they build up their position as they exchange their posts.

Referring to the approach suggested by George Lakoff and Mark Johnson,[44] we may say that it is time (not space) that is considered to be a container for travel experiences; it must fit the events. Space only provides scenery. This does not mean that it is not important, but the components for its construction are obtained from areas other than the basic, hard building blocks of the framework of travel. Images of distant lands, lost civilizations (and narratives about how the taste of life is experienced and its meaning is found on the road) are planted by various messages of popular culture; they are suitable to create the imaginary scenery of one's own travel.

Whereas time and money are factors that restrain the freedom of an individual, they also indicate their involvement in everyday life. However, it is difficult to argue with arrival and departure dates. Of course, the traveler can be amazed how inconsistent the local timetables are because in traveling, time can, in fact, be liquid and absurd; the "real" time that creates the framework of travel must be solid. The scenery (spatial) is incorporated in the sphere of the traveler's imaginary; it is like a liquid matter that pours out of a frame onto the plane of the image. This matter is subjected to various kinds of processing.

SUMMARY

Time and space are used in different ways by a traveler's imaginary; they also translate to travel practices in a different mode. Space seems to be flexible and moldable; it allows for manipulation much easier than the time factor in the process of constructing individual projects for travel practices. Covering space is becoming easier and easier because of the complex network of flights, special offers for tickets and tour packages. Various interesting "locations" (i.e., destinations of successive trips) are suspended within the network of economic and temporal systems.[45] While interpreting these locations, the traveler may use the meanings which have been previously suggested by mediascapes and ideoscapes.[46] The analyzed material allows to conclude that time constructs a rigid travel framework. It is conceived as a factor placing limitations on a traveler's freedom (and human freedom in general). Knowledge about what it means to be involved in social and economic structures seems to be the reverse side of this rhetoric of freedom; therefore, to construct a framework for travel, not only is time used, but money as well. It can be assumed that there is a fear of being totally dominated by these structures at the core (as yet, this psychologizing interpretation has gained the status of a hypothesis, which is referred to by the sources I have researched.) From the above, it may be clearly concluded that it is a calendar rather than a map that puts a tight rein on a traveler's imaginary.

The juxtaposition of the contemporary material and a bit historic examples demonstrate this phenomenon even more clearly. As far as Poland is concerned, the convenient point of reference are travel accounts concerning the Polish People's Republic period, both written at that time and of reminiscent nature. They direct attention to various aspects of the changing process. Due to the censorship, the earlier texts blurred pieces information, which in texts of reminiscent nature, are brought to light and used to exoticize the past. However, in both of them, the space categories were implemented to express freedom. Borders (physical and political; translatable into economic constraints) were an especially integral part of imagined space, due to difficulties in traveling experienced by Poles. A map seemed to be an obvious tool in representing primary travel conditions and, at the same time, it was an imaginary window on the world. A map was associated with cognitive experience, traveling in physical space as well. However, this cognitive experience could be transfigured into the emotional one. Therefore, the motif of flight that allows overview of space from above, gained a symbolic sense of liberation.

At present, under the time-space compression, flight is perceived as a translocation technique that takes place in time which is devoid of any meaning. Thus, people can move efficiently to a given location which in fact is well-known to them because of simulacric inversions. At this location, we find the utopia of life without a calendar for some time. However, this utopia has its beginning and its end, which means it has a solid, time-defined travel framework.

NOTES

1. Noel B. Salazar, "Tourism Imaginaries: A Conceptual Approach," *Annals of Tourism Research* 39 (2012): 836–82; Noel B. Salazar and Nelson Graburn, "Introduction Toward an Anthropology of Tourism Imaginaries," in *Tourism Imaginaries: Anthropological Approaches*, ed. Noel B. Salazar and Nelson Graburn (New York: Berghan Books, 2014), 1–28.

2. Daniel J. Boorstin, *The Image: A Guide to Pseudo-Events in America* (New York: Harper, 1964).

3. John Urry, *The Tourist Gaze: Leisure and Travel in Contemporary Societies* (London: Sage Publications, 1990).

4. Michael Haldrup and Jonas Larsen, *Tourism, Performance and the Everyday: Consuming the Orient* (London: Routledge, 2009).

5. Arjun Appadurai, *Modernity at Large Cultural Dimensions of Globalization* (Minneapolis: University of Minnesota Press, 1996).

6. Scott Lash and Celia Lury, *Global Cultural Industry* (Cambridge: Polity Press, 2007).

7. Tim Edensor, *Tourist at the Taj: Performance and Meaning at a Symbolic Site* (London: Routledge, 1998).

8. The interviews were part of workshop classes I gave at the Institute of Ethnology and Cultural Anthropology at the University of Warsaw over the period 2013–2016 with students' cooperation and, at this point, I would like to thank them for inspiring cooperation. In the same period, I followed forums and blogs.

9. While speaking of *topoi* [common places—gr. τόπος topoi, *loci communes*], I refer to the concept of Ernst Robert Curtius and its rhetorical antecedents, in which topos delivered a pattern for reasoning and persuasion, established (and supposed to be effective) presentation of a particular topic. In fact, as a conventionalized oratorical device, topos was a semi-finished form in which a variety of content could be captured by the orator in order to justify that the views held are valid. It appealed to audience's intelligence, emotions, habits, and preferences, while being suitable to prove a variety of—including contradictory ones—arguments. Topos did not have to be innovative—however, it had to be effective. It was used in multiple texts (hence its Latin name *locus communis* or "common place"). As it was effective, it was also used in everyday speech, and, to some extent, it was used automatically, see further: Ernst Robert Curtius, *European Literature and the Latin Middle Ages*, trans. Willard R. Trask (New York: Pantheon Books, 1953).

10. Monika Warneńska, *Tam, gdzie bogowie są wiecznie młodzi* (Warsaw: Krajowa Agencja Wydawnicza, 1984).

11. In Poland under the socialism, until 1956, the passport policy was hedged around with a variety of reservations. After 1956, it became easier to travel. However, trips to the West were still not an easy undertaking for formal and financial reasons. Journeys to European socialist countries were easier. Since 1972, journeys could be made based on the so-called "passport inserts" that were valid with ID cards. Until 1984, citizens each time before the journey had to apply to obtain a passport, and, upon returning, it was necessary to give the document back to the local headquarters

of Citizens Militia. In 1988, long-period passports began to be issued for all countries of the world.

12. Monika Warneńska, *Tam, gdzie bogowie są wiecznie młodzi*, 9.

13. Ibidem, 10.

14. Ibidem, 11.

15. Michel de Certeau. *Practices of Everyday Life*, vol. 1, trans. Steven Rendall (Berkeley: University of California Press, 2011), chapter 9; Beata Frydryczak, *Krajobraz. Od estetyki the picturesque do doświadczenia topograficznego* (Poznań: Wydawnictwo Poznańskiego Towarzystwa Przyjaciół Nauk, 2012), 40.

16. Michel de Certeau, *Practices of Everyday Life*, 120.

17. Beata Frydryczak, *Krajobraz*, 31.

18. Phil Macnaghten and John Urry, *Contested Natures* (London: SAGE, 1998), 120.

19. Ibidem, 121.

20. Artur Domosławski, *Kapuściński non-fiction* (Warsaw: Świat Książki, 2012), 92.

21. Ryszard Kapuściński, *Podróże z Herodotem* (Kraków: Znak, 2004), 15.

22. Ibidem, 20.

23. Ibidem.

24. Ibidem, 15–16.

25. Monika Warneńska, *Tam, gdzie bogowie są wiecznie młodzi*, 9.

26. Ryszard Kapuściński, *Podróże*, 14.

27. Ibidem, 38.

28. As cited in Artur Domosławski, *Kapuściński,* 138. Original in: Fatamorgana egzotyki "Sztandar młodych," August 23, 1955.

29. Ryszard Kapuściński, *Podróże*, 73.

30. Mark Augé, *Non-Places: Introduction to an Anthropology of Supermodernity* (New York: Verso, 2008).

31. Marzena Filipczak, *Jadę sobie. Azja. Przewodnik dla podróżujących kobiet* (Warsaw: Poradnia K, 2009), 9.

32. Ibidem, 240.

33. Ibidem, 7.

34. Ibidem, 162, emphasis by A. W.

35. David Harvey, *The Condition of Postmodernity* (Oxford: Blackwell, 1990).

36. Noel B. Salazar and Nina Glick Schiller, eds., *Regimes of Mobility: Imaginaries and Relationalities of Power* (London: Routledge, 2014); John Urry, *The Tourist Gaze: Leisure and Travel in Contemporary Societies* (London: SAGE, 1990).

37. Akhil Gupta and James Ferguson, "Beyond Culture: Space, Identity and the Politics of Difference," *Cultural Anthropology* 7 (1992): 6–23.

38. Marie Louise Pratt, *Imperial Eyes: Travel Writing and Transculturation* (London: Routledge, 1992).

39. Survey coding: survey number, sex of the interlocutor (W—woman, M—man), type of travels made (ti—individual tourism, ttr—organized tramping tourism, tm—package mass tourism).

40. www.gazeta.pl/forum, post dated October 24, 2014, accessed December 20, 2015.

41. www.travelbit.pl, dated November 29, 2015, accessed December 20, 2015.

42. www.travelbit.pl; dated November 30, 2015, accessed December 20, 2015.

43. www.travelbit.pl; dated November 30, 2015, accessed December 20, 2015.

44. George Lakoff and Mark Johnson, *Metaphors We Live By* (Chicago: The University of Chicago Press, 1980).

45. Manuel Castells, *The Rise of the Network Society* (Oxford: Blackwell, 2000).

46. Arjun Appadurai, *Modernity at Large: Cultural Dimensions of Globalization* (Minneapolis: University of Minnesota Press, 1996).

REFERENCES

Appadurai, Arjun. *Modernity at Large: Cultural Dimensions of Globalization*. Minneapolis: University of Minnesota Press, 1996.

Augé, Mark. *Non-Places: Introduction to an Anthropology of Supermodernity*. New York: Verso, 2008.

Bachórz, Agata. *Rosja w tekście i doświadczeniu. Analiza współczesnych polskich relacji z podróży*. Kraków: Nomos, 2013.

Boorstin, Daniel J. *The Image: A Guide to Pseudo-Events in America*. New York: Harper, 1964.

Castells, Manuel. *The Rise of the Network Society*. Oxford: Blackwell, 2000.

Cegielski, Max. *Masala*. Warsaw: Wydawnictwo WAB, 2008.

Certeau de, Michel. *Practices of Everyday Life*, vol. 1. Translated by Steven Rendall. Berkeley: University of California Press, 2011.

Curtius, Ernst Robert. *European Literature and the Latin Middle Ages*. Translated by Willard R. Trask. New York: Pantheon Books, 1953.

Domosławski, Artur. *Kapuściński non-fiction*. Warsaw: Świat Książki, 2012.

Edensor, Tim. *Tourist at the Taj: Performance and Meaning at a Symbolic Site*. New York: Routledge, 1998.

———. *National Identity, Popular Culture and Everyday Life*. Oxford: Berg, 2000.

Filipczak, Marzena. *Jadę sobie. Azja. Przewodnik dla podróżujących kobiet*. Warsaw: Poradnia K, 2009.

Firt, Jordan. "Splintered Space: Hybrid Spaces and Differential Mobility." *Mobilities* 7 (2012): 131–49.

Frydryczak, Beata. *Krajobraz. Od estetyki the picturesque do doświadczenia topograficznego*. Poznań: Wydawnictwo Poznańskiego Towarzystwa Przyjaciół Nauk, 2012.

Gupta, Akhil, and James Ferguson. "Beyond Culture: Space, Identity and the Politics of Difference." *Cultural Anthropology* 7 (1992): 6–23.

Haldrup, Michael, and Jonas Larsen. *Tourism, Performance and the Everyday: Consuming the Orient*. London: Routledge, 2009.

Harvey, David. *The Condition of Postmodernity.* Oxford: Blackwell, 1990.

Horolets, Anna. *Konformizm, bunt, nostalgia. Turystyka niszowa z Polski do krajów byłego ZSRR.* Kraków: Universitas, 2013.

Kapuściński, Ryszard. *Podróże z Herodotem.* Kraków: Znak, 2004.

Lakoff, George, and Mark Johnson. *Metaphors We Live By.* Chicago: The University of Chicago Press, 1980.

Lash, Scott, and John Urry. *Economies of Signs and Spaces.* London: SAGE, 1993.

Lash, Scott, and Celia Lury. *Global Cultural Industry.* Cambridge: Polity Press, 2007.

Macnaghten, Phil, and John Urry. *Contested Natures.* London: SAGE, 1998.

Pratt, Marie Louise. *Imperial Eyes: Travel Writing and Transculturation.* London: Routledge, 1992.

Rojek, Chris. "Indexing, Dragging and the Social Construction of Tourist Sights." In *Touring Cultures: Transformations of Travel and Theory,* edited by Chris Rojek and John Urry, 52–74. London: Routledge, 1997.

Salazar, Noel B. "Tourism Imaginaries: A Conceptual Approach." *Annals of Tourism Research* 39 (2012): 836–82.

Salazar, Noel B., and Nelson Graburn. "Introduction Toward an Anthropology of Tourism Imaginaries." In *Tourism Imaginaries: Anthropological Approaches,* edited by Noel B. Salazar and Nelson Graburn, 1–28. New York: Berghahn Books, 2014.

Salazar, Noel B., and Nina Glick Schiller, eds. *Regimes of Mobility: Imaginaries and Relationalities of Power.* London: Routledge, 2014.

Urry, John. *The Tourist Gaze: Leisure and Travel in Contemporary Societies.* London: Sage Publications, 1990.

———. *Mobilities.* Cambridge: Polity Press, 2007.

Warneńska, Monika. *Tam, gdzie bogowie są wiecznie młodzi.* Warsaw: Krajowa Agencja Wydawnicza, 1984.

Chapter 5

At a Crossroads of Cognition

Travels of Philosophy and Philosophy of Travels

Maria Zowisło

Travel is unquestionably a wide-ranging phenomenon of the human world and a meaningful image of man's curiosity and self-awareness. Its multifaceted presence in culture and thoughtful human life naturally makes it the right sort of matter about which to philosophize. Indeed, travel has been present in philosophy since the very dawn of its history and has appeared not only as a question of critical thought, but also as a lively experience in the lifetimes of a not inconsiderable number of philosophers. There are countless examples of philosophers' travel experiences and ruminations. In this article, I relate to selected comments and deliberations of philosophers concerning the travel motif and compare them with the accounts of modern world wayfarers: reporters, writers, essayists, and poets. From these colorful epic stories and reflections there emerges a very complex picture of travelers' experiences.

However, a philosopher could see two important modes in the tangle of wanderers' interests and intentions. These can help us to extract their distinct traits and make a tentative order, in the most general sense, of the variety of traveling attitudes. These modes appear to be travels of philosophy itself, that is, the wanderings of the restless philosophical mind that aspires to embrace with its cognitive powers the truth of being. What I mean here is the two types of philosophical experience present in past philosophical tradition and known in contemporary philosophy as phenomenology and hermeneutics. Interestingly, although these modes of cognition have inspired some philosophers to make creative syntheses (vide fundamental ontology of Martin Heidegger), their methodological premises are disjunctive. More significantly, these modes of philosophical cognition often manifest themselves in man's cultural practices, where their rigorous disjunction disappears and turns into a junction. (This means that philosophical modes of understanding in the framework of their cultural applications tend to be understood as ideal types according to Max Weber's *verstehende Soziologie*, interpretative sociology.) Real journeys are very often cocreated by both modes of experience; in the course of actual events they do not develop independently. What stays at a crossroads in pure thinking may come as conjunction in reality. Thus, travels of philosophy, when transferred to man's real travel experiences, encounter new areas of thinking, beyond some rigid logical divisions. This chapter takes up the issue of these two modes of wandering/cognition: the phenomenological and the hermeneutical. They are regarded here as tools to clarify meanings and directions of possible dialogue between philosophers and wanderers, travelers, and tourists.

TRAVEL IN CULTURE AND PHILOSOPHY

The travel motif has always attracted scholarly attention, both as a social phenomenon and as an idea residing in the collective consciousness. As a phenomenon, traveling is a real part of the historical dynamics of man's cultural practices. The ventures of the first humans out of Africa—nomadism, pilgrimages, mass migrations, geographical discovery, conquests and war campaigns, political and economic immigration, as well as contemporary tourism—these are only a few examples of real human travel activity. The idea of travel in turn manifests itself in the dynamics of human thinking and imagination. Here we can descry travel connotations inter alia in man's cognition and desire for knowledge, in artistic avant-garde creations, in social and religious structures of *rites de passage*, in the trances of shamans and mystics, in psychedelic trips, and in mythological images of the ultimate passing to the netherworld. The ongoing process of historical sedimentation and overlapping of these and other appearances and references has made traveling the root metaphor of human self-knowledge. According to Paul Ricoeur, root metaphors are peculiarly figurative images that enfold fundamental structures of the human attitude toward reality. As such, they are akin to symbols and archetypes (as understood by Philip Wheelwright and Mircea Eliade, among others) and endowed with a surplus of meaning that provokes "an endless exegesis."[1]

Philosophical interpretation of the travel motif seems to be the significant path of such a metaphor's exegesis. The idea that man is a wanderer, a nomad, a pilgrim has become an inherent part of the philosophical notion of *homo viator*. This notion, popularized in contemporary philosophy by French religious thinker Gabriel Marcel,[2] who adopted it from Saint Augustine's *homo inquietus,* expresses the essential truth about human creatures: wayfarers in existence between Earth and Heaven, restless and transgressive beings possessing curious minds, heading toward multiple lands and values.[3]

Like common travelers and contemporary tourists, philosophers engage in real travels and conceptualize their travel experiences. Their remarks or even broader considerations on meanings, functions, and values of wandering are important since they are rooted in critical thinking and frequently made with regard to the history of ideas. Thus, philosophical travels very often billow into some sort of philosophy of travel. We have to remember these two (real and ideal) levels of reference while considering philosophers' preoccupation with travel.

A willful ambition to study "the book of the world" is a motif that links philosophers with common travelers; exploration through unrestrained observation is the basis for both of reading the world. Visual examination was called *theorein* by the Greeks, thus combining knowledge with perception and scrutiny. It is obvious that the sense of sight is the door to the world and the lynchpin of cognition. In culture, this visual exploration adopts various incarnations, being a baseline in social communication, scientific research, philosophical investigations, and artistic visions; of course, it also is the core of a traveler's experience. The cognitive advantages of the sense of sight and its primacy in penetration of the world have been highlighted by numerous thinkers. Pythagoras was reported to (according to Cicero[4]) compare the world to athletic games and a philosopher to a spectator of this performance. Aristotle began the first book of *Metaphysics* with praise of visual experience.[5]

Of several motives, the curiosity to search is only one, strictly cognitive, aspect of the travel adventure that makes it similar to the philosophical experience. Naturally, there are other principal senses to consider. As mentioned previously, travel is a complex image of the human condition and its various existential, anthropological, metaphysical, and axiological dimensions have been constantly distinguished in philosophical reflection. In Western culture many philosophers were preoccupied with voyages. In this short essay I can give attention only to some examples.

PHILOSOPHERS ON THE ROAD

Among his other quests, Thales of Miletus, the father of European philosophy, sought to describe the objective world he toured in terms of geography. His disciple Anaximander drew world maps presenting it as a cylinder. Democritus, driven by a desire to know the world exhaustively, spent all his inheritance on traveling. His voyages helped him to develop knowledge in many directions, which fructified in the six hundred or so volumes he wrote on nature, astronomy, medicine, atomism, economics, politics, foreign languages, religions, customs, cultures, and many other subjects. To find a means to preserve freedom and political independence, the Sophists, "itinerant teachers of wisdom," moved on the roads, islands, and *poleis* of Hellas, recognizing how relative and subjective truth, laws, and customs were. There were the times when the philosophers Anaxagoras, Protagoras, and Aristotle were exiles. The only way of salvation from the threat of the death penalty for their bold scientific (astronomy), religious, or political views was to escape (from Athens). This, however, did not discourage them from continuing their philosophical activity; additionally, due to their nomadic life they became aware of the importance of cosmopolitanism. Thus, we could conclude that philosophizing and creative thought do not need any particular place to grow. The homeless state of a philosopher indicates a "homeless state of thought." This was indicated by Hannah Arendt in her reflections on the life of the mind, referring to, as a matter of fact, an exile-philosopher, Aristotle: "The thinking ego, moving among universals, among invisible essence, is, strictly speaking, nowhere; it is homeless in an emphatic sense—which may explain the early rise of a cosmopolitan spirit among the philosophers."[6]

Since for a thinker any place is suitable to engage in philosophical contemplation, it turns out that to know reality there is no necessary prerequisite to embark on a voyage; this was a conclusion drawn by Immanuel Kant, who did not move beyond the boundaries of Königsberg. This multicultural city of German, Polish, Lithuanian, and Jewish nations—the capital of East Prussia, a Baltic port successfully developing international trade, which was proud of its reputable university and cultural events—appeared to the philosopher to be the best model of the whole world. For this reason, the philosopher had no need to undertake voyages.[7] However, such an adamant attitude did not put him off his keen interest in physical geography. He gave lectures on this subject for many years and related the discipline to transcendental knowledge and pragmatic anthropology, seeing it as structured by a sensual a priori form of space and being the foundation for the enlightenment of human cosmopolitan education. He not only elaborated the methodological and scientific basis for modern geography, but also was fond of reading travel books and thus studied foreign and exotic cultures.[8] This hobby may be regarded as a kind of philosopher's "imaginative traveling." Perhaps such a virtual journey may prove more intense and inspiring than a real one, who knows?

This was not the case with René Descartes, who sought the Archimedean point for *clare et distincte* knowledge and therefore questioned bookish erudition and saw it as the first great obstacle on the path to the truth that had to be overcome by dubious *cogito*. So, at the starting point of philosophizing only the real world could be the right book (*fabula mundi*), the living one of study and learning that was more inspiring than printed books full of unproven claims. This was depicted by René Descartes in his *Discourse on Method*: "I entirely abandoned the study of letters, and resolved no longer to seek any other science than the knowledge of myself, or of the great book of the world. I spent the remainder of my youth in travelling . . . , in collecting varied experience . . . , and, above all, in making such reflection on the matter of my experience as to secure my improvement."[9] It was on the way, in Germany, in an inn near Ulm, the "city of mathematicians," in a chamber heated by a bread-oven, in the silence and solitude of the night of November 9 to November 10, 1619, that Descartes experienced the enthusiasm of discovering the right method of "conducting reason." Thus, real voyages, legitimate as a means of fresh cognition, turned out to be merely a first step to finally resettling in cogito habitation. In fact, on cogito and its innate ideas, Descartes based *itinerarium* of the rationalistic *methodos,* that is, an accurate and reliable way to the truth.

Nevertheless, the philosopher was en route all his life until his ultimate stop in Stockholm. For him—as for the ancient Sophists—traveling was the best vehicle for saving scientific and political independence. Seeking a friendly place for pursuing his research, the Frenchman chose a new home-land—the liberal Netherlands—where he stayed for many years. Another wandering philosopher, Jean-Jacques Rousseau, a Swiss contributor to French philosophy and political thought, experienced his early existential and intellectual divide in October 1749, while walking to Vincennes: taking a rest under a tree he read a note about a competition announced by the Academy of Dijon on the impact of scientific progress on people's customs and morality. In the retreat of nature, away from the hustle and bustle of cities, being inspired, Jean-Jacques experienced his illumination, in which "man of nature" won over "man of man" or "social man." Wandering became for him a way to escape from artificiality and the civilized world ruled by the laws of alienation; it became a means to return to nature.[10] Subsequently, in his later pedagogical treatise *Emile* (1762), the philosopher paid some attention to traveling and saw it as the complement of natural education. Yet, his philosophy of travel was not confined to educational remarks. It got its final shape in the philosophy of existential retreat and stillness, the utmost aims of any movement. We can distil the meaning of such an experience while following his succeeding "memoir strolls" in *The Reveries of the Solitary Walker,* his last writing and actually his final reckoning of life, created in the seclusion of Ermenonville (1778). What emerges little by little from them is the idea of the essential dream about the unity of man and nature. It seems to be a kind of original reconciliation of two opposite philosophical stances: the Stoic acceptance of fate and the Epicurean experience of the bliss of existence. In the *Fifth Walk,* we find a description of *sentiment de l'existence,* the sense of existential happiness that appears as we withdraw from the social world, from its temptations and concerns, to the bosom of nature. On the small Saint-Pierre island of Lake Biel in Switzerland, in two autumn months of 1765, Jean-Jacques experienced a state of relief and solace in an intense meditation on the here and now, *hic et nunc*: "What do we enjoy in such a situation? Nothing external to ourselves, nothing if not ourselves and our own existence. As long as this state lasts, we are sufficient unto ourselves, like God."[11] Wandering is here a means to reaching peace, tranquility, relaxation; movement tends here to stillness where the essence of existence is revealed, given in the communion of the subject and the object, in unity of man and the world. Of course, the philosopher was quite aware that such a dolce far niente, that is, idleness of ecstatic leisure, was a rare privilege and could not last permanently. As he enunciated earlier in *Du contrat social* (1762), man's destiny was to create a fair community, a state of sovereign *citoyens*. Here, it was the validity of the social contract based on the general will that could enable people to overcome common alienation. Yet, in *Reveries,* his interests did not focus on politics anymore and civic mutuality gave its place to moral solidarity. Thus, the philosopher escaped the threat of solipsism.

Philosophical rambles taken in an easy rhythm of body and mind, stimulating quiescence and meditation, were not an isolated spiritual adventure pursued just by Rousseau. In the middle of the nineteenth century, a similar experience was shared by an American romantic Henry David Thoreau, a tramp of the forests of New England. He went to Pond Woods near Concord, built a cottage on his own, and lived there for over two years, exercising self-reliance and social independence (we can see here the existential background of his later political idea of "civil disobedience"). Primarily, his stay in the severe natural milieu at Walden Pond can be seen as a particular American trapper variant of a universal motif of man's nostalgia to live authentically and consciously outside social limitations, in unity with nature. This sounded in tune with Ralph Waldo Emerson's philosophy of nature and his individualistic and heroic ethos of self-reliance. In fact, this prominent master of American transcendentalists was the owner of the plot where Thoreau set his cabin up. Recollecting his project in *Walden,* Thoreau indicated that his principal aim was to conduct a simple Spartan existence, removed from any social and civilized facilities, to feel the core of life.[12] In Thoreau's experiment, philosophy and life itself were made equal. As evolved and practiced in the bosom of nature, Thoreau's transcendentalism could be named *philosophia activa.* I mean here a pattern of vital thought that permeates thoughtful life. This style of attentive and deliberate philosophical life was advocated and uncompromisingly fulfilled by a few other thinkers: Socrates, the Cynics, Pascal, Kierkegaard, Nietzsche, and Wittgenstein. The latter also traveled much, and among his destinations were the countries of Northern Europe: Iceland, Norway, and Ireland. Norway with its gaunt and arresting landscapes of fjords and mountains seems to have been his favorite country. Near Skjolden, a village located in a faraway mountain place at the end of Sognefjord, he built a small hut in 1913 and fled to that place when tired of academic life in Cambridge. Although the philosopher did not seek any sentimental union with nature and actually needed human contact, the solitude of the fjord and closeness to nature conduced to clarify and shape his thoughts.[13]

Switching now to urban life and to another wandering philosopher, we can notice that things looked close enough to the famous educational tradition of the Grand Tour with regard to Arthur Schopenhauer's civic voyages. As with Descartes, traveling was for Schopenhauer an important experience of philosophical initiation that was better than the "vain words" of university learning. Actually, in his own reminiscence reported by his biographer Wolfgang Abendroth, he considered traveling to be the best life lesson. It could keep his mind open and fresh to see "things how they really were."[14] As a young man, this future "Buddha of Frankfurt" undertook a two-year voyage across Europe with his parents. He visited the Netherlands, England, France, Switzerland, Austria, Saxony, Silesia, and Prussia. In Lyon, he wept over the general indifference to the appalling terror of the revolution. In Toulon, he felt acute compassion upon seeing the suffering of the galley slaves. Later, in Lisbon, the misery of a beggar sitting tired on the street triggered another severe shock. The result of these and similar experiences was his deep insight into the nature of life as a "misbegotten affair." In such an existential hell, man unveiled the ambiguous character of a suffering being and, at the same time, a being that inflicts all sorts of abuse. In the end, Schopenhauer's Grand Tour lesson taught him that the ancient biblical wisdom of Ecclesiastes, that is, *vanitas vanitatum*, was by all means well founded. Thereafter, in his most important work *Die Welt als Wille und Vorstellung* (1819), he gave it a Buddhist setting by filling it with a pessimistic statement on universal suffering (*duhkha* in Sanskrit).

TWO PHILOSOPHICAL MODES OF TRAVEL EXEGESIS

There could be countless other examples of how travel developed self-awareness among philosophers. These examples highlight the importance of travel as an existential experience, a lesson on how to intently regard and understand data and the situations and events we encounter in the course of it. Travels afford distance toward cultural prejudices or claims to consider one's own position as absolute, thus casting light on relative ideas, laws, and customs. As such, travels are considered as a medium of freedom and free thinking; sometimes, in a more profound moral and emotional mind-set, they can elicit cosmopolitan and even mystical solidarity with nature, alien people, and cultures. Obviously, when undertaken with conscious personal engagement, voyages can catalyze intellectual, moral and spiritual transformation, and self-realization. To sum up, the travel motif, multifaceted in its ontological, cognitive, and axiological aspects, could be seen in the perspective of two different ideal types of philosophical experience—phenomenological or hermeneutic—although, most frequently, both types codetermine the course of travel and are not isolated and preclusive, because reality is by no means homogeneous.

What are the main traits of "phenomenological traveling"? As we have already mentioned, voyages can create a space of authenticity and free thinking. They offer for the flexible mind of a traveler the opportunity to check out stereotypes and to have a new perspective on reality, untainted with conventional opinions; to venture original experiences, with no premises and prejudices. In this sense, in some aspects the travel experience can get closer to the idea of the phenomenological reduction (*epoché*), according to Edmund Husserl. In his *Ideen I* (1913) and *Cartesianische Meditationen* (1931), Husserl explained *epoché* as a means of bracketing conceptual and conventional biases and assumptions of natural and scientific attitudes so as to extract the essence of the phenomena of the world. Phenomenological reduction can be perceived as a kind of meditation that grounds the consciousness in fresh wonderment so that it can see things straightforwardly as they are themselves beyond any preconceptions. This is Husserlian *zurück zu den Sachen selbst*: phenomenological-transcendental exercise of the mind. Sometimes travels are experienced and practiced as not unlike returns to the "things themselves."

And what do I mean by "hermeneutic travel"? It is a survey of reality mediatized by means of cultural texts we come to know before the travel starts or during its run (and even *post factum*). This is traveling with a store of prejudgments, preknowledge. Examples are Montesquieu's travels through "books and countries,"[15] contemporary voyages via classic routes paved by the great modern admirers of antiquity, like Winckelmann or Goethe; journeys to European museums and ancient ruins undertaken by the Polish poet and essayist, Zbigniew Herbert,[16] as well as *Travels with Herodotus* by Polish reporter Ryszard Kapuściński, describing the nooks and crannies of foreign lands, culture, and history. All these travels take place both in reality and in the mind and were embarked upon to share the meaningful atmosphere of the stuff and milieu of works of culture and current and historical events. Primarily, it is like a "path to the world through printed pages"[17]: books, traditions, and teachings make us deepen our cognition. Ryszard Kapuściński called such an experience the "iconographic journey": "These journeys were much more multidimensional than my original one. . . . What is more, they had a certain advantage over the actual trip—in an iconographic journey such as this, one could stop at any point, calmly observe, rewind to the previous image, etc., something for which on real journey there is neither the time nor the chance."[18] Thanks to traveling, man interiorizes both historical and spatial strangeness and ultimately achieves deeper self-knowledge. The hermeneutic experience is of circular structure: starting with his own position, which is determined by his specific historical and cultural context, the traveler confronts otherness, recognizes its values and meanings, and accepts them and makes them part of his own world. In this way, he expands and enriches his own identity and, at the same time, influences the ontic transformation of his own world. According to Hans-Georg Gadamer, this is what the dialectics of hermeneutical experience is all about: "Thus, the experiencing consciousness has reversed its direction—i.e., it has turned back on itself. The experiencer has become aware of his experience; he is 'experienced.' He has acquired a new horizon within which something can become an experience form him."[19] It seems that exactly this type of experience most frequently becomes present also in tourism: here strangeness appears in the shape of a stereotypic and exotic object that attracts the tourist's gaze and interest, and challenges him to a more concerned attitude. More profound tourist contact creates a chance to broaden a tourist's recognition of the real values of visited places as well as of his own personal limitations, barriers, and capabilities.

Perhaps, most of our travels run just like this, that is, in the hermeneutic mode of experience. The question is: is it really possible to phenomenologically bracket a store of cultural preknowledge, which today is even more intensive and additionally amplified by ubiquitous media advertising, travel movies, and travel brochures? Yet, very often many travelers contest misconceptions, rigid thinking habits, and stereotypes. Such travelers closely resemble romantics who are eager to stay authentic outside the beaten tracks of given patterns. Their attitude, although in some cases sentimental and naïve, approaches the ideal of pure phenomenological experience with no premises. The intentions of Descartes, Rousseau, and Schopenhauer were pretty similar to such a line. These philosophers also embarked upon journeys in order to feel life in a living "book of life," denying at the same time meditations in books printed with signs of tradition and authority. Here not "the printed pages" are "the path to the world," but the very desire to authentically experience pure being. Phenomenological wanderings reveal a truth that is different to the hermeneutic one: "There is no other way to the world, but the way of compassion."[20] What Zbigniew Herbert, a Polish poet, means here is empathic unity of man and being. In her poem "Raz jeden" [Once], another Polish poet, Julia Hartwig, says, "Take a look with the ant's eye . . . with the eye of the victim and with the eye of suffering /take a look once without resentment/But can you really handle it?"[21] In her self-commentary to the poem, the poet explains: "This is a call addressed to myself, to look at the world in a condition as clean as possible. . . . To get rid of prejudices, of everything that pushes us away from the world. At the same time, this is a plea for empathy, a plea to understand every object and every creature in its separate, autonomous existence. Not to impose myself to it. Not to place myself in the center of the world."[22]

In such a model of empathic and unprejudiced attitude, elements of landscape and gestures of ordinary people as well as common moments of everyday life are even more significant than works of art kept in museums. Being can emanate living meanings through insignificant fragments of the world. Polish aesthetician and historian of art Maria Poprzęcka conceives and practices traveling in such a fresh original sense close to phenomenological perceiving: her eye captures different fragments of the world without making any qualitative appraisal and grading between them. In the open fresh look of the open curious eye of a traveler, everything is equally significant and equally holds original beauty and value: a shack for cats on the edge of an estate and Vermeer's canvas in the Mauritshuis in The Hague.[23] One can see the closeness of such perception to a childish one. Nonetheless, it does not mean simply infantile unthinking staring. It carries far deeper meanings. A traveler's eye seizes things—views and fragments of the whole—and can consciously reveal flashes of truth in them. There arises an urge to save and maintain these epiphanies of absolute values in the phantasmagoria of phenomena, just as it is in the case of Japanese *haiku* poetry or Chinese meditative calligraphy. Many travelers fulfill this urge writing books, drawing sketches, or simply taking photos. Polish philosopher and travel writer Michał Paweł Markowski is a good example of the "phenomenological photographer." Traveling all over the world he keeps views cropped in the lenses of his camera, sometimes close-up and sometimes from far away, every time achieving an unusual effect. His pictures are really small pieces of art evoking through inconspicuous things their ultimate beauty and sometimes even an existential message. It may be a shadow on the wall, stones and dust in rubble, or woolly clouds flowing over railway tracks.[24]

A good illustration of the phenomenological travel experience is *La Route Bleue* (1983) by Scottish thinker Kenneth White. He is a conscious philosophical wayfarer who calls himself an "intellectual nomad." The book reported the journey he took to Labrador, the place he saw as the most forgotten land, "the land of Cain."[25] In an absolutely bare landscape, he felt he had reached the boundaries of human entity and in such a denuded condition he heard the poetic appeal of the earth. Referring to Martin Heidegger's idea of "the speech of being," he developed original "geopoetics," a project of poetical notebooks sketched by a man living and moving caringly in the abode of nature.[26]

RECAPITULATION

Discussing the above instances of travels, we must admit that the experiences we described here as phenomenological, these shared by Rousseau,

Schopenhauer, Thoreau, White, and others are not completely devoid of hermeneutical elements, that is, references to cultural texts (in a broad semiotic sense). The philosophers felt that all objects of their surveys were not absolutely free from subjective gaze and cultural associations and conventions. Moreover, it has to be stressed that all data clothed in lingual expressions loses its natural innocence. Man is not quite a pure natural entity because he is involved in many "institutions" (an idea subsequently developed by Arnold Gehlen) of cultural traditions.[27] The good habit of reading is one example of such "institution." In fact, at Walden Pond Thoreau read classical authors and even, to his little shame, travel novels. Man's readings are the mirror of culture, its history and tradition, but this mirror is equally a meniscus that refracts perception. Julia Hartwig, as mentioned above, appeals to human mindfulness and attentive empathy in observing the world to see things purely, without enforcing on them personal or other additions. Yet, she is pretty aware that human experience is inevitably well-equipped with the baggage of cultural knowledge. This equipment enriches human cognition with deep and trusty meanings. In her own journeys described in her journals, she admitted both lines of surveying the world: natural and cultural, phenomenological and hermeneutical. Her *American Journal* is a smart and elaborate fresco of the vast American continent, stretched between two oceans, which makes her feel the "broad wind" of the space. Yet, she also felt attracted by American culture, poetry, art, and politics. Living in Stony Brook on Long Island, she used to watch birds' behavior with the eye of an empathic poet, then sensitively carrying the observations to paper. Once, seeing an aggressive blue jay, she remembered a well-known Hitchcock movie, and this connotation was as natural for her, a cinema connoisseur, as nature itself.[28] Meanings of cultural texts are deeply anchored in human consciousness and this truth became the great problem for late Husserl when he tried to cope with the challenge of linguistic and historical turn in contemporary *Lebenswelt* philosophy. The phenomenological idea of transcendental *ego* was contested by proponents of this turn (Dilthey, Heidegger, Gadamer, Ricoeur, and others from the hermeneutical camp) and thus the phenomenological project of pure evidence was shaken to its foundations.

In philosophy, phenomenological and hermeneutical methods are preclusive since they start with different premises: immediate evidence (phenomenology) on the one hand and mediation of signs (hermeneutics) on the other.[29] However, as far as the living experience of travel is concerned, these modes seem to coexist; what is more, they complement each other's perspectives. The apparent disparity between theory and practice, philosophy and travel, can be explained by the fact that philosophy simply suggests its methods, creates them as pure and coherent projects, and consequently adheres to them when constructing and describing data. In addition, the philosophical quest pertains to reality in its wholeness and thus stays *in abstracto*. According to Kantian transcendentalism, the wholeness cannot be a constitutive idea of experience; it only is a boundary idea of thought. Thinking on the universe as such is a kind of metaphysical speculation that passes scientific experience but is possible thanks to the capacity of *reine Vernunft*, that is, pure reason. For this pure reason, it is not difficult to stick to the roads set out by itself in its intelligible space of thought.

As far as real traveling is concerned, we are facing a living experience of the world. Travel means to immerse in the road *in concreto*; therefore, it starts with a detail and does not exclude incoherence or straying and overlapping roads. Although it is dimensioned on maps, the world surprises us with its unpredictability as we travel. Therefore, travel forces us to revise measures and prejudgments and sometimes, as when experiencing illumination, it reveals hidden and unexpected sides of reality. Each of the "metaphysical nomads" sets off to travel, equipped with a store of his or her own biography, a store of historical and cultural contexts, some kind of scientific and literary tradition. Yet, that does not mean that he or she, if truly motivated, is deprived of the powers to make a private *epoché*, to "bracket" this store and to experience, even for a fleeting moment in a kaleidoscope of phenomena, the epiphany of being.

NOTES

1. Paul Ricoeur, *Interpretation Theory: Discourse and the Surplus of Meaning* (Fort Worth: Texas Christian University Press, 1976), 57, 64–65. On symbolical paradigms and archetypes in: Gilbert Durand, *L'imagination symbolique* (Paris: Presses Universitaires de France, 1964). Also, Maria Zowisło, *Między reliktem a archetypem. Krytyka rozumu mitologicznego* (Kraków: Akademia Wychowania Fizycznego, 2006), 89–99.

2. Gabriel Marcel, *Homo viator. Wstęp do metafizyki nadziei*, trans. Piotr Lubicz (Warsaw: Instytut Wydawniczy Pax, 1984), 158–59.

3. Augustyn, *Wyznania*, trans. Zygmunt Kubiak (Warsaw: Instytut Wydawniczy Pax, 1987), 7.

4. Marek Tulliusz Cyceron, *Pisma filozoficzne*, vol. III, trans. Jozef Smigaj (Warsaw: Państwowe Wydawnictwo Naukowe, 1961), 687.

5. Arystoteles, *Metafizyka*, trans. Kazimierz Leśniak (Warsaw: Państwowe Wydawnictwo Naukowe, 1984), 3.

6. Hannah Arendt, *The Life of the Mind: The Groundbreaking Investigation on How We Think* (San Diego, CA: Harcourt, 1978), 199.

7. Steffen Dietzsch, *Immanuel Kant. Biografia*, trans. Krystyna Krzemieniowa (Warsaw: Wiedza Powszechna, 2005), 17.

8. Paul Richards, "Kant's Geography and Mental Maps," *Transactions of the Institute of British Geographers* 61 (1974): 1–16.

9. René Descartes, *A Discourse on Method*, The Project Gutenberg EBook #59, http://www.gutenberg.org/files/59/59-h/59-h.htm, Part I.

10. Frédéric Gros, *Filozofia chodzenia*, trans. Ewa Kaniowska (Warsaw: Wydawnictwo Czarna Owca, 2015), 71–88.

11. Jean-Jacques Rousseau, *The Reveries of the Solitary Walker*, trans. Charles E. Butterworth (Indianapolis: Hackett Publishing Company, Inc., 1992), 69.

12. Henry David Thoreau, *Walden, czyli życie w lesie*, trans. Halina Cieplińska (Warsaw: Państwowy Instytut Wydawniczy, 1991), 122.

13. Knut Olav Åmås, "Ludwig Wittgenstein in Norway 1913–1950," in *Wittgenstein and Norway*, ed. Kjell S. Johannessen et al. (Oslo: Solum Vorlag, 1994), 9–57.

14. Wolfgang Abendroth, *Artur Schopenhauer*, trans. Ryszard Rozanowski (Wrocław: Wydawnictwo Dolnoslaskie, 1998), 19–20.

15. Paul Hazard, *Myśl europejska w XVII wieku od Monteskiusza do Lessinga*, trans. Halina Suwala (Warsaw: Państwowy Instytut Wydawniczy, 1972), 147.

16. Zbigniew Herbert, *Barbarzynca w ogrodzie* (Warsaw: Czytelnik, 1962); Zbigniew Herbert, *Martwa natura z wędzidłem* (Wrocław: Wydawnictwo Dolnośląskie, 1998).

17. Joseph Campbell, *Potęga mitu. Rozmowy Billa Moyersa z Josephem Campbellem*, trans. Ireneusz Kania (Kraków: Signum, 1994), 10.

18. Ryszard Kapuściński, *Travels with Herodotus*, trans. Klara Główczewska (London: Penguin Books, 2008), 49.

19. Hans-Georg Gadamer, *Truth and Method*, trans. revised Joel Weinsheimer and Donald G. Marshall (New York: Crossroad, 1989), 353–54.

20. Zbigniew Herbert, *Labirynt nad morzem* (Warsaw: Fundacja Zeszytow Literackich, 2000), 55.

21. Julia Hartwig, *Zobaczone* (Kraków: Wydawnictwo a5, 1999), 77.

22. Julia Hartwig, "O sztuce patrzenia," in *Rozmowy na nowy wiek*, vol. 1, ed. Katarzyna Janowska and Piotr Mucharski (Kraków: Wydawnictwo Znak, 2002), 129–30.

23. Maria Poprzęcka, *Na oko* (Warsaw: dwutygodnik.com—słowo/obraz terytoria, 2015), 52–55, 101–3.

24. Michał Paweł Markowski, *Dzień na ziemi. Proza podróżna* (Poznań: Wydawnictwo Poznańskie, 2014).

25. Kenneth White, *Niebieska droga*, trans. Radoslaw Nowakowski (Warsaw: Wydawnictwo Przedswit, 1992).

26. See more: Maria Zowisło, "The World and the Home: On the Paths of Contemporary Nomads," *Folia Turistica* 28, no. 2 (2013): 14–17.

27. Tadeusz Sławek, Ujmować. *Henry David Thoreau i wspólnota świata* (Katowice: Wydawnictwo Uniwersytetu Sląskiego, 2009), 77–79.

28. Julia Hartwig, *Dziennik amerykański* (Warsaw: Fundacja Zeszytow Literackich, 2015), 39.

29. Hanna Buczyńska–Garewicz, *Znak i oczywistość* (Warsaw: Instytut Wydawniczy Pax, 1981).

REFERENCES

Abendroth, Wolfgang. *Artur Schopenhauer.* Translated by Ryszard Rozanowski. Wrocław: Wydawnictwo Dolnoslaskie, 1998.

Åmås, Knut Olav. "Ludwig Wittgenstein in Norway 1913–1950." In *Wittgenstein and Norway*, edited by Kjell S. Johannessen, Rolf Larsen, and Knut Olaf Åmås, 9–57. Oslo: Solum Vorlag, 1994.

Arendt, Hannah. *The Life of the Mind: The Groundbreaking Investigation on How We Think.* San Diego, CA: Harcourt, 1978.

Arystoteles. *Metafizyka.* Translated by Kazimierz Leśniak. Warsaw: Państwowe Wydawnictwo Naukowe, 1984.

Augustyn. *Wyznania.* Translated by Zygmunt Kubiak. Warsaw: Instytut Wydawniczy Pax, 1987.

Buczyńska-Garewicz, Hanna. *Znak i oczywistość.* Warsaw: Instytut Wydawniczy Pax, 1981.

Campbell, Joseph. *Potęga mitu. Rozmowy Billa Moyersa z Josephem Campbellem.* Translated by Ireneusz Kania. Kraków: Signum, 1994.

Cyceron, Marek Tullisz. *Pisma filozoficzne*, vol. III. Translated by Jozef Smigaj. Warsaw: Państwowe Wydawnictwo Naukowe, 1961.

Descartes, René. *A Discourse on Method.* The Project Gutenberg EBook #59, http://www.gutenberg.org/files/59/59-h/59-h.htm, Part I.

Dietzsch, Steffen. *Immanuel Kant. Biografia.* Translated by Krystyna Krzemieniowa. Warsaw: Wiedza Powszechna, 2005.

Durand, Gilbert. *L'imagination symbolique.* Paris: Presses Universitaires de France, 1964.

Gadamer, Hans-Georg. *Truth and Method.* Translation revised by Joel Weinsheimer and Donald G. Marshall. New York: Crossroad, 1989.

Gros, Frédéric. *Filozofia chodzenia.* Translated by Ewa Kaniowska. Warsaw: Wydawnictwo Czarna Owca, 2015.

Hartwig, Julia. *Zobaczone.* Kraków: Wydawnictwo a5, 1999.

———. "O sztuce patrzenia." In *Rozmowy na nowy wiek*, vol. 1, edited by Katarzyna Janowska and Piotr Mucharski, 129–40. Kraków: Wydawnictwo Znak, 2002.

———. *Dziennik amerykański.* Warsaw: Fundacja Zeszytow Literackich, 2015.

Hazard, Paul. *Myśl europejska w XVII wieku od Monteskiusza do Lessinga.* Translated by Halina Suwala. Warsaw: Państwowy Instytut Wydawniczy, 1972.

Herbert, Zbigniew. *Barbarzyńca w ogrodzie.* Warsaw: Czytelnik, 1962.

———. *Martwa natura z wędzidłem.* Wrocław: Wydawnictwo Dolnośląskie, 1998.

———. *Labirynt nad morzem.* Warsaw: Fundacja Zeszytów Literackich, 2000.

Kapuściński, Ryszard. *Travels with Herodotus.* Translated by Klara Główczewska. London: Penguin Books, 2008.

Marcel, Gabriel. *Homo viator. Wstęp do metafizyki nadziei.* Translated by Piotr Lubicz. Warsaw: Instytut Wydawniczy Pax, 1984.

Markowski, Michał Paweł. *Dzień na ziemi. Proza podróżna.* Poznań: Wydawnictwo Poznańskie, 2014.

Poprzęcka, Maria. *Na oko.* Warsaw: dwutygodnik.com—słowo/obraz terytoria, 2015.

Richards, Paul. "Kant's Geography and Mental Maps." *Transactions of the Institute of British Geographers* 61 (1974): 1–16.

Ricoeur, Paul. *Interpretation Theory: Discourse and the Surplus of Meaning*. Fort Worth: Texas Christian University Press, 1976.

Rousseau, Jean-Jacques. *The Reveries of the Solitary Walker*. Translated by Charles E. Butterworth. Indianapolis: Hackett Publishing Company, Inc., 1992.

Sławek, Tadeusz. *Ujmować. Henry David Thoreau i wspólnota świata*. Katowice: Wydawnictwo Uniwersytetu Slaskiego, 2009.

Thoreau, Henry David. *Walden, czyli życie w lesie*. Translated by Halina Cieplinska. Warsaw: Państwowy Instytut Wydawniczy, 1991.

White, Kenneth. *Niebieska droga*. Translated by Radoslaw Nowakowski. Warsaw: Wydawnictwo Przedswit, 1992.

Zowisło, Maria. *Między reliktem a archetypem. Krytyka rozumu mitologicznego*. Kraków: Akademia Wychowania Fizycznego, 2006.

———. "The World and the Home: On the Paths of Contemporary Nomads." *Folia Turistica* 28, no. 2 (2013): 14–17.

Chapter 6

Traveling and Politics

A Reflection on Russian Tourism in the Past and Today

Magdalena Banaszkiewicz

This chapter discusses one of the key topics for the anthropology of tourism, namely cultural change conditioned by tourist mobility. The axis of discussion will be the tension between tourism preferred by the national authorities and outbound tourism that is largely perceived as a potential threat to a state's social and political order. In the following parts of the text, I will try to show that the dynamics of the development of the Russian tourism is sinusoidal in character—in more "liberal" times, when the authorities looked more favorably on Europe, foreign travel evolved, while in times of a more isolationist politics, a more intensive development of domestic tourism was observed. Tracing the development of the next decades, traveling in Russia will be an attempt to answer the question of who a Russian tourist is and what he or she wants, as well as how much the realization of their dreams depended on the current state politics.

IN THE FOOTSTEPS OF PETER THE GREAT

The residents of Russia[1] compared to other European countries were relatively less mobile. The breakthrough came only with Russia's gradual opening to Western culture in the second half of the seventeenth century, particularly the "opening of a window" to Europe by Peter I, whose youthful journey (between 1697 and 1698) can be clearly classified as a grand tour, which was then gaining in popularity. The tsar's expedition started a new habit in the culture of Russia's nobility: travel abroad for educational purposes. In 1777, Benjamin Gensz, the owner of a Moscow boarding school for boys, placed an advertisement in a contemporaneously popular newspaper, *Moscow News*, that read "A Benjamin Gensz's plan for a possible travel to foreign countries, organized at the request of some persons by the owner of a school for the nobles." It was probably the first tourist ad in the history of Russia. Gensz, himself willingly traveling in Europe, saw such travel as an excellent opportunity to deepen knowledge, acquire practical experience, and thus educate future generations to use their skills for the benefit of the state.[2]

While the trip to Europe was to stimulate the intellect, and "expand the horizons," traveling across Russia for cognitive purposes seemed "strange and senseless an activity"[3] to its residents. Although there are descriptions of trips across Russia from as early as the sixteenth or seventeenth century, the first Russian traveler who left and wrote an account of his journey was Nikolai Karamzin, who traveled abroad to Paris and Geneva. His "Pisma russkovo puteschestvennika" [Letters of a Russian traveler] (1791–1792)[4] became a model to follow for many decades and won the author considerable popularity. Karamzin's intellectual journey, during which he visited Kant in Königsberg, among others, coincided with the release of another work of art crucial for the Russian culture namely *Puteshestvie iz Peterburga v Moskvy*[5] by Alexander Radishchev. The author's journey across Russia provided a background for his thorough critique of serfdom, presenting his own concepts underpinned by the philosophy of the Enlightenment. Radishchev's philippics, overlapping the revolutionary ferment in France, had shaken Catherine II so firmly that, as a result, the empress not only condemned the author to death (a penalty that was eventually changed to prison), but also banned foreign travel, declaring it dangerous for the internal stability of the state.[6]

Foreign travels had already been perceived as a potential threat to social and political order and attitude from the authorities will also be visible later, becoming a characteristic feature of Russia's political culture. It is worth remembering that in the next decades of the nineteenth century, the tsar himself decided who could and who could not leave and enter Russia.[7] Nicholas I cautioned his oldest son, who later became Alexander II, about travel to Europe in an instruction handed to him in 1838, prior to the commencement of Alexander's grand tour. It reads as follows: "You will be ravished by many things, but having familiarized with them, you will find that not everything is worthy of imitation, and that many things, worthy of respect where they are, cannot be applied with us—we should maintain our nationality, our hallmark and woe betide us if we abandon it; our strength, salvation and inimitableness lie in it."[8] As Mikołaj Banaszkiewicz notes: "The same words (not mentioning that the instruction had been written by Nicholas) Alexander II will address in 1864 to his eldest son, Nicholas."[9] A journey to the West, although essential for the intellectual development of the heir to the throne, was treated as "a necessary evil."

Karamzin, whose trip to the West led to a more conservative attitude, and Radishchev, for whom a journey across Russia became an opportunity to present the liberal, Western-centric views, are characters personifying two extremely contradictory tendencies that have become a leitmotif of both the worldview-related orientations and a model for travelers throughout the entire nineteenth century. Westernizers[10] perceived the journey to the West as necessary to convince themselves of the civilizational superiority of Europe.[11] A well-known writer and professor of Moscow State University, Stepan Petrovich Shevyrev, in 1847, stated outright: "True are those who say that in Russia one can only go to settle matters, but in no way can he or she travel."[12] He continued to argue that the reason behind it was an intolerable lack of any amenities, while comfort, an outcome of development of European civilization, accompanying those who travel to the West, makes moving a real journey.[13] In turn, there was an increasing need for getting to know their own country and its people among the slavophiles.[14] They claimed that the innate innocence, not being contaminated with civilization and deep spirituality of the Russian province transferred since time immemorial, may healingly affect the nobility and foster its love for the country. Ivan Aksakov, one of the Slavophile movement leaders, in a letter to his fiancée, wrote: "One way or another, we will organize a journey through Russia: you need to see Russia as it is and maintain fidelity in love with it and be faithful to it."[15]

Before Russia entered the stage of the shaping of organized tourism in the second half of the nineteenth century, two significant phenomena characteristic for domestic mobility already existed in its culture. The first was pilgrimage, realizing the need for individual search for God *(bogoiskatelstvo),* which was a response to the increasing dependence of the Church from the State.[16] Desiring a more direct relationship with God, people strayed from the official ecclesiastical life, finding spiritual guides called *starets* (elder) in monasteries and hermitages (e.g., Optino hermitage, which became a center of religious revival in the mid-nineteenth century). Crowds of common people as well as intelligentsia and people of culture came to the *starets* seeking solace. The accounts of pilgrimages and meetings with the *starets* can be found in the works of Gogol,[17] Dostoevsky[18] and Tolstoy.[19]

The era preceding the period of organized tourism development is also the time of cognitive-cultural traveling. Both then and now, two capitals of the Empire enjoyed particular popularity: the former, Moscow, as well as the new,[20] St. Petersburg. However, priority has to be given to the city of Peter I, which, at the time of Catherine II, became the undisputed primary travel destination for many travelers, both foreign and domestic. It was with them in mind that the first Russian tourist guide was written.[21] In the first half of the nineteenth century, the capital was visited not only to settle matters in one of many offices, but also to see the beauty of its architecture or participate in cultural life.

THE BIRTH OF ORGANIZED TOURISM

The second half of the nineteenth century saw the first attempts of associating tourism lovers (e.g., Caucasian Alpine Club, Crimean Mountain Club, Tourists-Velocipede Riders Club)[22] and organizing joint trips both at home and abroad. In 1901, the most important association was founded: the Russian Society of Tourists (*Rossijskoe Obshchestvo Turistov*), which survived even the Bolshevik Revolution. The activity of associations anticipated a touring movement, which was very important for the tourist culture of the Soviet era (and currently resurging). The movement aims at traveling in order to get familiar with one's own country in terms of "little homeland," multidisciplinary forms of local study, which can be to some extent compared to a combination of educational, wildlife, and ethnic tourism.

In the second half of the nineteenth century, tourist traffic began to be operated by the first tourist companies; the "Imatra Joint Stock Company" was established in 1871. The enterprise organized trips to Imatra, a famous Finnish waterfall "discovered" by Catherine II a hundred years earlier. A few years after the company had been founded, Leopold Lipson founded a tourist company in St. Petersburg, which was based on the model of the one established by Thomas Cook.[23]

Traveling to resorts and spas, mostly foreign, was a very characteristic form of leisure time in the prerevolutionary period. However, Mineral Waters, Borjomi, and Crimea enjoyed increased popularity, and were not only treated as places for recuperation, but also for intensive social life and doing business.[24]

Dissemination of traveling at the turn of the century was largely favored by the development of railways, especially the main Trans-Siberian Railway, opening vast spaces of Siberia and the Far East for exploration by travelers and tourists. One consequence of the Revolution of 1905 was the abolition of transport restrictions, which largely contributed to the development on the mass scale of tourism. Political and social changes, even those pertaining to the situation of peasants, contributed to the emergence of new groups capable of participating in tourist life (e.g., from the first decade of the twentieth century, the regional councils organized trips for students to St. Petersburg or Moscow, so that children could become familiar with the legacy of the empire[25]). At the same time, militia reports from that period show that sport and tourism would often serve as socialist propaganda—trips, especially those organized for students, were led by socialist activists, who, while hiking, conducted more or less overt revolutionary agitation.[26]

POST-REVOLUTIONARY SEARCH FOR PATH

In terms of organization and structure, the October Revolution of 1917 did not bring about any rapid changes in tourism. Although the first years following the Bolshevik Revolution can hardly be called a period of peace and harmonious development, the country was in a state of civil war, basic survival products were scarce, and there were numerous acts of terror against the enemies of the new order. Yet, the structures of revolutionary power were still being formed. Therefore, in the first decade after the revolution, tourism developed as part of already existing organizations, who had suspended their activity for the tumultuous period of the First World War.[27]

Political turmoil in the first half of the 1920s, which was reflected in relatively independent and freely developing tourism, concluded with the strengthening role of Joseph Stalin in the Central Committee. The Soviet Union entered a new period—centralization of power, creation of the planned economy, clearing the party of people that could threaten the position of the leader. The process of taking total control over the lives of Soviet citizens did not spare tourism. Obviously, an average USSR citizen could only dream of foreign travels during the Stalinist period (although it could have been burdened with great risk).[28] The state gradually took control over mobility by introducing internal passports, and, in tourist traffic, the authorities introduced a system of vouchers only to be realized in predesignated places of leisure.

In 1929 the Society for Proletarian Tourism and Excursions RSFSR (*Obschestvo Proletarskovo Turizma and Ekskursji RSFSR*, in short, OPTE) was established.[29] The main objectives of the society's activities included

Promoting, among the working people, ideas of organized tourism i.e. amateur trips favouring raising culture level, ensuring cultural use of active leisure and giving the idea of their own country, as well as other ones. The trips fostered live contact between the people of USSR, shaped artistic taste and love of nature, quenching health and character; shaping tourism into a broad, organized social movement, which became possible only after the October Revolution, when coming to power of the working classes enabled the construction of socialism and the increase of material status of the society, which urged the masses to participate in culture; organized mutual help among tourists; supporting the defence of the USSR through militarization of tourism; organizing tourists' social work during their journey; introducing elements of sightseeing into tourism.[30]

The society, having its substructures at regional and city committees, schools, or workplaces, virtually monopolized domestic tourism. In addition to organizing trips, running tourist equipment renting facilities, developing accommodation facilities, and setting out new tourist trails, the OPTE conducted active educational politics. The main organs to promote proletarian tourism were two magazines: the biweekly *On Land and On Sea* (*Na sush'e i na mor'e*) with an appendix called "Tourist Library" (a brochure that published text written by tourists themselves), as well as the monthly *Tourist-activist*, intended for tour operators and training staff, rather than for tourists.[31]

TOURISM AS FORGING OF A NEW SOVIET MAN

Traveling, a form of spending leisure time in accordance with socialist ideology, had hardly anything to do with entertainment and rest in the Soviet Union. It was meant to be a time of intensive work on oneself and others. It is perfectly exemplified by slogans calling for engagement in tourism—for example, "Tourism for bourgeoisie—entertainment, for us—recreation in the name of socialism," "Proletarian tourism—a powerful weapon against idleness, religion and bourgeoisie," "Proletarian tourist—an eye of the worker-peasant inspection."[32]

Each trip aimed at raising political and cultural awareness, and also had to bring measurable results, helping to build socialism in the country. As Usyskin recalls: "One of the main tasks was tourist socio-political work during marches, conducting agitating conversations with the local people (especially in remote and inaccessible areas), delivering literature to the locals, physical help e.g. during harvest."[33] Regardless of the trail a tourist followed, the aim of the expedition was not only rest, but, above all, education and training. As one of the slogans read: "A well-organized trip is worth a stack of read books!"

Most tours of the Soviet citizens were amateur, independently-organized trips to natural areas. Propagated forms of tourism included hiking in the mountains, cycling trips, and long group marches. They were meant to pursue the cult of youth and a healthy body, which were so characteristic of the Soviet ideology because a Soviet man should burst with physical energy. As Maxim Gorky claimed, the Soviet man vocation was not only to understand the world, but to control it. Therefore, tourism also became a form of a special method of work organization—consisting of working at a slow pace throughout the entire period of carrying out a plan and rapidly intensifying just before the deadline when the plan implementation was threatened, forging a Soviet "hero."[34] Like in the movement of *stakhanovites*,[35] the objective was to encourage the Soviet tourists to social rivalry. The competition was also given institutional framework in the second half of the 1930s, when an official badge "Tourist of the USSR," of different classes, was introduced. The 1930s can also be perceived as a period when tourism became militarized, in accordance with the slogan: "Proletarian tourism raises brave fighters."[36]

Tourism was intended to develop physical culture, but, above all, traveling was the realm of ideological work, and that is why places connected with the revolution, as well as the life and work of Bolshevik leaders, were significant tourist destinations. From the first days after coming to power, the Bolsheviks treated the issue of ideological education very seriously, thus promoting the cult of revolution. Historical politics of the new authorities considered revolutionary activity as crucial. In addition, the main objective of the new government was to take power regardless of the length of process and number of victims it took to achieve it. New trails essentially covered areas where the Bolsheviks, underground, were preparing a coup, areas where fighting took place, or areas famous for prominent revolutionary deeds. Finally, the mandatory places to be visited were museums and memorial chambers of chief revolutionaries. Perhaps the life and work of Vladimir Ilyich Lenin was the most explored aspect illustrating the essence of the Bolshevik Revolution. Merely a few months after the death of the leader in 1924, a museum of Lenin was founded, which holds thousands of exhibits featuring life achievements of the Bolshevik leader.[37] Lenin's Mausoleum holds the embalmed body of Lenin, placed there in 1924.

Since the Lenin cult was one of the most pervasive features of the Soviet political practice, Lenin's Mausoleum has become one of the most recognizable symbols in the Soviet Union and the model for similar sites of political worship. According to Froese, "Although performing a religious blessing over a man who called the destruction of religion is certainly a curiosity, the symbolism and the aura of Lenin's mausoleum dry actually provokes a response. By placing Lenin in a state of suspended animation, Soviet officials intentionally imitated how the bodies of saints were displayed in monasteries throughout Russia."[38] Both in Moscow and in the rest of the Soviet Union, places of worship of Lenin created a universal network of symbolic meanings. In subsequent years, the consistent policy of atheism and destruction of the traditional religious cult, paralleled with the sacralization of the revolution and its leaders, made the places connected with the revolution a destination of communist "pilgrimage." Communist tours were a search for a form of "sacred," they met the need for security, strengthened the "ideological faith," not to mention the fact that, perhaps, to the greatest extent, they played a role of ritual-creating social relationships, and it was the tours that built the ideal collective of the Soviet people, deeply devoted to the slogans promoted by the Bolshevik leaders. During the discussed period, "trips-pilgrimages" considerably contributed to raising ideological awareness of the citizens—tourists.

Particular attention was paid to the creation of tourism offered for children and youth, which was to continue the educational activities of school. As early as 1919, in the vicinities of Petrograd[39] several tourist bases were created, where young people could spend time with class educators and teachers.[40] During stays at the bases, children were not to take a break from everyday hardships of education. Even if they stopped learning for some time, the education process was continued:

> We must make an entire generation of communists from the young generation. From children as soft as wax, we must mould them into real, honest Communists. . . . We must snatch children out of evil family influence. We must take them under our wings and clearly speaking nationalize them. From the first days of their lives they will be under salutary influence of the Communist kindergartens and schools. Here, they will learn the ABC of Communism and grow into real Communists.[41]

The above rules of pedagogy were obeyed during school trips and holiday camps. The most famous include Artek, an all-union pioneer camp founded in 1925 on the coast of Crimea. As one of Artek's enthusiasts wrote half a century later: "Artek became realization of Lenin's dreams of joyful childhood of young citizens of the Soviet country. The children's republic by the sea was becoming more popular each day. Similar camps were built in Siberia, Ural, Leningrad and Kazan."[42]

The forms of tourism varied and depended on the social status, just as in the nineteenth century. Contrary to propaganda slogans, Soviet society was not homogenous with working people of towns and villages. "The privileged part of nomenclature had access to scarce goods such as cottages, holidays in luxurious resorts or trips."[43] Resorts and sanatoriums were built in climate attractive areas at the beginning of the 1930s, with the said social group in mind. So-called resort-tourism, despite being passive, and thus not fitting the basic ideological assumptions of spending leisure time by a Soviet man, became a significant socio-cultural phenomenon.[44] The importance of tourism in the life of a Soviet man was proven by the mere fact of including it in the third five-year plan. According to its assumptions, ten million citizens of the Soviet Union were to practice tourism and fifteen million were expected to participate in one-day trips on days off work. Rapid expansion of tourism infrastructure was predicted. In addition, the creation of tourist facilities and tourist homes offering thirty-two thousand beds was envisaged, as well as plans for opening new tourist clubs, which were to become a "driving force of tourism massification among the working class."[45] The outbreak of war on the western front did not prevent the contemporaneous tourism activity. The season of 1940–1941 was considered as one of the most active, when it comes to practicing winter tourism. It was the attack of Nazi troops in June 1941 that blocked the development of Soviet tourism for a few years. The previous physical activity, promoted by tourist and sport sections, turned out useful in the harsh fighting front—for example, a group of Soviet climbers played a prominent role in warfare—operation "Elbrus," which they participated in, later became one of the Great Patriotic War myth motives.[46]

LEISURE OF THE WORKING MASSES

The tourist infrastructure was severely damaged by war. However, while the destroyed tourist homes or holiday bases could be rebuilt with time, the loss of staff, instructors, guides, and activists was irreversible (the number of up to twenty-seven million residents of the Soviet Union is estimated to have been killed in the Great Patriotic War[47]) Tourist activity gradually revived in the postwar period, and gained a rapid momentum within the years after Stalin's death in 1953.

In 1955, fifteen years after closing the borders for tourism, "Inturist" handled two thousand people. In subsequent years, the number of tourists steadily increased. In 1956, as many as half a million Soviet citizens went on trips to sixty-one countries, and 484 thousand tourists from eighty-four countries of the world visited the Soviet Union.[48] The working class usually limited its trips to countries of people's democracies, known as the "near abroad."[49] Travel to Bulgaria, Romania, Czechoslovakia, and Hungary was considered as a recognition and prize, but was available only for people enjoying excellent reputation as "genuine Soviet people."[50]

Although traveling abroad was possible, it pertained only to a very limited number of privileged people who had received foreign passport. The period under Khrushchev and then Brezhnev, however, brought rapid development of domestic tourism. Owing to the introduction of the five-day working week citizens had more free time. Since the 1960s the standard of living improved—earnings increased and supplies improved. In the 1960s, *Kraevedenije*, so important even before the revolution as in the first years following the takeover of power by the Bolsheviks,[51] but repressed from the end of the 1920s for its "bourgeois passéism" and Localista inclinations, began to experience revival. The reason for this was the fact that, according to Donovan, *kraevedenije* was as an important vehicle in the process of creating new narratives of Soviet patriotism on the basis of local heroes and myth.[52] Cyclical rallies of the youth aimed at discovering places of victory in the Great Patriotic War, through hiking, played a significant role in patriotic education of the young.[53] The relatively stable political and economic situation of the late socialism period was favorable for focusing more on leisure, being more physically active, as well as the desire to learn about new areas and meet new people. Package holidays, workers' holidays, and employees' trips with family and friends to dachas (Russian counterpart of "cottages")[54] are forms of a collective life through which a Soviet man's awareness was meant to be raised. As Koenker notices: "Even in post-Soviet times, the power of collective norms, for example, concerning dacha activities, exerts a strong influence. This delicate balance between the satisfactions of uniqueness and the comfort of collectivity may constitute one of the particular features of socialist tourism and travel."[55] The number of trips abroad by Soviet citizens is a significant indicator of liberalization taking place in the political-ideological sphere in the Soviet Union at that time. In the 1970s, the number reached a level of 1.7 million, while in the first half of the 1980s it was already 4.8 million.[56]

At the end of the Soviet Union, tourism occupied one of the most important places in the social space, as well as in the economy, despite dramatic collapse in the statistics of tourism, which occurred after the power plant disaster in Chernobyl in 1986. Soviet tourism actually became a mass phenomenon.[57]

Technical facilities, infrastructure, and a network of organizations and associations entangling the whole country, as well as the habit of participating in tourism, were later inherited by the Russian Federation, providing great tourism potential.

TOURIST PATRIOTISM OF TODAY'S RUSSIA

The collapse of the Soviet Union and the subsequent transition period adversely affected the development of domestic tourism.[58] Citizens of the Russian Federation, having received almost complete freedom to travel, began traveling abroad,[59] which was reflected in statistics: in 2000, 4.5 million Russians went abroad; in 2007, 9.3 million; and, in 2013, 18.3 million.[60] Warm countries with fairly attractive prices like Turkey, Egypt, Tunisia, Thailand, Italy, and Spain enjoyed the biggest popularity. Also, large tourism traffic was maintained with neighboring countries, especially the Baltic nations or Central Asia. In addition, the Russians would eagerly leave their country, during the winter break between Christmas and New Year's, for European ski resorts or more exotic locations like the Dominican Republic or Cuba.

The situation has radically changed as a result of the conflict over Crimea, which resulted in a sharp decline in the purchasing power of ruble and the strengthening of anti-Western sentiments among the Russian society. The year 2014 brought a significant decrease in the foreign trips of Russians (by about one and a half million compared to 2013). In 2015 the number grew and, according to estimates, it was less than ten million trips.[61] As a direct result of the decrease, two-thirds of companies that handled the outbound tourism market closed down or transformed in 2015.[62] Foreign trips became too expensive, and, according to many, too dangerous because of recently escalating terrorist attacks.[63] These two factors have become a "gift" for the government, which has been conducting an intensive policy of stimulating the development of domestic tourism.

In 2011, the government of the Russian Federation adopted a program of tourism development for 2011–2018, which is primarily aimed at the development of domestic and inbound tourism (*Federalnaia celevaia programma "Rozvitije vnutrennovo and vjezdnovo turizma v Rossijskoi Federacji, 2011–2018 gody"*).[64] Among the factors that inhibit the development of domestic tourism the following were highlighted: inadequate transport and accommodation infrastructure, high prices, poor staff training, and insufficiently innovative tourism products. Scarce knowledge of the tourist potential of Russia among its residents, as well as the negative image of national tourism products with the Russian citizens were also mentioned as the said inhibiting factors. The conclusions contained in the document are accurate reflections of reality. The Russians do not want to travel across the country for two reasons: the price compared to the standard is far too high and foreign trips enticed more effectively with advertisements (or at least they did). Paradoxically, observations made by the nineteenth-century travelers are still valid. Conversely, the Russian government seeks to emphasize, in the program, that domestic tourism is a manifestation of patriotism and indicates "the growth of patriotic sentiments in the society of the Russian Federation, as well as among the youth,"[65] as one of the factors contributing to its development. As the tourist potential of Russia is enormous, it is very difficult to accurately go through the propositions contained in the document. However, those that continue traditional ways of traveling across Russia—firmly rooted in the Russian culture, dominate. Firstly, it is tourism with a cultural-cognitive base. Significantly, one of the guidelines for its implementations is returning to the idea of sightseeing and ethnographic movement.[66] It has been suggested that better alignment of tourism programs for children and youth with the education system might result in creating favorable conditions for patriotic education and broadening the learners' horizons.[67] Much attention is paid to the recreational role of tourism, aimed at improving psycho-physical conditions of citizens in health and holiday centers. Expanding the range of leisure tourism in the Russian resorts has also been one of the adopted assumptions. The reason behind it is that the resorts become competitive in relation to foreign destinations preferred by the Russians to date. Great potential for the development of eco-tourism has been stressed, which could use values of Russia's natural environment, as well as pilgrimage tourism.

Obviously, supporting the development of domestic tourism is justified by economic factors. Nevertheless, it should also be regarded in terms of ideology: appreciating tourist attractions of one's own country can be a trendy form of expressing patriotism, as well as showing that the Russians do not need to leave their country because they can find everything at home. The example of Crimea and its annexation, depicted by the government of the Federation as a return of the land to where it originally belonged, is very vivid and one that launched an intensive promotional campaign, which now translates into a significant increase in the number of Russian tourists visiting the Peninsula.[68]

Such attitude is supported by various rankings created by means of organizing nationwide contests, in which the citizens themselves give their votes. In response to creating a list of the new seven wonders of the world (which did not include any object in Russia), the Russians decided to organize their own contest called "Seven Wonders of Russia," which was followed, in 2013, by a contest for the most visually recognizable places in Russia.[69] As of 2015, the Russian Geographical Society organizes a photo competition called "The Most Beautiful Country," which aims to show the unique wildlife of Russia. The last edition was attended by twenty-five thousand people who sent in more than 200 thousand photos.[70] Although the regulations of these actions raise controversies and the results cause lively debates, their presence in national media and support from political and cultural authorities stimulates the Russians to be more interested in their own country.

In the past couple of years, Russia has also become one of the most active players in the UNESCO, expressing remarkable interest in issues of world heritage and heritage presentation. As Plets suggests, politics toward heritage could be analyzed as a form of "soft power" both in national as well as international dimensions: "The material expressions and branding strategies of a national site are the 'signifiers' of a nation's ideology and ambitions in the present (the signified)."[71]

SUMMARY

It is not easy, in such a short text, to render the complexity of factors affecting patterns of traveling of the Russians. Depending on the time-period, different determinants were more or less influential. Although the development of tourism in Russia was impacted by changing technology or fashion, above all it was stimulated by the policy of authorities. Generally speaking, as it has been pointed out in the article, the authorities were reluctant to citizens traveling abroad, limiting their mobility by applying various administrative measures. Modern tourism is deeply rooted in the past. Even if it is a stimulus to cultural change, it is still a mirror of the existing socio-cultural system, which has evolved for centuries.

Therefore, in my opinion, anthropology of tourism—rather an approach that aims to describe and understand the deeper complexity of modern travel—can profit also by looking into the past and including the historical framework as one of the perspectives helpful in developing more sophisticated interpretations of the present phenomena.

NOTES

1. I mean Russia from the medieval period until the eighteenth century, therefore Muscovite Rus, the Tsardom of Russia, as well as the Russian Empire.
2. Genadij Petrovich Dolzhenko and Jurij Stepanovich Putrik, *Istorija turizma v Rossijskoi Imperii, Sovetskom Soiuze, i Rossijskoi Federacji* (Moscow: Izdatelskij Centr MarT, 2010), 16.
3. Nikolai Borisov, *Povsednevnaia zhizn russkovo puteshestvennika v epohu bezdorozhija* (Moscow: Molodaia Gvardija, 2010), 11.
4. Andrew Kahn, *Nikolai Karamzin: "Letters of a Russian Traveller"* (Oxford: Voltaire Foundation, 2003).
5. Aleksandr Nikolaevich Radishchev, *A Journey from Saint Petersburg to Moscow*, ed. Roderick Page Thaler (Cambridge, MA: Harvard University Press, 2013).
6. Nicholas V. Riasanovsky and Mark D. Steinberg, *A History of Russia*, 7th edition (Oxford: Oxford University Press, 2000).
7. Unintelligible restrictions of the travelers across Russia by the late 1930s of the nineteenth century are vividly depicted in a work of art by Marquis de Custine, see Astolphe De Custine, *Letters from Russia* (New York: New York Review of Books, 2012).
8. As cited in Mikołaj Banaszkiewicz "Refleksja polityczna rosyjskich elit z podróży po Europie w połowie XIX wieku" [*The Political Reflection of the Russian Elite After Journeys to Europe in the Half of 19th Century*], *Politeja* 26, no. 4 (2013): 391.
9. Banaszkiewicz, *Refleksja polityczna*, 391.
10. Supporters of the Western culture, expressing an opinion, that Russian should follow in the wake of the European modernization.
11. Reflections after journeys of famous Russians in the nineteenth century, see: Derek Offord, *Journeys to a Graveyard: Perceptions of Europe in Classical Russian Travel Writing* (Leiden: Springer, 2006); Sara Dickinson, *Breaking Ground: Travel and National Culture in Russia from Peter I to the Era of Pushkin* (Amsterdam: Rodopi 2006).
12. Stepan Petrovich Shevyrev, *Puteschestvije v Kirilo-Belozerskij monastyr* (Moscow, 2004), 9, in Borisov, *Povsednevnaia*, 14.
13. Shevyrev, *Puteschestvije*, 14.
14. The supporters of only "traditional Slavic" values (based on Orthodox Christianity, Tsarist autocracy, and folksiness) thought that Russia should not be inspired by the Western model, but follow its own "Slavic" way.
15. Ivan Sergeieievich Aksakov, *Ivan Sergeieievich Aksakov v evo pismah*, vol. 3 (Moscow, 2004), 327, in Borisov, *Povsednevnaia zhizn*, 16.

16. As a result of reform in 1721, traditional office of patriarch was removed, and the Russian Orthodox Church formally became a national institution. See: Richard Pipes, *Russia Under the Old Regime* (New York: Penguin Books, 2005).

17. Nikolai Gogol, *Selected Passages from Correspondence with Friends* (Nashville, TN: Vanderbilt University Press 2009).

18. Fiodor Dostojevsky, *The Brothers Karamazov* (New York: Oxford University Press, 2008).

19. Lev Tolstoy, *Anna Karenina* (Knoxville, TN: Wordsworth Classics, 1999).

20. Saint Petersburg was established as the capital by Tsar Peter the Great in 1712.

21. Andrey Ivanovich Bogdanow and Vasilyi Ruban, *Istoricheskoe, geografiches-koe opisanije Sankt Peterburga ot nachala zavedenija evo, s 1703 po 1751 god.* Cf.: Grigoryi Usyskin, *Ocherki ustorii rossijskovo turizma* (Moscow: Izdatelskyi Torgovyi Dom Gerda, 2000), accessed August 4, 2016, http://tourlib.net/books_history/usyskin03.htm, chap. 3.

22. Dolzhenko and Putrik, *Istorija turizma*, 24–51.

23. Usyskin, *Ocherki ustorii*, http://tourlib.net/books_history/usyskin03.htm, chap. 3.

24. On patterns of leisure time see: Boris Egorov. Praca i wypoczynek w życiu rosyjskim, in: *Oblicza Rosji. Szkice z historii kultury rosyjskiej XIX wieku* [The Faces of Russia: Essays on the History and the Culture of Russia in the 19th Century] (Gdańsk: Słowo obraz/terytoria, 2002), 307–17.

25. Dolzhenko and Putrik, *Istorija turizma*, 64–81.

26. Usyskin, *Ocherki ustorii*, http://tourlib.net/books_history/usyskin06.htm, chap. 6.

27. Dolzhenko and Putrik, *Istorija turizma*, 681–91.

28. Outbound tourism, which was mainly propagandist was controlled, in the 1930s, by a special department of the OPTE, while inbound tourism, from its origins until the collapse of the Soviet Union, was controlled by the legendary Inturist, see "Inturist—80 let vokrug sveta 1929-2009," special issue of journal *Inturist*, 7 (2009). Cf. Viktor Samoilovich, *Gid, gidessa i turik v pridachu* (Saint Petersburg: Osipov, 2006).

29. Valerij Aleksandrovich Kvartalov, Vladimir Kirlovich Fedorchenko, *Turizm socjalnyi: istorija i sovremennost* (Kiev, 1989), 45.

30. See Ustav (*Statute of) OPT RSFSR*, in: Igor Orlov, Elena Jurchikova, *Massovyi turizm v stalinskoi povsednevnosti* (Moscow: ROSSPEN, 2010), 169–78.

31. Orlov and Jurchikova, *Massovyi turizm*.

32. Dolzhenko and Putrik, *Istorija turizma*, 98–116.

33. Usyskin, *Ocherki ustorii*, tourlib.net/books_history/usyskin07.htm, chap. 7.

34. On the cult of heroes and creation of a new man, see Sheila Fitzpatrick, "Palaces on Monday," in *Everyday Stalinism: Ordinary Life in Extraordinary Times—Soviet Russia in the 1930s*, ed. Sheila Fitzpatrick (Oxford: Oxford University Press, 1999), 67–98; also: Mikhail Heller, *Cogs in the Wheel—The Formation of Soviet Man* (New York: Alfred A. Knopf, 1988)

35. The term for movement of record breaking labor leaders. The term was derived from Aleksey Stakhanov, a miner who, in 1935, called for competing in workplace.

36. Orlov and Jurchikova, *Massovyi turizm*, 126–43, por. Usyskin, *Ocherki ustorii*, http://tourlib.net/books_history/usyskin09.htm, chap. 9.

37. Vyacheslav Semyonov, *The Central Lenin Museum: A Guide* (Moscow: Raduga Publishers, 1986).

38. Paul Froese, *The Plot to Kill God: Findings from the Soviet Experiment in Secularization* (Berkeley: University of California Press, 2008), 40.

39. The name Saint Petersburg was used between 1914 and 1924, when it was changed to Leningrad.

40. Usyskin, *Ocherki ustorii*, tourlib.net/books_history/usyskin07.htm, chap. 7.

41. Heller, *Cogs in the Wheel*, 149.

42. Adriej Sidorenko, "Artek," *Здоровье*, 6 (1975), accessed August 4, 2016, http://www.bibliotekar.ru/464/2.htm. On the international significance of Artek see Margaret Peacock, "Mobilized Childhood Responds to the Threat," in *Innocent Weapons: The Soviet and American Politics of Childhood in the Cold War*, ed. Margaret Peacock (Chapel Hill: University of North Carolina Press, 2014), 94–122.

43. On the privileges of the elite, see Fitzpatrick, "A Magic Tablecloth," in *Everyday Stalinism*, 89–114.

44. Orlov and Jurchikova, *Massovyi turizm*, 151–59.

45. Usyskin, *Ocherki ustorii*, http://tourlib.net/books_history/usyskin09.htm, chap. 9.

46. On the role of climbing in the culture of the 1930s, see Eva Maurer, "Al'pinizm as Mass Sport and Elite Recreation: Soviet Mountaineering Camps under Stalin," in *Turizm: The Russian and East European Tourist under Capitalism and Socialism*, ed. Anne Gorsuch and Diane Koenker (Ithaca, NY: Cornell University Press, 2006): 141–63.

47. See Roger Marwick, "The Great Patriotic War in Soviet and Post-Soviet Collective Memory," in *The Oxford Handbook of Postwar European History*, ed. Dan Stone (Oxford: Oxford University Press, 2012), 669–732.

48. "Inturist—80 let vokrug sveta 1929–2009." Cf. Viktor Samoilovich, *Gid, gidessa i turik v pridachu*.

49. See more in: Anne Gorsuch, "Time Travelers: Soviet Tourists to Eastern Europe" in *Turizm*, ed. Gorsuch and Koenker (Ithaca, NY: Cornell University Press, 2006): 205–26.

50. Every citizen who wished to obtain a foreign passport was verified by the security service.

51. On a curious phenomenon of "virtual tourism" in the 1920s, in the context of relation between sightseeing and museum sciences, see further: Francine Hirsch, "Getting to Know 'The Peoples of the USSR': Ethnographic Exhibits as Soviet Virtual Tourism, 1923–1934," *Slavic Review* 62, no. 4, special issue: "Tourism and Travel in Russia and the Soviet Union" (2003): 683–709.

52. Victoria Donovan, "'How Well Do You Know Your Krai?' The Kraevedenie Revival and Patriotic Politics in Late Khrushchev-Era Russia," *Slavic Review* 74, no. 3, (2015): 464–83.

53. Usyskin, *Ocherki ustorii*, http://tourlib.net/books_history/usyskin13.htm, chap. 13.

54. For more on the Russian dacha, see Stephen Lovell, *Summerfolk: A History of the Dacha, 1710–2000* (Ithaca, NY: Cornell University Press, 2003).

55. Diane Koenker, "Travel to Work, Travel to Play: On Russian Tourism, Travel, and Leisure," *Slavic Review* 62, no. 4, (2003): 660.

56. Diane Koenker, *Club Red: Vacation Travel and the Soviet Dream* (Ithaca, NY: Cornell University Press, 2013).

57. Usyskin, *Ocherki ustorii*, http://tourlib.net/books_history/usyskin14.htm, chap. 14.

58. On the period of transformation in tourist economy of Russia, see Frederic Dimanche and Lidia Andrades, *Tourism in Russia: A Management Handbook* (Bingley, UK: Emerald Group Publishing, 2015): 14–26.

59. I mean Russia from the medieval period until the eighteenth century, therefore Muscovite Rus, the Tsardom of Russia, as well as the Russian Empire.

60. Statistical indicators of mutual trips by citizens of the Russian Federation and citizens of foreign states provided by Federal Agency for Tourism, Ministry of Culture of the Russian Federation, accessed August 4, 2016, http://www.russiatourism.ru/contents/statistika/statisticheskie-pokazateli-vzaimnykh-poezdok-grazhdan-rossiyskoy-federatsii-i-grazhdan-inostrannykh-gosudarstv/. Por. Dolzhenko and Putrik, *Istorija turizma*, 85–91.

61. Statistical indicators of mutual trips by citizens of the Russian Federation and citizens of foreign states provided by Federal Agency for Tourism, Ministry of Culture of the Russian Federation, accessed August 4, 2016, http://www.russiatourism.ru/contents/statistika/statisticheskie-pokazateli-vzaimnykh-poezdok-grazhdan-rossiyskoy-federatsii-i-grazhdan-inostrannykh-gosudarstv/ Dolzhenko and Putrik, *Istorija turizma*, 280–95.

62. Aleksandr Baklanov and Julija Dudkina, *Shto stało s turizmom v Rossiji*, accessed August 4, 2016, http://russiantourism.ru/main/main_15143.html.

63. Survey carried out by Levada Center show, that almost half of the respondents considers traveling abroad too dangerous. *Poezdki za granicu*, accessed August 4, 2016, http://www.levada.ru/2016/01/20/poezdki-za-granitsu-2/.

64. Federalnaia celevaia programma "Rozvitije vnutrennovo i vjezdnovo turizma v Rossijskoi Federacji (2011–2018 gody)," accessed August 4, 2016, http://www.russiatourism.ru/contents/deyatelnost/federalnaya-tselevaya-programma-razvitie-vnutrennego-i-vezdnogo-turizma-v-rossiyskoy-federatsii-2011-2018-gody-.

65. Federalnaia celevaia programma, 39.

66. Federalnaia celevaia programma, 53.

67. Federalnaia celevaia programma, 54.

68. On the consequences of the annexation of Crimea by Russia, see *European Tourism amid the Crimea Crisis, a report by the European Travel Commission and Tourism Economics* (Brussels, October 2014), accessed August 4, 2016, http://www.etc-corporate.org/news/european-tourism-amid-the-crimea-crisis.

69. Genadij Petrovich Dolzhenko, Jurij Stepanovich Putrik, *v Rossijskoi Imperii, Sovetskom Soiuze, i Rossijskoi Federacji* (Moscow: Izdatelskij Centr MarT, 2010), 16.

70. *Russkoe Geograficheskoe Obshchestvo vybiraet samyie krasivyie fotografii Rossiji*, accessed August 4, 2016, http://www.russiatourism.ru/news/10847/.

71. Gertjan Plets, "Ethno-nationalism, Asymmetric Federalism and Soviet Perceptions of the Past: (World) Heritage Activism in the Russian Federation," *Journal of Social Archeology* 15, no. 1 (2015): 80.

REFERENCES

Aksakov, Ivan Sergeieievich. *Ivan Sergeieievich Aksakov v evo pismah*, Vol. 3, Moscow: Izdatelstvo Russkaia Kniga, 2004.

Baklanov, Aleksandr, and Julija Dudkina. *Shto stało s turizmom v Rossiji*. Accessed August 4, 2016. http://russiantourism.ru/main/main_15143.html.

Banaszkiewicz, Mikołaj. "Refleksja polityczna rosyjskich elit z podróży po Europie w połowie XIX wieku" [The Political Reflection of the Russian Elite after Journeys to Europe in the Half of 19th Century]. *Politeja* 26, no. 4 (2013): 389–403.

Bogdanow, Andrey Ivanovich, and Vasilyi Ruban. *Istoricheskoe, geograficheskoe opisanije Sankt Peterburga ot nachala zavedenija evo, s 1703 po 1751 god.*

Borisov, Nikolai. *Povsednevnaia zhizn russkovo puteshestvennika v epohu bezdorozhija.* Moscow: Molodaia Gvardija, 2010.

de Custine, Astolphe. *Letters from Russia.* New York: New York Review of Books, 2012.

Dickinson, Sara. *Breaking Ground. Travel and National Culture in Russia from Peter I to the Era of Pushkin.* Rodopi: New York, 2006.

Dimanche, Frederic, and Lidia Andrades. *Tourism in Russia: A Management Handbook.* Bingley, UK: Emerald Group Publishing, 2015.

Dolzhenko, Genadij Petrovich, and Putrik Jurij Stepanovich. *Istorija turizma v Rossijskoi Imperii, Sovetskom Soiuze, i Rossijskoi Federacji.* Moscow: Izdatelskij Centr MarT, 2010.

Donovan, Victoria. "'How Well Do You Know Your Krai?' The Kraevedenie Revival and Patriotic Politics in Late Khrushchev-Era Russia," *Slavic Review* 74, no. 3 (2015): 464–83.

Dostojevsky, Fiodor. *The Brothers Karamazov.* New York: Oxford University Press, 2008.

Egorov, Boris. *Praca i wypoczynek w życiu rosyjskim.* In *Oblicza Rosji. Szkice z historii kultury rosyjskiej XIX wieku* [*The Faces of Russia: Essays on the History and the Culture of Russia in the 19th Century*], 307–17. Gdańsk: Słowo obraz/ terytoria, 2002.

European Tourism amid the Crimea Crisis, a report by the European Travel Commission and Tourism Economics. Brussels: October 2014. Accessed August 4, 2016. http://www.etc-corporate.org/news/european-tourism-amid-the-crimea-crisis.

Federalnaia celevaia programma "Rozvitije vnutrennovo i vjezdnovo turizma v Rossijskoi Federacji (2011–2018 gody)." Accessed August 4, 2016. http://www. russiatourism.ru/contents/deyatelnost/federalnaya-tselevaya-programma-razvitievnutrennego-i-vezdnogo-turizma-v-rossiyskoy-federatsii-2011-2018-gody.

Fitzpatrick, Sheila. *Everyday Stalinism: Ordinary Life in Extraordinary Times— Soviet Russia in the 1930s.* London: Oxford University Press, 1999.

Froese, Paul. *The Plot to Kill God: Findings from the Soviet Experiment in Secularization.* Berkeley: University of California Press, 2008.

Gogol, Nikolai. *Selected Passages from Correspondence with Friends.* Nashville, TN: Vanderbilt University Press, 2009.

Gorsuch, Anne. "Time Travelers: Soviet Tourists to Eastern Europe." In *Turizm: The Russian and East European Tourist under Capitalism and Socialism*, edited by

Anne Gorsuch and Diane Koenker, 205–26. Ithaca, NY: Cornell University Press, 2006.

Heller, Mikhail. *Cogs in the Wheel – The Formation of Soviet Man.* New York: Knopf, 1988.

Hirsch, Francine. "Getting to Know 'The Peoples of the USSR': Ethnographic Exhibits as Soviet Virtual Tourism, 1923–1934." *Slavic Review* 62, no. 4, special issue: Tourism and Travel in Russia and the Soviet Union (2003): 683–709.

"Inturist—80 let vokrug sveta 1929–2009," special issue of journal *Inturist*, Vol. 7, Moscow, 2009.

Kahn, Andrew. *Nikolai Karamzin: "Letters of a Russian Traveller."* Oxford: Voltaire Foundation, 2003.

Koenker, Diane. "Travel to Work, Travel to Play: On Russian Tourism, Travel, and Leisure." *Slavic Review* 62, no. 4 (2003): 657–65.

———. *Club Red: Vacation Travel and the Soviet Dream.* Ithaca, NY: Cornell University Press, 2013.

Kvartalov, Valerij Aleksandrovich, and Valerij Aleksandrovich Fedorchenko. *Turizm socjalnyi: istorija i sovremennost.* Kiev, 1989.

Lovell, Stephen. *Summerfolk: A History of the Dacha, 1710–2000.* Ithaca, NY: Cornell University Press, 2003.

Offord, Derek. *Journeys to a Graveyard: Perceptions of Europe in Classical Russian Travel Writing.* Leiden: Springer, 2006.

Orlov, Igor, and Elena Jurchikova. *Massovyi turizm v stalinskoi povsednevnosti.* Moscow: ROSSPEN, 2010.

Marwick, Roger. "The Great Patriotic War in Soviet and Post-Soviet Collective Memory." In *The Oxford Handbook of Postwar European History*, edited by Dan Stone, 669–732. New York: Oxford University Press, 2012.

Maurer, Eva. "Al'pinizm as Mass Sport and Elite Recreation: Soviet Mountaineering Camps under Stalin." In *Turizm: The Russian and East European Tourist under Capitalism and Socialism*, edited by Anne Gorsuch and Diane Koenker, 141–63. Ithaca, NY: Cornell University Press, 2006.

Peacock, Margaret. *Innocent Weapons: The Soviet and American Politics of Childhood in the Cold War.* Chapel Hill: University of North Carolina Press, 2014.

Pipes, Richard. *Russia Under the Old Regime.* New York: Penguin Books, 2005.

Poezdki za granicu, Accessed August 4, 2016. http://www.levada.ru/2016/01/20/poezdki-za-granitsu-2/.

Plets, Gertjan. "Ethno-nationalism, Asymmetric Federalism and Soviet Perceptions of the Past: (World) Heritage Activism in the Russian Federation." *Journal of Social Archeology* 15, no. 1 (2015): 67–93.

Radishchev, Aleksandr Nikolaevich. *A Journey from Saint Petersburg to Moscow.* Edited by Roderick Page Thaler. Cambridge, MA: Harvard University Press, 2013.

Riasanovsky, Nicholas V., and Mark D. Steinberg. *A History of Russia.* 7th edition. New York: Oxford University Press, 2000.

Russkoe Geograficheskoe Obshchestvo vybiraet samyie krasivyie fotografii Rossiji. Accessed August 4, 2016. http://www.russiatourism.ru/news/10847/.

Samoilovich, Viktor. *Gid, gidessa i turik v pridachu.* Saint Petersburg: Osipov, 2006.

Semyonov, Vyacheslav. *The Central Lenin Museum: A Guide*. Moscow: Raduga Publishers, 1986.

Shevyrev, Stepan Petrovich. *Puteschestvije v Kirilo-Belozerskij monastyr*. Moscow, 2004.

Sidorenko, Andriej. "Artek." *Zdorovi'e*, nr 6 (1975), Accessed August 4, 2016. http://www.bibliotekar.ru/464/2.htm.

Statistical indicators of mutual trips by citizens of the Russian Federation and citizens of foreign states provided by Federal Agency for Tourism. Ministry of Culture of the Russian Federation. Accessed August 4, 2016. http://www.russiatourism.ru/contents/statistika/statisticheskie-pokazateli-vzaimnykh-poezdok-grazhdan-rossiyskoy-federatsii-i-grazhdan-inostrannykh-gosudarstv/.

Tolstoy, Leo. *Anna Karenina*. London: Wordsworth Classics, 1999.

Usyskin, Grigoryi. *Ocherki ustorii rossijskovo turizma*. Moscow: Izdatelskyi Torgovyi Dom Gerda, 2000. Accessed August 4, 2016. http://tourlib.net/books_history/usyskin.htm.

Chapter 7

Mediating Central and Eastern Europe in Tourism Discourse

Sabina Owsianowska

At the end of the twentieth century, tourism in Central and Eastern Europe began to play an increasingly important role in promoting national, ethnic, and common European heritage. The transformation realities, including the challenges of economic development and the process of stronger European integration in the first decade of the twenty-first century, created a new mission for culture for the candidate and then admitted member states.[1] In the formation of relationships between culture and tourism in the pre-accession period and after the European Union enlargement, the following were considered: to what extent should indigenous cultural values serve the symbolic "return" to Europe? which elements are to be produced and which images are to be shaped for the needs of one's own society, and which for global tourism and the "heritage industry"? According to Sharon Macdonald,[2] who describes the "past presencing" process and emphasizes the special role memory plays in Europe, history is written by historians based on the analysis of source materials, while heritage is a product of contemporary times and the result of decisions about what "should be passed on to an imagined future," as Tunbridge and Ashworth argued.[3] Directions and assumptions of cultural policy meeting the requirements of globalization lead to initiating different transborder, interregional, and international projects, institutions, and networks, also within the tourist sector. Against the background of stereotypical images of post-transition Eastern Europe, attention should be paid to decisions that aim to provide regional resources within the framework of (branded) tourism products. This allows us to look at heritage through the prism of the process of formulating strategies of local development and modernization, which is particularly important for postsocialist states.

At the outset, a question about the referent concept of Central and Eastern Europe arises: which exact part of the continent are we considering (because even a cursory review of tourist offers makes it clear that the list of countries is not fixed)? After the fall of communism, there was a "fragmentation" of the former Eastern Europe, and the very notion of an Eastern Europe became increasingly blurry. Central, Eastern, Central-Eastern, East-Central, Southern, South-Eastern, Northern, North-Eastern Europe, and so on—the new subregions were delimited or renamed, even if there were no clear boundaries between them for historical, cultural, political, or geographical reasons. Noteworthy is the fact that, since the 1970s, from as far as the German Rhineland to the border between Lithuania and Belarus, one could encounter voices in favor of Central European identity,[4] complicating the simplified division of the continent into Western and Eastern Europe.

The source of the idea and the consequences of extracting Central Europe from the group of countries, which after the Second World War were under the common name of "Eastern Europe," refer to identity building and self-determination after decades of totalitarianism. Significantly, the effect of emancipation can be exclusion from supranational discourse for the sake of regional particularities that may, in fact, weaken the idea of European community. Of course, these are broader problems outside the phenomenon of traveling. The tourist industry, however, has become an important catalyst for action toward promoting the image of a place and people. What is more, as Shohamy and Waksman write: "Contemporary tourism is one of the key domains in which nations construct their discourses of national identity and unity."[5] Commemorative monuments, battlefields, castles, or other ideological landscapes, as well as memories of home and everyday life, values, rituals, and so on are the basis for creating and strengthening a sense of belonging. But they are also at the core of tourism products, and their meanings vary in response to the expectations, knowledge, and perceptions of different groups of "consumers," who might be domestic or foreign visitors.

As Scollon states, "Our social world is in fact a discursive world,"[6] which is why through discourse analysis we can examine how tourist texts mediate the process of creating "independent communities" and negotiate their place in a larger regional and global context. For inhabitants of the Central and Eastern Europe countries, heritage tourism, which has been developing dynamically in times of political, social, and cultural integration in the first decade of the twenty-first century, was an expression of the desire to strengthen their sense of identity and distinctiveness.[7] It was the response to the progressive unification in the sphere of everyday life that motivated people to define their individuality in terms of "global ecumene" and protection against pressure from mass culture. Tourism is thus an opportunity to reflect on the relationships between "local" and "global" ("glocalization"), on "the tension, which is visible between the world of anonymous panculturalism and the need for particular belonging to a community of local character."[8]

In this chapter, I propose reflections on the manner of representing Central and Eastern Europe in the language of tourism—in brochures and websites of tour operators who offer trips to the region; traditional, printed guidebooks and their online, interactive versions; and websites of national and local tourist organizations. As Pritchard and Morgan write: "Brochures, travel guides and websites available to tourists shape their expectations long before they arrive at their destination. Thus, the representations of local life presented in those texts become the codified and authorized versions of local culture and history."[9] I turn to the theory of G. Dann, who claims that tourism is grounded in discourse and that it seduces people and converts them into visitors via "static and moving pictures, written texts and audio-visual offerings."[10] As such, discourse can be identified with semiosis, and its critical analysis reveals inter alia the sources of knowledge and power, the asymmetry in social relations, and an ideological background of a multimodal message. In a broader sense, tourism discourses enable us to study "tourism imaginaries," which Salazar and Graburn conceptualize as "socially transmitted representational assemblages that interact with people's personal imaginings and that are used as meaning-making and world shaping devices."[11]

BETWEEN THE WEST AND THE EAST

Before going into further analysis, it is worth briefly explaining why the expression "Eastern Europe," according to the universal and unambiguous division into the East and West adopted by outsiders, is a far-reaching simplification, a remnant of the Cold War. Well, for a few reasons. First, according to insiders, this dichotomous division of the continent following the Second World War along the border demarcated by the victorious powers is not justified today and should not be reproduced. The nomenclature preserved in language from the times of the Iron Curtain dividing Europe into two zones of influence is, in fact, more complex and problematic. Second, one should take into account the broader global context of decolonization and the end of the world's division into opposing blocks in the mid-twentieth century. As a consequence, Eurocentrism became a subject of criticism; however, the postcolonial discourse in countries that are "in between" or "on the border" has its specific features, and it is characterized by different emphases in the debate over such global processes as integration and decolonization.

From Eastern Germany to Russia, there was a strong desire to prove that the nations belong to the center, to confirm their Europeanness. Europe became a "magnet," which clashed with the idea of Europe as a "fortress," accepting only the elect.[12] The reaction to this contradictory situation was creating an alternative vision of the center such as Central Europe, which refers to the Germanic idea of *Mitteleuropa* or, contrarily, to the concept of a supranational Slavic region. These projects were an expression of the dissent hegemonic position in Western Europe, the discourse of exclusion directed against the discourse of those who were/are in power.[13] After 1989, the issue also arises of treating the period of Soviet domination in Central and Eastern Europe as a form of colonialism. The formation of new states after the collapse of the former empire and the strengthening of individual and national identities, in which heritage is a key factor, may be considered similarities of postsocialism and postcolonialism; nevertheless, researchers point out the differences between both concepts, if only because of the specificity of regional history.[14]

The fact is that accurate determination of this area of the continent as a geographical unit always caused a great problem. The American historian L. Wolff, going back to eighteenth-century history, tries to describe the process of "inventing Eastern Europe" in reference to the tradition of the Enlightenment, based on maps, documents, and descriptions of travels that were created both thanks to the experience of the explorers, researchers, and tourists of the times (e.g., William Coxe), and were also the product of philosophical considerations (e.g., Voltaire) and the imagination of "armchair travelers."[15] Wolff critically analyzes the views linking the western and northern part of Europe with that which is "civilized" and modern, and the eastern countries with that which is "barbaric" and underdeveloped; he shows the sources of the division into the "center" and "periphery" predetermined in the consecutive centuries. The historical context outlined by Wolff highlights in a sense the genesis of relationships between Europeans from two sides of the Iron Curtain. The feeling of incessant belonging to Western civilization, expressed by those from the eastern part of Europe, is/was not always acknowledged with understanding and acceptance by Westerners, and this type of collision of different views is the essence of the debate on Central Europe. Undoubtedly, the need to underline the intra-regional differentiation—within the wider area of Eastern Europe—was justified from the point of view of identity dilemmas. Not surprisingly, an especially lively debate flared up when discussing the conditions of accession to the European Union. In the face of real unification, concerns were raised about the actual place among others, the possible profits and losses. Integration processes were carried out at the same time as the political and economic transformation, and it was not possible to analyze their effects separately; thus, the possible negative consequences of the transformation are attributed to the integration within the European Union and vice versa.[16]

In conclusion, Central Europe is more a historical and geopolitical concept, a symbolic—and even mythical—construction than a territory of precisely specified boundaries. Simona Škrabec, a Slovenian literary critic, who tries to explain why it is so difficult to define "Central Europe," claims that it is wrong to assume common history as a main factor forming the identity of the region. To redefine the notion of Central Europe, she refers to the concept of Michel Foucault and resigns from historical narrative. In her analysis, Škrabec works as an archaeologist and reveals subsequent layers of meaning, starting from the present.[17] The results of her investigation are not a clear answer to the question, what does the term "Central Europe" mean? They rather confirm that we should construct a "mental representation" of the region, taking into consideration its past, but above all, try to understand its contemporary diversity and future challenges.

CENTRAL AND EASTERN EUROPE IN TOURISM DISCOURSE

The strong relationship between tourism and imagination seems crucial in the tourist experience description and is the subject of interdisciplinary analyses.[18] On the one hand, researchers examine which signs, symbols, and myths are associated with a place—the projected image of a destination— and then disseminated through official and unofficial forms of tourism discourse. On the other hand, scholars concentrate on tourists' perception of the destination—its perceived image—examining both verbal and visual on-trip and post-trip narratives.[19] Analysis of the perception of the region by tourists, however, goes beyond the scope of this chapter, and I will not deal with this issue. I rather focus on mediation of the images of the region that occur in tourist media: first, the offers and brochures of tour operators specializing in Central and/or Eastern Europe; second, in travel guidebooks—for example, a Baedeker from the series Eyewitness Travel Guides titled "Eastern & Central Europe" (2010) and Wikitravel, a popular source of information for contemporary tourists; third, on the official websites of national tourist organizations—for example, Bulgarian Tourist Board, Czech Tourism Authority, German National Tourist Board, Hungarian Tourism Agency, Polish Tourist Organisation, Slovak Tourist Board, Slovenian Tourist Board, and suchlike.[20]

Guidebooks, brochures, and other tourist texts play an intermediary role in tourist experiences. The specificity of the genres and the features of the language of tourism are the reason that in each of these areas, we may have to deal with stereotypical images, patterns of traveling more connected with the culture of the sender and/or inherent for informational and marketing objectives than aiming to present the country from a local perspective. The official websites of national tourist organizations are not only a space for promotion, but in the case of Central and Eastern European countries, where the situation radically changed in the 1990s, they also serve to build and strengthen national identity and reshape the image of the country and its inhabitants.[21] In a sense, both tourist guidebooks and websites can also be treated as *"lieux de mémoire*/sites of memory"[22] themselves, because they represent not only physical space, but also symbolic objects, characters, practices, and performances.

What is worth noting is that not all countries presented today as part of Central and Eastern Europe share common experiences, that is, of communism and the (post)transition period (vide Austria and Switzerland, which are classified as part of Central Europe for geographical, administrative, and historical reasons—for example, in online guidebooks such as Wikitravel.[23] To compare, the United Nations World Tourism Organization (UNWTO) divides Europe into four regions, and the countries that are included in the Central and Eastern European tourist offer are in this classification part of Western Europe (e.g., Germany, Austria); Central-Eastern Europe (Bulgaria, Czech Republic, Estonia, Hungary, Latvia, Lithuania, Moldova, Poland, Romania, Slovakia); and Southern-Mediterranean Europe (Bosnia-Herzegovina, Croatia, Macedonia, Montenegro, Serbia, Slovenia).[24] Thus, the seemingly simple question about tourism in Eastern and—in particular—Central Europe, where the presence of some states depends on the adopted criteria (see also, e.g., European Travel Commission, ETC[25]), may be confusing. Even if the UNWTO classification, designed mainly for statistical purposes, does not reflect the key assumptions for this chapter, I refer to it as a starting point for further discussion. Admitting the limitations of this study, which results in an incomplete, and—in a sense—fragmented image of Central and Eastern Europe in tourism discourse, I am persuaded that both other countries and the whole region should be the subject of research in the future.

LEGENDARY, IMPERIAL, RURAL, UNSUNG . . . "AT THE CROSSROADS OF EUROPE AND ASIA"?

I will start with an overview of the trip offers to Central and Eastern Europe. They may include Austria, Croatia, Czech Republic, Hungary, Poland, and Russia (Homeric Tours, "Stimulate your intellectual curiosities in CEE"); and additionally Germany, Estonia, and other *pribaltik* and Balkan states (Jay Way Boutique Travel. Central & Eastern Travel Specialists since 2006[26]). Some organizers propose several countries—for example, the Czech Republic, Germany, Austria, Hungary, and Poland—in one package (Collette, "Europe's Magnificent and Legendary Cities"), while another tour operator demarcates between "Central and East Europe" (slogan: "Rising Nations Ready for Prime Time"), including among the destinations Bulgaria, Belarus, the Czech Republic, Poland, Romania, Slovakia, Hungary, and

Moldova. Consequently, Slovenia, Serbia, and Croatia are in this offer part of the "Balkans," while Estonia, Latvia, and Lithuania are part of the "Baltics" (MIR Corporation, "Journeys to the Legendary Destinations at the Cross-roads of Europe and Asia"). The examples below illustrate how the region is mediated in their proposals and what they believe to be the chief characteristics of particular destinations, which are waiting "to be discovered." The chief characteristics range from the destinations' imperial legacy and folk traditions to contemporary culture and the legendary past:

1. *"Stimulate your intellectual curiosities in Central & Eastern Europe"*[27] (Homeric Tours)
   Austria, Hungary, Poland, Germany, the Czech Republic: "Eastern European Highlights"
   Austria, Hungary, the Czech Republic: "Grand Capitals" (of Central Europe)
   Austria and Hungary or—Austria and the Czech Republic: "Imperial Highlights"
2. *"Europe's Magnificent and Legendary Cities"*[28] (Collette)
   Czech Republic, Germany, Austria, Hungary, and Poland
3. *"Journeys to the Legendary Destinations at the Crossroads of Europe and Asia"*[29] *(MIR Corp.)*
   "Rising Nations Ready for Prime Time"
   Belarus: "A step back in time"
   Bulgaria: "Roses and Roman Ruins"
   Czech Republic: "Hip and Historic: Cobbled Streets and Contemporary Culture"
   Hungary: "Imperial Legacy and Folk Traditions"
   Moldova: "Waiting to be Discovered"
   Poland: "New Europe Success Story"
   Romania: "Village Life, Vampires and Variety"
   Slovakia: "Sleeping Beauty"
   Belarus, Ukraine, and Moldova: "An In-depth Study of Three Unsung Countries"
   Bulgaria and Romania: "Through the Valley of the Roses to the Painted Monasteries"

I close this section with reference to the Central Europe Company, located in southern Poland, which invites us on a "journey beyond political borders and disputes." Tailor-made trips, sentimental routes, back-to-the-roots travels, and homecomings[30] bring much more than just the nostalgia or heritage tourism experience. The authors explain why it is worth exploring this part of the continent thus:

Central Europe is not a region you can mark on the map, as in the case of Central America. It is a kingdom of spirit, as British historian Timothy Garton Ash wrote. . . . This is what fascinates us in our part of the continent—Germany, Poland, Ukraine, the Czech Republic, Slovakia, Austria, Slovenia, Hungary and Romania. Its multiculturalism, multilingualism, its multi-religious character—often imaginary—after the tragedies of wars and forced migrations. This nostalgia . . . especially here in mitteleuropa, is a memory of something which has never existed.[31]

On the one hand, these words refer to the peculiarities of the region, today eagerly recalled to add color to the tourist offers, while on the other, they invoke endless debates on European identity. Historical sources and concepts are interpreted differently—the mentioned "mitteleuropa," which in the statements from the Central European Company tour guides has nothing to do with the Germanic concept, but refers to a certain worldview.

LOOKING BACK: GLORIOUS PASTS, TRAUMA, AND THE DIFFICULT HERITAGE

In the Wikitravel guide, Central Europe is presented as a region constituting the "heart of Europe." The authors have taken into account German-speaking countries (Germany, Austria), the Visegrad states (Poland, Slovakia, the Czech Republic, and Hungary), and Slovenia, a former republic of Yugoslavia, as well as Switzerland and Liechtenstein. There is also mention of the areas that are currently not considered as Central European: Western Ukraine, Kaliningrad (Russia), Alsace and part of Lorraine (France), and South Tyrol/Alto Adige (Italy), at least to some extent due to historical and cultural relationships (e.g., coexistence within the Polish-Lithuanian Commonwealth and the Austro-Hungarian Empire). In the past, Central and Eastern Europe experienced a multiplicity of mixed cultural influences, which makes it interesting not only for history lovers and cultural tourists. Until the twentieth century, the history of the region was shaped by powerful empires, not nation-states, and nowadays "the post-socialist Central and Eastern Europe is but the inheritor of an even more complicated pre-socialist Central and Eastern Europe!"[32]

In the "Eastern & Central Europe" Baedeker,[33] the authors introduce the signs that are typical for local landscapes: picturesque villages, the ruins of old castles, palaces, manor houses, huge monasteries, cathedrals, synagogues, wooden churches, tserkvas, etc. The appearance of historical cities such as Vienna, Budapest, Prague, and Krakow reflected their artistic and technical achievements, as well as ethnic diversity among the local population. The main facts are recalled, including the role of the "legendary" Alps, which formed a natural boundary, or rather, a transition territory, between the zones of influence of the Latin, Germanic, and Slavic cultures. Against this background, under the slogan "Understand," the list of key regional images of Central and Eastern Europe opens: "Castles and Fortresses," "Great Capitals," "Historic Cities," and "Jewish Culture."[34]

Remembering history expressed in residential and military architecture, reconstructing victorious battles, and emphasizing the glorious past are just one side of the coin. The second shows the tragic fate of many generations, partitions and occupation, Holocaust, totalitarian systems of the twentieth century, suppression of national and ethnic identity, emigration for political and economic reasons, genocide, and fratricidal struggles. This area was inhabited by various ethnic, national, and religious groups for centuries, but after the Second World War the situation changed completely. Some people were forced to leave their homeland; others stayed back. The unresolved disputes about the meaning of difficult and controversial events have impact on the interpretation of the legacy and are still a serious challenge that the people of this part of Europe have to face. D. Bechtel's[35] research in eastern Poland and western Ukraine (which were parts of former Galicia) shows how the search for the multicultural past can encourage tourism development (especially memory tourism). Studying memory as an important factor in tourism, S. Marschall concentrates on the arrival of Germans in Poland within the framework of so-called "homesick tourism" and notes that this type of travel should be distinguished from those such as "roots tourism" or "personal heritage tourism."[36]

MULTICULTURALITY REVISITED: MEMORIES OF HOME AND EVERYDAY LIFE IN TOURISM PRODUCTS

After the collapse of communism, multicultural heritage was "rediscovered," reconstructed, or even reinvented, and became the core of tourism products that enrich the region's offer and motivate residents to nurture and restore traditions. Homecomings thanks to tourism encourage exploring traces and signs of the "lost" world. In the promotions, there appear references to the memory of the former "cultural mosaic" and its traces, that is, the history of former Galicia and the borderland regions. The coexistence of different cultures and religions frames narratives about the places and people that were previously overlooked or marginalized. This very special meaning can be found in Jewish heritage, which is marked in different tourist media and products, and other ethnic and national minorities (e.g., Roma, Lemko) also take advantage of the chance to promote the heritage of their own group.[37]

As one can read on the website of the abovementioned Central Europe Company: "A few years ago we fell in love with this world of remote towns, with the world of Hutsuls, Jews and tens of other nationalities. Thanks to writer Joseph Roth, our kingdom of spirit was set in Galicia, his beloved Austro-Hungarian Empire and its borderlands."[38]

The trip organizers specializing in Central and Eastern Europe focus on the "bright myth" of the borderland regions,[39] on the idyllic, idealized past that is not only represented by material objects, ruins, and relics, but also by intangible heritage. Numerous trails, workshops, and festivals are based on the traditions associated with different ethnic groups, cultivating their lifestyles, music, crafts, language(s), etc. Culinary routes, restaurants, cooking, and having meals with locals popularize regional cuisine, which is anchored in the multiculturality of this "peripheral" area.

The notion of "being provincial or peripheral" relates to "the mechanisms of center-periphery dependencies and their symbolic effects on regional level."[40] The tourist industry, however, is one of the main factors of modernization of underdeveloped, rural areas in Central and Eastern Europe. The EU incentives opened the opportunity to promote multicultural legacy in the region and to construct a new identity, to revive it in terms of economy, and to strengthen its competitive position on the tourism market. The challenge for the future is to delineate new ways of interpreting the dissonance of heritage in the age of increasing nationalism.

POSTSOCIALIST/POSTCOMMUNIST LEGACIES

The legacy of the socialist/communist years and its reception play a special role in Central and Eastern Europe: from negation to projecting attractions based on significant objects, events, or even a way of life typical of the era. As we can read in the Wikitravel guide, it is important to recognize the diversity within the region and avoid stereotypes. One manifested attempt to understand the region's specifics is the abovementioned use of the name "Central Europe" instead of "Eastern Europe," as well as resignation from hasty comparisons and recognition of the diversity among nations, for example, in the field of language and traditions.

> It is a common mistake by outsiders to label all Slavic or the former Warsaw Pact (also called the Eastern Bloc) states in the region as located in Eastern Europe. Almost uniformly, inhabitants of Central Europe will be flattered and pleased if you correctly describe their countries as "central European" both geographically and culturally. Conversely, they may be upset if you lapse into Cold War stereotypes.[41]

In this sphere, however, there are many more nuances than names. They regard both society's attitude toward the times of communism/socialism and their traces preserved in space, culture, politics, and lifestyle. It happens that with the change of government, decisions are made to differently treat the remains of communism in a country—for example, moving monuments, renaming streets, etc.[42] In tourism, we can observe interest in trails, events, or museums, which bring the past closer, and for the elder generations of locals they are an opportunity for reminiscence or nostalgia (e.g., *Ostalgie* in former Eastern Germany, Yugo-nostalgia in Balkan countries), but for the younger ones, they are a tool in education and entertainment. For visitors from outside the system, these products are also a kind of lesson on little-known history and, usually, a form of fun.[43] As a result, it happens—out of necessity—that the simplified message mostly contains information about what was different, strange, surprising, or absurd from the point of view of a tourist, but it is devoid of references to the broader historical and political context—for example, information regarding the restriction of liberty, the victims, the prevailing terror. However, by including selected tangible or intangible testimonies of a bygone era into the circle of recognized heritage (e.g., in the process of certification of best tourism products[44]), their relevance is renegotiated for the heirs of an unwanted past. The yesterdays of this part of Europe should find their place in the general history of the continent, which may help in better understanding each other and caring for common heritage.

THE DILEMMAS OF COMMON EUROPEAN HERITAGE

As written by T. G. Ash, "Europe has lost the plot. As we approach the 50th anniversary of the treaty of Rome on 25th March 2007—the 50th birthday of the European economic community that became the European Union— Europe no longer knows what story it wants to tell."[45] Ten years later, this question provokes a discussion on contemporary Europe and on storytelling about its common legacy and future coexistence of different nations and ethnic groups. After the fall of communism, the previous narrative lost its raison d'être, summed around the idea of unification after the war and against the hostile regime. Over time, as there were more countries in the European Union, the need became greater for common symbols, myths, and shared memory locations.[46]

Referring to Pierre Nora, one can ask if it is possible to identify the European "sites of memory." Nora approached the proposal of indicating the *lieux de mémoire européens* with skepticism, resulting from the belief that such places need a community, which cannot be created by a group of several dozen countries. Notwithstanding, he proposed to include such sites as "historiographical" places (school textbooks, museums); "foundational" places (from antiquity onward); "decisive" places in the military or the diplomatic sense (battlefields, treaties); geographical places (rivers, mountains, etc.); cultural and economic places (universities, trade routes, economic centers); places of scientific discovery or artistic movements; and other symbolic places (pilgrimages, tourist routes, etc.).[47]

In the process of Europeanization, tourist attractions became important for building transnational identity and promoting events aimed to celebrate the community's values. Specific solutions included the funding of programs to facilitate popularization of cultural diversity, cross-border cooperation, and initiatives that exemplify institutional support of the idea of Europe, such as celebrating "European Heritage Days" or "European Capitals of Culture." This identity building is also encouraged through an inventory of places likely to gain the label European Heritage: "European Heritage sites are milestones in the creation of today's Europe. Spanning from the dawn of civilization to the Europe we see today, these sites symbolize European ideals, values, history and integration."[48]

CONCLUSIONS: TOWARD THE FUTURE

The above analysis of tourism discourse suggests two perspectives. According to the first, Central and Eastern Europe (or its subregions, e.g., Central Europe or Eastern Europe) is/are recognized and jointly promoted in a variety of tourist media as one destination. The senders/authors develop the framework of common topics, images, and myths to describe each region as a certain whole (which is especially important for travelers who decide to take a European "grand tour" and visit the most remarkable sites of the continent). In the second approach, we deal rather with the insiders' view exposed in self-promotional initiatives undertaken by official institutions responsible for development of the tourist sector. Their goal is to shape the new image of the country/region as an attractive, modern, and dynamically developing tourist destination.

The period of the Cold War divided Europe for several decades, and only after the changes in the 1990s, mobility between the two parts of the continent became possible without restriction. Invoking the postwar division of Europe can be an important reference point for shaping a new image of the region, an expression of "self-exoticization,"[49] and a difficult stereotype to overcome, which makes futile every effort toward a constant change. Different countries can work together to find the best solution for improving their competitiveness, as can be seen in the example of Baltic states. Worth mentioning are such actions as a call to stop describing them as "post-Soviet" or the shift of their status from Eastern to Northern Europe.[50] A different situation occurs in the so-called Visegrad countries. Currently, the relationship between the four countries is weakening—some of them are in favor of stronger integration with the European Union (the Czech Republic, Slovakia), while others seem to gravitate toward the opposite direction (Hungary, Poland). The choice of narrative strategies reflects the main directions of tourism promotion, including the pursuit of Europeanization or resistance toward the same process in shaping the image of a destination.

The events of recent years once again create concern throughout Europe due to the increasing significance of nationalism, threats to democracy, Euroskepticism, and the risk of disintegration. Tourism discourse, by mediating attractions and products that relate to the controversial, dissonant heritage; multiculturality; memories of home and everyday life of repatriated and "disinherited" inhabitants and their children; as well as to a common European future, contributes to the incorporation of selected themes into contemporary culture, entertainment, and public debate.

NOTES

1. Boris Vukonić, "Turning Point in European Tourism Development," in *Tourism in Scientific Research in Poland and Worldwide*, ed. Wiesław Alejziak and Ryszard Winiarski (Krakow and Rzeszow: AWF Krakow Press, 2006).

2. Sharon Macdonald, *Memorylands: Heritage and Identity in Europe Today* (London: Routledge, 2013).

3. John Tunbridge and Gregory Ashworth, *Dissonant Heritage: The Management of the Past as a Resource in Conflict* (Chichester: Wiley & Sons, 1996), 6.

4. Ullrich Kockel, Máiréad Nic Craith, and Jonas Frykman, eds., *A Companion to Anthropology of Europe* (Wiley-Blackwell, 2012), 3.

5. Elana Shohamy and Shoshi Waksman, "Building the Nation, Writing the Past: History and Textuality at the *Ha'apala* Memorial in Tel Aviv-Jaffa," in *Semiotic Landscapes: Language, Image, Space*, ed. Adam Jaworski and Crispin Thurlow (London: Continuum International Publishing Group, 2011), 241–55. See also: Michael Pretes, "Tourism and Nationalism," *Annals of Tourism Research* 30 (2003): 125–42; Caroline Scarles and Jo-Anne Lester, eds., *Mediating the Tourist Experience: From Brochures to Virtual Encounters* (London: Ashgate, 2013).

6. Ron Scollon, *Mediated Discourse: The Nexus of Practice* (London: Routledge, 2001), 11. See Richard W. Hallet and Judith Kaplan-Weinger, *Official Tourism Websites: A Discourse Analysis Perspective* (London: Channel View Publications, 2010), 7.

7. Monika Murzyn, "Heritage Transformation in Central and Eastern Europe," in *The Ashgate Research Companion to Heritage and Identity*, ed. Peter Howard P. and Brian Graham (London: Ashgate, 2012), 315–46; Andrzej Tomaszewski, "Europa Środkowa: dobra kultury a dziedzictwo kultury," in *Europa Środkowa—nowy wymiar dziedzictwa,* ed. Jacek Purchla (Kraków: MCK, 2002), 131–36.

8. Wojciech Burszta, *Antropologia kultury: tematy, teoie, interpretacje* (Poznań: Wydawnictwo Zysk i S-ka, 1998), 51.

9. Annette Pritchard and Nigel Morgan, "Representations of 'Ethnographic Knowledge': Early Comic Postcards of Wales," in *Discourse, Communication and Tourism*, eds. Adam Jaworski and Annette Pritchard (Clevedon: Channel View Publications, 2005), 94.

10. Graham Dann, *The Language of Tourism: A Sociolinguistic Perspective* (Wallingford: CABI, 1996). See Richard W. Hallet and Judith Kaplan-Weinger, *Official Tourism Websites;* Sabrina Francesconi, *Reading Tourism Texts: A Multimodal Analysis* (London: Channel View Publications, 2014).

11. Noel B. Salazar and Nelson H. H. Graburn, "Introduction: Towards Anthropology of Tourism Imaginaries," in *Tourism Imaginaries,* 1; Naomi Leite, "Afterword: Locating Imaginaries in the Anthropology of Tourism," in *Tourism Imaginaries,* 260–78.

12. Anna Horolets, *Obrazy Europy w polskim dyskursie publicznym* (Kraków: Universitas, 2006).

13. Milan Kundera, "The Tragedy of Central Europe," *The New York Review of Books*, 26 April 1984. See further Michal Buchowski and Hana Cervinkowa, "On Rethinking Ethnography in Central Europe: Toward the Cosmopolitan Anthropologies in the 'Peripheries'," in *Rethinking Ethnography in Central Europe*, eds. Michał Buchowski, Hana Cervinkova, and Zdenek Uherek (New York: Palgrave Macmillan, 2015), 1–20; Catherine Lee and Robert Bideleux, "East, West, and the Return of 'Central': Borders Drawn and Redrawn," in *The Oxford Handbook of Postwar European History,* ed. Dan Stone (Oxford: Oxford University Press, 2012), 79–97; Simona Škrabec, *Geografia wyobrażona. Koncepcja Europy Środkowej w XX wieku* (Kraków: MCK, 2013); Claudio Magris, *O demokracji, pamięci i Europie Środkowej* (Kraków: MCK, 2016); Emil Brix, *Z powrotem w Europie Środkowej. Eseje i szkice* (Kraków: MCK, 2012); Maria Todorowa, *Balkany wyobrażone* [see chapter "Między klasyfikacją a polityką. *Bałkany i mit Europy Środkowej*/Between Classification and Politics: Balkans and the Myth of Central Europe"] (Wołowiec: Wydawnictwo Czarne, 2008), 301–45.

14. Madina Tlostanova, "Postsocialist ≠ postcolonial? On Post-Soviet Imaginary and Global Coloniality," *Journal of Postcolonial Writing* 46 (2012): 130–42, accessed November 13, 2016, http://www.tandfonline.com/doi/abs/10.1080/17449855.2012.65 8244?journalCode=rjpw20; Jennifer Suchland, "Is Postsocialism Transnational?" *Signs: Journal of Women in Culture and Society* 36 (2011): 837–62; Hana Cervinkova, "Postcolonialism, Postsocialism and the Anthropology of East-Central Europe," *Journal of Postcolonial Writing* 48 (2012): 155–63.

15. Larry Wolff, *Inventing Eastern Europe: The Map of Civilization on the Mind of the Enlightenment* (Stanford, CA: Stanford University Press, 1994).

16. Anna Galasińska and Dariusz Galasiński, *The Post-Communist Condition: Public and Private Discourses of Transformation* (John Benjamins Publishing, 2010).

17. Simona Škrabec, *Geografia wyobrażona.*

18. Noel B. Salazar and Nelson Graburn, eds., *Tourism Imaginaries: Anthropological Approaches* (London: Berghahn, 2014); Maria Gravari-Barbas and Nelson

Graburn, eds. *Tourism Imaginaries at the Disciplinary Crossroads: Place, Practice, Media* (London: Routledge, 2016).

19. Kathryn Bell, "A Comparative Analysis in Projected and Perceived Image of Gloucester," in eds. Caroline Scarles and Jo-Anne Lester, *Mediating the Tourist Experience*, 105–22.

20. The analyzed sources of information are: http://www.bulgariantouristboard. com/; https://www.czechtourism.com/home/; https://www.czechtourism.com/home/; https://www.slovenia.info/en; http://romaniatourism.com/; https://www.polska.travel/ pl; http://gotohungary.com; http://www.germany.travel.

21. Richard W. Hallet and Judith Kaplan-Weinger, *Official Tourism Websites*; Sabina Owsianowska, "Tourism Promotion, Discourse and Identity," *Folia Turistica* 25 (2011): 231–48.

22. Pierre Nora, "Between Memory and History: *Les lieux de mémoire*," *Representations* 26 (1989): 7–25.

23. "Central Europe," Wikitravel: The Free Travel Guide, accessed November 15, 2016, http://wikitravel.org/en/Central_Europe.

24. UNWTO, http://europe.unwto.org/.

25. European Travel Commission, http://www.etc-corporate.org/.

26. http://www.jaywaytravel.com/itineraries.

27. http://www.homerictours.com/central-eastern-europe-travel/central-eastern-europe.asp.

28. http://www.gocollette.com/en/tours/europe/austria/magnificent-cities-of-central--eastern-europe.

29. http://www.mircorp.com/.

30. Sabine Marschall, ed., *Tourism and Memories of Home: Migrants, Displaced People, Exiles and Diasporic Communities* (Bristol: Channel View Publications, 2017); Delphine Bechtel, *Le tourisme mémoriel en Europe centrale et orientale* (Paris: Perta, 2013).

31. The Central Europe Company. Travel Culturally [Kompania Środkowoeuropejska. Podróżuj kulturalnie], accessed November 2016, http://mitteleuropa.pl/.

32. Magdalena Banaszkiewicz, Nelson Graburn, and Sabina Owsianowska, "Tourism in Post-Socialist Eastern Europe," *Journal of Tourism and Cultural Change* 15 (2017): 109–21.

33. Matthew Willis and Jonathan Bousfield, "Eastern & Central Europe," In *Eyewitness Travel Guide* (London: Dorling Kindersley, 2010).

34. Ibidem, 28.

35. Delphine Bechtel, "Le tourisme mémoriel vers la Galicie: retours sur les lieux du conflit interethnique entre Polonais, Ukrainiens et Juifs," in Delphine Bechtel and Luba Jurgenson, *Le tourisme mémoriel en Europe centrale et orientale* (Paris: Petra, 2013), 151–72.

36. Sabine Marschall, ed. *Tourism and Memories of Home.*

37. Anya Diekman and Melanie Smith, eds., *Ethnic and Minority Cultures as Tourist Attractions* (Bristol: Channel View Publications, 2015); Ruth Gruber, *Virtually Jewish: Reinventing Jewish Culture in Europe* (Berkeley: University of California Press: 2002).

38. The Central Europe Company.
39. Sabina Owsianowska, "Tourist Narratives about the Dissonant Heritage of the Borderlands: The Case of South-eastern Poland," *Journal of Tourism and Cultural Change* 15 (2017): 167–84.
40. Tomasz Zarycki, *Ideologies of Eastness in Central and Eastern Europe* (New York: Routledge, 2014), 176.
41. "Central Europe," Wikitravel.
42. Mariusz Czepczynski, *Emancipated Landscapes of Post-socialist Europe* (2007). Document online, accessed November 15, 2016, http://www.rali.boku.ac.at/ila/veranstaltungen-des-ila/archiv-veranstaltungen/lx-landschaft-denken/11-26042007/mariusz-czepczynski/.
43. Magdalena Banaszkiewicz, "A Dissonant Heritage Site Revisited—The Case of Nowa Huta in Krakow," *Journal of Tourism and Cultural Change* 15 (2017): 185–97.
44. Sabina Owsianowska and Magdalena Banaszkiewicz, "Dissonant Heritage in Tourism Promotion: Certified Tourism Products in Poland," *Folia Turistica* 37 (2015): 145–66.
45. Timothy G. Ash, "Europe's True Stories." *Prospect Magazine* 131 (2007): 36–39.
46. Sharon Macdonald, *Memorylands*.
47. Krzysztof Kowalski, "Inventing a Common European Memory: Reflections on the *European Heritage Label* Initiative," in *The Limits of Heritage: The 2nd Heritage Forum of Central Europe*, eds. Katarzyna Jagodzińska and Jacek Purchla (Kraków: International Cultural Centre, 2015), 627–42. See Pierre Nora, "Czy Europa istnieje?," *Gazeta Wyborcza*, August 11, 2007, http://wyborcza.pl/1,76842,4381316.html.
48. So far, twenty-nine sites with the label "European" have been designated, twelve of them are situated in the postsocialist countries, and four more in Austria and Germany. "European Heritage Label," European Commission, accessed March 15, 2017, https://ec.europa.eu/programmes/creative-europe/actions/heritage-label_en.
49. See Banaszkiewicz and Owsianowska, "Anthropological Studies on Tourism in Central and Eastern Europe" (in this book).
50. "Baltic states: please stop calling us *former* Soviet countries," Latvian Public Broadcasting English-language service, accessed January 2017, http://www.lsm.lv/en/article/politics/updated-baltic-states-please-stop-calling-us-former-soviet-countries.a217911/; "Countries or areas/ geographical regions," United Nations, Statistics Division, accessed January 2017, https://unstats.un.org/unsd/methodology/m49/.

REFERENCES

Ash, Timothy Garton. "Europe's True Stories." *Prospect Magazine* 131 (2007): 36–39.
Banaszkiewicz, Magdalena. "A Dissonant Heritage Site Revisited—The Case of Nowa Huta in Krakow." *Journal of Tourism and Cultural Change* 15 (2017): 185–97.

Banaszkiewicz, Magdalena, Nelson Graburn, and Sabina Owsianowska. "Tourism in (Post) Socialist Eastern Europe." *Journal of Tourism and Cultural Change* 15 (2017): 109–21.

"Baltic States: Please Stop Calling us *Former Soviet* Countries." Latvian Public Broadcasting English-language service. Accessed January 2017. http://www.lsm. lv/en/article/politics/updated-baltic-states-please-stop-calling-us-former-soviet-countries.a217911/.

Bechtel, Delphine. "Le tourisme mémoriel vers la Galicie: retours sur les lieux du conflit interethnique entre Polonais, Ukrainiens et Juifs." In *Le tourisme mémoriel en Europe centrale et orientale*, edited by Delphine Bechtel and Luba Jurgenson, 151–72. Paris: Petra, 2013.

Bell, Kathrine. "A Comparative Analysis in Projected and Perceived Image of Gloucester." In *Mediating the Tourist Experience: From Brochures to Virtual Encounters*, edited by Caroline Scarles and Jo-Anne Lester, 105–22. London: Ashgate, 2013.

Buchowski, Michał, and Hana Cervinkova. "On Rethinking Ethnography in Central Europe: Toward the Cosmopolitan Anthropologies in the 'Peripheries.'" In *Rethinking Ethnography in Central Europe*, edited by Michał Buchowski, Hana Cervinkova, and Zdenek Uherek, 1–20. New York: Palgrave Macmillan, 2015.

Burszta, Wojciech. *Antropologia kultury: tematy, teorie, interpretacje.* Poznań: Wydawnictwo Zysk i S-ka, 1998.

Buzalka, Juraj. "Scale and Ethnicity in Southeast Poland: Tourism in the European Periphery." *Etnográfica* 13 (2009): 373–93.

"Central Europe." Wikitravel: The Free Travel Guide. Accessed November 15, 2016. http://wikitravel.org/en/Central_Europe.

"Countries or Areas/Geographical Regions." United Nations, Statistics Division. Accessed January 2017. https://unstats.un.org/unsd/methodology/m49/.

Cervinkova, Hana. "Postcolonialism, Postsocialism and the Anthropology of East-Central Europe." *Journal of Postcolonial Writing* 48 (2012): 155–63.

Czepczynski, Mariusz. *Emancipated Landscapes of Post-socialist Europe* (2007). Document online. Accessed November 15, 2016. http://www.rali.boku.ac.at/ila/veranstaltungen-des-ila/archiv-veranstaltungen/lx-landschaft-denken/l1-26042007/mariusz-czepczynski/.

Dann, Graham. *The Language of Tourism: A Socioliguistic Perspective.* Wallingford: CABI, 1996.

Diekman, Anya, and Melanie Smith, eds. *Ethnic and Minority Cultures as Tourist Attractions.* Bristol: Channel View Publications, 2015.

Edensor, Tim. *National Identity, Popular Culture and Everyday Life.* Oxford: Berg, 2000.

"European Heritage Label." European Commission. Accessed November 15, 2016, https://ec.europa.eu/programmes/creative-europe/actions/heritage-label_en.

Francesconi, Sabrina. *Reading Tourism Texts: A Multimodal Analysis.* London: Channel View Publications, 2014.

Galasińska, Anna, and Dariusz Galasiński. *The Post-Communist Condition: Public and Private Discourses of Transformation.* Amsterdam: John Benjamins Publishing, 2010.

Gravari-Barbas, Maria, and Nelson Graburn, eds. *Tourism Imaginaries at the Disciplinary Crossroads: Place, Practice, Media.* London: Routledge, 2016.

Gruber, Ruth. *Virtually Jewish: Reinventing Jewish Culture in Europe.* Berkeley: University of California Press, 2002.

Hallet, Richard W., and Judith Kaplan-Weinger. *Official Tourism Websites: A Discourse Analysis Perspective.* Bristol: Channel View Publications, 2010.

Jagodzińska, Karolina, and Jacek Purchla, eds. *Limits of Heritage. The 2nd Heritage Forum of Central Europe.* Krakow: International Cultural Center [MCK], 2015.

Jaworski, Adam, and Crispin Thurlow, eds. *Semiotic Landscapes: Language, Image, Space.* London: Continuum, 2010.

Kockel, Ullrich, Máiréad Nic Craith, and Jonas Frykman, eds. *A Companion to Anthropology of Europe.* London: Wiley-Blackwell, 2012.

Kowalski, Krzysztof. "Inventing a Common European Memory: Reflections on the *European Heritage Label* Initiative." In *The Limits of Heritage: The 2nd Heritage Forum of Central Europe*, edited by Katarzyna Jagodzińska and Jacek Purchla, 627–42. Kraków: International Cultural Centre, 2015.

Kundera, Milan. "The Tragedy of Central Europe." *The New York Review of Books*, 26 April 1984.

Lee, Catherine, and Robert Bideleux. "East, West, and the Return of 'Central': Borders Drawn and Redrawn." In *The Oxford Handbook of Postwar European History*, edited by Dan Stone, 79–97. Oxford: Oxford University Press, 2012.

Leite, Naomi. "Afterword: Locating Imaginaries in the Anthropology of Tourism." In *Tourism Imaginaries: Anthropological Approaches*, edited by Noel Salazar and Nelson Graburn, 260–78. London: Berghan Books, 2014.

Macdonald, Sharon. *Memorylands: Heritage and Identity in Europe Today.* London: Routledge, 2013.

Magris, Claudio. *O demokracji, pamięci i Europie Środkowej.* Kraków: MCK, 2016.

Marschall, Sabine, ed. *Tourism and Memories of Home: Tourism and Memories of Home Migrants, Displaced People, Exiles and Diasporic Communities.* Bristol: Channel View Publications, 2017.

Murzyn, Monika. "Heritage Transformation in Central and Eastern Europe." In *The Ashgate Research Companion to Heritage and Identity*, edited by Peter Howard and Brian Graham, 315–46. London: Ashgate, 2012.

Nora, Pierre. "Between Memory and History: Les lieux de mémoire." *Representations* 26 (1989): 7–25.

Nora, Pierre. "Czy Europa istnieje?" *Gazeta Wyborcza*, August 11, 2007, http://wyborcza.pl/1,76842,4381316.html.

Owsianowska, Sabina. "Tourism Promotion, Discourse and Identity." *Folia Turistica* 25/1 (2011): 231–48.

Owsianowska, Sabina. "Tourist Narratives about the Dissonant Heritage of the Borderlands: The Case of South-eastern Poland." *Journal of Tourism and Cultural Change* 15 (2017): 167–84.

Owsianowska, Sabina, and Magdalena Banaszkiewicz. "Dissonant Heritage in Tourism Promotion: Certified Tourism Products in Poland." *Folia Turistica* 37 (2015): 145–66.

Pretes, Michael. "Tourism and Nationalism." *Annals of Tourism Research* 30 (2003): 125–42.

Pritchard, Annette, and Nigel Morgan. "Representations of 'Ethnographic Knowledge': Early Comic Postcards of Wales." In *Discourse, Communication and Tourism,* edited by Adam Jaworski and Annette Pritchard. Clevedon: Channel View Publications, 2005.

Salazar, Noel, and Nelson Graburn, eds. *Tourism Imaginaries: Anthropological Approaches.* London: Berghan Books, 2014.

Scarles, Caroline, and Jo-Anne Lester, eds. *Mediating the Tourist Experience: From Brochures to Virtual Encounters.* London: Ashgate, 2013.

Scolon, Ron. *Mediated Discourse: The Nexus of Practice.* London: Routledge, 2001.

Shohamy, Elana, and Shoshi Waksman. "Building the Nation, Writing the Past: History and Textuality at the *Ha'apala* Memorial in Tel Aviv-Jaffa." In *Semiotic Landscapes: Language, Image, Space,* edited by Adam Jaworski and Crispin Thurlow, 241–55. London: Continuum International Publishing Group, 2011.

Suchland, Jennifer. "Is Postsocialism Transnational?" *Signs: Journal of Women in Culture and Society* 36 (2011): 837–62.

Tlostanova, Madina. "Postsocialist ≠ postcolonial? On Post-Soviet Imaginary and Global Coloniality." *Journal of Postcolonial Writing* 46 (2012): 130–42.

Todorova, Maria. *Bałkany wyobrażone.* Wołowiec: Wydawnictwo Czarne, 2008.

Tomaszewski, Andrzej. "Europa Środkowa: dobra kultury a dziedzictwo kultury." In *Europa Środkowa—nowy wymiar dziedzictwa,* edited by Jacek Purchla, 131–36. Kraków: MCK, 2002.

Tunbridge, John, and Gregory Ashworth. *Dissonant Heritage: The Management of the Past as a Resource in Conflict.* Chichester: Wiley & Sons, 1996.

Vukonić, Boris. "Turning Point in European Tourism Development." In *Tourism in Scientific Research in Poland and Worldwide,* edited by Wiesław Alejziak and Ryszard Winiarski. Krakow: AWF Krakow Press, 2006.

Willis, Matthew, and Jonathan Bousfield. "Eastern & Central Europe." In *Eyewitness Travel Guide.* London: Dorling Kindersley, 2010.

Zarycki, Tomasz. *Ideologies of Eastness in Central and Eastern Europe.* New York: Routledge, 2014.

Part III

ANTHROPOLOGICAL INSPIRATIONS IN TOURISM STUDIES

From the Workshop of Central and Eastern European Researchers

Chapter 8

Here Come the Barbarians

Perceptions of Alcotourism in Golden Sands, Bulgaria

Carla Bethmann

On a warm evening in June 2007,[1] I was sitting in a sidewalk café in the Bulgarian tourist resort of Golden Sands, chatting with Mariya, who was in her sixties and had been working in the tourism industry for forty years.[2] We were talking about the development of tourism in the Varna region, when suddenly our conversation was interrupted by an incredible racket down the street. While I craned to see what was going on, Mariya remained unmoved. "It's just a pub crawl," she said, and indeed the source of the noise soon came into view. It was a large group of young people, all wearing identical T-shirts, surrounded by a wall of noise, and led by a man shouting incomprehensibly into a megaphone. The group passed us, and when it was possible to talk again, Mariya looked at me angrily and burst out, "You see what this place has become? The drinking hole of the European youth. The youngsters who come here only care about cheap booze, parties, and sex. They are like barbarians. No manners, no culture, nothing. It didn't used to be like that. People came here for our culture, our history. Yes, the beach, too. But they cared about other things as well. Now it's just these people who stay for a week in a cheap, all-inclusive hotel, and all they do is lie on the beach during the day and party at night. It breaks my heart to see that."

Three years later, Germany's largest tabloid ran a series that compared Golden Sands and the "Ballermann," a strip of beach bars in Majorca with a reputation for wild parties, dancing, and sex, fueled by copious amounts of alcohol.[3] In the series "Golden Sands: More Riotous Than Ballermann," the Bulgarian resort was painted in glowing colors, as being even wilder and more permissive, yet cheaper than Majorca. The tabloid stated that Golden Sands scored with its "pretty girls" and "organized benders" that included "boozing, snogging and party games with whipped cream." Golden Sands was referred to as "The Ballermann of the East" or "The Balkan-Ballermann," and it was concluded in the tabloid's "Great Party Showdown" that "Golden Sands is much more awesome than Majorca—the women are prettier, the bikinis tinier and, most importantly, the booze is cheaper."[4]

"CHEAP BOOZE" AND "POOR SAVAGES": TOURIST IMAGINARIES OF BULGARIA

This representation of Golden Sands echoed with elements of tourist imaginaries that were widespread in Germany. Bulgaria was imagined as rooted in the communist past, and thus more backward and less civilized than Western Europe. These imaginaries were circulated and reinforced by the media. In the wake of Bulgaria's EU accession, there was a flurry of reports on the country that shared some recurring themes. In one, its poverty was compared to Western Europe, the high incidence of corruption, prostitution, the presence of organized crime, and the high levels of emigration.[5] Similar to other Eastern Europeans, Bulgarians were generally viewed as less cultured and civilized than Western Europeans. For example, men from Eastern Europe were imagined as being heavy, but congenial, drinkers. Women were viewed as beautiful and available, just waiting for their Western Prince Charming.

It is also instructive in this regard to take a look at the "Atlas of Prejudice" by Bulgarian graphic designer Yanko Tsvetkov.[6] It contains a series of satirical cognitive maps of Europe according to the prejudices and stereotypes held by various nations. On the map where German views are depicted, Bulgaria simply bears the legend "Schnapps" [brandy]. From the Russian perspective, it is "Cheap Booze," the Dutch see it as part of the "Whore Belt," and for the French, it is a country of "Poor Savages."

Such stereotypes were promulgated in German media reports on Bulgaria as a tourist destination. These accounts emphasized Bulgaria's affordability compared to other holiday destinations favored by German tourists. However, from the mid-2000s, there also appeared a growing number of articles on the wild partying scene in the country's beach resorts. The gist of these write-ups was the same as in the series quoted above. Bulgarian resorts and clubs were cheap, the women were beautiful, alcohol was free-flowing, and the parties were wild and uninhibited.[7] This triad of alcohol, partying, and sex is also at the center of the academic literature on alcotourism.

TRANSGRESSION AND LIMINALITY: ACADEMIC PERSPECTIVES ON ALCOTOURISM

Like the mass media, the academic literature tends to associate party tourism with binge drinking, drug consumption, wild partying, dancing, flirting, and casual sex. Alcohol is of central importance here, facilitating social interaction, creating social bonds, and lowering inhibitions; hence the term "alcotourism."[8] Alcohol consumption enables people to "relax," "let go," and "let out their wild side." This often segues into transgressive behaviors such as public nudity, casual sex, violence, and the destruction of property. Therefore, both media and academic reports on alcotourism often carry undertones of disapproval and moral panic. They highlight the dangers of excessive alcohol consumption and the behaviors associated with it, as well as the risks to personal and public health, the public order, and general safety and security.[9]

In Europe, the expansion of alcotourism was paralleled by a growing body of research in the academic fields of alcohol studies, tourism studies, and urban studies. Earlier anthropological works on tourism often mentioned alcotourism in passim, but it has only recently become a focus of research.[10] Two main lines of inquiry that are rooted in older themes in tourism anthropology are of particular relevance here.

The first invokes the literature on the construction of places and spaces of consumption. Tourism anthropology has analyzed the construction of tourist space and the complex ways it is used and imbued with meaning by a variety of actors.[11] This approach has been extended to alcotourism, where Ana Maria Munar examined "beer tourism" and the enactment of German identities on the Ballermann;[12] Thomas Thurnell-Read analyzed the negotiation and use of Kraków's urban space by British stag parties;[13] and Hazel Andrews investigated how the Majorcan resorts of Palmanova and Magaluf ("Shagaluf") are imbued with a sense of "effervescent Britishness" through the consumption and bodily practices of British charter tourists.[14]

Another strand of research in the anthropology of tourism has focused on the tourists themselves, their motivations and the meanings of their activities. Here, tourists were variously described as searching for authenticity, for difference, or for an escape from ordinary life. Tourism was investigated as a liminal experience that contrasts with everyday reality.[15] This is also true for alcotourists who seek to leave their mundane lives behind and attain a state of being where ordinary norms and rules no longer apply, and behaviors that are normally viewed as transgressive become perfectly acceptable.[16] The practices of alcotourists are, however, not uncontested; they share tourist spaces with other tourists, tourism workers, and local inhabitants who may well be critical of their hedonistic and transgressive behaviors.

Yet, despite the growing academic interest in alcotourism, scant attention was paid to the perceptions of those who must frequently interact with alcotourists and mediate between them and the local population: the tourism workers. Hence, in this chapter, I will focus on resort workers, their interactions with alcotourists, and their perceptions of them. At the heart of my analysis is a paradox of alcotourism in Golden Sands: on one hand, tourism workers and the tourism industry actively contributed to it and benefited from its development, while, on the other hand, they were, like Mariya, highly critical of it. In order to understand the workers' perspective, it is necessary to first take a brief look at the history of tourism in Golden Sands.

FROM ELITE RESORT TO CHEAP MASS TOURISM DESTINATION: A BRIEF HISTORY OF TOURISM IN GOLDEN SANDS

The history of tourism on the Bulgarian Black Sea coast goes back to the 1950s, when the socialist government built the country's first beach resorts. These were meant to serve the domestic working class, but, from the late 1960s, became a destination for international tourists as well. In the 1970s, Golden Sands experienced a noticeable growth in tourist arrivals.[17] Since socialist Bulgaria viewed rest and recreation as a right of her citizens, a large share were domestic tourists whose holidays were heavily subsidized by the state. The vast majority of international tourists came from other socialist countries in Central and Eastern Europe, but there was also a growing share of tourists from the capitalist West. For the latter, traveling to Bulgaria offered a glimpse of life behind the Iron Curtain, in addition to experiencing the country's cultural and historical sights, beautiful landscapes, and friendly people.[18] The 1980s were considered the "golden years" of tourism by many of the older workers I talked to. International tourist numbers peaked and resort jobs were considered highly desirable, as they offered access to the glamorous resorts and opportunities to interact with foreigners.[19]

Among the citizens of the socialist bloc, Golden Sands enjoyed a reputation as a highly desirable and exclusive destination. Foreign travel was restricted, and for most tourists from Central Europe, the Bulgarian Black Sea coast was the closest they could get to a holiday on a sun-drenched beach. Vacation spots in Golden Sands were limited, and they were distributed through complex barter arrangements between the COMECON states. In fraternal socialist countries like the GDR, the lucky recipients were often well-connected members of the socialist elite, or distinguished workers who were rewarded for their efforts in building the socialist fatherland.[20]

Throughout the socialist period, culture and heritage were important elements of tourism in Golden Sands. This followed from the efforts of socialist countries to divest "high culture" of its elite status and make it accessible to the masses. Culture also played an essential role in the struggle to create a "socialist way of life" and mold a new type of "socialist personality" characterized by "high culture, high intellectual and material needs."[21] In addition, the resorts advertised the achievements of socialism; they were to demonstrate to both domestic and international tourists that socialist Bulgaria met not just the material, but also the intellectual needs of her citizens. This included providing them with opportunities for rest and recreation, as well as for continued self-improvement and personal growth.[22] Hence, throughout the tourist season, there was a plethora of cultural events and offerings in Golden Sands, ranging from folklore, musical, and theater performances, to visits to museums, lectures, and exhibitions, and day trips to sites of cultural and historical interest.

This came to an end with the collapse of socialism across Central and Eastern Europe in 1989–1990. In its wake, tourist arrivals in Bulgaria dropped sharply as a consequence of declining prosperity in the former socialist countries, the violent conflicts in the region, and the economic and political instability of the country.[23] The Bulgarian seaside resorts were privatized at the turn of the century. Privatization was driven by foreign tour operators who invested heavily in the upgrading of existing hotels, and the construction of new ones. Once again, tourist numbers rose dramatically, but the majority of tourists now came from Western Europe, with Germany, the United Kingdom, and Scandinavia providing the strongest segments. The share of tourists from Central and Eastern Europe remained low until the mid-2000s, when the number of Russian arrivals began to grow. Domestic tourism picked up with the recovery of the national economy, but during the high season, the resorts were dominated by international tourists.[24]

Following privatization, Golden Sands experienced massive development. Hotels were growing in size, and the building density in the resort increased. The coastline became increasingly urbanized due to resort expansion and the proliferation of private accommodation and service providers. By the time of my fieldwork, Golden Sands was a mass tourism destination that attracted international tourists looking for sun, sea, and sand, often supplemented by spirits, sex, and savings. The main draw and competitive advantage of the region was its affordability: tour packages to Golden Sands were still considerably cheaper than those to similar destinations in Spain, Greece, or Croatia.[25]

Thus, within the living memory of the older generation of tourism workers, Golden Sands had experienced massive changes in the organization of its tourism industry, the visitors it attracted, its reputation, and the associated tourist imaginaries. Resort workers used narratives and nostalgic memories of tourism under socialism to criticize the transformation of Golden Sands into a cheap mass tourism destination, and challenge its growing reputation as a party hotspot. However, as I will show in the next section, the rejection of party tourism and portrayals of alcotourists as "barbarians" ignored the active participation of the local tourism industry and the resort workers in the construction and development of alcotourism in Golden Sands.

CREATING A "BALKAN-BALLERMANN":
THE CO-CONSTRUCTION OF ALCOTOURISM

The emerging model of alcotourism in Golden Sands was bolstered by three interrelated factors: the structure and organization of the tourism infrastructure, the organization of consumption in the resort, and the economic interests of the resort workers. In this section, each of them will be addressed in turn.

The organization of the tourism infrastructure in Golden Sands facilitated the development and growth of alcotourism. Alcotourists, whether they traveled to Golden Sands, Majorca, or Ibiza, relied on an infrastructure that provided them with cheap flights, cheap hotels, and cheap alcohol. Golden Sands was served by the Varna airport that was connected via regular and charter flights to dozens of airports in Western and Northern Europe and Russia. Flight costs for tourists were low as they either bought their flights as part of the holiday package or used low-cost airlines.

Alcotourism was also facilitated by the affordability of Golden Sands' hotels. Room prices in Bulgaria's resorts were generally low compared to those of similar summer sun destinations in southern Europe; this was a consequence of the lower labor costs in Bulgaria, the oversupply of accommodation, fierce competition, and the strong position of tour operators vis-à-vis hotels. Further discounts were offered to tourists arriving outside the main season of July/August. Therefore, the shoulder season attracted many alcotourists, such as high school students celebrating their graduation.

Golden Sands had a number of hotels specifically targeting young alcotourists. The manager of one of them said, "This hotel has a specific reputation: It's young people who drink, smash things up, and go. . . . The very building and everything in it are designed with these people in mind. Everything is very basic. There are as few things as possible in the rooms, so there is not much they can destroy. We have pool bars and discos, that's all they need."

The prices of tour packages to Golden Sands had also become more affordable with the spread of all-inclusive deals. Hotels offered these packages to benefit from economies of scale, and tourists were able to minimize their costs by paying in advance for everything they would consume. Likewise, tour operators targeting a young clientele offered specialized all-inclusive "party trips" and "party packages" that were advertised as "the wildest week of your life." Besides flights, accommodation in a "party hotel," and meals and drinks, they included events like organized pub crawls, foam parties, and beach parties as well as free or discounted entry to night clubs.

The tourism infrastructure in Golden Sands also provided a wide array of bars, discotheques, clubs, and pubs. As emphasized by the German tabloids, it was their affordability that attracted alcotourists. It arose from lower prices in Bulgaria as compared to tourists' countries of origin. However, while tourists perceived prices in Golden Sands as being low, Bulgarians viewed the resort as exceedingly expensive, and unaffordable by most.

A second factor bolstering alcotourism was the organization of consumption in the resort. As all businesses in Golden Sands sought to earn a profit, tourists were encouraged to consume as much as possible, and that included the consumption of alcohol. Walking through the resort, one was struck by the abundance of restaurants, bars, and pubs, all advertising "special offers." Every single establishment had "happy hours" when drinks were discounted or offered in "buy one, get one free" deals. Restaurants attempted to attract patrons by offering free drinks with any hot meal. There were "ladies' nights," "pre-parties," beach parties, and pub crawls. Local organizers sold package deals and discount cards that gave tourists free entrance to clubs and discotheques, as well as discounts on drinks and food. Touts trying to lure tourists into their venues commonly did so with promises of free or discounted drinks, and all-inclusive packages included free alcoholic drinks as well.

Many forms of organized consumption that had been tried and tested in the well-established Mediterranean party resorts were imported into Golden Sands. One example was the organized pub crawls where, over the course of an evening, groups of participants visited a number of bars and clubs. The ultimate goal of pub crawls was getting completely and utterly drunk, and, to this end, tour guides instigated drinking games and competitions, constantly pressuring participants to drink as much as possible. In line with the emerging reputation of Golden Sands as the "Balkan-Ballermann," clubs and venues from Majorca and Ibiza had opened subsidiaries that were specifically aimed at the alcotourist and partying crowds. They had proven successful in Spain and were now branching out to other partying destinations.

To encourage consumption, laws and regulations were only selectively enforced in the resort. While private security services and the regular police were present, they were mostly concerned with preventing incidents that might disturb the tourists and puncture the tourist bubble. Security forces would oust beggars and unlicensed mobile vendors, but they often turned a blind eye to drunk and aggressive tourists, prostitution (which was illegal at the time of my fieldwork), the consumption of illegal drugs, public nudity, public sex, and other transgressions arising from excessive alcohol consumption. This nurtured a sense of licentiousness that was at the heart of Golden Sands' reputation as a party resort.

A third factor contributing to the pervasiveness of alcotourism was the economic interests of resort workers. Although tourism workers bemoaned the replacement of cultured middle class tourists by young alcotourists, and resented the various problems these tourists created, many of them still encouraged excessive alcohol consumption and contributed to the resort's permissive atmosphere. Alcohol consumption among tourists was actively encouraged by the employees of restaurants, bars, and clubs. Many of these workers earned only a minimum salary, while the majority of their incomes came from tips and commissions. Restaurant and bar employees received a percentage of the daily business turnover, which gave them an incentive to encourage tourists to consume more. A larger bill meant they would receive a larger tip and a larger commission at the end of the day. Drunk customers were also more susceptible to all kinds of scams that benefited servers and business owners, such as shortchanging customers, putting additional items on their bill, or substituting cheap for expensive drinks. Touts were also earning commissions and were thus motivated to persuade tourists to participate in pub crawls, club parties, or other alcohol-fueled events.

Workers' economic interests contributed to the permissive atmosphere prevailing in Golden Sands. Servers and bartenders would interact with tourists in ways the latter perceived as "flirty" in order to increase their tips. Beach boys and girls, as well as resort employees sought affairs with tourists in return for gifts or invitations to nights out. Prostitutes roamed the "party street" looking for customers. Although, officially, hotels did not permit guests to bring prostitutes to their rooms, doormen and front desk employees would look the other way for a tip. And often, resort workers who noticed behaviors or incidents that were not entirely within the boundaries of propriety or, indeed, legality, would turn a blind eye because they did not wish to get involved in any conflicts. They did not view it as their job to police the tourists, and had no desire to get involved in the unpleasantness and potential hassle involved in calling them to order. All this resulted in a sense of "anything goes," encouraging tourists to transgress the boundaries of acceptable and appropriate behavior, seemingly with no particular consequences.

It thus emerges that alcotourism in Golden Sands was facilitated and fueled by the tourism infrastructure, the organization of consumption in the resort, and the economic interests of the resort workers, many of whom benefited financially from at least tacitly encouraging excessive drinking and partying. This raises the question as to why so many workers criticized and challenged the practice of alcotourism and the growing reputation of Golden Sands as a party hotspot.

"PROLES," "PLEBS," AND "BARBARIANS": CONTESTING ALCOTOURISM

Although alcotourism was co-constructed by tourists and resort workers, its growth was contested by workers and business owners in Golden Sands. Their criticism focused on its profitability and on the consequences of tourists' transgressive behavior, and it was underpinned by workers' sense of social class and national identity.

It cannot be doubted that for some groups of resort workers, alcotourists were a profitable source of income. Among them were owners and employees of bars, pubs, clubs, and discotheques, specialized tour operators and the employees of party hotels, as well as individual entrepreneurs like beach boys and prostitutes. However, there were also businesses that lost out, such as agencies organizing day trips and cultural events, the more expensive bars and restaurants, and high-end retailers. The owners and employees of such businesses were critical of the rise of alcotourism because they did not particularly benefit from it.

Most workers and business owners I talked to in Golden Sands complained about declining incomes and revenues. They mourned the loss of the cultured and affluent middle-class tourists of yesteryear, and their replacement by alcotourists and the party-going crowd. In reality, the reasons behind the overall decline of incomes were more complex: resort fragmentation and competition, the oversupply of businesses, the shifting balance of power between hotels and tour operators, the growth of all-inclusive packages, but also changing trends in tourism, as well as conditions in the countries the tourists originated from. Alcotourists, however, made a convenient symbol of many of these trends, as they were indeed less affluent, more likely to be on all-inclusive packages, and more inclined to spend money on only a narrow range of activities. They also stood out, and their high visibility, coupled with their frequently excessive behavior, made them a potent symbol of all that was wrong with tourism in Golden Sands.

But, equally importantly, alcotourists shared the resort space with other, more desirable types of tourists who consumed a wider array of goods and services: pensioners arriving in the shoulder season, couples with children who came in the high season, and middle-class tourists in general. Resort workers feared that the presence and behavior of alcotourists would drive out the remaining "good tourists." The latter would not wish to spend their holidays surrounded by drunk and unruly crowds, and would choose other destinations if the growth of alcotourism continued.

Alcotourism was also criticized because resort workers were directly affected by tourists' transgressive behavior. All workers in frontline service jobs I talked to had at one time or another been slighted, insulted, harassed, or attacked by intoxicated tourists. The most extreme cases of drunk tourists beating up resort workers made it into the media, but, in their daily work, employees routinely defused potential or actual conflicts with tourists. These ranged from aggressive drunks verbally assaulting or threatening workers, to female workers being sexually harassed, to tourists damaging—accidentally or on purpose—property and merchandise. This side of alcotourism was one of the reasons terms like "proles," "plebs," "barbarians," and "trash" were bandied about when resort workers talked about the "new type" of tourists at Golden Sands.

Resort workers' contempt was also rooted in class issues. The vast majority of workers in Golden Sands were highly educated members of the Bulgarian middle class. Foreign language skills were a prerequisite for being hired in the resorts, and many workers held university degrees. They were rich in cultural capital and they scoffed at foreign tourists they perceived as uncultured and poor. However, despite their behavior, and the resulting perceptions formed by resort workers, many alcotourists did, in fact, have a middle-class background. In line with tourist imaginaries of "the Wild East," they viewed and treated Golden Sands as a space that offered release from social constraints and freedom to do all the things they would never even consider doing at home. They were encouraged in this by guides, reps, and entertainers whose role in organized parties was helping tourists overcome their inhibitions.[26]

A final reason why resort workers criticized alcotourism was national pride. Many workers were proud of their country's long history, rich culture and heritage, and its beautiful and modern resorts. They found it insulting that these were all ignored and dismissed by alcotourists who simply saw Golden Sands as a place that had a beach, plenty of discos and bars, and cheap booze. One bar owner said, "We have Scandinavian tourists here who come just for the cheap alcohol. They arrive at the airport and they don't know where they are. They just know they are by the sea, and that their hotel has a pool bar and plenty of alcohol. That's all they care about." Resort workers resented discourses that constructed their country as nothing more than a place where drinks were cheap, parties were wild, and women were pretty. They were offended not just by the actual behavior of tourists, but also by the imaginaries they produced and perpetuated. Compared to the past reputation of Golden Sands, this was seen as a decline.

CONCLUSION: ALCOTOURISM AS A SYMBOL OF DECLINE

Contrary to widespread narratives that likened the growth of alcotourism to a barbarian invasion that the tourism industry and workers in Golden Sands were helpless to prevent, alcotourism was co-constructed. The tourism industry and the resort workers actively contributed to its growth, both out of sheer necessity ("alcotourism is better than no tourism"), and a desire for individual financial gain. Nevertheless, resort workers were highly critical of this "new type" of tourism. Their criticism was based on a number of tangible reasons, such as alcotourists' lower spending, excessive behavior, propensity for conflict and destruction, and the likelihood of them driving out the remaining "good tourists."

I would, however, argue that the trend towards alcotourism was also challenged by tourism workers because it had become a symbol of decline, namely, the decline of their country, their resort, and of resort workers individually and as a social group. For older tourism workers in particular, alcotourism was a constant reminder of the changing image and reputation of Golden Sands. In the course of their working lives, people like Mariya had experienced the resort's transformation from a desirable destination of the socialist elite to a cheap mass tourism destination, and from a favored holiday spot of the cultured middle class to "the drinking hole of the European youth." Workers' awareness of foreign media reports describing Golden Sands as "The Balkan-Ballermann" and "The Wild East," and their perceptions of deteriorating "tourist quality" added to the general sense of loss of resort status and reputation.

Alcotourism was also a potent symbol of the declining social status of resort work. Positions in the international tourist resorts were highly desirable under socialism, when they offered good year-round incomes, in addition to numerous perks and privileges. In the postsocialist period, many resort jobs were seasonal, and the incomes they brought had dropped with the decline in tourist affluence. Resort work had become less desirable and respected; workers felt that some tourists treated them like "servants," "punching bags," and "prostitutes," and many of the highly trained and experienced members of the hospitality industry had left and found work elsewhere.

The tensions between alcotourists and tourism workers were exacerbated by the diverging levels of cultural and economic capital the two groups possessed. Golden Sands was a tourist space where a highly educated and cultured workforce met and interacted with alcotourists who chose to behave like "proles" and "plebs" for the duration of their holidays. Irrespective of tourists' actual levels of income and education, on the basis of their behavior, they were perceived by resort workers as being uneducated, ill-mannered, and of a lower class. Yet, these tourists were able to pay for a holiday in a resort that had become unaffordable to many Bulgarians, including those who worked in the tourism industry. This highlighted the relative social decline of resort workers who, despite their superior levels of education and culture, did not possess the affluence of the Western tourists or the local newly rich. Ultimately, this situation was a symptom of the downward social mobility among the educated Bulgarian middle class, whose relative social and economic status had declined in the previous two decades.

Finally, alcotourism was also viewed as symptomatic of Bulgaria's loss of international reputation and status. The country that was once a valued member of the socialist camp was now imagined by foreigners as a poor, corrupt, crime-ridden place at the margins of Europe. Bulgaria used to be a desirable holiday destination offering history, culture and heritage, in addition to sunny beaches. Now, it was depicted as a country of wild parties, cheap booze, and easy sex; a place where common rules of civilized behavior could be suspended, and tourists could do whatever they pleased.

The contested practice of alcotourism was thus paralleled by contested imaginaries. On the one hand, Western European alcotourists imagined Bulgaria as an underdeveloped country on the European periphery with an exuberant drinking and partying culture. Economic, cultural, and civilizational backwardness were closely linked in Western tourist imaginaries: Bulgaria was constructed as a poor and wild country where the rules of civilized behavior did not apply, and where it was perfectly acceptable for tourists to let loose. It was simply assumed that in the interest of maintaining flows of tourists and currency, the more excessive and transgressive aspects of alcotourism would be ignored.

From the perspective of resort workers, on the other hand, it was the alcotourists who lacked culture and civilization. This was shown by their low interest in Bulgaria's culture and heritage, as well as by their hedonistic and transgressive behavior in Golden Sands. But like the tourists, workers were also acutely aware of existing economic inequalities. They knew that, for the time being, they were indeed dependent on the revenues derived from alcotourism. No matter how they felt about it, for the foreseeable future, they would have to cope with the annual invasion of "Western barbarians."

NOTES

1. The material in this chapter was collected in thirteen months of ethnographic fieldwork carried out on eight trips to the Varna region between June 2004 and October 2008. In addition to participant observation and numerous informal talks and conversations, I also conducted sixty-two semi-structured interviews with people working in the tourism industry. They were held in Bulgarian, German, or English, according to the preferences of the interviewees, recorded with their permission, and later transcribed and translated. All direct quotations in this chapter are excerpts from these interviews.

2. I am grateful to the tourism workers in the Varna region who contributed to this research by taking the time to share their stories and experiences and answer my numerous questions. To protect their identities, all names in this chapter were replaced by pseudonyms. I also wish to thank the editors of this book for their helpful comments and suggestions. Last but not least, a big thank you goes to Anke Reichenbach and Mehrdad Mozayyan for carefully reading and commenting on the draft of this chapter. All remaining mistakes are, of course, my own.

3. See: Sacha Szabo, *Ballermann – Das Buch. Eine wissenschaftliche Analyse eines ausseralltaeglichen Erlebnisses* (Marburg: Tectum Verlag, 2011).

4. "Goldstrand – Wilder als der Ballermann. Mallorca oder Bulgarien – der grosse Party-Vergleich," *Bild*, September 6, 2010, accessed September 8, 2010, http://www.bild.de/reise/2010/goldstrand-bulgarien-mallorca-party-vergleich-wild-13798006.bild.html.

5. E.g. Renate Flottau, "Bulgarien: Im Wuergegriff der Mafia," *Spiegel Online*, April 22, 2008, accessed April 22, 2008, http://www.spiegel.de/panorama/justiz/bulgarien-im-wuergegriff-der-mafia-a-548353.html; Johannes Voswinkel, "Das Recht des bösen Wolfs. EU-Erweiterung I: Warum Bulgarien, einst der Musterschüler des Balkans, in Korruption und Lethargie stecken bleibt," *Die Zeit*, May 11, 2006.

6. Yanko Tsvetkov, *Atlas of Prejudice*, Vol. 1, no. 1 (Create Space Independent Publishing Platform, 2013).

7. E.g. Mikka Bender, "Amore in Italien, Doener in der Turkei? Klischees!" *Die Welt*, June 26, 2012; Elena Lalowa, "Bulgariens Schwarzmeerkueste: Reiseziel Exzess," *Spiegel Online*, September 26, 2010, accessed September 26, 2010, http://www.spiegel.de/reise/aktuell/bulgariens-schwarzmeerkueste-reiseziel-exzess-a-719411.html.

8. David Bell, "Destination Drinking: Toward a Research Agenda on Alcotourism," *Drugs: Education, Prevention and Policy* 15 (2008): 291–304.

9. See the overview in Ilse van Liempt et al., "Introduction: Geographies of the Urban Night," *Urban Studies* 52 (2015): 413–14. See also: Sébastien Tutenges and Morten Hesse, "Patterns of Binge Drinking at an International Nightlife Resort," *Alcohol and Alcoholism* 43 (2008): 595.

10. Juxtaposing tourists and barbarians is also not new to tourism anthropology. Thus, in *The Golden Hordes: International Tourism and the Pleasure Periphery* (London: Constable, 1975), Louis Turner and John Ash compared tourists to barbarian invaders that destroy local cultures and livelihoods. Unlike Turner and Ash, however, my Bulgarian interlocutors did not condemn mass tourism as a destructive force, nor did they label all tourists as barbarians. Their criticism was aimed at a specific tourist segment, namely, alcotourists. Other tourist segments were highly welcome. In fact, objections to alcotourism were, among other things, based on fears that it might drive out more desirable sun, sea, and sand tourists, such as families or the elderly.

11. Simon Coleman and Mike Crang, eds., *Tourism: Between Place and Performance* (New York: Berghahn, 2002).

12. Ana Maria Munar, "Sun, Alcohol and Sex: Enacting Beer Tourism," in *The Global Brewery Industry: Markets, Strategies, and Rivalries*, ed. Jens Gammelgaard and Christoph Dörrenbächer (Cheltenham, UK: Edward Elgar, 2013).

13. Thomas Thurnell-Read, "Tourism Place and Space: British Stag Tourism in Poland," *Annals of Tourism Research* 39 (2012): 801–19.

14. Hazel Andrews, *The British on Holiday: Charter Tourism, Identity and Consumption* (Bristol, UK: Channel View Publications, 2011).

15. Nelson H. H. Graburn, "The Anthropology of Tourism," *Annals of Tourism Research* 10 (1983): 9–33.

16. E.g. Daniel Briggs, *Deviance and Risk on Holiday: An Ethnography of British Tourists in Ibiza* (Basingstoke, UK: Palgrave Macmillan, 2013).

17. N. Enev, "Razvitie na turizma vav varnenski okrag," *Izvestiya: Spisanie na visshiya institut za narodno stopanstvo 'Dimitar Blagoev'—Varna* 2 (1984): 14–25.

18. Francis W. Carter, "Bulgaria," in *Tourism and Economic Development in Eastern Europe and the Soviet Union*, ed. D. R. Hall (London: Belhaven Press, 1991).

19. See also: Kristen Ghodsee, *The Red Riviera: Gender, Tourism, and Postsocialism on the Black Sea* (Durham, NC: Duke University Press, 2005).

20. Heike Wolter, *'Ich harre aus im Land und geh, ihm fremd' – Die Geschichte des Tourismus in der DDR* (Frankfurt: Campus, 2009).

21. Ulf Brunnbauer, "Making Bulgaria Socialist: The Fatherland Front in Communist Bulgaria, 1944–1989," *East European Politics and Societies* 22 (2008): 56.

22. Lothar A. Kreck, "Tourism in Former Eastern European Societies: Ideology in Conflict with Requisites," *Journal of Travel Research* 36 (1998): 62–67.

23. Marin Bachvarov, "End of the Model? Tourism in Post-Communist Bulgaria," *Tourism Management* 18 (1997): 43–50.

24. Marin Bachvarov, "Tourism in Bulgaria," in *Tourism in the New Europe: The Challenges and Opportunities of EU Enlargement*, ed. D. Hall et al (Wallingford, UK: CABI, 2006).

25. Carla Bethmann, *'Clean, Friendly, Profitable'? Tourism and the Tourism Industry in Varna, Bulgaria* (Münster: LIT, 2013).

26. See also: Sébastien Tutenges, "Stirring Up Effervescence: An Ethnographic Study of Youth at a Nightlife Resort," *Leisure Studies* 32 (2013): 233–48.

REFERENCES

Andrews, Hazel. *The British on Holiday: Charter Tourism, Identity and Consumption*. Bristol, UK: Channel View Publications, 2011.

Bachvarov, Marin. "End of the Model? Tourism in Post-Communist Bulgaria." *Tourism Management* 18 (1997): 43–50.

———. "Tourism in Bulgaria." In *Tourism in the New Europe: The Challenges and Opportunities of EU Enlargement*, edited by Derek Hall, Melanie Smith, and Barbara Marciszewska, 241–55. Wallingford, UK: CABI, 2006.

Bell, David. "Destination Drinking: Toward a Research Agenda on Alcotourism." *Drugs: Education, Prevention and Policy* 15 (2008): 291–304.

Bender, Mikka. "Amore in Italien, Doener in der Turkei? Klischees!" *Die Welt*, June 26, 2012.

Bethmann, Carla. *'Clean, Friendly, Profitable'? Tourism and the Tourism Industry in Varna, Bulgaria*. Münster: LIT, 2013.

Bild. "Goldstrand – Wilder als der Ballermann. Mallorca oder Bulgarien – der grosse Party-Vergleich." *Bild*, September 6, 2010. Accessed September 8, 2010. http://www.bild.de/reise/2010/goldstrand-bulgarien-mallorca-party-vergleich-wild-13798006.bild.html.

Briggs, Daniel. *Deviance and Risk on Holiday: An Ethnography of British Tourists in Ibiza*. Basingstoke, UK: Palgrave Macmillan, 2013.

Brunnbauer, Ulf. "Making Bulgaria Socialist: The Fatherland Front in Communist Bulgaria, 1944–1989." *East European Politics and Societies* 22 (2008): 44–79.

Carter, Francis W. "Bulgaria." In *Tourism and Economic Development in Eastern Europe and the Soviet Union*, edited by Derek R. Hall, 220–35. London: Belhaven Press, 1991.

Coleman, Simon, and Mike Crang, eds. *Tourism: Between Place and Performance*. New York: Berghahn, 2002.

Enev, N. "Razvitie na turizma vav varnenski okrag." *Izvestiya: Spisanie na visshiya institut za narodno stopanstvo 'Dimitar Blagoev'* – Varna 2 (1984): 14–25.

Flottau, Renate. "Bulgarien: Im Wuergegriff der Mafia." *Spiegel Online*, April 22, 2008. Accessed April 22, 2008. http://www.spiegel.de/panorama/justiz/bulgarien-im-wuergegriff-der-mafia-a-548353.html.

Ghodsee, Kristen. *The Red Riviera: Gender, Tourism, and Postsocialism on the Black Sea*. Durham, NC: Duke University Press, 2005.

Graburn, Nelson. "The Anthropology of Tourism." *Annals of Tourism Research* 10 (1983): 9–33.

Kreck, Lothar A. "Tourism in Former Eastern European Societies: Ideology in Conflict with Requisites." *Journal of Travel Research* 36 (1998): 62–67.

Lalowa, Elena. "Bulgariens Schwarzmeerkueste: Reiseziel Exzess." *Spiegel Online*, September 26, 2010. Accessed September 26, 2010. http://www.spiegel.de/reise/aktuell/bulgariens-schwarzmeerkueste-reiseziel-exzess-a-719411.html.

Munar, Ana Maria. "Sun, Alcohol and Sex: Enacting Beer Tourism." In *The Global Brewery Industry: Markets, Strategies, and Rivalries*, edited by Jens Gammelgaard and Christoph Dörrenbächer, 310–33. Cheltenham, UK: Edward Elgar, 2013.

Szabo, Sacha. *Ballermann – Das Buch. Eine wissenschaftliche Analyse eines auseralltaeglichen Erlebnisses*. Marburg: Tectum Verlag, 2011.

Thurnell-Read, Thomas. "Tourism Place and Space: British Stag Tourism in Poland." *Annals of Tourism Research* 39 (2012): 801–19.

Tsvetkov, Yanko. *Atlas of Prejudice*. Vol. 1, no. 1. Create Space Independent Publishing Platform, 2013.

Turner, Louis, and John Ash. *The Golden Hordes: International Tourism and the Pleasure Periphery*. London: Constable, 1975.

Tutenges, Sébastien. "Stirring Up Effervescence: An Ethnographic Study of Youth at a Nightlife Resort." *Leisure Studies* 32 (2013): 233–48.

Tutenges, Sébastien, and Morten Hesse. "Patterns of Binge Drinking at an International Nightlife Resort." *Alcohol and Alcoholism* 43 (2008): 595–99.

van Liempt, Ilse, Irina van Aalst, and Tim Schwanen. "Introduction: Geographies of the Urban Night." *Urban Studies* 52 (2015): 407–21.

Voswinkel, Johannes. "Das Recht des bösen Wolfs. EU-Erweiterung I: Warum Bulgarien, einst der Musterschüler des Balkans, in Korruption und Lethargie stecken bleibt." *Die Zeit*, May 11, 2006.

Wolter, Heike. *'Ich harre aus im Land und geh, ihm fremd'* – *Die Geschichte des Tourismus in der DDR*. Frankfurt: Campus, 2009.

Chapter 9

Making Tourists Engaged by Vulnerable Communities in India

Natalia Bloch

The residents of Dharamshala and Hampi—two popular tourist destinations in India—are subjected to power structures imposed on them by both postcolonial state and international regimes. In the case of Dharamshala, this is "the international refugee regime,"[1] strongly rooted in what Liisa Malkki calls "the national order of things,"[2] which makes statelessness an inferior form of existence in the face of citizenship. In the case of Hampi, the regime is that of UNESCO and its attendant Eurocentric concept of material heritage preservation,[3] shared by the Archaeological Survey of India, a body created by the British in the colonial era, which is presently responsible for maintaining archaeological remains "of national importance."[4] Despite being vulnerable, Tibetan refugees from Dharamshala and the evicted residents of Hampi try to exercise agency, employing varied and nuanced strategies to achieve their goals.

This chapter aims to demonstrate how tourism can be skillfully used by local communities to overcome their subalternity. It reveals that encounters between "hosts" and "guests"—long-studied within the anthropology of tourism[5]—have the potential to empower the former. I analyze this empowering use of tourism in relation to both the political struggles of subaltern communities and their collective social benefits. In other words, I examine the strategies employed by vulnerable communities to engage tourists as their allies and supporters on a level more nuanced than simply generating individual profits.

The power relations inscribed into tourism have been widely studied by cultural anthropologists.[6] In the early stage of tourism studies' development, the workings of tourism were often perceived through the opposition of domination and subordination as neocolonial and neoliberal practices associated with the commodification of culture, the instrumentalization of social relations, environmental degradation, and the fostering of global economic

181

inequalities.[7] Today many researchers trace the continuity of colonial discourse in tourist imaginaries and representations of the Other,[8] often referring to the concept of Orientalism.[9] However, employing postcolonial theory as an analytical framework for tourism studies[10] and acknowledging tourism in postcolonial countries as part of the colonial legacies[11] enable us to overcome a binary approach that reduces tourists to superficial consumers of mystifications and local communities to passive victims of the tourists' imaginations. The postcolonial critique cuts across the dichotomous divide between the (former) colonizer and the (post-)colonized Other, thus unveiling the ambiguity of the power relations involved. It attempts to recover "the voice of the subaltern,"[12] to be sensitive to less obvious, more nuanced forms of agency. In this chapter, I argue that tourism can serve as a platform for such an exercise.

The fall of the Iron Curtain offered scholars from Central and Eastern Europe the opportunity to research parts of the world that had previously been described only by so-called "First World" scholars. I believe that the experience of being in a subaltern position makes one particularly sensitive to the issues of power structures and the subtle ways these structures are challenged. The postcolonial perspective, along with the bottom-up position employed in an anthropological research, offer insight into the complex and dynamic relations that take place between tourists and their "hosts" on a level of everyday interactions.[13] It embraces both power and agency, the global and the local.[14]

This chapter is based on ethnographic fieldwork conducted within a multisited research project in 2013 and 2014 between Dharamshala in the northern state of Himachal Pradesh and Hampi in the southern state of Karnataka, India.[15] Both these sites provide primarily budget services to mostly individual tourists or those traveling in small groups, and as such create a "heterogeneous space" where tourists and locals get a chance to mingle and where their worlds overlap.[16] This gives anthropologists a great opportunity to employ "deep hanging-out" research technique,[17] that is, roaming around, making friends, meeting friends' friends, being invited and taking part in events, and moving back and forth between tourists, tourism service providers, and other members of host communities. I spent five months in each field site, trying to grasp the perspective of the "hosts" on tourism. This fieldwork was combined with mobile ethnography conducted among tourists.[18]

SETTING THE STAGE

Dharamshala: Refugee Settlement as a Tourist Highlight

Dharamshala, and more specifically its upper part called McLeod Ganj,[19] was a hill station that served British soldiers and their families as a summer spot to escape the heat of the Indian plains. When India won her independence, the Parsi family, which had been providing supplies to the British since the middle of the nineteenth century, was unsure about how to revitalize the area. Therefore, when the first Indian prime minister Jawaharlal Nehru was searching for a site to settle newly arrived refugees from Tibet, the Parsis proposed McLeod Ganj as a suitable place. The fourteenth Dalai Lama and the first group of Tibetans arrived at the hill station in 1960. Since then Dharamshala has been the seat of the exile government and the "capital" of the Tibetan diaspora, with approximately 5,000 refugees inhabiting McLeod Ganj and another 8,000 living in the surrounding areas. After the Dalai Lama was awarded the Nobel Peace Prize in 1989, foreign tourists started visiting McLeod Ganj, many in search of Buddhist spirituality. Their presence attracted other migrants who now work as providers of goods and services. However, Tibetans, as non-Indian citizens even in the second and third generation, are not allowed to purchase land or real estate. In most cases, they are forced to live and run their enterprises on a rental basis, which to some extent limits their access to profits from tourism.

Hampi: "Living" versus Material Heritage

Hampi was the capital of the now-ruined Hindu Vijayanagara kingdom, founded in the fourteenth century and abandoned soon after the invasion of the local sultanates two centuries later. However, it is believed that worship in the Virupaksha Temple has endured and the place continues to be an important pilgrimage destination in Southern India, a "living temple."[20] In the 1940s severe droughts in neighboring areas brought people desperately seeking job opportunities to Hampi, where they settled, initially within the temple walls. When their number increased, many of them began occupying the *mandapas*, that is, colonnaded pavilions that originally accommodated a market, lining the main bazaar in front of the Virupaksha Temple. Apart from farming, they provided services to pilgrims, selling souvenirs, food, and drinks.

Following the discovery of the area by hippies in the 1970s, and the designation of Hampi as a World Heritage Site by UNESCO in 1986, foreign tourists started visiting the site. As a consequence, most residents gave up less profitable farming and shifted toward the tourism sector, turning their dwellings—in and around the *mandapas*—into family-run guest houses, eateries, and shops to serve the needs of backpackers. However, since 2011, under the pretext of a lawsuit in the High Court of Karnataka and orders from the local executive authority, an ongoing eviction of people has been taking place, followed by demolition of their homes and enterprises. The Eurocentric paradigm of material heritage conservation prevailing since the colonial era has led to the stigmatization of Hampi residents as those who have posed a threat to the national and global heritage.[21] Also the anti-colonial, Occidentalist perspective on tourism as moral contamination employed by Hindu leaders has legitimized the partial removal of tourism service providers from Hampi.[22] To date, almost two-thirds of the village population of two and a half thousand have been displaced.

ENGAGING TOURISTS FOR A POLITICAL CAUSE

Political Souvenirs and Awareness Talks

Dharamshala itself is an outstanding example of refugees' agency, as they have managed to turn a refugee settlement into a popular tourist destination. Many Tibetans living in McLeod Gunj earn their day-to-day living from tourism by operating guest houses, restaurants, bakeries, shops, and stalls. But the presence of tourists is used by Tibetans in many other ways. First of all, foreigners visiting this Indian hill station are engaged into the struggle for a Tibet's cause. Tourism here is employed in the diaspora's identity politics as a platform to strengthen the image of Tibetan culture as exceptional and distinct from that of the Chinese, and to build knowledge of the political goals of the Tibetan exile community. Therefore, a significant number of souvenirs available on the local tourist market refer to the "Free Tibet" slogan. As a result, one can observe tourists wearing T-shirts that call for us to "Stand for Tibet," or pronounce the wearer is "Proud to be a Tibetan"; one can also find them carrying cotton bags with the motif of the Tibetan national flag and umbrellas that encourage us to "Save Tibet." "Free Tibet" has become a brand featured on caps, hats, scarves, jackets, stickers, and laptop covers. The creativity in this cultural and political production seems to be unlimited. One producer, for instance, adapts global capitalist brands into Tibetan ones, making the North Face or Coca-Cola call for "Free Tibet." Another one calls for boycotting products made in China by changing the slogan to "Made in Tibet." Although obviously commodified, these engaged souvenirs raise awareness of the Tibetan cause, and tourists are strongly encouraged to purchase them to support the community and its political goals. Even if they do not, they still remain an audience for the Tibetans' political self-representations, as national symbols and political statements are omnipresent in the tourist space of Dharamshala. Young refugees, practicing everyday nationalism,[23] employ them on their garments, motorbikes, and tattoos. These are used to decorate stores, hotel reception desks, and restaurants. Even passwords for wireless internet—"gototibet," "savetibet," or "tibetwillbefree"—carry a political message that tourists simply cannot escape.

Moreover, many events organized by Tibetan refugees for their international guests are educational in character. One of the numerous NGOs in

Dharamshala screens documentaries twice a week, mostly on human rights violations in Tibet, while serving dinner that provides the organization with financial support. On Tuesdays tourists can attend a meeting with a former political prisoner. On Wednesdays another NGO organizes lectures—called "awareness talks"—with Power Point presentations on the history of Tibet's independence and Chinese occupation, during which tea and snacks are served. One of the last slides asks on behalf of the tourist audience: "How can I support Tibet?," and then provides answers:

> *Be a member of different NGOs to know more about Tibet.*
> *Give gifts that are Tibet related such as scarves, prayer flags etc.*

> *Wear T-shirts, scarves and something which is Tibetan* [the speaker comments: "There are many people already tired of helping Tibetan people. When they see other guys wearing a 'Free Tibet' T-shirt, they will be encouraged, you will give them new energy. It is like a handshake with those who support Tibetans"].

> *Write articles on your blog, Facebook, local newspaper, school magazine etc.*
> *Organize events such as screening documentary, talks etc.*

> *Put Tibet stickers wherever you can* [the speaker comments: "If you place such a sticker on your laptop, on your car or in the bus, then people who will see it may one day sit down in front of their computers and google 'Free Tibet'"].

> *Donate time, money and ideas.*
> *Become a volunteer.*

In a nearby café, run by newly arrived refugees, jam sessions take place on the occasion of *Lhakar*,[24] that is, White Wednesday. It is a movement initiated in Tibet and aimed at cultural resistance by doing "something Tibetan"—such as wearing traditional dress, speaking Tibetan, doing shopping in Tibetan stores—on every Wednesday, which is considered to be an auspicious day for the Dalai Lama.[25] Tourists are encouraged to participate in *Lhakar* by listening to Tibetan songs performed by local Tibetans. The food served during such events is also an interesting reinterpretation of Tibetan "traditional" cuisine: *momo*,[26] steamed dumplings, are stuffed with Nutella, and "Tibetan pizza" is on the menu.

Both the NGOs and the exile government organize political tours in Dharamshala for foreign and Indian tourists, mostly students. Such political tourism aims at involving the participants in the cause (otherwise, as one NGO activist said, "The tourists come here, and when they leave, the only thing they know about Tibet is *momo*"), while skillfully playing up the more conventional, natural, and cultural attractions of Dharamshala. One such tour is advertised in this way:

> If you want to explore Tibet's current political situation and experience its socio-cultural heritage, the Little Lhasa program will be a great opportunity for you. We will spend one week in beautiful McLeod Ganj, learning about the different organizations within the Tibet movement, meeting activists, Tibetan government in exile and monks and nuns. You will also have time to explore the amazing natural surroundings of the Himalayan mountains, visit Buddhist monasteries and eat traditional Tibetan food.[27]

How important this tourism is for Tibetan political elites proves that participants have personal meetings not only will the local NGO activists, but also with respected former political prisoners, and even with the head of the exile government himself.

Some researchers suggest that making Buddhism the main export product of the Tibetan diaspora is a reinterpretation of the historical *chö-yon*,[28] that is, "patron-priest" relationship. It was a distinctive political and cultural institution based on reciprocity: the lay external ruler—initially Mongol, then Manchurian—offered the Tibetan high religious leaders and their schools care and protection (including military one), while the latter in return offered their patrons spiritual services (and legitimization of their rule).[29] Tibetan refugees seem to perceive their relationships with the so-called "West"—and the various stakeholders that constitute "the international refugee regime"—in a similar way. Creating seductive self-representations they offer "to the world" the precious heritage of Tibetan Buddhism, expecting in return support for their political cause.[30] As such they do not position themselves as those who beg for help, but as equal partners in this symbolic exchange. Tourists, perceived as representatives of "the West," are involved in this local practice of reciprocity, transformed into a new political context.[31] I would even argue that they are made morally obliged by their Tibetan "hosts" to become engaged. For the tourists themselves, the events described above add value to their experience, making their holidays something more than just a pleasure.[32] Taking part in tours as that of "Little Lhasa" gives them a chance to transform themselves from being simply "see-ers"—those who merely consume places visually[33]—into real "doers," if ones recalls the imagined hierarchy that tourists visiting Dharamshala construct to distinguish the former from the latter.[34]

Campaigning and Advocating

In an effort to prevent eviction and demolition of their homes and premises, the inhabitants of Hampi also engage tourists in their struggle against the authorities. With the help of a Bangalore-based NGO that works for sustainable tourism, villagers have attempted to resist the manner in which they have been stigmatized as illegal encroachers commercially exploiting the national heritage. To do that they countered the idea of "dead monuments" with the concept of "living heritage," of which they feel a part. Tourists were invited to support this resistance. During the demolition of the bazaar in 2011, tourists spoke to the media about the unique atmosphere that the people of Hampi had brought to this place. One tourist from Australia, who had befriended one of the guest house owners, initiated the "Save Hampi People" campaign on Facebook. Together they created a video that revealed abuses of power by the authorities against the local people and called for international support: "This short documentary film has been made as a direct appeal to UNESCO to step in now and stop the demolition of Hampi's long-established community." On the video Hampi was presented not only as a set of monuments, but also as "a vibrant community who has lived and worked here for generations" and who "preserves Hampi's intangible cultural heritage," while "evidence from the Vijayanagara Empire shows Hampi as a living community with a busy bazaar . . . full of people selling all kinds of goods." One of the arguments employed to support villagers' claims to the site and its heritage was that "we created Hampi as a safe and welcoming place for tourists."[35] Under the "Save the village of Hampi and the citizens life" petition to UNESCO, created on the change.org website by a guest from the United States, tourists expressed their support in comments, such as: "Save the people of Hampi like the Architecture. They are living treasures"; "I visited Hampi just recently, and loved it. The people, the atmosphere, the sights, the markets, is what makes Hampi. . . . People lived there 600 years ago. Why not now. Preservation is one thing, but to make it a deserted coffin is not the feel anyone wants."[36]

Hampi residents present themselves as those who in fact developed the site, creating not only a necessary tourist infrastructure—when no authorities were there to do so—but also making a friendly atmosphere that attracted tourists. Tourists, therefore, are positioned on the same side of the barricades as the local people in their struggle against the authorities. On the video they express their sympathy and support directly: "I have talked to some of the people in the town who are being forced to move. One guy spent his life from having a street stall to finally renting a tiny shop. He's so distressed. It distresses you [when] hearing the story"; "Although we can understand that it's supposed to be an archaeological site, we really hope the people of Hampi can keep their little businesses."[37]

In some cases, this declared support took a more concrete form. When the most disadvantaged among the evicted residents moved to a shack encampment set up on the outskirts of their former village, another tourist from Australia collected money to purchase metal beds that people could survive nights when monsoon flooded their shelters.

ENGAGING TOURISTS INTO DIRECT WORK
FOR THE BENEFIT OF THE COMMUNITY

Reciprocal Spaces of Volunteer Tourism

Engaging tourists in community-based initiatives is another example of the agency exercised by the inhabitants of Dharamshala and Hampi. Dharamshala is literally packed with local NGOs which existence is based on volunteer tourism. They seek tourists to volunteer for different kinds of work, such as child-care, web design, public relations, or simply office work, but mostly volunteers are needed for capacity building, such as teaching languages and computer skills. Although everybody admits that long-term volunteers are the most valued, those who come on a drop-in basis are very welcome. One of the NGOs—Tibet World—states it clearly in its flyer: "Needed Volunteers! Appreciate to join with us, no matter how long you can, do volunteer." Thus, every tourist who comes to Dharamshala can become a volunteer, even for a couple of days or hours. The previously mentioned events, such as "movie and Tibetan pizza night" or "talk with a former political prisoner and noodles," are aimed not only at spreading awareness of Tibet's cause, but also at recruiting volunteers. As one young Tibetan announced at the end of a "movie night": "And tomorrow at 2 p.m. we have English conversation classes, you are all welcome, you don't have to do anything, just show up."

In the last few years the number of NGOs offering language—mostly English, but also French and German—classes to refugees has increased to such an extent that Dharamshala has become known in India as a place where one can attend conversation classes with foreigners for free. Only one single organization claims that during its six years of existence it scrolled almost 9,000 volunteers from sixty-five countries. It seems that supply has exceeded demand, and one can see unemployed volunteers roaming around Dharamshala, trying to find at least part-time jobs in various NGOs. Initially, these organizations were created in order to support the adaptation process of the newcomers from Tibet by improving their language skills. However, the mass protests and the crackdown in Tibet in 2008 drastically reduced the number of newly arriving refugees due to a very strict border control by Chinese and the political situation in Nepal which used to be a transit country for Tibetans on their way to India. As a result now the conversation classes serve largely to monks, in many cases already born in India, who lacked foreign languages education in monasteries and want to study English to "speak about Buddhism to the world." This declared motivation reflects the idea behind the "patron-priest" relationship, which I have already discussed. Among the students there are also Ladakhis, Sikkimese, Mongolians, Burmese, and Thais—all those who "look Tibetan" and have Buddhist background. They exercise their own agency, trying to participate in the benefits from tourism that the Tibetanness generates.

The phenomenon of international volunteer tourism—along with the concept of development it often supports[38]—has been widely criticized, mostly for continuing the "civilizing mission" of European colonialism by imposing the ideas of modernization developed in the societies of the Global North onto the rest of the world. It has been argued that it may even contribute toward maintaining global economic inequalities, as poverty in an aestheticized and depoliticized form seems to be the main factor which attracts tourists.[39] Tibetan refugees, however, do not construct their attractiveness to the tourists on the basis of poor economic condition, but on their pride in their unique culture and just political struggle. As a result, they are perceived as "rich refugees" by some members of the host society.[40] There is also an issue of leakage, when volunteers' money goes to organizations that specialize in volunteers' enrollment—money that, if contributed directly to the community, could be used more efficiently, for instance, to employ local labor.[41] This, however, does not as yet relate to Dharamshala, as most of the NGOs operating there are grassroots organizations directly recruiting volunteers and most of which do not charge fees for the opportunity to be involved.[42] Tibetans themselves define their goals, although they try to adjust to "global standards" (such as speaking English or being technically skilled). Still, these NGOs are generally community-based initiatives, such as Tibet Hope Centre, which aims at "building confident, self-sufficient individuals" and declares in its mission that it seeks to "empower refugees with education, language skills, and resources for continued nonviolent resistance to China's occupation of Tibet."[43] This quotation shows how the social and political goals of the Tibetan diaspora combine, and how volunteer work performed by tourists on behalf of community members is at the same time perceived as a support for a Tibet's cause.

One could of course question the teaching efficiency of such a language education, given the volunteers' usual lack of professional skills and experience, and their high rotation. However, if looked at from another angle, volunteer tourism brings different benefits as well. Conversation classes, for instance, provide a platform for informal, interpersonal encounters, giving students who are not directly involved in the tourism sector access to foreigners. Such contacts are often later fostered on other levels and have the potential to transform into reciprocal relationships. Friendships or love relations that are the outcomes of these encounters provide Tibetans with diversified social networks, cultural capital,[44] and even financial support, and may result in emigration to a "better world."[45] In other words, local NGOs have created a space for reciprocity in a similar way to how trekking expeditions help Sherpas in Nepal build reciprocal commitments with Westerners that result in sponsorships and invitations to the tourists' home countries.[46] As such they have the potential to empower unprivileged individuals whose sociopolitical position is an outcome of the community's vulnerability. For tourists, in turn, this provides both a chance for non-commodified interactions with locals, thus fulfilling their need for "hot authenticity,"[47] and an opportunity to become "new moral tourists."[48]

Moving between Charity and Tourism

Similar processes take place in Hampi. Although much smaller than Dharamshala, and not as focused on volunteer tourism, it has created its own organizations which are strongly supported by tourists, their work, and donations. The NGOs themselves are often the outcomes of the tourists and locals' mutual encounters. The NGO from Dharamshala that organizes "documentary and *momo* nights" was started by a young Tibetan man and his then Australian girlfriend. The trust from Hampi that supports children from disadvantaged families (after the evictions particularly those from a shack encampment) was founded by a local tourist guide and his friend, a British tourist, who provided funds for renting a guest house to accommodate a child daycare center. Both Australian tourists who engaged themselves in supporting the struggle of Hampi people against evictions had volunteered at this NGO. The trust's director told me that he considered new projects, this time to support elder people or even street dogs. He moved smoothly between the sectors of charity and tourism. The job of a tourist guide—working both in English and French—gave him an access to tourists and an opportunity to win sponsors and volunteers (when we first met—and he did not yet know that I was not a "typical" tourist—he asked me what I thought about the trust; I answered that it was fine, but there was very little space for children; he reacted immediately: "So when you come back home, you may find some sponsors for a bigger building!"). This can also work in an opposite way: the NGO tag helps the man to acquire customers for his newly opened restaurant. This is a quite common situation in Hampi, where most community-based activities are combined with tourism. It is often the contacts with tourists and the opportunities they offer in regard to social, cultural, and financial capital that inspire local people to start an NGO.

CONCLUSIONS

These few examples from two different tourist destinations in India demonstrate that tourism has a potential to contribute to overcoming the structural constraints imposed on local residents by various regimes. Both vulnerable communities—the Tibetan refugees in Dharamshala and the Indian inhabitants of Hampi facing eviction—use the presence of tourists to support their political goals and their communities' well-being. They employ reciprocal strategies to build bonds with tourists, which might then be transformed into both symbolic and material capital. As such they are "active agents responding to the opportunities available to them."[49] Tourists, on the other hand, receive authentic, intimate, and non-commodified experiences they search for, thereby adding meaningfulness to their holidays. Instead of being merely superficial tourists, they become—albeit temporarily—supporters of a just cause, teachers, and step-parents. The residents of Dharamshala and Hampi, aware of this desire—called by Kristin Lozanski a "desire to be desired"[50]—provide tourists with the "self-development programmes,"[51] and at the same time benefit from them. In other words, they skillfully appeal to the phenomenon of the "moralization of tourism" and the imperative it imposes on tourists to become "new moral tourists," that is, culturally sensitive, globally responsible, and politically aware.[52] The fact that the residents of Dharamshala and Hampi are able to use tourism that it could operate to their advantage, is related to the character of tourism itself. Contrary to postcolonial countries which have primarily developed "enclave tourism" that separates "hosts" from "guests,"[53] the high level of heterogeneity which characterizes most of the tourist spaces in India offers the residents a relatively democratic access to foreigners and an opportunity to personally interact with them. This not only enables local communities to integrate with the tourism market,[54] but also provides them with intangible benefits which can be employed to overcome their subalternity and vulnerability.

NOTES

1. Gil Loescher, "The International Refugee Regime," *Journal of International Affairs* 47, no. 2 (1994); Gil Loescher, *Beyond Charity: International Co-operation and the Global Refugee Crisis* (Oxford: Oxford University Press, 1993); see: Aristide R. Zolberg, Astri Suhrke, and Sergio Aguayo, *Escape from Violence: Conflict and the Refugee Crisis in the Developing World* (Oxford: Oxford University Press, 1989), 3–33.
2. Liisa H. Malkki, "Refugees and Exile: From 'Refugee Studies' to the National Order of Things," *Annual Review of Anthropology* 24 (1995).
3. Thomas H. Eriksen, "Between Universalism and Relativism: A Critique of UNESCO Concept of Culture," in *Culture and Rights: Anthropological Perspectives*, ed. Jane K. Cowan, Marie-Bénédicte Dembour, and Richard A. Wilson (Cambridge: Cambridge University Press, 2001).
4. Natalia Bloch, "Evicting Heritage: Spatial Cleansing and Cultural Legacy at the Hampi UNESCO Site in India," *Critical Asian Studies* 48 (2016): 556–78, accessed September 23, 2016, doi:10.1080/14672715.2016.1224129; see: Helaine

Silverman, ed., *Contested Cultural Heritage: Religion, Nationalism, Erasure, and Exclusion in a Global World* (New York: Springer, 2011).

5. See: Valene L. Smith, ed., *Hosts and Guests: The Anthropology of Tourism* (Oxford: Blackwell, 1977) and Valene L. Smith and Maryann Brent, eds., *Hosts and Guests Revisited: Tourism Issues in the 21st Century* (New York: Cognizant Communication Corporation, 2001).

6. Donald V. L. Macleod and James G. Carrier, eds., *Tourism, Power and Culture: Anthropological Insights* (Bristol, UK: Channel View Publications, 2010).

7. Theron A. Nuñez, "Tourism, Tradition, and Acculturation: Weekendismo in a Mexican Village," *Ethnology* 2 (1963); Louis Turner and John Ash, *The Golden Hordes: International Tourism and Pleasure Periphery* (London: Constable, 1975); Dennison Nash, "Tourism as a Form of Imperialism," in *Hosts and Guests: The Anthropology of Tourism*, ed. Valene L. Smith (Oxford: Blackwell, 1977). There was, however, a contrary tendency to see international tourism as a tool of development and a key player in poverty alleviation. See discussions on this issue: George Young, *Tourism: Blessing or Blight?* (Harmondsworth, UK: Penguin Books, 1973); Emanuel de Kadt, ed., *Tourism: Passport to Development?* (New York: Oxford University Press, 1979).

8. Noel B. Salazar, "Tourism Imaginaries: A Conceptual Approach," *Annals of Tourism Research* 39 (2012); Noel B. Salazar and Nelson Graburn, eds., *Tourism Imaginaries: Anthropological Approaches* (Oxford: Berghahn Books, 2014).

9. Edward W. Said, *Orientalism* (New York: Vintage Books, 1978).

10. C. Michael Hall and Hazel Tucker, eds., *Tourism and Postcolonialism: Contested Discourses, Identities and Representations* (London: Routledge, 2004).

11. Benoît de L'Estoile, "The Past as It Lives Now: An Anthropology of Colonial Legacies," *Social Anthropology* 16 (2008).

12. Gayatri Ch. Spivak, "Can the Subaltern Speak?" in *Marxism and the Interpretation of Culture*, ed. Cary Nelson and Lawrence Grossberg (Basingstoke, UK: Macmillan Education, 1988).

13. See: Tim Winter, *Post-Conflict Heritage, Postcolonial Tourism: Culture, Politics, and Development at Angkor* (London: Routledge, 2007).

14. Compare the main principles of a hopeful tourism approach based on an engaged critical tourism enquiry: Annette Pritchard, Nigel Morgan, and Irena Ateljevic, "Hopeful Tourism: A New Transformative Perspective," *Annals of Tourism Research* 38 (2011), 950.

15. The project was financed by the National Science Center, Poland, decision number DEC-2011/03/B/HS2/03488.

16. Tim Edensor, *Tourists at the Taj: Performance and Meaning at a Symbolic Site* (London: Routledge, 1998), 41–68, 149–80.

17. James Clifford, *Routes: Travel and Translation in the Late Twentieth Century* (Cambridge, MA: Harvard University Press, 1997), 351. The term "deep hanging-out" was used by Renato Rosaldo during a conference on the meaning of the anthropological "field" in a postmodern context. This situation was recalled by Clifford in his book. See also: Graeme Rodgers, "'Hanging out' with Forced Migrants: Methodological and Ethical Challenges," *Forced Migration Review* 21 (2004).

18. Natalia Bloch, "Overheating with Authenticity: Between Familiarity and Otherness in Multisensory Experiencing of India by Tramping Tourists," *Déjà Lu* 4 (2016), accessed February 25, 2016, http://www.wcaanet.org/dejalu/.

19. This is the name given after Lieutenant Governor of Punjab, a British official who administrated the area during the colonial era.

20. John M. Fritz and George Michell, *City of Victory: Vijayanagara, the Medieval Hindu Capital of Southern India* (New York: Aperture Press, 1991); Anila Verghese, *Hampi: Monumental Legacy* (New Delhi: Oxford University Press, 2002).

21. Bloch, "Evicting Heritage."

22. Natalia Bloch, "Barbarians in India: Tourism as Moral Contamination," *Annals of Tourism Research* 62 (2016): 64–77.

23. Natalia Bloch, *Urodzeni uchodźcy. Tożsamość pokolenia młodych Tybetańczyków w Indiach* [Born Refugees: The Identity of the Young Generation of Tibetans in India] (Wrocław: Wydawnictwo Uniwersytetu Wrocławskiego, 2011), 523–39.

24. In Wylie's transliteration: *lhag dkar*. Turrell V. Wylie, "A Standard System of Tibetan Transcription," *Harvard Journal of Asian Studies* 22 (1959).

25. Tenzin Dorjee, "Why *Lhakar* Matters: The Elements of Tibetan Freedom," *Tibetan Political Review*, January 10, 2013, accessed November 25, 2015, http://www.tibetanpoliticalreview.org/articles/whylhakarmatterstheelementsoftibetanfreedom.

26. In Wylie's transliteration: *mog mog*.

27. "Little Lhasa 2012. Explore the Home of the Dalai Lama," Students of a Free Tibet India Official Blog, accessed September 12, 2015, https://lhasarising.wordpress.com/2012/05/01/little-lhasa-2012-explore-the-home-of-the-dalai-lama/.

28. In Wylie's transliteration: *mchod yon*.

29. Tsepon W. D. Shakabpa, *Tibet: A Political History* (New Haven, CT: Yale University Press, 1967), 64–70; Dawa Norbu, *China's Tibet Policy* (Richmond, UK: Curzon Press, 2001), 7.

30. Paul Christiaan Klieger, *Tibetan Nationalism: The Role of Patronage in the Accomplishment of a National Identity* (Berkeley, CA: Folklore Institute, 1992), 84–120.

31. See Vincanne Adams, *Tigers of the Snow and Other Virtual Sherpas: An Ethnography of Himalayan Encounters* (Princeton, NJ: Princeton University Press, 1996).

32. Jim Butcher, *The Moralisation of Tourism. Sun, Sand . . . and Saving the World?* (London: Routledge, 2003).

33. John Urry, *The Tourist Gaze: Leisure and Travel in Contemporary Societies* (London: Sage Publications, 1990); John Urry, *Consuming Places* (London: Routledge, 1995).

34. Eric McGuckin, "Postcards from Shangri-la: Tourism, Tibetan Refugees, and the Politics of Cultural Production" (PhD diss., New York University, 1997), 361–62.

35. All quotations come from the "Save Hampi People" video: https://www.youtube.com/watch?v=N9docvUG0mM, accessed November 23, 2015.

36. The quotations come from the comments to the "Save the village of Hampi and the citizens life" petition: https://www.change.org/p/unesco-save-the-village-of-hampi-and-the-citizens-life, accessed November 25, 2015.

37. All quotations come from the "Save Hampi People" video: https://www.youtube.com/watch?v=N9docvUG0mM, accessed November 23, 2015.

38. Kate Simpson, "'Doing Development': The Gap Year, Volunteer-tourists and a Popular Practice of Development," *Journal of International Development* 16 (2004).

39. Mary Mostafanezhad, "The Politics of Aesthetics in Volunteer Tourism," *Annals of Tourism Research* 43 (2013); see John Hutnyk, *The Rumour of Calcutta: Tourism, Charity, and the Poverty of Representation* (London: Zed Books, 1996), 56–57.

40. Audrey Prost, "The Problem with 'Rich Refugees,' Sponsorship, Capital, and the Informal Economy of Tibetan Refugees," *Modern Asian Studies* 40 (2006).

41. Jim Butcher and Peter Smith, "'Making a Difference': Volunteer Tourism and Development," *Tourism Recreation Research* 35 (2010), 33.

42. Only the oldest NGO charges fees for additional services it provides, such as pick-up service from the Delhi airport, accommodation in the form of a homestay, or taking part in excursions.

43. Tibet Hope Centre, accessed November 28, 2016, http://www.chicagomanualofstyle.org/tools_citationguide.html.

44. It is usually the tourist volunteers who are perceived as being motivated by the need to accommodate cultural capital (see Sue Heath, "Widening the Gap: Pre-University Gap Years and the 'Economy of Experience'," *British Journal of Sociology of Education* 28 (1997)), while this motivation may also refer to the members of host communities.

45. See Stanley Cohen and Laurie Taylor, *Escape Attempts: The Theory and Practice of Resistance to Everyday Life* (Harmondsworth, UK: Penguin Books, 1978). One NGO, Tibet Hope Centre, openly admits: "Each year, there [are] around 300 students leave[ing] the center with fluent English and now many of them are in Europe, US, Canada and many are working [in] the town in different job positions" (accessed November 28, 2016, http://tibethopecenterindia.blogspot.in/p/our-project.html).

46. Adams, *Tigers of the Snow*, 206–32.

47. Tom Selwyn, introduction to *The Tourist Image: Myth and Mythmaking in Tourism* (Chichester, UK: Wiley, 1996).

48. Butcher, *The Moralisation of Tourism*, 5–30, 77–94.

49. Kristin Lozanski, "Defining 'Real India': Representations of Authenticity in Independent Travel," *Social Identities* 16 (2010): 751.

50. Lozanski, "Defining 'Real India'," 756.

51. Anna Wieczorkiewicz, *Apetyt turysty. O doświadczaniu świata w podróży* [*The Tourist Taste: On Experiencing the World during Travel*] (Kraków: Universitas, 2008), 251.

52. Butcher, *The Moralisation of Tourism*.

53. Tilman G. Freitag, "Enclave Tourism Development: For Whom the Benefits Roll," *Annals of Tourism Research* 21 (1994).

54. Harold Goodwin, "Pro-poor Tourism: A Response," *Third World Quarterly* 29, no. 5 (2008): 869.

REFERENCES

Adams, Vincanne. *Tigers of the Snow and Other Virtual Sherpas: An Ethnography of Himalayan Encounters.* Princeton, NJ: Princeton University Press, 1996.

Bloch, Natalia. *Urodzeni uchodźcy. Tożsamość pokolenia młodych Tybetańczyków w Indiach* [*Born Refugees: The Identity of the Young Generation of Tibetans in India*]. Wrocław: Wydawnictwo Uniwersytetu Wrocławskiego, 2011.

———. "Overheating with Authenticity: Between Familiarity and Otherness in Multisensory Experiencing of India by Tramping Tourists." *Déjà Lu* 4 (2016). Accessed February 25, 2016. http://www.wcaanet.org/dejalu/.

———. "Evicting Heritage: Spatial Cleansing and Cultural Legacy at the Hampi UNESCO Site in India." *Critical Asian Studies* 48 (2016): 556–78.

———. "Barbarians in India: Tourism as Moral Contamination." *Annals of Tourism Research* 62 (2016): 64–77.

Butcher, Jim. *The Moralisation of Tourism: Sun, Sand . . . and Saving the World?* London: Routledge, 2003.

Butcher, Jim, and Peter Smith. "'Making a Difference': Volunteer Tourism and Development." *Tourism Recreation Research* 35 (2010): 27–36.

Clifford, James. *Routes: Travel and Translation in the Late Twentieth Century.* Cambridge, MA: Harvard University Press, 1997.

Cohen, Stanley, and Laurie Taylor. *Escape Attempts: The Theory and Practice of Resistance to Everyday Life.* Harmondsworth, UK: Penguin Books, 1978.

de Kadt, Emanuel, ed. *Tourism: Passport to Development?* New York: Oxford University Press, 1979.

de L'Estoile, Benoît. "The Past as It Lives Now: An Anthropology of Colonial Legacies." *Social Anthropology* 16 (2008): 267–79.

Dorjee, Tenzin. "Why *Lhakar* Matters: The Elements of Tibetan Freedom." *Tibetan Political Review*, January 10, 2013. Accessed November 25, 2015. http://www.tibetanpoliticalreview.org/articles/whylhakarmatterstheelementsoftibetanfreedom.

Edensor, Tim. *Tourists at the Taj: Performance and Meaning at a Symbolic Site.* London: Routledge, 1998.

Eriksen, Thomas H. "Between Universalism and Relativism: A Critique of UNESCO Concept of Culture." In *Culture and Rights: Anthropological Perspectives*, edited by Jane K. Cowan, Marie-Bénédicte Dembour, and Richard A. Wilson, 127–48. Cambridge: Cambridge University Press, 2001.

Freitag, Tilman G. "Enclave Tourism Development: For Whom the Benefits Roll." *Annals of Tourism Research* 21 (1994): 538–54.

Fritz, John M., and George Michell. *City of Victory: Vijayanagara, the Medieval Hindu Capital of Southern India.* New York: Aperture Press, 1991.

Goodwin, Harold. "Pro-poor Tourism: A Response." *Third World Quarterly* 29 (2008): 869–71.

Hall, C. Michael, and Hazel Tucker, eds. *Tourism and Postcolonialism: Contested Discourses, Identities and Representations.* London: Routledge, 2004.

Heath, Sue. "Widening the Gap: Pre-University Gap Years and the 'Economy of Experience'." *British Journal of Sociology of Education* 28 (1997): 89–103.

Hutnyk, John. *The Rumour of Calcutta: Tourism, Charity, and the Poverty of Representation*. London: Zed Books, 1996.

Klieger, P. Christiaan. *Tibetan Nationalism: The Role of Patronage in the Accomplishment of a National Identity*. Berkeley, CA: Folklore Institute, 1992.

Loescher, Gil. *Beyond Charity: International Co-operation and the Global Refugee Crisis*. Oxford: Oxford University Press, 1993.

———. "The International Refugee Regime." *Journal of International Affairs* 47 (1994): 351–77.

Lozanski, Kristin. "Defining 'Real India': Representations of Authenticity in Independent Travel." *Social Identities* 16 (2010): 741–62.

Macleod, Donald V. L., and James G. Carrier, eds. *Tourism, Power and Culture: Anthropological Insights*. Bristol, UK: Channel View Publications, 2010.

Malkki, Liisa H. "Refugees and Exile: From 'Refugee Studies' to the National Order of Things." *Annual Review of Anthropology* 24 (1995): 495–523.

McGuckin, Eric. "Postcards from Shangri-la: Tourism, Tibetan Refugees, and the Politics of Cultural Production." PhD diss., New York University, 1997.

Mostafanezhad, Mary. "The Politics of Aesthetics in Volunteer Tourism." *Annals of Tourism Research* 43 (2013): 150–69.

Nash, Dennison. "Tourism as a Form of Imperialism." In *Hosts and Guests: The Anthropology of Tourism*, edited by Valene L. Smith, 33–47. Oxford: Blackwell, 1977.

Norbu, Dawa. *China's Tibet Policy*. Richmond, UK: Curzon Press, 2001.

Nuñez, Theron A. "Tourism, Tradition, and Acculturation: Weekendismo in a Mexican Village." *Ethnology* 2 (1963): 347–52.

Pritchard, Annette, Nigel Morgan, and Irena Ateljevic. "Hopeful Tourism: A New Transformative Perspective." *Annals of Tourism Research* 38 (2011): 941–63.

Prost, Audrey. "The Problem with 'Rich Refugees,' Sponsorship, Capital, and the Informal Economy of Tibetan Refugees." *Modern Asian Studies* 40 (2006): 233–53.

Said, Edward W. *Orientalism*. New York: Vintage Books, 1978.

Salazar, Noel B. "Tourism Imaginaries: A Conceptual Approach." *Annals of Tourism Research* 39 (2012): 863–82.

Salazar, Noel B., and Nelson H. H. Graburn, eds. *Tourism Imaginaries: Anthropological Approaches*. Oxford: Berghahn Books, 2014.

Selwyn, Tom. "Introduction." In *The Tourist Image: Myth and Mythmaking in Tourism*, edited by Tom Selwyn, 1–32. Chichester, UK: Wiley, 1996.

Shakabpa, Tsepon W. D. *Tibet: A Political History*. New Haven, CT: Yale University Press, 1967.

Silverman, Helaine, ed. *Contested Cultural Heritage: Religion, Nationalism, Erasure, and Exclusion in a Global World*. New York: Springer, 2011.

Simpson, Kate. "'Doing Development': The Gap Year, Volunteer-tourists and a Popular Practice of Development." *Journal of International Development* 16 (2004): 681–92.

Smith, Valene L., ed. *Hosts and Guests: The Anthropology of Tourism*. Oxford: Blackwell, 1977.

Smith, Valene L., and Maryann Brent, eds. *Hosts and Guests Revisited: Tourism Issues in the 21st Century*. New York: Cognizant Communication Corporation, 2001.

Spivak, Gayatri Ch. "Can the Subaltern Speak?" In *Marxism and the Interpretation of Culture*, edited by Cary Nelson and Lawrence Grossberg, 271–313. Basingstoke, UK: Macmillan Education, 1988.

Turner, Louis, and John Ash. *The Golden Hordes: International Tourism and Pleasure Periphery*. London: Constable, 1975.

Urry, John. *The Tourist Gaze: Leisure and Travel in Contemporary Societies*. London: Sage Publications, 1990.

———. *Consuming Places*. London: Routledge, 1995.

Verghese, Anila. *Hampi: Monumental Legacy*. New Delhi: Oxford University Press, 2002.

Wieczorkiewicz, Anna. *Apetyt turysty. O doświadczaniu świata w podróży* [*The Tourist Taste: On Experiencing the World during Travel*]. Kraków: Universitas, 2008.

Winter, Tim. *Post-Conflict Heritage, Postcolonial Tourism: Culture, Politics, and Development at Angkor*. London: Routledge, 2007.

Wylie, Turrell V. "A Standard System of Tibetan Transcription." *Harvard Journal of Asian Studies* 22 (1959): 261–67.

Young, George. *Tourism: Blessing or Blight?* Harmondsworth, UK: Penguin Books, 1973.

Zolberg, Aristide R., Astri Suhrke, and Sergio Aguayo. *Escape from Violence: Conflict and the Refugee Crisis in the Developing World*. Oxford: Oxford University Press, 1989.

Chapter 10

"Tasting East?" Food in Polish Travel Accounts from Russia

Encounters, Sensual Experience, and Cultural Discourses

Agata Bachórz

WHY FOOD AND WHAT KIND OF FOOD?

The purpose of this chapter is to explore culinary themes as a dimension of travel experience from postsocialist Poland to Russia. I was interested in the ways of presenting culinary topics in oral and written travel narratives of Poles going to Russia. Both the tourist observations of local food and their interpretations of their own bodily experiences (what is the taste of local food? how does it influence the body?) were taken into consideration. Emotional descriptions of hospitality and shared meals consumed with local residents were included too. More importantly, I attempt to explain how these culinary motifs are inscribed into a more general and complex Polish image of the Russian Federation.

Culinary topics as strongly intertwined with tourist experience have already been discussed by scholars. Food and mobility overlap in various configurations, dealing with questions related to personal and collective identity, intercultural relations, locality and globalization, time and space.[1] This results from the fact that sensory perception is not merely a physical act, but a culturally constructed process.[2] Eating has become important in tourism analysis due to culturally structured dietary habits anchored to destinations accompanied by the fact that some degree of contact with local food is unavoidable and often desirable. Food is literally incorporated in (tourists') bodies.[3] This is the reason why a potential for overcoming embodied barriers and therefore modifying individual identity is inevitably inscribed in tourism, despite the declining role of food aversions and taboos in the global world.[4]

Collective, shared meals also create a context for encounters or—at least—provide an opportunity to build a narrative about them. Images of shared meals "evoke the sense of returning to pure, unmediated relations"[5] between hosts and guests. Contact with other people's food symbolizes contact between cultures—from cosmopolitan "games" with easily acceptable otherness, symbolic domination over cultures expressed by the act of metaphorical consumption of the Other, to overcoming deeply rooted distances.[6] Due to their multi-sensual character, experiences connected to dining and cuisine are also particularly important as means of contesting mass tourism patterns and therefore a way of achieving the sense of authenticity.[7]

While the senses are used to build meanings of places,[8] cuisine is not only a frame and metaphor for encounters between people and cultures, but also helps to express relations to space and time. Tension between food products' connection to a place (as a part of local heritage, which, due to biological characteristics, is not always suitable for transportation) and their mobility (may be in certain circumstances carried as gifts and tourist souvenirs) seems to be important, too. Descriptions of foreign flavors included in travel narratives have become a way of expressing distances and borders, as well as constituting wider symbolic geographies.[9] They also contribute to understanding of time by becoming a medium for memory.[10]

Heterogeneous culinary experience of tourists detaches from bodies of individuals, either by becoming a medium for stories about the place, time, and people or by blending into ready-made cultural narratives about them.

Therefore, this chapter looks at Russian food perceived by tourists not through the prism of its importance for individual biographies, as in the case of gastronomic tourism in its relation to the identity of cosmopolitan tourists.[11] At the forefront of this chapter are both collective and discursive dimensions of sensory experiences. I am interested in how historically formed cultural discourses—in this case, particular Central European discourses framed in the postcolonial perspective—become an "actor" mediating between people's encounters, sensual sensations, and emerging narratives.

Empirical material for this chapter has been gathered during research conducted in 2008–2011, which has already found its detailed discussion.[12] The general aim of the study was to understand Russia as a tourist destination perceived by contemporary Poles. Thus, the study of tourism served as a starting point to analyze the meaning of Russia in transforming Polish social reality. In this chapter, I refer to the same sources, focusing on the passages that relate to food and eating. The main core of the study consisted of twenty-eight individual in-depth interviews with people of different ages (between twenty and fifty) who traveled as tourists to Russia after the collapse of the Soviet Union. Particular destinations of my interviewees were varied, but only four of them limited their experience to the European part of the country (mostly Moscow or Sankt Petersburg), whereas the majority chose Siberia or Russian North (with a large share of mountain hiking). Interviewees were mostly backpackers; however, other types of tourists were also included. What they had in common was the fact that they traveled by local means of transport and—in the case of the vast majority (twenty-five)—the independent character of the trip undertaken.

The interviews were complemented by the analysis of travel writing—books by Polish authors who described their trips to Russia after 1991 (the original analysis consisted of seventeen books; in this chapter, however, I quoted only some of them and included books published after the original research). The written narratives, similarly to the interviews, mostly concerned non-European, rural, often peripheral areas of Russia, while metropolitan areas turned out to be rather underrepresented.

In both cases—interviews and books—it must be remembered that I refer to what people say or write, which is only the part of their experience considered worth recalling and narratively processed, that is, interpreted by tourists themselves. The configuration of both hosts' and guests' determinants, expectations, and limits allowed access to certain kinds of food, while it closed access to other kinds. The analysis of the cuisine tourists encounter on their way takes into account not only Russian internal tensions between local and global (for example, both growing interest[13] and distrust[14] toward foreign cuisines), but also characteristics of the particular model of traveling and chosen destinations' profile. Independently organized, budget tours in non-urbanized areas with limited or developing tourist infrastructure dominating in the empirical material conduced to a particular type of culinary experience.

Based on the material gathered, it is also difficult to discuss Russian national cuisine as a clear and coherent construct. The visited territory is naturally and culturally diverse (with a visible proportion of non-Russian ethnic groups), while the Polish tourists' routes, however clearly repeatable, run across more than one location. Cuisine—national or regional—understood as a ready-made "message" created by hosts and experts and targeted at clearly defined guests is not the case here either.

What is more, for Poles, the food is neither the principal attraction nor the main purpose of visiting Russia (as it is in the case of culinary tourism in the narrow sense). On the contrary, the culinary experience is rather the "side effect" of activities growing from diverse motivations, while the food-related topics represent only a small part of more complex narratives. A certain randomness of culinary choices results from the logistics of travel. It is intertwined with the importance of observing residents' daily lives typical for this model of traveling (e.g., in a Trans-Siberian train), accompanied by the imitation of local consumption practices or direct participation in them (in people's homes, during common repasts, etc.).

Tourist observations, however, relate to several types of food. Firstly (perhaps the most frequently mentioned and most eagerly associated with a journey to Russia), it is easily accessible home-like food offered usually by small, bottom-up (sometimes informal and not legalized) entrepreneurship (e.g., pastries with fillings, smoked or dried fish, self-grown fruits and vegetables, simple home dinners—potatoes and meat or dumplings are very popular among tourists, but also snacks or beer sold with an additional profit margin). This kind of trade is commonly associated with Trans-Siberian railway platforms, although similar street stalls appear in other places, such as Baikal resorts. Open-air markets can also be included in this category. Secondly, tourists observe and eat industrial food products at local stores (also locally adapted global supermarkets) and various booths. In the narratives, they are not described in detail since they are labeled as "usual," but some products may be mentioned either because of their otherness, unavailability at home, or their connection to the place and good memories. Thirdly, restaurants and local bistros are not entirely absent in the narratives. For various reasons, however, the places are usually not of a high standard. Fourthly, some participants of the study and book authors mention situations of being hosted in private or semiprivate areas (invitations to local people's homes, summer houses, workplaces, campfires, etc.). The issue of food products brought from Poland, not so uncommon, is deliberately omitted in this chapter.[15]

In the narratives and interviews, tourists obviously refer to food remembered as tasty; however, this is not the only reason to recall culinary experiences. Sometimes the link between particular meals and places may become more important than the taste itself (e.g., smoked fish may be "ordinary" in flavor, but it gains added meaning by becoming the nostalgic symbol of a stay on Baikal Lake). Moreover, experiences of dislike, disgust, and food uncertainty are particularly important in the case of this destination, where the food has been adapted by the tourism industry to the needs of tourists in a very limited way.[16] In general, negative or insecure feelings toward food may metonymically express the complexity of social relationships and hierarchies,[17] but also induce the positively evaluated risk,[18] which is afterward reinterpreted as an adventure.

In the collected material, culinary encounters are a mixture of contradictory elements with blurred boundaries: private and public, pleasure and disgust, disinterestedness and commodification, locality and universalization. They participate in constructing the image of "Russian cuisine" and "Russian culinary heritage" arising among tourists actively interpreting accidental or deliberately induced experiences. This image, however, is gaining coherence within the framework that takes into account the historically shaped Polish-Russian relations.

RUSSIA AS A TOURIST DESTINATION—
RUSSIA IN POLISH CONSCIOUSNESS?

Tourism from Poland to Russia (and other countries of the former Soviet Union) has been recently recognized as niche.[19] Russia should be seen as a rather unpopular destination, poorly mirrored in tourism statistics and declining after 2004.[20] Political transformation has been reflected clearly in people's choices related to leisure, consumption, and trajectories of mobility. Since the 1990s Poles have not only been more likely to travel, but there has also been a growing tendency to choose foreign destinations, which were for many people under socialism the unavailable objects of aspiration,[21] namely, Western and Southern European countries.[22] At the same time, postcommunist countries (with exceptions, such as Croatia or neighboring Czech and Slovakia) ceased to attract Poles and lost their status as attractive destinations. Despite opening for foreigners some parts of the former Soviet Empire after 1991, in common perception Slavic East, Russia in particular, is hardly associated with vacation spots. It should be noted that this results not only from a shift in cultural orientation, but also from a change of mobility regimes in Europe after the collapse of the Soviet Union and EU enlargement, especially after 2004, when the opening of the Western borders for Poles was accompanied by implementation of a visa regime to Russia and Belarus.

Despite the small quantitative scale of the mobility flow in this direction, it is not omitted by tourism studies due to strong cultural meanings that go far beyond tourism as such.[23] I assume that understanding of the phenomenon must be sought beyond the field of tourism, consumption, and leisure studies. I agree with the scholars who situate contemporary Polish-Russian relations within the postcolonial frame,[24] indicating the importance of both the former Russian/Soviet Empire and Western Europe in Polish consciousness. Relations to these two political and cultural centers explain today's ambivalence associated with the Slavic East. I have offered the detailed analysis of Polish-Russian tourism within this perspective elsewhere.[25] I argued that the perception of Russia as a destination is to a large extent conditioned historically, but it also responds to the needs of Polish hybrid identity. The latter combines European aspirations with suppressed, but in some contexts regarded as lost, belonging to the Eastern cultural circle.[26] For these reasons, in Polish travel narratives exoticization and orientalization of Russia meet the motives of community, similarity, or even the return to the roots.

Russia is perceived as a backward, uncivilized, or even wild and dangerous area that should be looked upon with a sense of superiority. Some scholars interpret this attitude as compensational orientalization of the former hegemon, whose strength was solely based on political domination.[27] It has also been argued that labeling other postsocialist societies as "Eastern" serves as a means of inscribing Polish society into European discourses.[28] When it comes to travel, themes of backwardness, danger, dirt, or decay may become a basis for adventure-like narratives. At the same time, as Anna Horolets argued, that belittling of post-Soviet countries by Poles is accompanied by attaching new meanings to them in tourism—partly based on imitating Western discourses.[29] Traveling to the former Soviet Union together with the whole package of accompanying attitudes became the intentional resistance to mass tourism. According to Horolets, it is also a highly distinctive choice made by new middle-class representatives, who—like the Western middle class—seek status confirmation.

This should be complemented by another interpretation. In an earlier publication, I described contemporary Polish tourism to Russia as not only a contestation of dominant tourism practices, but also as a resistance to the new, Western dominance, perceived as neocolonial.[30] Traveling to Slavic East is sometimes literally understood as a search for family roots,[31] which is reminiscent of historical—often resulting from colonial situations—interdependencies between two nations at institutional, biographical, and cultural levels. Yet it is also searching for the roots in a rather metaphorical sense—as a reactivation of a repressed sense of (Eastern, Slavic, postsocialist) community. Based on accounts of my interlocutors, I claim that practicing tourism in Russia should be partly interpreted in terms of opposing some aspects of Polish political and cultural transformation as imitative modernization,[32] perceived as uprooting.

RUSSIA ON A PLATE? BETWEEN FAMILIAR TASTE AND INDIGESTION

In this section, I present selected interpretations of culinary themes extracted from Polish stories about Russia. I focus on the images that fit the most orientalizing pattern in order to compare them with those that become a part of the story about cultural similarity and the sense of deep communion occurring during host-guest encounters. In my opinion, both of them may be interpreted not only within the universal framework of tourism studies, but also as a compensation of postsocialist and modernization tensions experienced by Polish society.

The significant part of Russian food that Polish tourists selectively describe seems to be "premodern"—in terms of biological risk connected to preindustrial modes of production, as well as the nostalgic image of "simple" and "natural" food products. A good example of the latter may be focusing on closeness between man and nature. Healing properties of Siberian herbs and exceptional knowledge that local residents are supposed to have about them is recalled in some travel writings. Similarly, both books and interviewees notice that local people in Russian mountains or Siberia know how to produce food out of natural resources (herbs, plants, mushrooms, fish, wild animals), while people in Poland already forgot this skill. According to the narratives, the closeness to nature sought in Russia is believed to be a remedy for the ailments of civilization.[33]

Another dimension of this allegedly preindustrial character of food is attributing nostalgia to homemade meals (mostly different kinds of pastries) sold by elderly women (called by the interviewees *babushkas*, i.e., grandmas) met especially on the train platforms. Although often caused by the economic necessity of local residents, this cheap, simple, and easily accessible food together with the context of informal trade is widely mentioned by the majority of my interlocutors, mostly with positive feelings.

This rather typical motif for Western tourism discourse, where travel becomes not only a form of mobility in space, but also a time shift, gains new meanings while performed inside the postsocialist block. The diagnosis of the allegedly premodern character of Russia becomes an ambivalent message about the modernity of Polish society.[34] This message resonates even more strongly in the context of negative sensual feelings. The body may become a means for stories about impassable difference.[35] In another article, I demonstrated a similar phenomenon in the Polish-Icelandic case, where gastronomic otherness was strongly present.[36] The language of biology intertwines with the language of culture where senses, by their alleged transparency,[37] naturalize the claims about differences, borders, hierarchies, and distances. Some tourists directly stated that certain meals offered in Russia were difficult to accept not so much in terms of bad taste or look, but because they were completely alien, impossible to swallow or digest. This happened, for example, in the case of pork fat, which a tourist (woman, age twenty-three) received from a travel companion on a train. In another interview a quasi-biological figure of adapting one's stomach to the local food appeared. A young participant in the study reiterated her concern about the possibility of food poisoning during the trip, recalled the gastric problems her friends experienced, but also reconstructed the process of gradual bodily habituation to this culinary otherness. Thus, intercultural distance became deeply embodied, while its decreasing was described in the language referring to nature, not culture:

> Usually the first things . . . when we tried something for the first time—well, it was bad. But, for example, the second, the third, the fourth and so on—then everything was fine. The stomach just had to switch to the fact that we did not eat what we do in Poland. Because, well, it is different. (woman, age twenty)

In the analyzed material, however, the descriptions of far-reaching incompatibility of food[38] met in Russia perceived as biological were not so common.
In fact, we are not dealing with food much different from what tourists know
(there are some exceptions, including meetings with indigenous ethnic groups
living in the Asian part of the Russian Federation[39]). On the contrary, Russian
cuisine was often represented by food considered rather easily understandable, *familiar* (woman, age thirty-four), *home-like* (man, age thirty-three),
and the meals were usually described as tasty. For example, the interviewee
answering the question about what she was buying on her train journey said:
"Pork chops, potatoes, sauerkraut—typical dinner" (woman, age twenty).
Similarly, in one of the travel writings, the author describes his local com-
panions on the train eating eggs, tomatoes, and smoked fish.[40] Another author
recalls how the residents of Moscow celebrate Victory Day with sausages,
dried squid, bread, and alcohol, while the field kitchen feeds with bread and
buckwheat with meat.[41] The author also mentions boiled potatoes, fresh veg-
etable salads with mayonnaise, and dried fish sold in the local market.[42] Also,
young tourists not so rarely buy at local shops the same basic food products
they do at home, treating it as a cheap necessity (e.g., bread and cheese).
Therefore, the guests from Poland may be curious about some eating habits or
particular food products, but in general there seems to be little culinary mys-
tery for them in Russia. One of the interviewees summed up his experience:

> *I think the cultural differences between Poland and Russia are not so big. I think
> that maybe for somebody who is not familiar with Polish or with Russian cuisine
> it could be something exciting, something new. But for a Pole these are not so
> great differences. There is no novelty or anything crazy in trying something
> Russian.* (man, age twenty-four)

If this is the case, feelings of uncertainty, anxiety, or disgust, as well as
digestive difficulties and other bodily sensations, are directly associated with
food going bad due to insufficient—according to tourists—sanitary conditions in which it was prepared, stored, or sold.[43] This is more a characteristic
motif than a clear impression of otherness. For example, some tourists would
advise drinking vodka after eating in order to carry out some kind of internal
disinfection. Others may directly express the feeling of insecurity when looking for a place to dine:

> *We decided to improve our moods by eating lunch, but in the whole town we
> could not find virtually any eatery. And we were certainly not looking for chic
> restaurants, but for any place where there would be at least twenty percent
> chance that our digestive systems would continue to function properly after a
> meal.*[44]

Descriptions of "suspicious" food perceived as "dirty" were sometimes accompanied by olfactory sensations assessed as either too close, or too dominant, or too aggressive. They are the opposite of modern attempts to remove natural fragrances[45] and bear associations with precapitalist times.[46] For example: "It was stuffy in the train compartment. Bitter smell of sweat was mixing with the smell of pork fat and apple aromas. It was a truly explosive mixture."[47] The repetition of similar motives obviously results from the fact that many tourists and travelers may be defined as niche, with limited budget, and therefore—as indicated above—their trajectory deliberately leads to peripheries, away from standardized eateries. This is how one of the interviewees explained her experience with Russian food, at the same time revealing new senses hidden behind experiences of taste and disgust:

> Well, I know that dinner in the elegant Russian restaurant will be also "Russian dinner," "Russian food." But I practiced the other type of tourism in my life, different than wandering around expensive restaurants. Thank you very much. In any case, [my fellow traveler] who noticed me buying pastry from an old woman in the street—he was shocked. I thought he was going to harm me because of that, thinking I would definitely be poisoned and he would have to save me. . . . When he saw that I was eating, he said, "Hey, but it smells good." I said, "Yes, it does." "What is inside the pie?" . . . And suddenly it turned out that he was okay after trying, he was healthy and he was surprised. But that's the point, that if not for me, if I had not showed him that I was not poisoned, I am not running to the toilet, I am not vomiting—he would have never tried it. (woman, age twenty-six)

I have already used the term "fear of poisoning" in relation to Russian food,[48] but it requires a closer look in this context. The statement quoted above illustrates the kind of anxiety tourists can experience toward food in Russia, but it also indicates that sensual data and their interpretations are, in fact, in between nature and culture.[49] One can also notice that the links between social and natural dimensions do not refer only to taste, but are inscribed in people's interpretation of the whole digestive process.[50] It is evident that the whole bodily experience, also that "beyond the palate"—connected to the digestion and indigestion—is interpreted as a "means of engaging in and responding to larger cultural phenomena."[51] It turns out that the focus on what happens after eating is not only the site of national politics, as Caldwell indicates,[52] but also part of "micro-politics" inscribed in tourism.

The entanglement of individual experience and particular (civilizational) discourse co-creating the tourist imagery is evident in the quotation given above: in this case his presumptions stopped the tourist from reaching for some type of food. At the same time, it is also evident that the all-encompassing discourse may be partly modified under the influence of face-to-face encounter. At any rate, we can say that if there is a doubt regarding food tourists meet on their way in Russia, it is not an expression of geographical distance and far-reaching cultural otherness. Instead, it would indicate the time distance, if we agree that focusing on sanitary deficiencies can be an indicator of civilizational assessments.

CONCLUSION: "DIRTY FOOD" AND CULTURAL INTIMACY

However, there is another, perhaps more important and less obvious meaning of "food pollution" in the context of host-guest relationship. Dirt as a relational and culturally constructed category is unveiled in the situation of people's encounters.[53] The guests' arrival triggers a look at the private space through the eyes of a newcomer and results in cleaning procedures:

> Hospitality . . . is closely tied with cleanliness. "Purifying one's space is an act of welcoming," proposes philosopher Michel Serres. In other words, hospitality is the opposite of appropriation: while appropriation is to take what is public and common and make it one's own by way of fouling or enclosing, hospitality means opening up one's private property and transforming it into something public and accessible for others.[54]

Nevertheless, the issue is not so simple. A tourist system that requires literal or metaphorical cleaning of the tourism space—polishing, removing undesirable elements, neutralizing odors; that is, staging—is what independent tourists explicitly or implicitly contest. To some extent, they do not want to be "guests"—they want to be "one of them." Drawing inspiration from the category of tourist "disruptions,"[55] it is worth asking whether "untidy hosts" are necessarily the element that breaks the host-guest relationship.

The food that may raise tourists' anxiety becomes a repository of authenticity with at least two meanings. The most obvious one is an impression of lack of staging: inviting tourists to a familiar and home-like atmosphere. Accordingly, the "dirt" spotted by the guests gives them a feeling of getting into the private space of the hosts. Another meaning of authenticity is more important for the analysis of links between individual experience and discursive symbolic geography. "Home-like," more natural and less processed, sometimes perceived as dangerous or disgusting meals are related to searching for the "authentic" life in Russia; that is, life devoid of uprooting tensions of modernity.[56]

An example from a slightly different but useful context may be recalled here. Ola Bilewicz, in her blog column, draws an image of Polish "unfashionable eateries" (cafés, bistros, restaurants)—beyond global chains, rather inexpensive and often established before 1989, visited more willingly by elderly people than the young. They still exist in some places, contrasting with new homogeneous spaces for the middle class, springing up like mushrooms after rain, which often imitate global fashions and became a hallmark of peripheral capitalism.[57] This contrast has a strong sensual dimension since it is based, according to the author, on the smell of the place:

> Places that smell like this must be probably linked by an underground tunnel, a secret route of last modest cafes and homespun bars, which have quietly signed an agreement to support each other in their existence, and at night, when no one sees, they blink to each other from different parts of the country in silent, discreet solidarity.[58]

Bilewicz names these places—local, non-perfect, and opposed to global capitalism—as "real." In the context of tourism, authenticity seems to be the right term to juxtapose with "real."[59] The participants of the study also visited places similar to the ones described above during their trips; however, it is not just about the literal associations relating to appearance, smell, or general profile of eateries. Deeper analogies should be sought. Tourists from Poland refer to an intangible feeling of loss they experience at home, a sense of truth they found in Russia, or the impression of familiarity and being as if "at home," even though in other contexts they may describe their destinations in a critical or ironic manner.

"Dirt" or disorder becomes a symbol of desirable social relations, considered as "real." Eating a risky (e.g., raw fish[60]) or unhygienic shared meal is not only a matter of politeness or reciprocity, but it becomes a direct sign of being "one of them." Tourists obviously eat in their own exclusive groups too, but they evoke memories of hospitality they experienced in Russia— whether during the trip on the Trans-Siberian Railroad or while camping, where they were invited to common meals, or in local homes. In fact, Russian food is rarely seen from the outside as an element of the ready-made cultural heritage. Instead, it becomes an important part of building social relations. Sometimes—this is fairly evident in travel writing—relations with local residents are described explicitly beyond the commodification system with food being given, not bought. For example:

> Guests set up their tents and pulled out their food, which turned out to be delicacies. There were potatoes, which I had not seen for months, dry sausage, pickled cucumbers and vodka, of course. The supper menu was completed by fishes

I caught. We feasted long and passionately, after that we sat together by the fire telling the stories until dawn. I can still remember this encounter, the surrounding nature, the shared evenings and natural, beautiful friendship, which is only possible away from civilization.[61]

Obviously, similar statements—and there are relatively many of them in the research material—can be interpreted using the universal category of *communitas*.[62] It seems, however, that this is not wrong, but rather insufficient interpretation. It was the particular Russian (Siberian or Slavic) hospitality that was described by Polish guests as going far beyond the purely pragmatic dimension.[63] Paradoxically, the culinary taste and the smell of food often become secondary. For some tourists, it does not really matter what they eat, while the overall situation, for which the food is the pretext, is certainly very meaningful. It is more about "being given a treat of authenticity" inscribed into the logic of gift exchange than about the cosmopolitan omnivorism inscribed into the global model of culinary tourism.[64] Interpersonal intimacy turns into cultural intimacy,[65] which is based on resistance against the expectations coming from the Western center. Creating Polish-Russian internal common space, as well as performing the "hidden" part of Polish identity, is at play. However, this contradicts with the equally important European part of Polish identity; hence, the peripherization of Russia does not disappear. In fact, these two parallel processes feed each other. While the "primitive" or "dirty" food is the flip side of "pure" social relations, both are inscribed in the same frame of postcolonial ambivalence concerning superiority and inferiority, tradition and uprooting, and finally, East and West.

NOTES

1. Ian Cook and Philip Crang, "The World on a Plate: Culinary Culture, Displacement and Geographical Knowledges," *Journal of Material Culture* 1 (1996), doi: 10.1177/135918359600100201; Melissa L. Caldwell, "Tasting the Worlds of Yesterday and Today: Culinary Tourism and Nostalgia Foods in Post-Soviet Russia," in *Fast Food/Slow Food: The Cultural Economy of the Global Food System,* ed. Richard Wilk (Altamira Press, 2006); Jennie Germann Molz, "Eating Difference: The Cosmopolitan Mobilities of Culinary Tourism," *Space and Culture* 10 (2007). doi:10.1177/1206331206296383. See also Agata Bachórz, "Disgusting Shark Meat and the Taste of North: Icelandic Food in the 'mouth' of Polish Tourists and Migrants," in *Mobility to the Edges of Europe: The Case of Iceland and Poland,* ed. Dorota Rancew-Sikora and Unnur Dis Skaptadottir (Warsaw: Scholar Publishing House), 2015.
2. Michael Herzfeld, *Anthropology: Theoretical Practice in Culture and Society* (London: Blackwell Publishing Ltd., 2001), chapter *Senses.*
3. Claude Fischler, "Food, Self and Identity." *Social Science Information* 27 (1988): 279, doi:10.1177/053901888027002005.

4. Winfried Menninghaus, *Wstręt: Teoria i historia,* translated from German by Grzegorz Sowiński (Cracow: Universitas, 2009), 22–3.

5. Anna Wieczorkiewicz, *Apetyt turysty: O doświadczaniu świata w podróży* [Tourist's Appetite: About Experiencing the World in Travel] (Cracow: Universitas, 2008), 303.

6. Cf. Ian Cook, "Geographies of Food: Mixing," *Progress in Human Geography* 32 (2008), doi:10.1177/0309132508090979.

7. John Urry, *The Tourist Gaze,* 2nd ed. (London: Sage, 2002), 142; Graham Dann and Jens Kristian Steen Jacobsen, "Tourism Smellscapes," *Tourism Geographies: An International Journal of Tourism Space, Place and Environment* 5 (2003): 3–4, doi:10.1080/1461 668032000034033; Molz, "Eating Difference," 84–88; Sally, Everett, "Beyond the Visual Gaze? The Pursuit of an Embodied Experience through Food Tourism," *Tourist Studies* 8 (2008): 340–42, doi:10.1177/1468797608100594; Wieczorkiewicz, *Apetyt turysty,* 260.

8. Paul Rodaway, *Sensuous Geographies: Body, Sense and Place* (London: Routledge, 2002).

9. Elżbieta Rybicka, "Kuchnia, mapa, mit środkowoeuropejski (wokół Cafe Museum Roberta Makłowicza)" [Cuisine, Map, Central European Myth (around Cafe Museum by Robert Makłowicz)], in *Terytoria smaku. Studia z antropologii i socjologii jedzenia* [*Territories of taste. Studies in anthropology and sociology of food*], ed. Anna Wieczorkiewicz and Urszula Jarecka (Warsaw: IFiS PAN, 2014), 116–19, 125–30. Cf. Bachórz, "Disgusting Shark Meat and the Taste of North."

10. Herzfeld, *Anthropology,* chapter *Senses;* Gediminas Lankauskas, "Sensuous (Re) Collections: The Sight and Taste of Socialism at Grūtas Statue Park, Lithuania," *The Senses and Society* 1 (2006): 30, 39–43, doi:10.2752/174589206778055682.

11. Cf. Molz, "Eating Difference."

12. Agata Bachórz, *Rosja w tekście i w doświadczeniu. Analiza współczesnych relacji z podróży* [Russia in Text and Experience: An Analysis of Contemporary Polish Travel Narratives] (Cracow: Nomos, 2013).

13. Caldwell, "Tasting the Worlds of Yesterday and Today," 97–104.

14. Melissa Caldwell, "Digestive Politics in Russia: Feeling the Sensorium beyond the Palate," *Food and Foodways: Explorations in the History and Culture of Human Nourishment* 22, no. 1–2 (2014): 113–15, 117, doi:10.1080/07409710.2014.892740.

15. See: Bachórz, *Rosja w tekście i w doświadczeniu,* 186.

16. Cf. Erik Cohen and Nir Avieli, "Food in Tourism: Attraction and Impediment," *Annals of Tourism Research* 31 (2004), doi:10.1016/j.annals.2004.02.003.

17. Jon Holtzman, "Remembering Bad Cooks: Sensuality, Memory, Personhood," *The Senses and Society* 5 (2010), doi:10.2752/174589210X12668381452881.

18. Molz, "Eating Difference," 84–88; Cf. Anna Horolets, "Kulturowe znaczenie ryzyka w narracjach Polaków podróżujących po Rosji" [Cultural Meaning of Risk in the Narratives of Poles Traveling to Russia], in *Wizje kultury własnej, obcej i wspólnej w sytuacji kontaktu* [Images of One's Own, Foreign and Shared Cultures in the Situation of Contact], ed. Monika Kostaszuk-Romanowska and Anna Wieczorkiewicz (Białystok: Galeria im. Ślendzińskich w Białymstoku, 2009), 140–44.

19. Anna Horolets, *Konformizm, bunt, nostalgia. Turystyka niszowa z Polski do krajów byłego ZSRR* [Conformity, Rebellion, Nostalgia: Niche Tourism from Poland to the Former Soviet Union] (Cracow: Universitas, 2013).

20. Bachórz, *Rosja w tekście i w doświadczeniu,* 10–11.

21. Paweł Sowiński, *Wakacje w Polsce Ludowej* [Vacations in the People's Republic of Poland] (Warsaw: Trio, 2005).

22. Krzysztof Podemski, *Socjologia podróży* [Sociology of Travel] (Poznań: Wydawnictwo Naukowe UAM, 2005), 126–37; *Polacy poznają świat, czyli o zagranicznych wyjazdach i znajomości języków obcych. Komunikat z badań* [Poles Learn about the World, i.e. about foreign trips and knowledge of foreign languages. Research report] (Warsaw: CBOS [Public Opinion Research Center], 2012), accessed July 15, 2016, http://cbos.pl/SPISKOM.POL/2012/K_148_12.PDF; *Wyjazdy wypoczynkowe Polaków w 2015 roku i plany na rok 2016. Komunikat z badań* [Poles' Holiday Trips in 2015 and Their Plans for 2016. Research Report] (Warsaw: CBOS [Public Opinion Research Center], 2016), accessed July 15, 2016, http://www.cbos.pl/SPISKOM.POL/2016/K_021_16.PDF.

23. Magdalena Banaszkiewicz, *Dialog międzykulturowy w turystyce. Przypadek polsko-rosyjski* [Intercultural Dialogue in Tourism: Polish-Russian Case] (Cracow: Wydawnictwo Uniwersytetu Jagiellońskiego, 2012); Bachórz, *Rosja w tekście i w doświadczeniu;* Horolets, *Konformizm, bunt, nostalgia.*

24. Maxim Waldstein, "Observing *Imperium*: A Postcolonial Reading of Ryszard Kapuscinski's Account of Soviet and Post-Soviet Russia," *Social Identities* 8 (2002), doi:10.1080/1350463022000030010; Tomasz Zarycki, "Uses of Russia: The Role of Russia in the Modern Polish National Identity," *East European Politics and Societies* 17 (2004), doi:10.1177/0888325404269758; Tomasz Zarycki, "Polska i jej regiony a debata postkolonialna" [Poland and Its Regions in Postcolonial Debate], in *Oblicze polityczne regionów Polski* [Political Face of Polish Regions], ed. Małgorzata Dajnowicz (Białystok: Wyższa Szkoła Finansów i Zarządzania, 2008); Maria Janion, "Poland between the West and East," translated from Polish by Anna Warso, *Teksty Drugie* 1 (2014) *Special Issues English Edition* (for the discussion about postcolonialism in Eastern Europe see also the whole volume).

25. Bachórz, *Rosja w tekście i w doświadczeniu.*

26. Maria Janion, *Niesamowita Słowiańszczyzna: Fantazmaty literatury* [This Amazing Slavdom: The Phantasms of Literature] (Cracow: Wydawnictwo Literackie, 2006), 7–46.

27. Ewa Thompson, *Imperial Knowledge: Russian Literature and Colonialism* (Westport, CT: Greenwood Press, 2000).

28. Waldstein, "Observing *Imperium*"; Merje Kuus, "Europe's Eastern Expansion and the Reinscription of Otherness in East-Central Europe," *Progress in Human Geography* 28 (2004), doi:10.1191/0309132504ph498oa; Zarycki, "Uses of Russia," 599–607.

29. Horolets, *Konformizm, bunt, nostalgia,* 75–124.

30. Bachórz, *Rosja w tekście i w doświadczeniu,* 74–80, 275–82.

31. Agata Bachórz and Anna Horolets, "Historical Blueprints of Tourists' Paths from Poland to the Former USSR," *Journal of Tourism and Cultural Change* 15 (2017): 152–66.

32. Marek Ziółkowski, "O imitacyjnej modernizacji społeczeństwa polskiego" [Imitative Modernization of Polish Society], in *Imponderabilia wielkiej zmiany* [Imponderables of Great Change], ed. Piotr Sztompka (Warszawa, Kraków: PWN, 1999).

33. Bachórz, *Rosja w tekście i w doświadczeniu,* 144–50.

34. Waldstein, "Observing *Imperium*"; Kuus, "Europe's Eastern Expansion," Zarycki, "Uses of Russia."

35. Menninghaus, *Wstręt: Teoria i historia.*

36. Bachórz, "Disgusting Shark Meat," 124–28.

37. Herzfeld, *Anthropology,* chapter *Senses.*

38. Cf. Molz, "Eating Difference," 86–88.

39. For the best example see: Magdalena Skopek, *Dobra krew. W krainie reniferów, bogów i ludzi* [Good Blood: In the Land of Reindeer, Gods and Men] (Warsaw: PWN, 2012).

40. Igor T. Miecik, *14:57 do Czyty: Reportaże z Rosji* [14:57 Train to Chita: Reportages from Russia] (Wołowiec: Wydawnictwo Czarne, 2012), 6.

41. Piotr Milewski, *Transsyberyjska: Drogą żelazną przez Rosję i dalej* [Trans-Siberian Train: By Railroad through Russia and Beyond] (Cracow: Znak 2014), 76–77.

42. Milewski, *Transsyberyjska,* 105.

43. Cf. Cohen and Avieli, "Food in Tourism."

44. Tomasz Cyrol, *Transsibem nad Bajkał* [On Baikal Lake by Transsiberian Train] (Łomianki: LTW, 2008), 53.

45. Dann and Jacobsen, "Tourism Smellscapes," 13.

46. Cf. Christoph Neidhart, *Russia's Carnival: The Smells, Sights and Sounds of Transition* (Lanham, MD: Rowman & Littlefield, 2003).

47. Milewski, *Transsyberyjska,* 223.

48. Bachórz, *Rosja w tekście i w doświadczeniu,* 198.

49. Herzfeld, *Anthropology,* chapter *Senses.*

50. Caldwell, "Digestive Politics."

51. Ibidem, 112.

52. Ibidem, 125.

53. Mary Douglas, *Purity and Danger: An Analysis of Concept of Pollution and Taboo* (London: Routledge, 1966).

54. Soile Veijola et al., "Introduction: Alternative Tourism Ontologies," in *Disruptive Tourism and its Untidy Guests: Alternative Ontologies for Future Hospitalities* (London: Palgrave Macmillan UK, 2014), 1.

55. Veijola et al., "Introduction: Alternative Tourism Ontologies," 4.

56. See: Dean MacCannell, *The Tourist: A New Theory of the Leisure Class* (New York: Schocken Books, 1976).

57. Ola Bilewicz, "Realność poznaje się po zapachu (noworoczna dygresja na błahy temat)" [Reality is Known by the Smell (New Year's Digression on Fiddling Topic)], *Blog Nowych Peryferii: Spół-dzielenie* [New Peripheries' Blog], accessed July 15, 2016, http://olabilewicz.nowe-peryferie.pl/2015/01/01/realnosc-poznaje-sie-po-zapachu-noworoczna-dygresja-na-blahy-temat/.

58. Ibidem.

59. Dean MacCannell, "Staged Authenticity: Arrangements of Social Space in Tourist Settings," *American Journal of Sociology* 79 (1973): 591, doi:10.1086/225585.

60. Hieronim Żygadło, *Drzemiąca tajga: Wspomnienia* [Dormant Taiga: Memories] (Wrocław: Wektory, 2006), 92.

61. Romuald Koperski, *Przez Syberię na gapę* [Through Siberia without a Ticket] (Gdańsk: Stratus, 2000), 104.
62. Victor Turner, *Dramas, Fields and Metaphors: Symbolic Action in Human Society* (Ithaca, NY: Cornell University Press, 1975).
63. Żygadło, *Drzemiąca tajga,* 18; Cyrol, *Transsibem nad Bajkał,* 79.
64. Molz, "Eating Difference."
65. Michael Herzfeld, *Cultural Intimacy: Social Poetics in the Nation-State.* Second Edition. (London: Routledge, 2005).

REFERENCES

Bachórz, Agata. *Rosja w tekście i w doświadczeniu. Analiza współczesnych relacji z podróży.* Cracow: Nomos, 2013.

Bachórz, Agata. "Disgusting Shark Meat and the Taste of North: Icelandic Food in the 'Mouth' of Polish Tourists and Migrants." In *Mobility to the Edges of Europe: The Case of Iceland and Poland,* edited by Dorota Rancew-Sikora and Unnur Dis Skaptadottir, 109–35. Warsaw: Scholar Publishing House, 2015.

Bachórz, Agata, and Anna Horolets. "Historical Blueprints of Tourists' Paths from Poland to the Former USSR." *Journal of Tourism and Cultural Change* 15 (2017): 152–66.

Banaszkiewicz, Magdalena. *Dialog międzykulturowy w turystyce. Przypadek polsko-rosyjski.* Cracow: Wydawnictwo Uniwersytetu Jagiellońskiego, 2012.

Bilewicz, Ola. "Realność poznaje się po zapachu (noworoczna dygresja na błahy temat)." *Blog Nowych Peryferii: Spół-dzielenie.* Accessed July 15, 2016. http://olabile-wicz.nowe-peryferie.pl/2015/01/01/realnosc-poznaje-sie-po-zapachu-noworoczna-dygresja-na-blahy-temat/.

Caldwell, Melissa L. "Digestive Politics in Russia: Feeling the Sensorium beyond the Palate." *Food and Foodways: Explorations in the History and Culture of Human Nourishment* 22, no. 1–2 (2014): 112–35. doi:10.1080/07409710.2014.892740.

Caldwell, Melissa L. "Tasting the Worlds of Yesterday and Today: Culinary Tourism and Nostalgia Foods in Post-Soviet Russia." In *Fast Food/Slow Food: The Cultural Economy of the Global Food System,* edited by Richard Wilk, 97–112. Lanham, MD: AltaMira Press, 2006.

Cohen, Erik, and Nir Avieli. "Food in Tourism: Attraction and Impediment." *Annals of Tourism Research* 31 (2004): 755–78. doi:10.1016/j.annals.2004.02.003.

Cook, Ian. "Geographies of Food: Mixing." *Progress in Human Geography* 32 (2008): 821–33. doi:10.1177/0309132508090979.

Cook, Ian, and Philip Crang. "The World On a Plate: Culinary Culture, Displacement and Geographical Knowledges." *Journal of Material Culture* 1 (1996): 131–53. doi:10.1177/135918359600100201.

Cyrol, Tomasz. *Transsibem nad Bajkał* [On Baikal Lake by Transsiberian Train]. Łomianki: LTW, 2008.

Dann, Graham, and Jens Kristian Steen Jacobsen. "Tourism Smellscapes." *Tourism Geographies: An International Journal of Tourism Space, Place and Environment* 5 (2003): 3–25. doi:10.1080/1461668032000034033.

Douglas, Mary. *Purity and Danger: An Analysis of Concepts of Pollution and Taboo.* London: Routledge, 1966.

Everett, Sally. "Beyond the Visual Gaze? The Pursuit of an Embodied Experience through Food Tourism." *Tourist Studies* 8 (2008): 337–58. doi:10.1177/1468797608100594.

Fischler, Claude. "Food, Self and Identity." *Social Science Information* 27 (1988): 275–92. doi:10.1177/053901888027002005.

Herzfeld, Michael. *Anthropology: Theoretical Practice in Culture and Society.* London: Blackwell Publishing Ltd., 2001.

Herzfeld, Michael. *Cultural Intimacy: Social Poetics in the Nation-State* (Second Edition). London: Routledge, 2005.

Holtzman, Jon. "Remembering Bad Cooks: Sensuality, Memory, Personhood." *The Senses and Society* 5 (2010): 235–43. doi:10.2752/174589210X12668381452881.

Horolets, Anna. "Kulturowe znaczenie ryzyka w narracjach Polaków podróżujących po Rosji." In *Wizje kultury własnej, obcej i wspólnej w sytuacji kontaktu*, edited by Monika Kostaszuk-Romanowska and Anna Wieczorkiewicz, 138–46. Białystok: Galeria im. Śleńdzińskich w Białymstoku, 2009.

Horolets, Anna. *Konformizm, bunt, nostalgia. Turystyka niszowa z Polski do krajów byłego ZSRR.* Cracow: Universitas, 2013.

Janion, Maria. *Niesamowita Słowiańszczyzna. Fantazmaty literatury.* Cracow: Wydawnictwo Literackie, 2006.

Janion, Maria. "Poland between the West and East." Translated from Polish by Anna Warso. *Teksty Drugie. Special Issues English Edition* 1 (2014): 13–33.

Koperski, Romuald. *Przez Syberię na gapę.* Gdańsk: Stratus, 2000.

Kuus, Merje. "Europe's Eastern Expansion and the Reinscription of Otherness in East-Central Europe." *Progress in Human Geography* 28 (2004), 472–89. doi: 10.1191/0309132504ph498oa.

Lankauskas, Gediminas. "Sensuous (Re)Collections: The Sight and Taste of Socialism at Grūtas Statue Park, Lithuania." *The Senses and Society* 1 (2006): 27–52. doi: 10.2752/174589206778055682.

MacCannell, Dean. "Staged Authenticity: Arrangements of Social Space in Tourist Settings." *American Journal of Sociology* 79 (1973): 589–603. doi: 10.1086/225585.

MacCannell, Dean. *The Tourist: A New Theory of the Leisure Class.* New York: Schocken Books, 1976.

Menninghaus, Winfried. *Wstręt. Teoria i historia,* translated from German by Grzegorz Sowiński. Cracow: Universitas, 2009. [English translation: *Disgust: Theory and History of a Strong Sensation.* Albany, NY: SUNY Press, 2003].

Miecik, Igor T. *14:57 do Czyty. Reportaże z Rosji* [14:57 Train to Chita: Reportages from Russia]. Wołowiec: Wydawnictwo Czarne, 2012.

Milewski, Piotr. *Transsyberyjska. Drogą żelazną przez Rosję i dalej.* Cracow: Znak, 2014.

Molz, Jennie Germann. "Eating Difference: The Cosmopolitan Mobilities of Culinary Tourism." *Space and Culture* 10 (2007): 77–93. doi:10.1177/1206331206296383.

Neidhart, Christoph. *Russia's Carnival: The Smells, Sights and Sounds of Transition.* Lanham, MD: Rowman & Littlefield, 2003.

Podemski, Krzysztof. *Socjologia podróży*. Poznań: Wydawnictwo Naukowe UAM, 2005.

Polacy poznają świat, czyli o zagranicznych wyjazdach i znajomości języków obcych. Komunikat z badań [Poles Learn about the World, i.e., about foreign trips and knowledge of foreign languages. Research report]. Warsaw: CBOS [Public Opinion Research Center], 2012. Accessed July 15, 2016. http://cbos.pl/SPISKOM. POL/2012/K_148_12.PDF.

Rodaway, Paul. *Sensuous Geographies: Body, Sense and Place*. London: Routledge, 2002.

Rybicka, Elżbieta. "Kuchnia, mapa, mit środkowoeuropejski (wokół Cafe Museum Roberta Makłowicza)." In *Terytoria smaku. Studia z antropologii i socjologii jedzenia*, edited by Anna Wieczorkiewicz and Urszula Jarecka, 115–32. Warsaw: IFiS PAN, 2014.

Skopek, Magdalena. *Dobra krew. W krainie reniferów, bogów i ludzi* [Good Blood: In the Land of Reindeer, Gods and Men]. Warsaw: PWN, 2012.

Sowiński, Paweł. *Wakacje w Polsce Ludowej*. Warsaw: Trio, 2005.

Thompson, Ewa. *Imperial Knowledge: Russian Literature and Colonialism*. Westport, CT: Greenwood Press, 2000.

Turner, Victor. *Dramas, Fields and Metaphors: Symbolic Action in Human Society*. Ithaca, NY: Cornell University Press, 1975.

Urry, John. *The Tourist Gaze*, 2nd edition. London: Sage, 2002.

Veijola, Soile et al. "Introduction: Alternative Tourism Ontologies." In *Disruptive Tourism and its Untidy Guests: Alternative Ontologies for Future Hospitalities*, edited by Veijola, Soile et al., 1–18. London: Palgrave Macmillan UK, 2014.

Waldstein, Maxim. "Observing *Imperium*: A Postcolonial Reading of Ryszard Kapuscinski's Account of Soviet and Post-Soviet Russia." *Social Identities* 8 (2002): 481–99. doi:10.1080/1350463022000030010.

Wieczorkiewicz, Anna. *Apetyt turysty. O doświadczaniu świata w podróży*. Cracow: Universitas, 2008.

Wyjazdy wypoczynkowe Polaków w 2015 roku i plany na rok 2016. Komunikat z badań [Poles' Holiday Trips in 2015 and Their Plans for 2016. Research Report]. Warsaw: CBOS [Public Opinion Research Center], 2016. Accessed July 15, 2016. http://www.cbos.pl/SPISKOM.POL/2016/K_021_16.PDF.

Zarycki, Tomasz. "Uses of Russia: The Role of Russia in the Modern Polish National Identity." *East European Politics and Societies* 17 (2004): 595–627. doi: 10.1177/0888325404269758.

Zarycki, Tomasz. "Polska i jej regiony a debata postkolonialna." In *Oblicze polityczne regionów Polski*, edited by Małgorzata Dajnowicz, 31–48. Białystok: Wyższa Szkoła Finansów i Zarządzania, 2008.

Ziółkowski, Marek. "O imitacyjnej modernizacji społeczeństwa polskiego." In *Imponderabilia wielkiej zmiany*, edited by Piotr Sztompka, 38–64. Warszawa, Kraków: PWN, 1999.

Żygadło, Hieronim. *Drzemiąca tajga. Wspomnienia* [Dormant Taiga: Memories]. Wrocław: Wektory, 2006.

Chapter 11

"Let's Make Laces in the Garden"

Creative Tourism in Rural Poland

Anna Sznajder and Katarzyna Kosmala

This chapter explores the complex relations between tourism and creativity. In particular, tourists' experience of local culture and craft in Bobowa, a small town in Southern Poland, will be discussed. Creative tourism in Bobowa is associated with a local craft revival coordinated by local activists, and in association with the Center for Culture and Promotion and Association for Handicraft Protection. As the result of creative interaction between people, place, processes, and products,[1] this type of "heritage" tourism has the potential for future development based on place-making strategies and rich cultural, social, and symbolic capital. "Heritage" tourism in the Bobowa region relies on the community's tangible heritage and intangible cultural resources related to bobbin lacemaking in Bobowa since the beginning of the nineteenth century.[2] The development of a flourishing cottage industry, supported by traders and nobility, led to the creation of a Bobowa lacemaking school in 1899. In the following years, this school brought fame to the region as its students won a silver medal during the World Craft Exhibition in 1904 in Saint Louis, Missouri, and later, a gold medal in 1905 in San Francisco.[3] The school's original prewar patterns were distributed among lacemakers by instructors and traders, which enriched lace designed after the opening of the Cooperative "Koronka" in 1949.[4] The lace-centered cottage industry employed lacemakers as home workers providing a salary, insurance, and pension package and organized sales across the country and abroad. Political changes after 1989 created much turbulence for craft development and left many individuals without employment. Recognizing the risk of craft disappearance, local activists started to engage in a revival project, renaming the former cottage industry as a heritage craft and encouraging local women to preserve their skills. These efforts commenced in 1995 and since the year 2000 continued through a national lacemaking contest: the International

Bobbin Lace Festival. In 2008, increasing awareness of lacemaking heritage materialized in the form of a working lacemaker monument erected in Bobowa,[5] situated at the Main Square's fountain. The monument commemorates women's work and local heritage, and on an international level, links Bobowa with European lacemaking heritage and the history of its cottage industry. The monument is an expression of these women's identities, which were formed by socioeconomic conditions of a particular historical period, and in a broader context, it underlines the fragmented and fluid nature of Central and Eastern European geographies.[6] To understand the processes of heritage construction, McDowell[7] suggests investigating "the connections between memory, identity and heritage through the cultural landscape," which, in the case of Bobowa, requires further studies. As an artifact and also as an outcome of the cultural landscape of Bobowa, the monument expresses the collective identity: a tribute to women's work.

CREATIVE TOURISM IN THE CONTEXT
OF BOBOWA CRAFT HERITAGE

It could be argued that one of the key roles of cultural heritage is as a resource for safeguarding local identities and a stimulus for sustainable development.[8] "Heritage is not the historic monument, archaeological site, or museum artifact, but rather the activities that occur at and around these places and objects."[9] The intimate relationship of heritage industry to a locality, its territory, and the community that lives there,[10] in terms of creative tourism, receives new meaning. In Bobowa, the skills-based workshops immerse outsiders in the historical background of a craft-based cottage industry and a center of creative identity. The long and rich history of Bobowa makes it an attractive destination for tourists. Bobowa's origins are dated from the Middle Ages, confirmed by a document detailing the town's location in 1339.[11] The cultural and religious attractions of the place include the eighteenth-century synagogue and two churches from the fifteenth and sixteenth centuries; the medieval architecture of the town; the eighteenth-century Jewish graveyard; the seventeenth-century mansion house of the Długoszewski family;[12] St. Florian's chapel from the eighteenth century on the Main Square; and the First World War cemetery.[13] Cultural tourism in the region is enriched by the International Festival of Bobbin Lace and the Gallery of Bobbin Lace located in the Cultural Center.[14] In the literature about Bobowa, there is a visibly dominant masculine approach to the place's heritage.[15] We argue that this strategy is undervaluing the role of lacemakers in tourism development. Possibilities of using bobbin laces and lacemakers in the town's promotion are not discussed beyond the annual festival. The reason for that might be a lack of awareness about the activity of local women and a lack of understanding regarding a heritage based on skills, techniques, and old patterns. Lacemaking could attract more tourists. Tourism started to increase on a small scale through the development of agro-farms based on lacemaking workshops. The concept of creative tourism,[16] which is oriented on the creative process, experience, and active skill development (learning) and is embedded in a locally lived-in experience, could be particularly useful for advancing strategies around local heritage development. Bobowa's municipality is the only place where bobbin lacemakers are active in emphasizing its distinguishable character across Poland and beyond. Indeed, lacemaking and related occupations are not recognized in the town's official development strategy. The twenty-first century brought to Bobowa a perception of crafts not only as an artisanal and sometimes even artistic work, but as a tourist object[17] and a fashion accessory. Importantly, it also unveiled the value of the lacemaking process and lacemakers' lifestyle through the tourist experience itself. Such opportunities were recognized by few local individuals as a source of income in the form of weekly agro-tourism holidays with lacemaking courses at the center, the possibility of attending embroidery workshops, and courses for visitors in Bobowa as part of a folk craft experience.

These forms of creative tourism (however unnamed as such and defined rather as examples of agro-tourist holidays) are recognized and accepted in this community, becoming part of both a formal and an informal economy.

We define creative tourism as an experiential activity that "offers visitors the opportunity to develop their creative potential through active participation in courses and learning experiences which are characteristic of the holiday destination where they are undertaken."[18] Creative tourism stimulates place-making and its reinvention on the basis of its local people and resources. Often perceived as the "next generation" of cultural tourism,[19] creative tourism, as we understand and theoretically apply it, is rooted in the local culture.

Authenticity, active participation, crafts-based creativity, skill development, and a search for meaningful experience are essential components of creative tourism. Richards[20] pointed out the need for creative experience among tourists visiting cultural places and recognized the shift from passive to active participation in the place, as well as involvement in intangible heritage rather than exploration of its tangible assets. He enumerated factors that encouraged people to search for creativity in tourism, which included discontentedness with modes of consumption, blending the time for work and leisure, the need for self-development and expression, and the construction of biography and identity. The term—"creative tourist"—reflects back to the "active co-creator or co-producer of his own experience," defined as novelty seekers, knowledge and skills learners, green issues aware, and leisure types.[21] In other words, creative tourists are consumers responsible for producing their own goods and services; in the case of Bobowa this experience revolves around laces and lacemaking. Exploring tourists' motivations for involvement in creative tourism, Tan, Luh, and Kung[22] highlighted the importance of participation in acts of everyday creativity (craft, cultural refinement, self-expressive creativity, interpersonal creativity, and sophisticated media consumption), which bring visitors closer to local lives. Interestingly, some have argued that the need for creative experiences supporting personal psychological health, positive development, enjoyment, and fulfillment does not exactly relate to a need to make innovative or effective items. Instead, new knowledge, self-insight, and relationships become sources of strength, empowerment, or resilience.[23] It seems that creative tourists search for innovative experience, or alternatively, opt to utilize local resources for personal reasons, engaging in community experience and participating in a peripheral lifestyle. As identity is intimately connected with place,[24] lacemakers may be perceived as guardians of authentic craft experience.

In order to understand the reasons behind participation in lacemaking courses by women (there is little evidence that men are interested in craft experiences in agro-tourism, perhaps considering it a typically female-centered activity) from different age groups, backgrounds, and occupations, we draw on a concept of activity-related authenticity in tourism, named also as *existential authenticity*. This "refers to a potential existential state of Being that is to be activated by tourist activities," not to authenticity of objects seen during the journey.[25] We recognize the existential authenticity experienced by tourists in Bobowa in the way they organize their holidays, which is a daily routine of learning and making lace stitches, time spent on and upon the roller, a feeling of exhaustion and experience of physical pain, as well as satisfaction from completed work. A training experience in an original craft that is set in an indigenous place, contact with its local dialect and freshly made home food, and the ability to immerse oneself in the history of the place are of particular value in building one's identity in the context of the creative tourism, lacemaking, heritage experience. The educational aspect of these workshop-centered trips,[26] considered in literature as an essential element of contemporary tourism, apart from entertainment per se,[27] creates new categories of tourist products that allow the local community to construct visible signs of local heritage (a monument, a gallery, a craft shop).

Different profiles of the creative tourists mean that lacemakers have to adjust their behavior to create an appropriate in-house atmosphere. Often, they negotiate between "housewifization of labour"[28] (being tied to traditional cooking and cleaning for guests), presenting themselves as skilled craftswomen and tutors, and mediating between visitors and the rest of the community. Clients rarely come with their partners, so they are able to enjoy this intimate space[29] as well as immerse themselves in this rural idyll. This experience supports original and creative processes as well as independent tourist creativity,[30] expressed, for example, by the choice of thread color or pattern.

Creative tourism activity in Bobowa is gendered, and happens in gendered spaces that are historically associated with women lacemakers' initiatives and work. Creative experiences are linked to historical contexts, historically constructed identities, and gender bias, which include elements of self-expression while supporting collectivity as people work, but still allowing learning of the craft codes of the Bobowa region. Plurality of identities supports gendered construction and organization of private and public spaces for tourists,[31] which, in the case of lacemakers, contributes to reinforcement of enterprising individuals through interaction, involvement, and becoming visible.

We strongly disagree with the idea that tourists need knowledge about how "the creative process has been constructed" in order to "maximize their creative experience."[32] In fact, creativity in touristic experiences relies largely on the authenticity of people, language, and processes, whose expression is often spontaneous and unplanned.

METHODOLOGY

Data was collected during fieldwork in the lacemaking community of Bobowa in 2010–2012, accompanied by further and ongoing research. While investigating three case studies closely, we saw our respondents within the community context, alongside which were interviews from other participants. Observational techniques have also been used to widen the angle of the study in order to provide supplementary information on tourists, hosts, and practices. Data collection included participation in lacemaking workshops, interviewing lacemakers and tourists, and photographing both groups in leisure and work spaces. Weekly participation in the daily life of the agro-tourism farm owner exposed the intimacies of her relations with tourists and the sensitivity of her work as a lacemaking heritage transmitter. This highlighted to us that "heritage is intimately linked with identity."[33] We argue that in order to be recognized as such, a particular set of intangible cultural and social values are required. Thus, individuals are responsible for emotional engagement in workshops between participants and forms of heritage. Here, the researchers' role was to support such actions by involving the self in emotional and sensual craft experiences and becoming a craft practitioner.

Valuing female experience and knowledge,[34] and taking subjective rather than objective positions, allowed for a more in-depth inquiry and thus increased the quality of collected material.[35] Active participation in workshops exposed the nuances of creating an atmosphere related to place, a variety of teaching styles, and the responses and involvement of clients into tangible and intangible heritage that was connected to place. Qualitative interviews permitted respondents to narrate their experiences and provide insight into the evolution of becoming a lacemaker. Tracing the role of tourists' participation in the domestic life of the host exposed the role of creative tourism as reflective interaction[36] that enhanced involvement into both practice and community life.

LACEMAKERS' SPACES: THE WORKSHOPS

Creative tourists search for a unique experience that allows them to immerse in a particular context and space as part of creative processes and practices, which merge livelihoods with local histories and people. Bobowa's lacemakers' workshops, as private spaces for expression of creativity and inspiration, are, first of all, a material expression of identity, and secondly, spaces that allow a relationship with the memory of family, history, and the collective past to be maintained. Through the making process, the individual is linked to the place's lacemaking heritage, embodying one's genealogy through things.[37] Workshops of contemporary lacemakers in Bobowa are an expression of individuality and identity. Creative tourists' workshops need to be something to be attracted to from the first; it can be the shape of the pillow, dynamic movements of hands spotted during the lacemakers' presentation, or the pose of the craftswoman bent over in a sitting position with the roller held carefully between her knees. This image is something that the tourist is confronted with at the moment of participation—workshops become spaces of struggle. Soon, however, relaxing sounds of blocks and clear instruction evolve into a rhythm of thread and pattern that slowly follows the move of bobbin blocks from left to right, from up to down. After weekly workshops many tourists end up buying tools, patterns, and laces from the lacemakers. Craft identities are co-constructed by a creative experience.[38] Richards[39] argues that creative experiences are co-created between hosts and tourists. Within this partnership and collaboration, the tools for making bobbin laces, including a pillow, bobbin blocks, threads, pins, and a crochet needle, serve as a medium between a relationship on the edge of which authentic experiences emerge. In Bobowa and its neighborhood, different tools were used over the decades that were original to the region. The tools from lacemakers' workshops are part of craft tradition: "the craft artifacts, the associated lifestyles and structures at a given time and a given place."[40] The objects are designed to suit the place; moreover, they are gendered and are a form of gender-based representation. Following the line of thought of King,[41] it could be argued that gender dynamics in cultural representations of objects appear in terms of who is allowed to make things, the value assigned to women's making, and the ways in which women are supposed to respond to artifacts. The form of bobbin laces and the knowledge of how to make them were transmitted through generations. Creative tourists, participating in the process of knowledge and pattern sharing, are included in the community scheme and play an important role in the symbolic continuation of tradition.

In order to illustrate the character of creative tourism in Bobowa, different profiles of women and their entrepreneurial ideas will be presented. The three accounts are based on experiences of everyday practices of active lacemakers.

AUTHENTICITY OF EVERYDAY LIFE: EWA SZPILA AND HER AGRO-TOURISM FARM WITH LACEMAKING COURSES

The experience of an everyday lacemaker's life in a small town can be seen through Ewa Szpila, whose life is underpinned by a rustic, idyllic landscape that embraces an authenticity that relates to both objects and activities. She is currently one of the most specialized people in contemporary bobbin lace-making in the community of Bobowa and in Europe. She has obtained great proficiency in laces by winning national and international contests, designing, judging others, lecturing, and presenting on lacemaking themes. She learned laces in the late 1990s and was trained by her colleague. As an outsider who came to Bobowa after her husband, she was not particularly limited by family or neighbors. Her confidence was strengthened after she participated in a course about entrepreneurship in rural areas that was organized by the Regional Development Center for the unemployed. She started a farm that embraced agro-tourism, and as part of a strategy of diversification, she began offering pillow lace workshops. The agro-tourism farm, with lacemaking workshops, was a successful idea that linked training in craft with a landscape that greatly added to its touristic appeal, making it an attractive holiday for women in their forties to sixties. Szpila's entrepreneurial success is a result of her marketing skills and her easygoing personality. During the initial stages (meeting potential customers during a festival), Ewa describes lacemaking as a special practice worth learning. She highlights the originality of the craft as well as her exceptional teaching approach to lacemaking.

Next is the preparation of a place that reflects an authentic rural idyll for clients in Ewa's own home and garden. Here, the children become involved with the mother's project, supporting, if necessary, the service in the household and entertaining the guests. The husband also at times contributes to a positive atmosphere with his occasional cooking, offering conversations and stories about the community life of Bobowa. The involvement of the whole family is crucial for a service provision. Ewa's experience as a lacemaker who makes and promotes laces, is involved with contests locally, or travels with them abroad, helped her create a mini exhibition on lacemaking in her house. It can be seen as part of a strategy not only to encourage other women to learn, but also to enter into a lifelong relationship with the "magic world of laces." Famous among incomers is the arbor (built by Szpila's husband), which is a perfect place for workshops in the summer. Here, laces can be made in fresh air in a blooming garden.

Following this home and arbor space experience, which strengthens authenticity of practice, there is time for special lacemaking training, described in the form of a story. This approach, besides introducing ritualized lacemaking behavior, is an excellent way to teach others almost without using technical vocabulary characteristic of this type of craftsmanship. Ewa's illustrative language, which might seem to be infantile at first glance, effectively implements skills in her students:

A treasure: "During making leaves a pair, which is leading a thread, is interwoven between other pairs and called 'a treasure.'" "Keep this pair in your hands as your little treasure, you are not allowed to release it."
A false cord—a chain screwed a few times depending on the length of the interval.
Lazybones—a pair used to make a garland named as State Agricultural Farms [PGR-y[42]].

> Garland . . . is a stripe with margin. So there is a stripe made, and then pair with blue thread is left aside [Ewa previously depicted pair with color, so it will not be lost]—these are so called lazybones. Up-down, down-up, etc. till next pin and stripe with margin. These pairs make business. Then down-up-down-up, we came to pair so called slacking. Those are so called PGR's, they don't want to work. We add the pair, which also wants to slack, hand around and drink. So they could drink together. And we move left pairs: down-up-down-up, till those, which works, they have own businesses.

In the last example, the language that relates to the past appears very naturally with the description of the *lazy* non-working pairs and active pair in garland technique. It reflects the perception of the difference between the past (slow, passive socialism) and the present (progressive, fast-moving capitalism) and, in a broader sense, between the people in the community who negotiate between the past and present.

Organization of the client's work and discipline during workshops are essential for a trainee's progress and satisfaction, as well as the promotion of the farm idea and overall satisfactory performance of creative tourism.

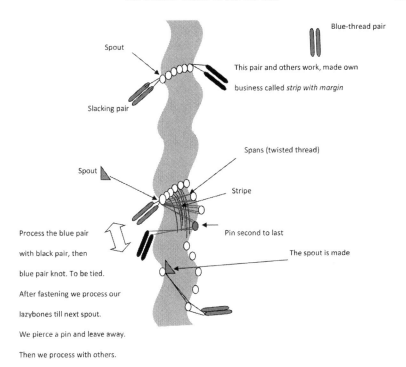

Blue-thread pair

Spout

This pair and others work, made own

business called *strip with margin*

Slacking pair

Spans (twisted thread)

Spout

Stripe

Process the blue pair

Pin second to last

with black pair, then

The spout is made

blue pair knot. To be tied.

After fastening we process our

lazybones till next spout.

We pierce a pin and leave away.

Then we process with others.

Figure 11.1 Instruction of making a garland drawn by the workshop participant in **2012.** Adapted from: Ethnographic Journal. *Source*: Diagram by Anna Sznajder.

During six days of workshops some standards, even for beginners, need to be met, which include learning basic stitches and making simple traditional lace using five techniques. Techniques are trained in a particular order each day. The routine (8 am—waking up/breakfast; 9 am—work starts; 11 am—coffee break; 12–12:30 pm—end of work; 12:30–2:00 pm—free time for guests, including shopping and other forms of tourism; 2:00–2:30 pm—lunch; 3:00–5:00 or 6:00 pm—lacemaking workshops; 6:30–7:00 pm—dinner, free time, or evening together) helps to make sure that, by the end of the week, the trainee has learned the basics and ended up with a final product from their creative tourism experience. Sometimes Ewa completes more complicated patterns only a few hours before the train departs on Sunday.

The final stage of Ewa's workshops is an invitation to be included in her elite circle of lacemakers, which is centered on the International Bobbin and Needle Lace Organization (OIDFA). Recognizing the benefits of membership in an organization, Ewa became its representative for Poland and encouraged her trainees to join OIDFA. This should be considered a significant contribution in bobbin lacemaking promotion on the national and international level.

This is not about the local heritage keepers—citizens of Bobowa—but about building networks with those who can help promote it.

Successful creative tourism initiatives result in contemporary creative products and processes that include craft taken home, and skills and techniques that can be practiced. Engagement in collective making of laces, while talking, singing, gossiping, and spending time together, is a reconstruction of feminine labor from Bobowa's past. Similarly, engaging with storytelling over the hundred-year-old patterns or tools and learning about their originality, destination, and link to family stories enrich the experience of creative tourism and morph into an authentic attachment to community history. Finally, Ewa introduces innovations in lacemaking by presenting contemporary designs, advertising in local shops with lace jewelry, or encouraging women to belong to a lacemaking community so that visitors can regularly interact with the site. Manipulation of culture and creative resources and their adaptation to particular conditions show that authenticity can be retained;[43] it determines continuation with tradition and its reinterpretation by creative tourists.

The variety of local lacemaking craft workshops exposes a diversity of authentic creative experience discourses considered as indigenous, through which "power relations are constantly organized."[44] Such experiences are in a dominant position in regard to the translation of heritage between the community and tourists. Jadwiga Śliwa highlighted her professional experience as key to authentic lacemaking practice in Bobowa. Secondly, she introduced an extra element of passive participation in embroidery workshops in her private and intimate atelier.

The idea of a lacemaking and embroidering craft studio appeared a few years after she lost her job in a vocational school (in lacemaking class) in 1999 and was a catalyst for her search for a new identity as an unemployed lacemaking instructor. Joblessness was challenging for her family. She returned home after some negative experiences as a migrant worker in the United Kingdom. She decided to return and start from the beginning; firstly, teaching children lacemaking in a local cultural center, and secondly, searching for clients of handmade embroidery banners requested by schools, associations, and churches. Participation in Bobowa's events (contests and the festival), as well as a craft revival across Poland and her travels abroad, accelerated the transformation into individual workshops for craft lovers, "Holidays with Lace" [Wakacje z koronką]. The central attraction of the workshops was her craft studio, where she demonstrates a process of making embroidered banners. Five-day holidays include accommodation, food, and course materials using the company logo, and also a certificate confirming participants' attendance in a course led by a professional lacemaking instructor and teacher from a vocational school. The slogan on her professionally

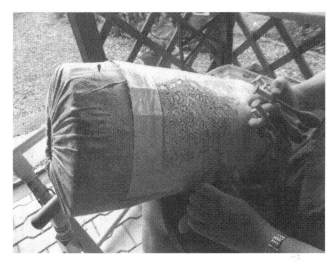

Figure 11.2 Advanced student making the laces; Western European fan pattern with Bobowa's techniques, 2011. *Source*: Photo by Anna Sznajder.

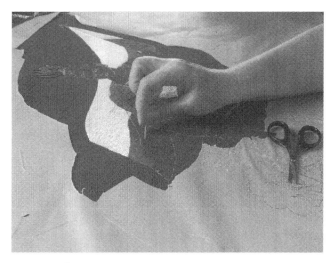

Figure 11.3 Jadwiga Śliwa during work, making the Saint Florian banner for the local Fire Brigade, Bobowa 2010. *Source*: Photo by Anna Sznajder.

designed leaflet was, "choose your favorite technique and come for training," which highlights an approach opposite to the teaching of Ewa Szpila, who presents a planned lacemaking schedule. Differentiation comes also with the concept of the craft studio, which has the character of a craft atelier rather than an idyllic rural holiday on a farm. On the company website[45] short descriptions introduce the idea of the craft studio and a creative experience in the house of a professional. A gallery of laces and embroidery demonstrates the skills of the instructor, showcasing examples of inspirational old and modern lace patterns. Diplomas, certificates, and referral letters from Poland and abroad are official proofs of Śliwa's skills as a teacher, instructor, and lacemaker displayed on the walls. She designed her own-shaped pillow, stand, and bobbin blocks, which vary from those traditionally known in the region and used by lacemakers. Her studio is to be developed into a gallery on the hills of nearby Brzana village, with the help of her daughters.

EXPERIENCING LIVE FOLKLORE: MARIA SIKORSKA'S FOLK-BASED WORKSHOPS

Heritage is a process whereby the past is constantly interpreted through people's memory and choices.[46] These meanings overlap, linking the local with the global, the past with the present, and the rural with the urban. Some have argued that tourism must rely on "seductive as well as restrictive imaginaries about people and places,"[47] which drives both tourists and services for them in place. Contrary to skilled and experienced instructors working in the idyllic garden or professional modern craft studio, the image of folk artisan, coarse and simple, brings out the flavor of a past collective life in a rural community. Unlike Ewa and Jadwiga, who utilize the ideas of rural idyll or

Figure 11.4   The wooden house of Maria Sikorska on Bobowa's Main Square (first from the right) and the monument of a Lacemaker, Bobowa 2010. *Source*: Photo by Anna Sznajder.

professional craft teaching, Maria Sikorska introduces folklore elements to her touristic product. Workshops are conducted in her living room decorated with handmade folklore and sacred images from laces. Sharing her private space and her own story with the trainees, similarly to Ewa and Jadwiga, she engages participants with the craft-making environment and multiple dimensions of Bobowa community. She even kept a special chronicle of her lacemaking livelihood.

The example of Maria Sikorska, as that of Jadwiga, demonstrates how unemployment becomes a factor in making money from lacemaking. A former nursery teacher in the nearby city of Nowy Sącz, she started learning laces when she became unemployed. After a two-year process of skills development, she started participating in local lacemaking contests, winning prizes and promoting laces during events and exhibitions. After building an artisan portfolio, she finally applied for a nationally recognized The Folk Craftsman title, which she received in 2008 from the Folk Craftsmen Association

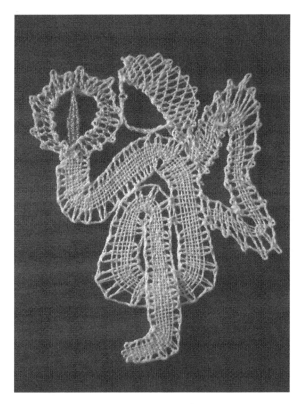

Figure 11.5   Six-hour workshops with Maria Sikorska in Bobowa, 2010. *Source:* Photo by Anna Sznajder.

in Lublin. This title allowed Maria to improve her selling, network, travel, and meet other craftsmen and craftswomen across Poland. These experiences encouraged her to construct the image of folk artisan—a woman in folk floral scarf or red corals emphasizing her regional and peripheral authenticity. In time, Maria Sikorska was the only one in Bobowa who became registered with the Heritage Trail,[48] Krakow's charity that supports local craftsmen in Southern Poland through promotion and events; places where they can sell their craft. Her profile and achievements were presented on the website along with her home address, inviting tourists for creative experiences in an old prewar house in the center of Bobowa's Main Square. Her entrepreneurial skills significantly developed during this time and, currently, she is actively selling the crafts of her neighbors and friends, cooperating with designers she met during events, and teaching one- or half-day workshops in her home.

CONCLUSIONS

This chapter examined some of the links between tourism development and women's innovative working strategies in rural areas, drawing on the example of lacemaker entrepreneurs from Bobowa, Southern Poland. By applying the concept of creative tourism, we have sought to define authentic experiences of local culture and their role in creative work among hosts and guests, exploring how the opportunities to use creative skills happen through active participation in lacemaking—an activity that is characteristic of the region. Increasing involvement in local cultural heritage by experiencing, participating, and learning occurs through the interaction, immersion, and experience of the craft, craftmakers, and their place.

Despite the continuing influences of the historical (rural and socialist) discourses, there are signs that Bobowa is witnessing a melding of neoliberal economic processes, shaping creative tourism locally. In Bobowa, activity-based creative tourism is supported by the uniqueness of the local identities of enterprising lacemakers. The presented case studies of women who decided to start a business using local tangible and intangible heritage-based resources—bobbin laces and lacemaking skills—expose the potential of creative tourism, framed as a new, gender-specific experience. A rich environment and its natural, cultural, and traditional qualities enrich the experience of tourists. Creative tourism grants the visitors a glimpse of the private sphere of local women's lives. Reflecting upon how private spaces are constructed, reconstructed, and co-constructed by hosts and guests, and what are further implications for the self-realization and self-expression as well as sustainable livelihoods of both groups, creative tourism can play a crucial role in negotiating identities as well as balancing power relations.

Implementing innovations in a lacemaking community through creative persons, processes, and products exposes cultural change in Bobowa over the last decade and demonstrates the role of gender-specific forms of tourism based on local craft heritage. Innovative ideas developed from year to year demonstrate how creative tourism contributes to recognition of Bobowa as a lacemaking place that supports rural development in broader terms, and simultaneously, reveals tensions arising between tradition and innovation.

This process includes further challenges for authenticity of laces, lace patterns, tools, and accessories, which must be redesigned and remade to meet creative tourists' expectations. Guest-host relations are also transformed and renegotiated in the form of long-term acquaintances, friendships, and master-trainee relations. These relationships are carefully maintained not only for the purpose of future income, but also for participation in the real and symbolic life of a craft community. The fact that creative tourism is usually based on family assets, such as the private space of house and garden, exposes its potential to change by developing small-scale enterprises led by individual lacemakers. It could be argued that, in the case of Bobowa's creative tourism, specific focus is oriented on exploitation of entrepreneurial opportunity and draws on active skills development and demand for self-actualization in lacemaking.

The landscape of Bobowa became, to use a literary term, "emblematic." A town's iconic monument is an artifact signifying the cultural status of the place; hence, it fulfills "the need to connect the present to the past."[49] Authenticity of the creative tourism experience relies on the uses of history, which construct multiple layers of meanings that are grouped around the following themes: creative skills, creative products, creative people, and finally, creative places that include organization of work, production, and distribution. We conclude that there remains a crucial challenge to develop conceptualizations of creative tourism that encompass multiple worldviews of hosts and visitors in co-producing heritage.

NOTES

1. Greg Richards, "Creativity and Tourism. The State of the Art," *Annals of Tourism Research* 38 (2011): 1225–53, accessed November 15, 2015. doi:10.1016/j.annals.2011.07.008.

2. Maria Gutkowska-Rychlewska, *Historia ubiorów* (Wrocław: Ossolineum, 1968).

3. Józef Kochmański, *100 lat Szkolnictwa Zawodowego w Bobowej 1899–1999* (Bobowa: Komitet Organizacyjny Obchodów 100-lecia ZSZ im. S. Wyspiańskiego w Bobowej, 1999).

4. Wojciech Molendowicz, *Bobowa od A do Ż* (Nowy Sącz: Nova Sandec, 2009), 56.

5. Łaś, "Święto tradycji, Międzynarodowy Festiwal Koronki Klockowej w Bobowej," in *Gazeta Krakowska*, October 7, 2008.

6. Katarzyna Kosmala, "Expanded Cities in Expanded Europe: Resisting Identities, Feminist Politics and their Utopianism," *Third Text* 24 (2010): 541–55, accessed February 13, 2013. doi:10.1080/09528822.2010.502773; Katarzyna Kosmala, "Introduction: Politics of Gender, Video, New Media Arts and Post-Socialist Europe," in *Sexing the Border. Gender, Art and New Media in Central and Eastern Europe,* ed. Katarzyna Kosmala (Newcastle upon Tyne: Cambridge Scholars Publishing, 2014), 1–12.

7. Sara McDowell, "Heritage, Memory and Identity," in *The Ashgate Research Companion to Heritage and Identity*, ed. Brian Graham and Peter Howard (Aldershot: Ashgate Publishing, 2008), 37.

8. Ummu Hani, Azzadina Ima, Sianipar Corinthias, Setyagung Estav, and Tomohisa Ishii, "Preserving Cultural Heritage through Creative Industry: A Lesson from Saung Angklung Udjo," *Procedia Economics and Finance* 4 (2012): 194, accessed November 15, 2015. doi:10.1016/S2212-5671(12)00334-6; Rossitza Ohridska-Olson and Stanislav Ivanov, "Creative Tourism Business Model and Its Application," in *Bulgaria*. 2010, accessed November 15, 2015. http://culturalrealms.typepad.com/files/creativetourismbm_article_1_lr.pdf, 3.

9. Laurajane Smith, "The 'Doing' of Heritage: Heritage as Performance," in *Performing Heritage: Research, Practice and Innovation in Museum Theater and Live Interpretation*, ed. Anthony Jackson and Jenny Kidd (Manchester: Manchester University Press, 2011), 70.

10. Ahmed Skounti, "The Authentic Illusion: Humanity's Intangible Cultural Heritage, the Moroccan Experience," in *Intangible Heritage*, ed. Laurajane Smith and Natsuko Akagawa (London: Routledge, 2009), 74.

11. *Strategia Rozwoju Gminy Bobowa na lata 2008–2013*, 2007, accessed January 15, 2013, 1. http://www.bobowa.pl/userfiles/file/pliki/strategia.pdf.

12. Bobowa Miastem od 1.01.2009 r. Kraków: Urząd Statystyczny w Krakowie oddział w Tarnowie. 2009, accessed January 10, 2015, 11–12, http://www.bobowa.pl/pliki/inne/stat-bobowa.pdf.

13. *Strategia Rozwoju Gminy Bobowa na lata 2008–2013*, 2007, 17, accessed January 15, 2013. http://www.bobowa.pl/userfiles/file/pliki/strategia.pdf.

14. Anna Sznajder, "Connecting European Lacemaking Traditions—Reflections on 16th International Bobbin Laces Festival in Bobowa, Southern Poland 2015. Relier les traditions dentelliéres européennes—Pensées sur le 16éme Festival International de Dentelle de Bobowa, sud de la Pologne 2015," *Quarterly Journal of the International Bobbin and Needle Lace Organisation* 34 (2016): 28.

15. Anna Sznajder, "Women, Bobbin Lace Histories and the Formation of Lacemaking Heritage in Bobowa, Southern Poland: An Ethnographic Case Study" (PhD diss., The University of the West of Scotland, 2014), 110.

16. Greg Richards and Julie Wilson, "Developing Creativity in Tourist Experiences: A Solution to the Serial Reproduction of Culture?" *Tourism Management* 27 (2006), accessed June 15, 2015. doi:10.1016/j.tourman.2005.06.002, 1218–20.

17. According to respondents, before the Second World War laces were sold as tourist objects in nearby Krynica. Now, in Krynica, there is a shop with laces. Linking laces from Bobowa with Krynica mineral waters resort through trading, exposes links between the tourism industry and product development. With strong development of Bobowa as a bobbin lacemaking heritage center in recent decades, lace becomes a local product assigned exclusively to its locality.

18. Greg Richards and Crispin Raymond, "Creative Tourism," *Atlas News* 23 (2000): 18.

19. Rossitza Ohridska-Olson and Stanislav Ivanov, *Creative Tourism*, 3.

20. Greg Richards, "Creativity and Tourism: The State of the Art."

21. Siow-Kian Tan, Ding-Bang Luh, and Shiann-Far Kung, "A Taxonomy of Creative Tourists in Creative Tourism," *Tourism Management* 42 (2014): 249.

22. Siow-Kian Tan, Ding-Bang Luh, and Shiann-Far Kung, "A Taxonomy of Creative Tourists in Creative Tourism," *Tourism Management* 42 (2014): 248–53.

23. Paul Silvia, Roger Beaty, Emily Nusbaum, Kari Eddington, Holly Levin-Aspenson, and Thomas Kwapil, "Everyday Creativity in Daily Life: An Experience—Sampling Study of 'little c' Creativity," *Psychology of Aesthetics, Creativity, and the Arts* 8 (2014), accessed November 15, 2015. doi:10.1037/a0035722, 183–88.

24. Helen Berry, "Regional Identity and Material Culture," in *History and Material Culture: A Student's Guide to Approaching Alternative Sources*, ed. Karen Harvey (London: Routledge, 2009), 149.

25. Ning Wang, "Rethinking Authenticity in Tourism Experience," *Annals of Tourism Research* 26 (1999): 352.

26. Anna Brzezińska, Marek Krajewski, ed., "Wakacje z koronką. Oferta kształcenia w zakresie rękodzieła (wybrane przykłady)," in *Handmade. Praca rąk w postindustrialnej rzeczywistości* (Warszawa: Fundacja Nowej Kultury Bęc Zmiana, 2010), 276.

27. Zygmunt Kruczek, *Atrakcje turystyczne. Fenomen, typologia, metody badań* (Kraków: Wydawnictwo Proksenia, 2011), 49.

28. Kristine McKenzie Gentry, "Belizean Women and Tourism Work: Opportunity or Impediment?" *Annals of Tourism Research* 34 (2007): 478, accessed November 15, 2015. doi:10.1016/j.annals.2006.11.003.

29. For instance, intimacy of women only craft spaces has been recognized in *Weranda Country* magazine (Ross 2015) as an alternative lifestyle from the city. Meanwhile, it also promotes the idea of actively and creatively spent leisure time.

30. Anna Wieczorkiewicz, *Apetyt turysty. O doświadczaniu świata w podróży* (Kraków: Universitas, 2008), 39.

31. Cara Aitchison and Fiona Jordan, "Gender, Space and Identity: Introduction," in *Gender, Space and Identity: Leisure, Culture and Commerce*, ed. Cara Aitchison and Fiona Jordan (Eastbourne: Leisure Studies Association, 1998), vi.

32. Siow-Kian Tan, Shiann-Far Kung, and Ding-Bang Luh, "A Model of 'Creative Experience' in Creative Tourism," in *Annals of Tourism Research* 41 (2013): 154, accessed November 15, 2015. doi:10.1016/j.annals.2012.12.002.

33. Laurajane Smith and Natsuko Akagawa, "Introduction," in *Intangible Heritage*, ed. Laurajane Smith and Natsuko Akagawa (London: Routledge, 2009), 1–9.

34. Barbara Pini, "Feminist Methodology and Rural Research: Reflections on a Study of an Australian Agricultural Organisation," *Sociologia Ruralis* 43 (2003): 419, accessed January 15, 2015. doi:10.1046/j.1467-9523.2003.00253.x/pdf.

35. Lorraine Dowler, "Participant Observation," in *A Feminist Glossary of Human Geography*, ed. Linda McDowell and Joanne Sharp (London: Arnold Publishers, 1999), 195–96.

36. Greg Richards and Julie Wilson, "Developing Creativity in Tourist Experiences," 1219.

37. Nicolette Makovicky, "Closet and Cabinet: Clutter as Cosmology," in *Home Cultures* 4 (2007): 298, accessed November 15, 2015. http://connection.ebscohost.com/c/articles/28334458/closet-cabinet-clutter-as-cosmology.

38. Fiona Hackney, "CAREful or CAREless? Collaborative Making and Social Engagement through Craft," in *Engage 33: Critical Craft*, ed. Karen Raney (London: The National Association for Gallery Education, 2013), 34.

39. Greg Richards, "Creativity and Tourism."

40. Sirpa Kokko and Patrick Dillon, "Crafts and Craft Education as Expressions of Cultural Heritage: Individual Experiences and Collective Values among an International Group of Women University Students," *International Journal of Technology & Design Education* 21 (2011): 488, accessed October 15, 2015. doi:10.1007/s10798-010-9128-2.

41. Catherine King, "Making Things Mean: Cultural Representations in Objects," in *Imagining Women: Cultural Representations and Gender*, ed. Frances Bonner, Lizbeth Goodman, Richard Allen, Linda Janes, and Catherine King (Cambridge: Polity Press in Association with The Open University, 1992), 15.

42. A State Agricultural Farm [Państwowe Gospodarstwo Rolne, PGR] was a form of collective farming in the People's Republic of Poland between years 1949 and 1991.

43. Betty Duggan, "Tourism, Cultural Authenticity, and the Native Crafts Cooperative: The Eastern Cherokee Experience," in *Tourism and Culture: An Applied Perspective*, ed. Erve Chambers (Albany: State University of New York Press, 1997), 31.

44. Jarkko Saarinen, "Representations of 'Indigeneity': Sami Culture in the Discourses of Tourism," in *Indigeneity: Construction and Re/presentation*, ed. James Brown and Patricia Sant (Commanck: Nova Science Publishers, 1999), 242.

45. Sztuka Koronki. 2015, accessed November 15, 2015. http://www.sztuka-koronki.art.pl.

46. Jacek Purchla, "Dziedzictwo kulturowe," in *Kultura a rozwój*, ed. Jerzy Hausner, Anna Karwińska, and Jacek Purchla (Warszawa: Narodowe Centrum Kultury, 2013), 39.

47. Noel Salazar, "Tourism Imaginaries: A Conceptual Approach," *Annals of Tourism Research* 39 (2012): 863, accessed January 15, 2014. doi:10.1016/j.annals.2011.10.004.

48. Szlak Rzemiosła. 2015, accessed August 14. http://szlakrzemiosla.pl/Maria-Sikorska.html.

49. Gregory J. Ashworth and Brian Graham, "Senses of Place, Senses of Time and Heritage," in *Senses of Place: Sense of Time*, ed. Gregory John Ashworth and Brian Graham (Aldershot: Ashgate Publishing, 2005), 8–9.

REFERENCES

Aitchison, Cara, and Jordan Fiona. "Gender, Space and Identity: Introduction." In *Gender, Space and Identity: Leisure, Culture and Commerce*, edited by Cara Aitchison and Fiona Jordan, v–ix. Eastbourne: Leisure Studies Association, 1998.

Ashworth, Gregory J., and Brian Graham. "Senses of Place, Senses of Time and Heritage." In *Senses of Place: Sense of Time*, edited by Gregory John Ashworth and Brian Graham, 3–12. Aldershot: Ashgate Publishing, 2005.

Berry, Helen. "Regional Identity and Material Culture." In *History and Material Culture: A Student's Guide to Approaching Alternative Sources*, edited by Karen Harvey, 139–57. London: Routledge, 2009.

Bobowa Miastem od 1.01.2009 r. Kraków: Urząd Statystyczny w Krakowie oddział w Tarnowie, 2009. Accessed January 10, 2015. http://www.bobowa.pl/pliki/inne/stat-bobowa.pdf.

Brzezińska, Anna. "Wakacje z koronką. Oferta kształcenia w zakresie rękodzieła (wybrane przykłady)." In *Handmade. Praca rąk w postindustrialnej rzeczywistości*, edited by Marek Krajewski, 272–78. Warszawa: Fundacja Nowej Kultury Bęc Zmiana, 2010.

Dowler, Lorraine. "Participant Observation." In *A Feminist Glossary of Human Geography*, edited by Linda McDowell and Joanne Sharp, 195–96. London: Arnold Publishers, 1999.

Duggan, Betty. "Tourism, Cultural Authenticity, and the Native Crafts Cooperative: The Eastern Cherokee Experience." In *Tourism and Culture: An Applied Perspective*, edited by Erve Chambers, 31–57. Albany: State University of New York Press, 1997.

Gutkowska-Rychlewska, Maria. *Historia ubiorów*. Wrocław, Warszawa and Kraków: Ossolineum, 1968.

Hackney, Fiona. "CAREful or CAREless? Collaborative Making and Social Engagement through Craft." In *engage 33: Critical Craft*, edited by Karen Raney, 23–37. London: The National Association for Gallery Education, 2013.

Hani, Ummu, Ima Azzadina, Corinthias Sianipar, Estav Setyagung, and Ishii Tomohisa. "Preserving Cultural Heritage through Creative Industry: A Lesson from Saung Angklung Udjo." *Procedia Economics and Finance* 4 (2012): 193–200. Accessed November 15, 2015. doi:10.1016/S2212-5671(12)00334-6.

King, Catherine. "Making Things Mean: Cultural Representations in Objects." In *Imagining Women: Cultural Representations and Gender*, edited by Frances Bonner, Lizbeth Goodman, Richard Allen, Linda Janes, and Catherine King, 15–20. Cambridge: Polity Press in Association with The Open University, 1992.

Kochmański, Józef. *100 lat Szkolnictwa Zawodowego w Bobowej 1899–1999*. Bobowa: Komitet Organizacyjny Obchodów 100–lecia ZSZ im. S. Wyspiańskiego w Bobowej, 1999.

Kokko, Sirpa, and Patrick Dillon. "Crafts and Craft Education as Expressions of Cultural Heritage: Individual Experiences and Collective Values among an International Group of Women University Students." *International Journal of*

Technology & Design Education 21 (2011): 487–503. Accessed October 15, 2015. doi:10.1007/s10798-010-9128-2.

Kosmala, Katarzyna. "Expanded Cities in Expanded Europe: Resisting Identities, Feminist Politics and their Utopias." *Third Text* 24 (2010): 541–55. Accessed February 13, 2013. doi:10.1080/09528822.2010.502773.

Kosmala, Katarzyna. "Introduction: Politics of Gender, Video, New Media Arts and Post-Socialist Europe." In *Sexing the Border: Gender, Art and New Media in Central and Eastern Europe*, edited by Katarzyna Kosmala, 1–12. Newcastle upon Tyne: Cambridge Scholars Publishing, 2014.

Kruczek, Zygmunt. *Atrakcje turystyczne. Fenomen, typologia, metody badań.* Kraków: Wydawnictwo Proksenia, 2011.

Łaś, L."Święto tradycji. Międzynarodowy Festiwal Koronki Klockowej w Bobowej." *Gazeta Krakowska*, October 7, 2008.

Makovicky, Nicolette. "Closet and Cabinet: Clutter as Cosmology." *Home Cultures* 4 (2007): 287–310. Accessed November 15, 2015. http://connection.ebscohost. com/c/articles/28334458/closet-cabinet-clutter-as-cosmology.

McDowell, Sara. "Heritage, Memory and Identity." In *The Ashgate Research Companion to Heritage and Identity*, edited by Brian Graham and Peter Howard, 37–54. Aldershot: Ashgate Publishing, 2008.

McKenzie Gentry, Kristine. "Belizean Women and Tourism Work: Opportunity or Impediment?" *Annals of Tourism Research* 34 (2007): 477–96. Accessed November 15, 2015. doi:10.1016/j.annals.2006.11.003.

Molendowicz, Wojciech. *Bobowa od A do Ż.* Nowy Sącz: Nova Sandec, 2009.

Ohridska-Olson, Rossitza, and Stanislav Ivanov. *Creative Tourism Business Model and Its Application in Bulgaria.* 2010. Accessed November 15, 2015. http://culturalrealms.typepad.com/files/creativetourismbm_article_1_lr.pdf.

Pini, Barbara. "Feminist Methodology and Rural Research: Reflections on a Study of an Australian Agricultural Organisation." *Sociologia Ruralis* 43 (2003): 418–33. Accessed January 15, 2015. doi:10.1046/j.1467-9523.2003.00253.x/pdf.

Purchla, Jacek. "Dziedzictwo Kulturowe." In *Kultura a rozwój*, edited by Jerzy Hausner, Anna Karwińska, and Jacek Purchla, 39–56. Warszawa: Narodowe Centrum Kultury, 2013.

Richards, Greg. "Creativity and Tourism: The State of the Art." *Annals of Tourism Research* 38 (2011): 1225–53. Accessed November 15, 2015. doi:10.1016/j. annals.2011.07.008.

Richards, Greg, and Crispin Raymond. "Creative Tourism." *Atlas News* 23 (2000): 16–20.

Richards, Greg, and Julie Wilson. "Developing Creativity in Tourist Experiences: A Solution to the Serial Reproduction of Culture?" *Tourism Management* 27 (2006): 1209–23. Accessed June 15, 2015. doi:10.1016/j.tourman.2005.06.002.

Ross, Sonia. "Królowa Koronek." In *Weranda Country*, February, 2015. Accessed November 15, 2015. http://www.werandacountry.pl/hobby-i-praca/rzemioslo/ 16345-krolowa-koronek.

Saarinen, Jarkko. "Representations of 'Indigeneity': Sami Culture in the Discourses of Tourism." In *Indigeneity: Construction and Re/presentation*, edited by James Brown and Patricia Sant, 231–49. Commanck: Nova Science Publishers, 1999.

Salazar, Noel. "Tourism Imaginaries: A Conceptual Approach." *Annals of Tourism Research* 39 (2012): 863–82. Accessed January 15, 2014. doi:10.1016/j.annals.2011.10.004.

Silvia, Paul, Roger Beaty, Emily Nusbaum, Kari Eddington, Holly Levin-Aspenson, and Thomas Kwapil. "Everyday Creativity in Daily Life: An Experience—Sampling Study of 'little c' Creativity." In *Psychology of Aesthetics, Creativity, and the Arts* 8 (2014): 183–88. Accessed November 15, 2015. doi:10.1037/a0035722.

Skounti, Ahmed. "The Authentic Illusion: Humanity's Intangible Cultural Heritage, the Maroccan Experience." In *Intangible Heritage*, edited by Laurajane Smith and Natsuko Akagawa, 74–92. London: Routledge, 2009.

Smith, Laurajane. "The 'Doing' of Heritage: Heritage as Performance." In *Performing Heritage: Research, Practice and Innovation in Museum Theatre and Live Interpretation*, edited by Anthony Jackson and Jenny Kidd, 69–81. Manchester: Manchester University Press, 2011.

Smith, Laurajane, and Natsuko Akagawa. "Introduction." In *Intangible Heritage*, edited by Laurajane Smith and Natsuko Akagawa, 1–9. London: Routledge, 2009.

Strategia Rozwoju Gminy Bobowa na lata 2008–2013. 2007. Accessed January 15, 2013. http://www.bobowa.pl/userfiles/file/pliki/strategia.pdf.

Szlak Rzemiosła. 2015. Accessed August 14. http://szlakrzemiosla.pl/Maria-Sikorska.html.

Sznajder, Anna. "Women, Bobbin Lace Histories and the Formation of Lacemaking Heritage in Bobowa, Southern Poland: An Ethnographic Case Study." PhD diss., The University of the West of Scotland, 2014.

Sznajder, Anna. "Connecting European Lacemaking Traditions—Reflections on 16th International Bobbin Laces Festival in Bobowa, Southern Poland 2015. Relier les traditions dentelliéres européennes—Pensées sur le 16éme Festival International de Dentelle de Bobowa, sud de la Pologne 2015." *Quarterly Journal of the International Bobbin and Needle Lace Organization* 34 (2016): 22–28.

Sztuka Koronki. 2015. Accessed November 15, 2015. http://www.sztukakoronki.art.pl.

Tan, Siow-Kian, Shiann-Far Kung, and Ding-Bang Luh. "A Model of 'Creative Experience' in Creative Tourism." *Annals of Tourism Research* 41 (2013): 153–74. Accessed November 15, 2015. doi:10.1016/j.annals.2012.12.002.

Tan, Siow-Kian, Ding-Bang Luh, and Shiann-Far Kung. "A Taxonomy of Creative Tourists in Creative Tourism." *Tourism Management* 42 (2014): 248–59.

Wang, Ning. "Rethinking Authenticity in Tourism Experience." *Annals of Tourism Research* 26 (1999): 349–70.

Wieczorkiewicz, Anna. *Apetyt turysty. O doświadczaniu świata w podróży.* Kraków: Universitas, 2008.

Chapter 12

Toward Interpretative City Guiding

New Approaches and Services on the Example of Selected European Cities

Armin Mikos von Rohrscheidt

TOUR GUIDING AS A FIELD OF INQUIRY FOR TOURIST STUDIES

The analysis of tour-guiding phenomena indicates that slightly over 10 percent of 265 research papers published within the last 35 years regarded Europe.[1] This implies that the subject matter, situated on the intersection of applied cultural studies and research on tourist phenomena, is not treated with enough significance. The growing gap between guests' preferences and interests and the host-interpreters' offers might result in decreased demand and gradual decline of this ancient profession, which would lead to the disappearance of another medium of personal heritage sharing. At the same time, a few more creative guides, particularly those who make a living from that profession, are in search of new methods and tools, testing them at work and on their clients. Guides tend to alter, or at least diversify their offer profile, by implementing the element of heritage interpretation to an even greater degree.

The research was performed in July and August 2015 by cataloging and analyzing offers available on proposed websites of one dominating or a few leading tour operator(s) in several dozen historical European cities brimming with well-developed guiding offers. Such offers were studied, and they contained almost 500 detailed proposals with an explicit element of interpretation. Although the research does not provide total results, a group of cities may be considered as representative, equally for the so-called old European Union (from before enlargement in 2004), as well as its new part. The examples of offers specified as alternative and interpretative are further described in the form of case studies in the third part of this chapter.

ON HERITAGE AND THE TENETS
OF ITS INTERPRETATION

The most useful definition of heritage for the contemporary interpreter, and the most understandable for a tourist, is the one proposed by Robert Hewison. According to the author, heritage is "that which a past generation has preserved and handed on to the present and which a significant group of population wishes to hand on to the future."[2] The definition does not focus on isolated objects with unchangeable, once-given meaning and message, but it subsumes the heritage contextually and dynamically. In individual or collective consciousness, the heritage gains its full meaning when it dissolves into emotional engagement and exhaustion in knowledge; it becomes a part of identity when people endow it with new, personal meanings and use in establishing group or local bonds.

Even though sites, facilities, and objects can have their own values, they do not have their own meanings stretching beyond material or resource evaluation. In fact, everything that makes them part of heritage is their relation to people as authors, creators, and heroes—with the history of local communities that are still under their influence, with identity and the demeanor of those who stay connected with them. This is what makes heritage out of them. Any action undertaken alongside all forms of heritage not only preserves its existence, but also endows it with new social and cultural values.

According to the pioneer of heritage interpretation theory, Freeman Tilden, interpretation is "an educational activity which aims to reveal meanings and relationships through the use of original objects, by firsthand experience, and by illustrative media, rather than simply to communicate factual information."[3] It stands for something particularly different than simply the flow of information based on facts. Another, half-century-younger definition of interpretation proposed by the Interpretation Australia Association defines it in terms of "a means of communicating ideas and feelings which help people enrich their understanding and appreciation of their world, and their role in it."[4] The definition above concentrates on something far different from simple educational content. In this light, interpretation plays a vital role through sharing and receiving experiences connected with heritage, as well as building relations between heritage and its audience. Interpretation, as it is understood today, makes allowances for recipients' interests and engages their activity not only with the aim of provoking excitement, but also reflecting on the past, the present, and the future in the context of experienced heritage.

Apart from the necessary attractiveness of a message, which determines its effective heritage interpretation as part of education,[5] the dialogue with a recipient (treated as culture's participant) should be one of the paramount postulates in the process of creating heritage interpretation programs. The aforementioned heritage should not be interpreted as an entirety, but as an occasion and introduction to establish a more intense dialogue between a spectator (a tourist) and the reality it represents. An essential, but basic at the time, level of that postulate realization is to create interpretation programs (including the concept of tour guiding) so that the recipient has access to various forms of interpretation while sightseeing. The second level comprises allowing spectators to voice their own opinions on a given reality. By illustrating a world different from the one known to the audience, it expands their knowledge and gives them opportunities to reflect on their values and codes of conduct. This may influence the personality-shaping process, and in the case of inhabitants of a certain region or country, also deepen their identity.

In 2008, ICOMOS (International Council on Monuments and Sites), an important document regarding heritage interpretation and preservation, was published.[6] The majority of principles contained in it refer predominantly to heritage site administrators and their supervisors, that is, public authorities. However, some of them apply to people participating in the interpretation process: heritage site and interpretation center workers, tourist guides working as individual interpreters, oftentimes setting up their own interpretation programs. Responsibility for preparing interpreters to handle such activities rests upon hosts of heritage sites, including historical cities. Precise practical postulates contained in the document require from each interpretation to encourage individuals and communities to reflect on their own perception of a site and assist them in establishing a meaningful connection to it. The aim should be to stimulate further interest, learning, experience, and exploration. Some of the good realizations of the postulate are the forms of touring discussed in the following part of the chapter, in particular perspective sightseeing, with alternative narration, or the creative one, inviting to self-engagement in the phase of the first contact with the heritage. Furthermore, the document proposes that the authors and interpretation programs identify the diversity of their recipients—both demographically (children, disabled) and culturally (place of origin). In reference to the programs for disabled people, heritage should be physically accessible to the public. Discussed hereinafter, multisensory sightseeing offers this group of tourists access to a particular heritage and its interpretation. In the authors' reckoning, all groups that contributed to the historical and cultural meaning of a site have to be taken into account in interpretation. The postulates of perspective and alternative narration sightseeing easily find their way to realization in city guiding. Lastly, there is a need to incorporate elements of immaterial heritage into interpretation—even though just some of them are directly listed: music, dance, theater, literature, local habits, visual arts, and cultural heritage. Their realization in many European cities is fictionalized and creative forms of sightseeing—and, in reference to cuisine, multisensory sightseeing with culinary elements or creative sightseeing embracing culinary workshops. Exemplary realization of contemporary heritage interpretation in tourism, fully adequate to the intentions of the aforementioned authors, is the fruit of scholarly work, partially from Australia, published in the form of a comprehensive collection of principles and tips.[7]

NEW CITY TOURISTS AND GUIDES

Over the last thirty years, tourists' behavior and expectations have altered so dramatically that now one can talk about nothing else than an essential change. Today's city tourists are in the know of the world beyond their countries' borders and, accordingly, better prepared for touring than former generations. Having gained at least a communicative command of a foreign language, they are able to plan their own journey. They have numerous and far cheaper possibilities of relocation at their disposal, which increases self-reliance in selecting tours as well as organizing them. For a guide, this results in an increased percentage of orders from individual clients, yet simultaneously, a necessity to conform with the new groups of recipients who do not share, for example, collective knowledge or experience within the framework of a national or even European canon.

Said individualization of demand and tourist services continues to develop faster in cities than elsewhere. A growing group of tourists sells out the offers without mediation of tour organizers. For an active guide, this implies a necessity to create individual sightseeing programs, self-presentation on profiled and tourist portals, building up a direct contact with a client, as well as negotiating and offering professional consulting with him.

Under the influence of education, a significant number of tourists attribute different types of sensitivity; they are open-minded to the culture of groups that were formerly disregarded in dominating cultural narration (e.g., ethnic, sexual, and religious minorities; women). The times of typical, but constantly repeating, historical urban walks come to an end. They will still exist for organized tours, but for tourists interested in precise types of values or events, new offers will evolve. In order to remain in business, a city guide has to align his offer with the demand change.

"New" cultural tourists are characterized by significantly less respect toward noble authorities, formal ones in particular, such as a teacher or guide-educator (in the capacity of his "tourist" representation). They are more critical toward the content of dominating so far cultural narratives, including national ideologies and heritage. Influenced by modern education, including group classes, they become more daring by prompting discussions without hesitation and frankly expressing both approval and criticism in relation to the message and the whole guiding service.

City tourists, along with expected entertainment in leisure time, eagerly accept the element of confrontation with the heritage. Studies conducted in various sightseeing whereabouts of visiting and not only leisure tourists (to whom the city tourists are assigned), confirm that the presence of thoroughly realized interpretation in visited areas has a bigger impact on their satisfaction than elements of services and the majority of other features of a place.[8] Tourists' acceptance of new technologies is growing. Smartphones connected to Wi-Fi or GPS systems give them the possibility of autonomous selection of information in the form of images and sounds. QR codes and mobile applications are only the frontlines of the subsequent revolution—augmented reality. They already enable tourists to see an object in its non-existing, historical form and listen to a commentary as well as display professional films that present the object's history.

Independently of directing their actions toward tourists' satisfaction, which translates into financial profits,[9] tourist guides (including city guides) are specified as (1) leaders of tourist groups and tour managers ensuring program realization and tourist satisfaction; (2) educators and brokers of information; however, only recently they have started to be perceived as (3) the mediators between hosts and guests as well as heritage professionals.[10] Depending on vocational background and intellectual horizons, their awareness of existing interpretation principles and states differs. Nevertheless, as will be shown further in this chapter, elements of interpretation in their offers are becoming more and more numerous, and its contribution more explicit.

In this day and age, a tourist guide needs to confront yet another competitor, the technological excellence of which regarding illustration and preciseness of information one cannot exceed. Notwithstanding this, the thing that still makes a real-life guide unique is the element of interpretation: personal, subjective, inimitable—as it creates the atmosphere of exploring, goes beyond what might be considered the perfect illustration, and persuades tour participants to engage in a dialogue and active cognition of heritage as well as to prompt their own reflections. The guide should enable tourists to encounter the site's "unicum," that is, the unique elements of its identity. Such uniqueness stands for a worthwhile value that is adjusted to the material attractions or feeling connected with event participation. Their "firsthand" presentation—from the viewpoints of a host, local inhabitant, daily user, or an enthusiast—always involves the element of subjective interpretation, which is a great asset of a guide.

A quaint discourse to open up interpretation is the content of local histories that become "encysted" with time by local "histories" functioning as legends, fairy tales, myths, biographies, urban tales, and anecdotes—all of which create cultural contexts and constitute elements of inhabitants' identification. The asset of a guide-person is the multifarious interpretation of presented elements and phenomena in question, reflecting the complexity of a certain object (including ethnically unfamiliar and controversial motives), diverse perspectives, and varied evaluations of phenomena or events that result from, for example, their areas of origin, professional profiles, or a tour theme. Some tourists look forward to sightseeing sites that are important regarding their ideas or a more comprehensive illustration of figures and historical events, meaningful for the social movement or the group they belong to. Full consideration of all these postulates in the structure and content of guided touring develops into the so-called engaged narration.

A higher level of interaction, more demanding for a guide, is migrating between certain narrations that are "giving voice" to different attitudes, heroes, or groups. This creates the atmosphere of a "multi-textual game." While sightseeing, a multisensory message is also demanded: directed at a few senses and varied in form.

A guide must properly assess the specification, expectations, and interests of each group and match the tour practice with them. Thus, a city guide might be defined as *a person who professionally prepares and realizes the illustration and interpretation of heritage in terms of service for tourists within the space of one city and its historical surroundings.* According to leading researchers, interpretation is the principal means through which guides communicate with visitors,[11] pass experiences, and generate satisfaction.[12] The work of a growing group of today's guides can be qualified as *interpretative guiding* that is guiding in which the main goals are accomplished by using interpretation rules.[13] An interpretative variant of guiding is distinguished from the instrumental one (with a dominant role for the tour manager), still the most popular one in tour pilotage and field guiding (e.g., in the mountains)—and from the educational one (with the manager's dominant function as knowledge and experience), still common in cities and predominant in many museums.[14]

In the third part of the chapter, we are going to present examples of city-guiding forms that fulfill the principles of today's heritage interpretation in reference to existing forms of tour guiding.[15]

CASE STUDY OF INTERPRETATIVE URBAN TOUR GUIDING

The study consists of the analysis and classification of offers of 73 operators from 28 cities, which altogether amounts to 484 propositions. According to the classification proposed by the author in his city-guiding monography,[16] they fulfill all the criteria of alternative sightseeing, including fictionalized (62 programs), stylized (145), multisensory (97), creative (73), alternative

Table 12.1 Alternative Sightseeing with Elements of Interpretation in Selected European Cities

City	F	S	C	M	P	A	O	City	F	S	C	M	P	A	O
Augsburg	2	10	2	1	2	0	0	Milan	2	5	6	4	2	0	0
Barcelona	2	3	4	4	4	0	0	Münster	3	5	3	3	6	4	1
Berlin	3	6	5	2	3	1	1	Paris	3	12	5	13	5	2	2
Brussels	2	3	3	2	4	0	0	Poznan	3	3	1	1	1	1	0
Budapest	2	4	3	3	2	1	0	Prague	2	6	3	2	4	1	1
Bucharest	1	1	2	1	2	1	1	Riga	0	2	2	1	1	0	1
Dublin	4	7	3	5	2	0	1	Rome	2	4	2	6	2	0	0
Freiburg in Br.	6	8	2	3	5	1	1	Seville	2	6	2	4	2	1	1
Gdansk	1	5	2	2	1	0	0	Toulouse	1	3	1	1	2	1	0
Heidelberg	2	4	2	3	3	1	0	York	3	2	2	1	2	2	1
Cracow	1	9	3	2	2	0	1	Verona	2	4	1	3	0	0	0
Lisbon	1	3	2	4	1	0	1	Vienna	3	8	3	5	2	1	0
London	5	11	4	6	6	2	1	Vilnius	0	2	1	1	0	0	0
Madrid	4	8	3	9	3	2	1	Zagreb	0	1	1	5	0	0	1

Note: Sightseeing: F – Fictionalized, S – Stylised, K – Creative, M – Multisensory, A – Alternative narrations, P – Perspective, O – Other types of interpretative tour-guiding.
Source: Own research.

narrations (22), and perspective sightseeing (69). For each of those forms—regardless of earlier popularized sightseeing in historical disguises or special guiding for kids[17]—a more comprehensive description was presented together with an example of an offer realized in one of the cities that might appear helpful in figuring out the typical features, applied elements of heritage interpretation, as well as advantages and disadvantages of a certain form. Several interpretative tours were excluded from all the types due to their mixed structure, a few others due to the occurrence of features incongruent to any scheme. A detailed overview of identified offers is presented in Table 12.1.

Applied in some European cities, review of interpretative tour-guiding forms that can be found below is based on primary interpretation principles. This enables us to show congruence regarding tourist guide methods of interpretation and tools familiar or unfamiliar to them for heritage interpretation.

Type 1: Perspective Tour Guiding

Description: Interpretation represents a viewpoint of an "ordinary man" (an average inhabitant), a representative of a particular class (e.g., a peasant), or a vocational group (e.g., a craftsman, merchant, soldier, clergyman). A popular form of its realization is stylized sightseeing, wherein the costume and historical form of a language make the presentation of a particular point of view more substantial, a message more vivid, and reception deeper. In "perspective storytelling," a guide creates a coherent story on the basis of verified facts and their predominant interpretations—however, he consistently presents them from the perspective of a particular person. This allows for unconventional understanding of the whole process from "below," through the eyes of ordinary people experiencing historic events (e.g., inhabitants of the beleaguered castle) or those suffering from a form of harm (e.g., victims of persecution).

Advantages: Education subsumes and passes common heritage as the reality referring to large communities ("nations," "societies") impersonally—its recipients do not process information personally and very occasionally reflect on heritage values and impact. Heritage interpretation from the perspective of an individual (or a group) feeling opens to new possibilities of understanding it and makes the tour a more individual, personalized experience. The result is deeper reflection and the influence of experience on shaping individual attitudes. Another asset of this form of sightseeing is reading anew the "canonical" versions of the heritage interpretation along with the reality by guide, participants, and even inhabitants, which, in turn, enriches the heritage and enhances its impact.

Disadvantages: Many guides have neither perspective sightseeing experience, nor the academic background on a certain field of study, while the realization of message formed by others is easily recognized and critically evaluated.

Example: The Hidden City Tour (Classic)—Metropolis through the eyes of the homeless.

Organizer: Hidden City Tours, Barcelona (social project). *Duration:* approx. 1.5–2 hours, walk.

Description: Sightseeing proceeds in small groups (five to ten participants). It is led by homeless people or those who were homeless until recently, trained to perform duties in the capacity of a guide. They demonstrate and interpret field attractions, while providing information interesting for each tourist (including the historical or cultural meaning of an object), diversified with legends and anecdotes. Moreover, they introduce to tour guiding their own viewpoint and the sites particularly important for them. From the perspective of a homeless person, monumental buildings and city symbols gain new meanings—benches in parks appear to be safer and peaceful (for an overnight stay), bridges and flyovers turn out to be the links between districts, meeting sites of vital relevance for dynamically transforming communities, points of information exchange, goods, support, help, and vivid social life. The message is completed with anecdotes about original inhabitants remaining unknown for medial descriptions as well as descriptions of dilemmas that remain unfamiliar to an average inhabitant of the house next door with electric power and hot water. According to the participants' opinion, sightseeing not only conveys loads of new information, but also changes an image of the city in their eyes and inspires them to reflect on attitudes toward the rest of the inhabitants.

Places: Gothic district, El Raval, traditional city markets, Las Ramblas, other.

Use: From the moment of its emergence, perspective sightseeing has attracted literature lovers of different currents and biographies of interesting personae (when a story was constructed from "their" angle). Among their audience, there are also groups traveling on ethnical tours, including the ancestors of former inhabitants who do not live in a certain country anymore, or their countrymen. The "perspective" narration has the potential to be attractive for the representatives of social groups (e.g., farmers, workers) and their families.

Type 2: Sightseeing with Alternative Narration

Description: In this case, the starting point is the uncommon interpretation of historical events or social processes based on the same facts and logically compatible. Alternative narration dwells on research results and utilizes hypotheses that offer different interpretations of certain historical events, processes, and phenomena. A guide creates a coherent story out of them, showing a history supplemented with new facts and figures or a "might-have-happened" one. The guide's message involves undisputed facts, but in order to explain them, he uses alternative sources, interpretations, details on objects' purpose, or hypotheses regarding the characters' motivations.

Advantages: Sharing alternative narration not only animates the history and heritage, but also makes it a subject of intense reflection already "on the spot." Not only does it connect the interpretation with the sightseeing site, but also with the mediator who becomes a living, personally experienced spokesman of the given version of history (social attitude, cultural values, etc.), which can also be a source of dispute.

Disadvantages: The arrangement of sightseeing requires the tedious study of sources, relations, and plots that have so far remained missing in analyses or have been completely ignored in terms of their critical evaluation and reconstruction. Hence, the scriptwriter has to have an academic background or cooperate with experts. The criticism of those who do not accept neglecting temporarily the "more justified"—or so far predominant—vision of history and heritage evaluation (guides, inhabitants, etc.), seems to be the next problem. The introduction of each theme requires subtleness of form in which the information is passed, but also courage and resistance.

Example: Frauenhistorische Stadtrundgänge von Frauen für Frauen in Münster (the walks of female history—from women to women in Münster)

Organizer: Arbeitsgruppe Frauengeschichte Münster. *Duration:* 1.5 hours.

Description: It is the group of proposals realized by female guides and historians from a local university. Tours proceed once a month, throughout the whole year, and contribute to a coherent vision of the alternative interpretation of the city's history and the origin of its material and immaterial heritage. They are not limited to narration from the viewpoint of women as participants of a history (which would only be a perspective sightseeing). The contents of the historical walks are based on reinterpretation of historical sources relating to the most significant events and social processes, indicating their female initiators (until recently anonymous), coauthors, sturdy heroes, charismatic leaders, resilient producers, outgoing female rebels, and firebrands acting under the rebels' shadow. However, each of the sightseeing tours is committed not to people, but themes, thanks to which they co-produce the complete picture. The tours that have been organized so far are "women and religion," "women and medicine," "old and new female movements," "women in times of war and peace," "national socialism in Münster and resistance," "fight for women's rights," "work," and "upbringing and education." In many cases, new inspirations are found; in others, a determinative influence of famous and unknown women on fateful decisions of city rulers, their participation in the inception of urban movements and initiatives (religious and social), as well as spontaneous strikes and rebellions, a participation in great investments, and their role in the wake of commercial undertakings.

Places: As part of the series, every walk proceeds on the basis of its own script, in accordance with its subject matter, so that the whole city constitutes the setting for it.

Use: Occasions to demonstrate alternative narrations are provided by classical forms of tour guiding: the historical and thematic walks that can become vivid. Alternative narration can also be attractive for participants of educational tours that realize academic programs, that is, history- and ethnography-based ones or thematic and study trips.

Type 3: Fictionalized Sightseeing

Description: Fictionalized sightseeing ("*adventure performance,*" "*adventure city tour,*" "*dramatized city tour,*" in German: "*Erlebnisführung*"— experience touring) is *theme-based sightseeing of a township or place with the assistance of a tourist guide, embracing an element of history or theme-based stylization, taking place according to a meticulously prepared script that includes, for example, event staging, and makes allowances for one or several forms of activity on the part of visitors, connected with their presence in the following points of the tour.* It might be a walk with elements of script performance or action that develops in other places—performed by one actor playing various roles or many actors performing a number of scenes at each point—or sightseeing that comprises an active participation of tourists in the spectacle. The script is realized by the guide or a small team, and all (or some) participants are engaged to stage-play as secondary characters or to interact in specified places and within the capacity specified by the guide or actors.

Advantages: Dramatization enriches experiencing history or an aspect of heritage on the part of visitors, which gives a sense of finding oneself "in the midst of action." A feeling of "firsthand" experience is intensified by language and costume stylization. Employing various elements of the message, including "lively scenes," promotes participants' concentration. It is easier to encourage participants to engagement and gain a high level of interaction in the form of questions, verbal answers, and cooperation in the realization of script elements, which fosters a fuller and more effective memorization.

Disadvantages: Time- and effort-consuming preparation; high cost of realization caused by the necessity to pay the team and buy or rent costumes; preparation and realization of multimedia effects; and, when using foreign languages, script translation. The difficulties in realization might be caused by the third party. In the case of unfavorable weather, it is necessary to role-play the scenes in enclosed or covered spaces.

Example: Die Hexe von Freiburg.

Organizer: Freiburg Living History, Freiburg in Breisgau. *Duration:* 2 hours.

Description: The plot includes the last hours at large of a widow, Catherine Stadelmein, who was the inhabitant accused of witchcraft in the sixteenth century.

Places: Rathausplatz, Obere Altstadt (medieval city center), Münsterplatz.

Realization: Touring takes place in the form of sightseeing across the old town and seven fictionalized scenes with the participation of others. The tourist guide outlines the context of an event and creates the narration in the form of her farewell to the city and relatives, presenting historical buildings and heritage sites. In the following scenes, visitors meet particular protagonists. Finally, the walk turns into an escape from pursuers. In the end, the guide summarizes the historic event and asks questions to evoke reflections on the part of visitors. After that, the visitors are invited to take a supplementary stroll during which other crucial heritage sites are shown.

Elements of the message: Continuous storytelling (guide as the narrator), dialogues with three inhabitants (prostitute, executioner's daughter, Franciscan monk), three communal scenes (with friends, monks, and city representatives), sound and illumination effects (switched on by the guide).

Use: Fictionalized sightseeing is offered mostly on request of tourist groups. In Western Europe it is also used for student and theme-based trips. In cities with much tourist traffic it might be contained as part of the regular offer (e.g., in the season at a particular time and on a particular day of a week) and might be enjoyed for consideration. It happens to be organized on request of companies and their staff, for conference and congress participants, as well as celebration of tourist events.

Type 4: Multisensory Tours

Form: Sightseeing in which a participant's experience of the heritage and its interpretation by a tourist guide are based not only on seeing and hearing might be defined as multisensory. It engages the senses of taste, touch, and smell (or more) and endows this experience with a paramount (or at least major) role in sightseeing. This form oftentimes appears in the offer of tourist guides in cities wherein smell, taste, or touch considerably contribute to the cultural heritage—for example, in places where food, perfume, and the leather industry or some traditional crafts (such as tanning or pursemaking) were developed—or in cities with vast resources for using one of the aforementioned senses. In the contemporary tourist guide offer, one can find four main subtypes: (1) theme-based culinary tours; (2) tours based on sites where sensations experienced by one more sense apart from seeing and hearing are interpreted by a tourist guide as of equal value; (3) "compensatory" tours for people with seeing or hearing disorders, with a range of places about which one can learn through other senses (e.g., tactile), along with the interpretation of sensations experienced; and (4) "all-sensory tours" organized with the predominant use of one particular sense to experience a place where that sense is of utmost importance and what makes it a subject of interpretation.

Advantages: The basic advantage is the possibility of confronting city space and heritage through many senses, which offers a totality effect and validates tourists' sensory feedback. For people with limited perception, the lack of one sense is a natural recompensation for the unfavorable difference comparing to other visitors. In many cities, such a type of sightseeing enables introduction into an offer of the vital elements of local heritage and allows for the full employment of its potential (industrial, culinary, etc.). Multisensory tours also require deeper engagement of participants, which evokes a sense of individual engagement and multiplies one's satisfaction.

Disadvantages: Touring requires more effort from a tourist guide on the level of program construction and persistent care for the presence of multisensory experience by participants in each of the visited places.

Example: Budapest Locals.

Organizer: Anita Barta—a tourist guide; via: Budapest Travel Guide. *Duration:* 3–3.5 hours.

Description: The offer employs all five senses to present a particular message. Along with the history of a city and heritage sites' presentation, a guide tries to draw special attention to more than just seeing and hearing (even though these ways of perception are also interpreted in an unconventional way—for example, when it comes to street hustle and bustle). In a local pursemaking workshop, leather products and materials are presented; in a traditional covered market, tastes and smells are described and some samples are offered; in a wine tavern, café, and restaurant, participants are invited to taste soup, salami, wine, cakes, and vodka. After sightseeing, participants are invited to enjoy a meal.

Places and dominant/interpreted sensory feedback: heritage sites (sight), cityscapes (sight), Budapest *streets* (hearing, sight), Strudl Hous (taste), Great Market Hall (smell, taste, sight, hearing, touch), pursemaking workshop (touch, smell, sight), traditional wine tavern (taste).

Use: Multisensory sightseeing might be organized in almost any city—however, it is of paramount significance in places where developed culinary traditions along with rich offers in this capacity exist and where culinary tours are already open to visitors together with a set visitors' agenda and proposed meals.

Type 5: Creative Sightseeing

Description: Its distinguishing element is a combination of two modules: tour guiding within city space and creative engagement of visitors. There is an almost unlimited spectrum of topics and subjects: photography, culinary art (preparation of traditional dishes and desserts, etc.), painting (including street art), music (folk singing, re-creation of a local composer's, artist's, or band's pieces of art), theater (acting workshop based on local art), dance (folk or contemporary), and others. The first element of sightseeing is a walk (touring) that is theme-based (respectively to the field of participants' creative activity). Visitors engage in sightseeing (e.g., by taking photos) during a theme-based workshop led by a specialist (could be a tourist guide) in a selected place that is oftentimes important insofar as the main theme is concerned (museum, biographical site, photography atelier).

Advantages: One of the advantages that is of utmost importance is a high level of participant engagement. Visitors gain new skills, and some of them may develop into full-time hobbies. They become more sensitive to various dimensions of human creativity and improve their skills to make more weighty and deeper aesthetic points on the basis of their firsthand experience.

Disadvantages: The organization of creative sightseeing is more expensive. It requires utilization of materials and/or renting a place for a workshop after which some cleaning might have to be done. The tour guide, in turn, must have a good command of creative skills in a particular field or employ a specialist while limiting oneself to elements of introduction and interpretation of sites and materials.

Example: Riga Street and Urban Photography Tour.

Organizer: Eat Riga Tours and Events. *Duration:* 2.5–4 hours.

Description: The proposed offer involves (1) a walking tour with a guide who is a professional photographer along the most popular streets and sites in Riga, as well as less-known among tourist characteristic sites of local city life. Next to a typical description of heritage sites, their artistic interpretation in the form of beforehandedly taken professional photos is demonstrated, after which practical instruction and photo taking with the assistance of a professional photographer (also with the use of analogue or "soviet" cameras) takes place. The tour is crowned with a workshop during which photos are selected and retouched, and a photo album of Riga is created with the possibility of taking it on an electronic medium or on paper.

Places: Areas brimming with landmarked buildings, blocks with characteristic architectural objects (from gothic to secession), workshop in a professional photography atelier.

Use: A creativity postulate in the last years led to the emergence of a separate form of cultural tourism (*creative tourism*). The popularity of various ways in which visitors are engaged varies depending on trends of tourists' interests—though some ways are less popular in different countries: in Italy, culinary tours with workshops; in Germany, artistic tours (including street art); in Central European countries, photography. Frequently, said offers are addressed to children and involve touring with elements of drawing or painting of visited places. A group of interest embraces also enthusiasts of some arts and crafts, as well as students of art classes and courses.

SUMMARY

Prepared for the present analysis, this overview of innovative guiding forms in local tour operators across European cities enables us to state that in the face of demand, change has resulted predominantly from individualization of city tourism and tourist preferences—different from the previous ones—as well as competition from illustrative media. The guides more frequently tend to look for programs, methods, and tools that could increase their chance to compete for the client. As they are aware that they cannot outpace the more and more advanced forms of urban heritage illustration, they start to focus on its flexible and interactive interpretation. In the process of said interpretation, it is another human—perceived more as a natural partner for exploration of a city than a tool—who breathes some life into the local heritage through "voicing" opinions on its behalf and depicting it from different angles. The tour guide employs his personal skills and charisma to promote individual experience and further reflections as well as creates a natural opportunity to prompt a dialogue with particular values and demeanor. These modern qualities of tour guiding decidedly fulfill the principles of contemporary heritage interpretation.

NOTES

1. Betty Weiler and Rosemary Black, *Tours Guiding Research: Insights, Issues and Implications* (Bristol: Channel View Publications, 2015), 19.

2. Robert Hewison, "Heritage: An Interpretation," in *Heritage Interpretation, Volume 1*, ed. David Uzzell (London: Belhaven, 1989), 16.

3. Freeman Tilden, *Interpreting our Heritage* (Chapel Hill: University of North Carolina Press, 1957), 8.

4. *Sharing our Stories: Guidelines for Heritage Interpretation* (The National Trust of Australia, 2007), 8.

5. Interpretation theorists widely describe and justify, among others, the postulate of educational offer modernization by implementing the experience element in objects and exhibitions related to the heritage. "Experience" sightseeing is presumed as the expansion of the classical sightseeing of the authentic relics of the cultural heritage. Its introduction is a natural consequence of so-called "experience education" (promoted by school education) and desired element of time management by a contemporary person, who is oriented on the experience consumption.

6. *The ICOMOS Charter for the Interpretation and Presentation of Cultural Heritage Sites, Ratified by the 16th General Assembly of ICOMOS Quebec, Canada, 4 October 2008,* Accessed August 24, 2016. http://icip.icomos.org/downloads/ICOMOS_Interpretation_Charter_ENG_04_10_08.pdf.

7. *Sharing our Stories: Guidelines for Heritage Interpretation* (The National Trust of Australia, 2007).

8. Sam Ham and Betty Weiler, "Isolating the Role of On-site Interpretation in a Satisfying Experience," *Journal of Interpretation Research* 12, no. 2 (2007): 18.

9. Heidi Dahles and Karin Bras, eds., *Tourism and Small Entrepreneurs: Development, National Policy and Entrepreneurial Culture: Indonesian Cases* (New York: Cognizant, 1999), see also: Noel B. Salazar, "Tourism and Glocalization: 'Local Tour Guiding,'" *Annals of Tourism Research* 32, no. 3 (2005): 630.

10. Cf. Erik Cohen "The Tourist Guide: The Origins, Structure and Dynamics of a Role," *Annals of Tourism Research* 12, no. 1 (1985): 17 and following; Betty Weiler and Rosemary Black, *Tours Guiding Research: Insights, Issues and Implications* (Bristol: Channel View Publications, 2015), 32–36; see also: Noel B. Salazar, "Culture Broker, Tourism," in *Encyclopedia of Tourism*, ed. Jafar Jafari and Honggen Xiao (Vienna: Springer-Verlag, 2015), 1–2.

11. Cf. Erik Cohen "The Tourist Guide: The Origins, Structure and Dynamics of a Role," *Annals of Tourism Research* 12, no. 1 (1985): 5–29; Kathleen Pond, *The Professional Guide: Dynamics of Tour Guiding* (New York: Van Nostrand Reinhold,

1993); Betty Weiler and Sam Ham, "Tour Guides and Interpretation," in *Encyclopedia of Ecotourism*, 2001; see also Betty Weiler and Rosemary Black, *Tours Guiding Research: Insights, Issues and Implications*.

12. Betty Weiler and Rosemary Black, *Tours Guiding Research: Insights, Issues and Implications*, 56.

13. Cf. John Pastorelli, *Enriching the Experience—An Interpretative Approach to Tour Guiding*, French Forest: Pearson Education Australia, 2003.

14. Sharon Macdonald, "Mediating Heritage: Tour Guides at the Former Naziparty Rally Grounds," *Tourist Studies* 6, no. 2 (2006): 122; see also Betty Weiler and Rosemary Black, *Tours Guiding Research: Insights, Issues and Implications*, 45–47.

15. Armin Mikos v. Rohrscheidt, *Współczesne przewodnictwo miejskie. Metodyka i organizacja interpretacji dziedzictwa* [Modern City Tour-guiding: Methodoly and Organization of Heritage Interpretation] (Kraków: Proksenia, 2014), 3–4 and 117–232.

16. Armin Mikos v. Rohrscheidt, *Współczesne przewodnictwo miejskie*.

17. Cf. Armin Mikos v. Rohrscheidt, *Współczesne przewodnictwo miejskie*, 161–70 and 244–52.

REFERENCES

Cohen, Erik. "The Tourist Guide: The Origins, Structure and Dynamics of a Role." *Annals of Tourism Research* 12, no. 1 (1985): 5–29.

Dahles, Heidi, and Karin Bras, eds. *Tourism and Small Entrepreneurs: Development, National Policy and Entrepreneurial Culture: Indonesian Cases*. New York: Cognizant, 1999.

Ham, Sam, and Betty Weiler. "Isolating the Role of On-site Interpretation in a Satisfying Experience." *Journal of Interpretation Research* 12, no. 2 (2007): 5–24.

Hewison, Robert. "Heritage: An Interpretation." In *Heritage Interpretation*, volume 1, edited by David Uzzell, 15–23. London: Belhaven, 1989.

Macdonald, Sharon. "Mediating Heritage: Tour Guides at the Former Naziparty Rally Grounds." *Tourist Studies* 6, no. 2 (2006): 119–38.

Mikos v. Rohrscheidt, Armin. *Współczesne przewodnictwo miejskie. Metodyka i organizacja interpretacji dziedzictwa* [Modern City Tour-guiding: Methodology and Organization of Heritage Interpretation]. Kraków: Proksenia, 2014.

Mikos v. Rohrscheidt, Armin. "Kierunki badań i naukowa bibliografia turystyki kulturowej w Polsce i na świecie." *Turystyka Kulturowa* 8 (2014): 86–135. Accessed August 24, 2016. http://turystykakulturowa.org/ojs/index.php/tk/article/download/485/458.

Salazar, Noel B. "Tourism and Glocalization: 'Local Tour Guiding.'" *Annals of Tourism Research* 32, no. 3 (2005): 628–46.

Salazar, Noel B. "Culture Broker, Tourism." In *Encyclopedia of Tourism*, edited by Jafar Jafari and Honggen Xiao, 1–2. Vienna: Springer-Verlag, 2015.

Sharing our Stories: Guidelines for Heritage Interpretation, The National Trust of Australia, Text: Shar Jones, 2007.

The ICOMOS Charter for the Interpretation and Presentation of Cultural Heritage Sites. Ratified by the 16th General Assembly of ICOMOS Quebec, Canada, October 4, 2008.

The Nara Document on Authenticity. Nara: ICOMOS, 1994.

Tilden, Freeman. *Interpreting our Heritage.* Chapel Hill: University of North Carolina Press, 1957.

Pastorelli, John. *Enriching the Experience—An Interpretative Approach to Tour Guiding.* French Forest: Pearson Education Australia, 2003.

Pond, Kathleen. *The Professional Guide: Dynamics of Tour Guiding.* New York: Van Nostrand Reinhold, 1993.

Weiler, Betty, and Rosemary Black. *Tours Guiding Research: Insights, Issues and Implications.* Bristol: Channel View Publications, 2015.

Weiler, Betty, and Sam Ham. "Tour Guides and Interpretation." In *Encyclopedia of Ecotourism,* edited by David Bruce Weawer, 549–63. Wallingford: Cabi Publishing, 2001.

Chapter 13

Urban Exploration as an "Interior Tourism"

Contemporary Ruins behind the "Iron Curtain"

Małgorzata Nieszczerzewska

If we consider different factors shaping space and culture of the city, the status of a derelict architecture of a recent past seems very problematic. Modern, contemporary ruins (first and foremost derelict and abandoned industrial sites, hospitals, churches, private residences, and schools), which are not included on the lists of national or world heritage are considered as needless and negative spaces which destroy urban harmony and bring elements of chaos to the themed realm of the contemporary city. Urban ruins, in the past an integral part of the city space and culture, have now become redundant. Because they are sites with a problematic status and belonging, they are successfully "erased" from the official urban politics and culture in a symbolic way. For sure, they are traces of the past and traces of culture. And, as Andreas Schönle and Julia Hell suggest, these architectural remnants, which had lost their functionality and meanings, can be invested with various attributes: historical, aesthetic, and political.[1]

Stefan Symotiuk emphasizes that "place" situated against "space" is introducing another ontological question of the relation between "a part" and "the whole." This relation is ruled by many disproportions.[2] In the case of ruins it is the question of human being that is the reason of many paradoxes and ontological dilemmas. His absence in the place that has been forgotten and abandoned for a long time impacts the radical change of the building's ontological status. Ruins then begin to signify something more primary and fundamental: life as a natural and spiritual phenomenon.

We can use a metaphor and say, that derelict and collapsing architecture exists somewhere behind "the iron curtain" in the contemporary urban space—unseen by the eyes of the average city's inhabitants—because its existence is characterized by peculiar social and imaginary boundaries and limits. Decaying and defunct buildings could then be symbols of a "deformed" space of human products and experiences that comes into contact with his geographical and "symmetrical" space.[3] As Brian Dillon points out, in recent years many artists and researchers have turned to themes and imagery of ruination and destruction, especially to the remains of the architecture that seem like relics of the last century. There has been a proliferation of works that explore the ruins of modernist architecture, the defunct infrastructure of the Cold War, and other relics of the last decades of the twentieth century. Modern ruins appear first and foremost as an allegory for global or regional political forces that change the ways and circumstances of human being.[4]

Since contemporary ruins have not been "rationalized" as historically significant, but relegated to the wasteland, they provoke quite different considerations and can easily be defined as tourist destinations *à rebours*. Therefore, although they lack everyday experience on the one hand and have not been entrenched in the sphere of the heritage industry on the other, modern urban ruins became the main destination for urban explorers. In spite of the fact that the scholarly discourse concerning modern ruins or the process of modern culture's ruination has developed very fast recently,[5] there is still a lack of research about urban exploration as one of urban practices both in Poland and in other countries. As a discourse, exploration is first and foremost the domain of the Internet.[6] According to Cosmo Howard, discursive fields offer individuals "a range of modes and subjectivity" and that means they provide a number of alternative ways of experiencing the world and interpreting life experiences.[7] Urban exploration is one of the practices that enable tourists to experience the city space and human condition in quite a new way. Experience and meaning are possible here through un-social and "negative" surroundings, which are collapsing and decaying buildings, forgotten and abandoned, hidden behind an imaginary curtain.

The purpose of this study is then to "explore the narrative of urban exploration" and investigate how this practice is considered by the explorers at first, especially by those who live and explore in Poland. This chapter presents the results of an initial qualitative analysis of the narratives and declarations made by the explorers that can be found on the photo sharing websites, in online articles written by explorers and in some commentaries placed, for example, on Facebook. Considering the subject area of the book I tried to focus only on the analysis of Polish field of urban exploring, but, by virtue of the fact that the scope within which I was able to demonstrate the problem is necessarily limited, in some cases I used the narratives and commentaries made by foreign explorers as well.

EXPLORATION AS AN URBAN NICHE PRACTICE

In the photo book *Beauty in Decay* one can read that it is easy to describe what urban explorers do. They infiltrate abandoned buildings and industrial areas, often taking photographs along the way. Urban exploration can be approximately defined as a practice that seeks to reveal, through intentional infiltrations of the urban environment, areas normally veiled from view and closed to encounter.[8] Explorers do not steal, vandalize, or even leave graffiti behind them. But, on the other hand, it is not so easy to describe the whys and wherefores. Urban exploration (often called *urbex*), as a form of recreational trespass, has been perceived to be on the margins of legality, routinely misunderstood, dismissed, and discredited by society at large. "Urbexing" is a very materially embedded subculture, where community formation happens around specific physical locations, even though, as a global phenomenon, it is almost entirely facilitated by the Internet. Currently, there are different branches and genres of urban exploration, based on different agendas and philosophies, and hybrid groups that combine "urbexing" with other pursuits.[9]

Although the most known groups and individuals who practice urban exploration come from the United States and Western Europe, in recent years many urbexers have appeared in Poland as well. The practice of "urbexing" became a new way of experiencing the "blots on the Polish urban landscape" and an exciting way of spending free time. The most known Polish teams and photo sharing sites are[10]: Opuszczone.com, Trójmiejska Grupa Exploracyjna, Urbex Polska, Urb-Ex.pl, Double Penetration Urban Exploration Team, Deadzone.pl, Fotokomórka, and In-Dust-Real. Urban exploration in Poland, as in other countries which lay behind the Iron Curtain, implicates yet an additional meaning, because exploring relates, in large part, to the postcommunist architecture. Communist architecture was an exercise in architecture as an expression of ideology. Wandering through these ruins is very much like being in a graveyard where a dead way of life is buried, a graveyard of a system that collapsed. Industrial ruins are reminiscent not only of concrete historical experiences and technical and industrial progress, but also of an increasing unemployment and the change of everyday status as well. They reflect the tragic Soviet Era in Poland, but, on the other hand, they are often used for mythologizing the past. As Alicja Gzowska points out, "In an official parlance and agitprop of communist Poland, the workers were strongly appraised (especially those who were employed in heavy industry). They were defined as the main builders of the socialist country, its pride and strength, and therefore were offered a lot of privileges. But, on the other hand, it was the fabric and the industrial culture in the center, not the individual."[11]

The end of the Soviet era appeared actually a decade after the official date of the transformation's beginning, when a systematic reduction of the employment and decrease of the industry level really began. The processes of globalization forced a new division of work, and the fall of most production plants was a sign of the world passing away. A degradation of the worker's ethos and a change of his social status brought another kind of emptiness and a sense of loss. Many factories became needless. Their empty and decaying structures could be used as a metaphor of a *mise-en-scene* of the performance that had suddenly ended. Although the meaning of ruins depends on different contexts, there always remains pensiveness that obscures the perspectives of a new beginning.[12] As Johannes von Moltke claims, contemporary ruins become in this case a sign of melancholy in a productive sense: the melancholic gaze elaborates a ruin's aesthetic that allows the decaying structures to reveal themselves as objects beyond modernity's circuits of exchange.[13]

But, except the communist past of Poland and some kind of its nostalgic vision, the reasons for exploring abandoned architecture are just the same as in other parts of the world. As we can read in one of the Polish websites about urban exploration: "I admit, that it seems to be a strange interest, but it helped me to survive the hardest time in my life. It is for four years now as I am searching for and visiting places forgotten by other people. They may seem ugly and dirty, waiting for death, but for me these places are amazing and beautiful. It's enough to stop for a while and listen to their unique story."[14] Although urban exploration appeared as a niche activity in Poland many years after the Iron Curtain had fallen, it is getting more and more trendy nowadays. It seems that urbexers are inspired by the words of Ignasi de Solà-Morales Rubió, who wrote that the most exciting thing about empty places (which he calls *terrain vague*) are the relationships between the absence of use, of activity, and the sense of freedom, of expectance. It is all fundamental to understanding the evocative potential of the city's abandoned places.[15] The characteristic void and absence, but also some kind of a promise makes these places sites of the possible and of expectation for urbexers.

URBAN EXPLORATION AS AN "INTERIOR TOURISM"

One of the most interesting features of urban exploring activity is a possibility of viewing it as some sort of an "interior tourism." "Interior" means here a kind of a journey "towards the within," an escape from everyday reality and a type of contemplation (therefore one of the female Polish urbexers calls her website *In-dust-real* "a diary of feelings"[16]). The exploration of modern ruins concerned as an "interior tourism" is possible due to the impalpability of these "tourist" destinations. Contemporary ruins became thus a kind of screen on which explorers project their perceptions, fears, or phantasms. As places situated somewhere outside the official space of the city, thanks to their amorphism and peculiar indefinable existence, derelict buildings of a recent past enable numerous creative visualizations and conceptualizations. Therefore, they are not constant in our experience. Their changeability depends on us and the ways we read, imagine, and look at them. It is confirmed by the words of explorers which often treat abandoned architecture as a place that prompts them to make reflections about the human condition in late modernity. Infiltrating modern ruins is, on the one hand, a desire for new experiences and sensations and a test of courage, on the other, it is concerned as a way to discover explorer's subjectivity. Urbexers, as other tourists, use their own imagination, features, and cultural distinctions not only to construct their own senses of historic sites, but also to create the individual "inner adventures." The book *Beauty of Decay* states as follows: "You can lose yourself in derelict buildings and contemplate quietly about life, away from the noise and distraction of other people."[17] When explorers talk about "the atmosphere of a location," perhaps this is what they are trying to say. In this case, ruins provide a kind of objectivity chamber, a place outside the routinized world. Escaping from reality also means, that once outside of the world an explorer can drop his/her roles and stop playing for advantage and step back from his/her own subjectivity.

According to Symotiuk, every empty space is a space of freedom.[18] What this Polish philosopher has in mind here are such spaces as steppes, deserts, oceans, and outer space, but for urban explorers such a role can be played by modern ruins as well, because their "empty space" can be situated against the comfort of safeness and coziness of places connected with everyday life. For urbexers, such places offer the type of contemplation not only about time, death, or the past. First and foremost, derelict and collapsing buildings put into question our experience of a place in the city. Being a "city slicker," a philistine, an inhabitant of a metropolitan area or a small town, or a traveler visiting different cities is a process of trying oneself on the place. Thus the city offers many dimensions of negotiating oneself, it allows finding and constructing spaces of identity.[19] Our lives are abundant in "somethingness" and we are constantly overstimulated, especially if we live in a big city. A modern ruin with no functioning purpose—as Dylan Trigg points out—has the antidote we require to all of that. Trigg names it "nothingness" that is the vantage point in which the absent past is traceable in the unformed present. Nothingness is thus a volatile and active force, which gathers thought rather than destroying it.[20] Urbexers are attracted to modern urban ruins because of the possibility they give them to think of society and themselves in a new way as well. Urban exploration concerned as an "interior tourism" is based on the idea that the urban environment is a physical objectification of people's thinking and that it defines what types of practice and, therefore, what types of thought are able or are likely to take place within it. This implication results from the premise that urban space is an articulation of a society's thinking. Our ideas as a society are expressed by the architecture and the ways we use the space. Exploring abandoned architecture also wakes up thoughts, that it is a kind of arrogance toward history to think that the buildings we are putting up now are much better, and that they are going to age better, than the ones being torn down. It is then interesting to consider the situation from the point of view of entropy.[21] The explosion of new means and techniques of production known as the Industrial Revolution left behind some of the most fascinating and coveted abandoned sites in the urbex scene. In the early modern period in Europe, the birth of mass production cut the costs of building, allowing architects to focus more on the aesthetics including industrial, institutional, and residential construction. The myth of progress is used to justify our continuing acceptance that our society is being organized the only way it could possibly be. However, the ruined factory is a "fly in the ointment." It does not fit into the grand narrative of progress.[22] As explorers emphasize, these buildings were just born to be ruins. The pathos of the strident certainty of their design juxtaposed against the poetry of their decay is hard to ignore. Exploring an abandoned, huge factory also enables us to consider how much stuff we need to live as we do and how little we know about making it. This is the phantom haunting the desolate factory. "Maybe we don't want to work production lines anymore, but we are still addicted to what they produce. The industrial ruin brings us squeamishly close to facing those who now do our work so that we don't have to."[23] Explorers often suggest that space suffuses and informs our thought processes to a much deeper extent than we tend to notice. Ruined factories signify the failure of industrial production in an area. This is a subtext of urban exploration: a revealed secret story of what is happening now.[24] The ruined factory symbolizes the old modern world that had been conquered by the new, but, for explorers, it is a sign that this new one will be conquered too, because the ruin, as Russell A. Berman stresses, is the shadow of democratic process. That is why the term "modern ruin" indicates not only the destruction of prior human construction, but it suggests human agency,[25] human condition, and human subjectivity, that have been shaped within a democratic process of individualization as well.

"Interior tourism" means also the journey to the explorer's own past and memories. Or, as urbexers often underline, to the idea of childhood. Urbexing is a process of discovering the urban space and looking at it in a way that is elusive for a common passer-by. Contrary to appearances, it is not a very difficult task to perform. As Polish urbexers advise, "just remember as you used to be a little kid. The neighborhood was not secret and uncanny for you, because you knew every building, every tree and every hole in a fence. This child-like sensitivity to the details seems to disappear as one grows up, because we begin to notice, that everything around us is very well-known, typical and dead boring. Very often we are of the opinion that we know our surrounding as the back of our hand and we must leave to find something interesting. That's not true."[26] This point of view is also mentioned in *Beauty in Decay:*

> Think back to your childhood for a moment and it all begins to make sense. Do you remember the terrifying yet seductive draw of the archetypal haunted house? Every neighborhood and every childhood has one. At the very point we cross the border from childhood into adolescence we cross real physical borders too. It's the moment in our lives when we test the boundaries. We finally pluck up the courage to break into the haunted house and take a look around. You can probably remember your own experiences of this.[27]

Entering the empty and collapsing building also means testing the boundaries: of one's strength, emotions, skills, and imagination. But first of all, it demands to overcome the fear. On the one hand, individuality means freedom. On the other hand, it is bounded with uncertainty.[28] Urbexers feel uniquely (they certainly can signify a personality vis-à-vis society[29]) but, at the same time, they are afraid of what can happen to them while exploring. This "journey towards the within" can then be a possibility to experience fear as well. The explorers always remember that they are capable of having unmediated, bodily experiences of reality and they welcome the fear that may come with them. The fear is considered here as the gateway that leads explorers to the "wonderland" of abandoned places. "This is the world through the looking glass that in some dark corner of every soul, we are all looking for."[30] The most desired location to feel the fear is undoubtedly a derelict and ruined hospital (for Polish urbexers the most coveted place is the famous abandoned psychiatric hospital that sits in Owińska/Greater Poland[31]). It signifies a gateway between this world and the next and symbolizes a place where the new generation comes in and, often, where the old generation leaves. It can be called a vulnerable institution too, irrevocably tarred in the public mind with notions of malpractice, underfunding, and mismanagement. For urbexers, derelict hospitals mean institutions heavy under the weight of their own symbolism (especially when the goal of infiltration is a mental hospital), because it used to be the triumph of science and reason over "centuries of quackery." Therefore, the explorers emphasize that there is something terribly sad about a derelict hospital.

> Once the lights go out in a building in which so many pivotal moments of so many lives have occurred, the old life of the institution continues to resonate in the imagination of the explorer. Full of intimate mementoes and intriguing details, it's easy for the witness to become absorbed in visions and reverie.[32]

The dead hospital is then an even stronger symbol of death.

URBEX AND THE QUESTION OF INDIVIDUAL
FREEDOM AND CONTROL

Ruins are "free" in their collapsing process. But, according to Robert
Ginsberg, this freedom is uncertain, unsteady, and insecure, because the
form can disappear easily.[33] Therefore, another important question about
exploration as an "interior tourism" is a problem of freedom within the
instruments of control. Contemporary culture is characterized by ubiquitous supervision and invigilation. Postmodern cities are socially and
aesthetically controlled spaces, not only by CCTV systems. Individual
freedom does not then mean total freedom. Humans liberated from traditional determinations had to take greater control of and responsibility for
their own lives. Besides, they are much more dependent on modern institutions and structures,[34] and, what is more important, totally invigilated
by a new kind of media. Derelict and forgotten buildings are attractive to
explorers because they cannot be totally controlled, neither in their shape,
nor in their meaning. Although they threaten to imprison explorers in the
unguarded labyrinths of the past, they also promise to open imaginary
escapes.[35] As Bradley Garrett—one of the explorers—points out, urbexing
is a project of localized knowledge production born of a desire to connect
in a meaningful way to a world rendered increasingly mundane by commercial interests and an endless state of "heightened" security.[36] Explorers
are fascinated by the uncontrolled freedom of a building that collapses in
a quite unplanned way. Ruins are anamorphic, not only because they collapse uniquely, but because they morph into different shapes in the imagination of explorers. And "they make up the invisible cities of our dreams
and nightmares, conjuring them to life, and they reveal the *memento mori*
in every lively tableau."[37] Exploring derelict architecture is then an activity of creating a new narrative of the place. In an abandoned building, the
narratives of decay, entropy, and the encroachment of nature contrast with
the intended narrative of the architect. This results in some kind of spatial
poetry. In a blog on *In-dust-real*, the author writes:

> I am 30 and I am able to take shelter only in my head. The serial dreams about
> chases and impossibility of getaway had gone. But the no-name pursuer left.
> I am looking for him holding the camera in a building with no windows. The
> deeper we are going, the darker it is getting. I will get my hands on him, but
> the camera won't perpetuate anything. Such a place that will shelter you from
> something you are afraid of most of all does not exist.[38]

The "freedom" of a collapsing and derelict building also means the
authenticity of it. The question of "being authentic" is often highlighted

by touristic discourse and therefore is primary for urban exploration considered as an "interior tourism." Some would claim that authenticity was only possible in the past when the world was not under the shadow of media representation and distortion. According to Andreas Huyssen, the desire for the authentic always reflects the fear of inauthenticity, the lack of existential meaning, and the absence of individual originality: "The more we have learned to understand all images, words, and sounds as always already mediated, the more we desire the authentic and the immediate."[39] Abandoned buildings seem to be an answer to searching for something that is really authentic in a postmodern simulated urban realm, so "interior tourism" implies looking for traces left behind by other people, hidden under the official surface of a city space. As Kamilla—one of the Polish urbexers—summarizes, living people always leave traces: things, interferences, creations, and destructions. The main purpose for urban explorers is to find the "traces of the traces on photographs and in narratives." Traces in all of this that is unspeakable but can change anybody who has seen the abandoned place. The most important are the small parts of time and space, which create a new kind of reality around the explorers. The reality that can be dreamed, this one that is extremely real.[40] Urbexers often claim that the history they try to discover is in the whispers that surround them in an abandoned place and the tales passed on from those who came before. It is a history of people like them who did what they did, just like we do, as a response to the strange world they found themselves in. "Explorers have stumbled across this history, this folk history. It may be an irrational impulse to leap over a metaphorical wall into the ruined gardens of the haunted house but once there the treasure found is very real in an unexpected way."[41] As the explorers from Trójmiejska Grupa Exploracyjna claim, "Sometimes while exploring we are not searching for or expecting anything. On the contrary, we just know that the place is abandoned, we enter and the abandoned things are finding us."[42]

The form of a derelict building obliges our movement. As Ginsberg writes "we and it move around one another, backing off, moving in too close, and occasionally losing sight of one another. We must watch our step while gazing upward, or we may fall in the moat. The ruin does not have clearly prepared paths to follow or enjoyment of its forms. Any paths are meant didactically to aid appreciation of the intentions of the invisible original."[43] Modern ruins can then be a metaphor for contemporary life. Lack of charted and planned paths, many traps and a feeling of loneliness (many urban explorers infiltrate the abandoned building alone) can symbolize an existence of an individual in the time of individualism and its efforts in "searching for oneself." Abandoned and forgotten architecture is a proper place, when we can really feel something that Krzysztof Tyszka names a "loneliness of the soul." The modern world is heterogeneous and colorful, but modern man experiences some kind of homogeneity and the sameness in the same time. This heterogeneity is not a source of communication and reciprocal understanding, but it is the reason of isolation, uncertainty, and loss.[44] Modern ruins become then an existential metaphor, because they are an architectural witness of an existential void. The metaphor of a lonely soul also implicates a question of a human being in a secularized contemporary metropolis. As Michael Roth suggests, only in a secularized world can ruins be a site of contemplation.[45] In 1,791 Comte de Volney wrote: "Hail, solitary ruins! holy sepulchers and silent walls! you I invoke; . . . it excites in my heart the charm of delicious sentiments—sublime contemplations."[46] Contemporary urbexers underline that exploration is a kind of "reclaiming the sacred." Abandoned churches are symbols of a "death of sacrum" in the modern world and loss of faith. As one can read in *Beauty of Decay*, entering the ruined church contains a delicious sense of sacrilege and tasting the forbidden. And, of course, these sites have borne witness to the multiplicity of prayers of thousands of people over the years. "Even a deconsecrated church can make you question what it is exactly that you believe."[47] Although many of us believe that we are in the secular age of mass communication, quantum physics, and the genetic codes and manipulations, exploration of a ruined church can be a way to remind us that this is something more about the human condition—its spiritual dimension that had been lost. In opposition to many countries in Western Europe, in Poland there are very few of the derelict churches (most of them are the protestant sanctuaries or synagogues). But even these few can be symbols for urban explorers of what can happen if the process of "westernization" of Polish culture, that began after the Iron Curtain had fallen, continues.

Alicja Gzowska claims that modern ruins are becoming the central figure for the theory of modernity that wants to be much more than the triumph of progress and democratization. They wake the awareness of the dark side of progress and are the warning sign that reminds us about the resonance of forgetting the past. Although contemporary ruins are an oppressive space, that is somewhere in-between past and present, nature and culture, death and life,[48] they create an opportunity to the contemplation not only about modern processes of production and consumption, but about the condition of an individual human being as well. In a similar vein, Dylan Trigg suggests: "If rational progress undergoes doubt by the way of the ruin, then the prospect of our being-in-place needs to be called into question. In doing so, the ruin takes on a significance which exceeds its aesthetic merits and impressionistic evocations and becomes a symbol able to redefine the concept of dwelling."[49]

CONCLUSIONS: A DERELICT BUILDING AS A HUMAN

Urban explorers by definition go to places that most people do not enter. We may ask then, if they are having mental experiences that most other people are not having? Infiltration of abandoned buildings could imply that they are entering states of mind beyond the everyday. Explorers always "revive" the spirit of a location as part of their work. It is, as if, by investing their imagination into the practice of exploring the space, they are performing some important ritual, the results of which may seem invisible but, perhaps, can be essential to people who are not urbexers as well. Urban exploration as an "interior tourism" means a practice that symbolizes a kind of interior journey of an urban individual. This also implicates a metaphorized meaning of a collapsing building as a man, therefore explorers very often anthropomorphize decaying buildings in their narratives. Abandoned architecture symbolizes then a feeling and experiencing human being, just like in a poem of Claude Esteban:

> Someone, and no matter who, inhabits my head like it's an empty house; he enters, he leaves, he bangs each door behind him, powerless I put up with this ruckus. Someone, and maybe it's me, palms my most private thoughts; he crumples them, returns them to dust. Someone, and it's much later now, slowly walks across the room and, not seeing me, stops to contemplate the havoc. Someone, and no matter where, collects the pieces of my shadow.[50]

Christopher Woodward states in characteristic words: "When we contemplate ruins, we contemplate our own future."[51] To an urban poet, the decay of a building can easily represent dissolution of the individual ego in the flow of time. The more recent the ruins are, the greater emotions can appear, because derelict buildings symbolize our own transiency. Exploring the architecture that has been a place of everyday experience a few or dozens of years ago, causes other feelings and emotions than visiting some ancient ruins, because the ruins of contemporary society, latent on the urban landscape behind some "invisible curtain," are privileged spaces, which simultaneously invoke reactions of repulsion and sublime, and feelings of curiosity and fear. For many urban explorers, infiltrating decaying modern architecture is an activity that gives their lives another meaning. Because, according to Samuel Johnson, "whatever withdraws us from the power of our senses—whatever makes the past, the distant, or the future, predominate over the present, advances us in the dignity of human beings."[52] The fragmented and collapsing architecture from recent past can easily signify a fragmented life of the individual in the time of individualization. But, in contradiction to everyday experience of this life, makes the contemplation of the fragmented existence possible. At least, in urban explorers' minds and imaginations.

NOTES

1. Julia Hell and Andreas Schönle, "Introduction," in *Ruins of Modernity*, ed. Julia Hell and Andreas Schönle (Durham, NC: Duke University Press, 2010), 5.

2. Stefan Symotiuk, "Miejsce i czas," in *Genius loci. Studia o człowieku w przestrzeni*, ed. Zbigniew Kadłubek (Katowice: FA Art., 2007), 124.

3. Ibidem, 125.

4. Brian Dillon, "Introduction. A Short History of Decay," in *Ruins: Documents of Contemporary Art*, ed. Brian Dillon (Cambridge, MA: MIT Press, 2011), 10.

5. See e.g. Hanna K. Göbel, *The Re-use of Urban Ruins: Atmospheric Inquiries of the City* (New York: Routledge, 2015); Dylan Trigg, "The Aesthetics of Decay: Nothingness, Nostalgia and the Absence of Reason," *New Studies in Aesthetics* 37 (New York: Peter Lang Publishing, 2006); Tim Edensor, "Sensing the Ruin," *Senses and Society* 2 (2007): 217–32; Tim Edensor, *Industrial Ruins: Spaces, Aesthetics and Materiality* (Oxford: Berg, 2005); Tim Edensor, "The Ghosts of Industrial Ruins: Ordering and Disordering Memory in Excessive Space," *Environment and Planning D: Society and Space* 23 (2005): 829–49; Robert Ginsberg, *The Aesthetic of Ruins* (Amsterdam: Rodopi, 2004); Christopher Woodward, *In Ruins* (London: Vintage, 2002).

6. See e.g. Jeffrey Eugenides, *Against Ruin Porn*, accessed August 24, 2016, http://www.boat-mag.com/2014/02/05/against-ruin-porn; Julia Polter, *Beyond "Ruin Porn,"* accessed August 24, 2016, http://sojo.net/magazine/2013/08/beyond-ruin-porn; Matthew Christopher, *Confessions of a Ruin Pornographer*, accessed August 24, 2016, http://www.abandonedamerica.us/life-as-a-ruin-pornographer; John P. Lear, *Detroitism,* accessed August 24, 2016, http://www.guernicamag.com/features/leary_1_15_11/; Richard B. Woodward, *Disaster Photography: When is Documentary Exploitation?*, accessed August 24, 2016, http://www.artnews.com/2013/02/06/the-debate-over-ruin-porn/; Paulina Jaroszyńska, *Oswajanie dzikich miejsc*, accessed August 24, 2016, http://projektmiasto2.blox.pl/html/1310721,262146,14,15.html?6,2008; Brian Dillon, *Ruin Lust: Our Love Affair with Decaying Buildings*, accessed August 24, 2016, http://www.theguardian.com/artanddesign/2012/feb/17/ruins-love-affair-decayed-buildings.

7. Cosmo Howard, "Introducing Individualization," in *Contested Individualization: Debates about Contemporary Personhood*, ed. Cosmo Howard (New York: Palgrave Macmillan, 2007), 4.

8. Bradley L. Garrett, *The Fragmentation of Urban Exploration*, accessed October 12, 2014, http://www.domusweb.it/en/op-ed/2011/06/01/the-fragmentation-of-urban-exploration.html.

9. Veronica Davidov, *Urban Exploration: A Subculture at a Glance*, 2008, accessed August 24, 2016, http://www.materialworldblog.com/2008/03/urban_exploration_a_subculture.html.

10. http://opuszczone.com, http://3ge.pl; https://www.facebook.com/UrbexPolska/?fref=ts; http://www.urb-ex.pl; http://dpuet.blogspot.com; http://www.deadzone.pl; http://fotokomorka.com; http://www.in-dust-real.pl, accessed August 24, 2016.

11. Alicja Gzowska, "Sit Transit Gloria Mundi," *Widok* 4 (2013): 3.

12. Ibidem, 4.

13. Johannes von Moltke, "Ruin Cinema," in *Ruins of Modernity*, 413.

14. http://fotokomorka.com, accessed July 20, 2016.

15. Ignasi De Solà-Morales Rubió, "Terrain Vague." In *Anyplace*, ed. Cynthia C. Davidson (New York: Anyone Corporation, 1995), 118–24.

16. http://in-dust-real.pl/, accessed April 5, 2016.

17. Romany W. G., *Beauty in Decay* (Carpet Bombing Culture, 2011), pages not numbered.

18. Symotiuk, *Miejsce i czas*, 126.

19. Aleksandra Kunce, "Miejsce i rytm. O doświadczaniu miejsc w kulturze," in *Genius loci. Studia o człowieku w przestrzeni*, 98–99.

20. Dylan Trigg, *The Aesthetics of Decay*, accessed July 20, 2016. https://www.academia.edu/6218534/The_Aesthetics_of_Decay_Nothingness_Nostalgia_and_the_Absence_of_Reason; in the on-line version pages not numbered.

21. Francesca Picchi, *Modern Ruins*, accessed July 17, 2016, http://www.domusweb.it/en/architecture/2009/06/17/modern-ruins.html.

22. Trigg, *The Aesthetics of Decay*.

23. Romany W. G., *Beauty in Decay*.

24. Ibidem.

25. Russell A. Berman, *Democratic Destruction*, in *Ruins of Modernity*, 106–107.

26. http://figeneration.pl/urban-exploration-odkryj-na-nowo-miejska-dzungle/, accessed April 5, 2016.

27. Romany W. G., *Beauty in Decay*.

28. About individualism see e.g. *Essays on Individuality*, ed. Felix Morley (Philadelphia: University of Pennsylvania Press, 1958).

29. Weaver, *Individuality and Modernity*, 63.

30. Romany W. G., *Beauty in Decay*.

31. The mental hospital in Owińska (*Provinzial-Irren-Heilanstalt zu Owinsk*) was founded in 1838 by Germans which had occupied the Polish territory. One thousand and a hundred patients of the hospital were murdered during the Second World War within the T4 action.

32. Romany W. G., *Beauty in Decay*.

33. Ginsberg, *The Aesthetic of Ruins*, 21.

34. Howard, *Introducing Individualization*, 2.

35. Svetlana Boym, "Ruins of the Avant-garde: From Tatlin's Tower to Paper Architecture," in *Ruins of Modernity*, 83.

36. Garrett, *The Fragmentation of Urban Exploration*.

37. Boym, "Ruins," 83.

38. http://in-dust-real.pl/strefa-wykluczenia/, accessed April 5, 2016.

39. Andreas Huyssen, "Authentic Ruins," in *Ruins of Modernity*, 53.

40. http://in-dust-real.pl/strefa-wykluczenia/, accessed April 5, 2016.

41. Romany W. G., *Beauty in Decay.*
42. http://3ge.pl/onas/, accessed July 17, 2016.
43. Ginsberg, *The Aesthetic of Ruins*, 17.
44. Krzysztof Tyszka, *Samotność duszy. Dziedzictwo wiary i rozumu w (po) nowoczesności* (Warsaw: Wydawnictwo Uniwersytetu Warszawskiego, 2014), 59.
45. Quoted in Julia Hell and Andreas Schönle, *Introduction*, 5.
46. Quoted in Brian Dillon, *Introduction: A Short History of Decay*, 12.
47. Romany W. G., *Beauty in Decay.* On a question of abandoned and forgotten churches see also Małgorzata Nieszczerzewska, "Ruiny architektury sakralnej. Śmierć miejsca—śmierć sacrum?" *Wobec śmierci, Zeszyty Naukowe Centrum Badań im. Edyty Stein* 9 (2012): 273–89.
48. Gzowska, "Sit Transit," 6.
49. Trigg, *The Aesthetics of Decay.*
50. Bo Mackison, *Abandoned Door—A Metaphor for Transition*, http://bomackison.com/abandoned-door-a-metaphor-for-transition, accessed December 19, 2013.
51. Woodward, *In Ruins*, 2.
52. Ibidem, 4.

REFERENCES

Berman, Russell A. "*Democratic Destruction.*" In *Ruins of Modernity*, edited by Julia Hell and Andreas Schönle, 106–17. Durham, NC: Duke University Press, 2010.

Boym, Svetlana. "Ruins of the Avant-garde: From Tatlin's Tower to Paper Architecture." In *Ruins of Modernity*, edited by Julia, Hell and Andreas Schönle, 58–88. Durham, NC: Duke University Press, 2010.

Christopher, Matthew. *Confessions of a Ruin Pornographer.* Accessed August 24, 2016. http://www.abandonedamerica.us/life-as-a-ruin-pornographer.

Davidov, Veronica. *Urban Exploration: A Subculture at a Glance.* Accessed October 12, 2014. http://www.materialworldblog.com/2008/03/urban_exploration_a_subculture.html.

De Solà-Morales Rubió, Ignasi. "Terrain Vague." In *Anyplace*, edited by Cynthia C. Davidson, 118–24. New York: Anyone Corporation, 1995.

Dillon, Brian. "Introduction: A Short History of Decay." In *Ruins: Documents of Contemporary Art*, edited by Brian Dillon. Cambridge, MA: MIT Press, 2011.

———. *Ruin Lust: Our Love Affair with Decaying Buildings.* Accessed August 24, 2016. http://www.theguardian.com/artanddesign/2012/feb/17/ruins-love-affair-decayed-buildings.

Edensor, Tim. *Industrial Ruins: Spaces, Aesthetics and Materiality.* Oxford: Berg, 2005.

———. "The Ghosts of Industrial Ruins: Ordering and Disordering Memory in Excessive Space." *Environment and Planning D: Society and Space* 23 (2005): 829–49.

———. "Sensing the Ruin." *Senses and Society* 2 (2007): 217–32.

Eugenides, Jeffrey. *Against Ruin Porn.* Accessed August 24, 2016. http://www.boatmag.com/2014/02/05/against-ruin-porn.

Garrett, Bradley L. *The Fragmentation of Urban Exploration.* Accessed October 12, 2014. http://www.domusweb.it/en/op-ed/2011/06/01/the-fragmentation-of-urban-exploration.html.

Ginsberg, Robert. *The Aesthetic of Ruins.* Amsterdam: Rodopi, 2004.

Göbel, Hanna K. *The Re-use of Urban Ruins: Atmospheric Inquiries of the City.* New York: Routledge, 2015.

Gzowska, Alicja. "Sit Transit Gloria Mundi." *Widok* 4 (2013): 1–9.

Hell, Julia, and Andreas Schönle. "Introduction." In *Ruins of Modernity*, edited by Julia Hell and Andreas Schönle. Durham, NC: Duke University Press, 2010.

Howard, Cosmo. "Introducing Individualization." In *Contested Individualization: Debates about Contemporary Personhood*, edited by Cosmo Howard. New York: Palgrave Macmillan, 2007.

Huyssen, Andreas. "Authentic Ruins." In *Ruins of Modernity*, edited by Julia Hell and Andreas Schönle, 17–28. Durham, NC: Duke University Press, 2010.

Jaroszyńska, Paulina. *Oswajanie dzikich miejsc.* Accessed August 24, 2016. http://projektmiasto2.blox.pl/html/1310721,262146,14,15.html?6,2008.

Kunce, Aleksandra. "Miejsce i rytm. O doświadczaniu miejsc w kulturze." In *Genius loci. Studia o człowieku w przestrzeni*, edited by Zbigniew Kadłubek. Katowice: FA Art, 2007.

Lear, John P. *Detroitism.* Accessed August 24, 2016. http://www.guernicamag.com/features/leary_1_15_11/.

Mackison, Bo. *Abandoned Door–A Metaphor for Transition.* Accessed December 19, 2013. http://bomackison.com/abandoned-door-a-metaphor-for-transition.

Moltke von, Johannes. "Ruin Cinema." In *Ruins of Modernity*, edited by Julia Hell and Andreas Schönle, 395–417. Durham, NC: Duke University Press, 2010.

Morley, Felix, ed. *Essays on Individuality.* Philadelphia: University of Pennsylvania Press, 1958.

Nieszczerzewska, Małgorzata. "Ruiny architektury sakralnej. Śmierć miejsca – śmierć sacrum?" In *Wobec śmierci. Zeszyty Naukowe Centrum Badań im. Edyty Stein* 9 (2012): 273–89.

Picchi, Francesca. *Modern Ruins.* Accessed July 17, 2016. http://www.domusweb.it/en/architecture/2009/06/17/modern-ruins.html.

Polter, Julia. *Beyond "Ruin Porn."* Accessed August 24, 2016. http://sojo.net/magazine/2013/08/beyond-ruin-porn.

Romany W. G. *Beauty in Decay.* London: Carpet Bombing Culture, 2011.

Symotiuk, Stefan. "Miejsce i czas." In *Genius loci. Studia o człowieku w przestrzeni*, edited by Zbigniew Kadłubek. Katowice: FA Art, 2007.

Trigg, Dylan. "The Aesthetics of Decay: Nothingness, Nostalgia and the Absence of Reason." *New Studies in Aesthetics* 37. New York: Peter Lang Publishing, 2006.

Tyszka, Krzysztof. *Samotność duszy. Dziedzictwo wiary i rozumu w (po) nowoczesności.* Warsaw: Wydawnictwo Uniwersytetu Warszawskiego, 2014.

Weaver, Richard M. "Individuality and Modernity." In *Essays on Individuality*, edited by Felix Morley. Philadelphia: University of Pennsylvania Press, 1958.

Woodward, Christopher. *In Ruins.* London: Vintage, 2002.

Woodward, Richard B. *Disaster Photography: When is Documentary Exploitation?* Accessed August 24, 2016. http://www.artnews.com/2013/02/06/the-debate-over-ruin-porn/.

Online:

http://opuszczone.com.
http://3ge.pl, https://www.facebook.com/UrbexPolska/?fref=ts.
http://www.urb-ex.pl.
http://dpuet.blogspot.com.
http://www.deadzone.pl.
http://fotokomorka.com.
http://www.in-dust-real.pl.
http://figeneration.pl/urban-exploration-odkryj-na-nowo-miejska-dzungle/.

Chapter 14

Recalling the Ruins of the Socialist Modernity

Touring Lost Places in Yugoslavia between Private Search for Identity and Cultural Heritage Tourism

Michael Zinganel

This chapter does not place emphasis on the shared or divided memories of the peoples of Yugoslavia during the socialist period nor on the immediate revision of the dominant views of modernist, post-Second World War buildings and monuments which, after the federation's painful disintegration, were dedicated to neoliberal and, more frequently, nationalist purposes. Instead I am interested in the perception of protagonists from abroad—including myself—who were not completely involved in local, conflicting discourses and investigate the current imaginary of travelers who consume and reproduce the striking images and powerful narrations produced by non-Yugoslav artists and scholars. In the words of Noel B. Salazar these are acts of "picturing paradise," of stimulating a sort of "safari dream"[1] and seducing an increasing number people into visiting these spectacular ruins. The case study chosen for this chapter, the ruin of the Haludovo tourist resort on the island of Krk, was once upon a time a real jewel of late modern architecture and landscape design but it also represents the most frivolous kind of "third way" joint venture between socialist self-management and the US-American entertainment industry during the Cold War. Additionally, it analyses a series of modernist Second World War and partisan monuments. But, in my own professional research and teaching practice and in my naïve imaginary of the Austria's favorite communist neighbor, Yugoslavia, both modernism and monuments play a crucial role.

My own interest in contested socialist and modernist heritage on the territory of former SFR of Yugoslavia is based on my autobiographical experience of being a typical Austrian middle-class kid of the 1960s and 1970s who frequently went on summer holidays to the beautiful landscape of the Eastern

Adriatic coast to enjoy the fruits of Tito's "third way" policies between the eastern and western blocs. Back then, Yugoslavia's coastline was an "afford-able arcadia"[2] for feeling "really modern"[3]—a real but reasonably priced paradise for those Western European tourists not hunting for the higher status conferred by more prestigious travel destinations.[4] The adjacent peninsula of Istria was, and still is, a perfect place to study masterpieces of Roman, Early Christian, and Venetian heritage[5] with which Austria cannot compete. So, Istria was also one of the favorite destinations for the Graz Faculty of Architecture field trips in which I participated both as a student before the end of socialist period, and as a university teacher after the end of disintegra-tion wars (1991–1995). Typically, (for architects) we were also interested in the ambitious modernization programs launched during this socialist period. They resulted in modernist architecture of outstanding quantity and qual-ity, especially when compared to the anti-modernist style of the blown-up imitations of rural farmhouses complete with cozy rustic interiors that were built for tourist purposes in the Austrian Alps at the same time. Many of my colleagues from Austria and former Yugoslavia feared that this modernist socialist heritage would be in danger of demolition and reconstruction in the wave of "anti-socialist" resentment and the "neoliberal" building boom that we expected would follow the collapse of socialism.[6]

Instead of a peaceful transformation from Yugoslavia's "third way econ-omy" to pure market capitalism, the federation was shattered by nationalist aspirations and years of warfare and ethnic cleansing. This was, of course, a shocking experience for us as immediate neighbors too. Although in 1995 the Dayton Accords ended five years of war between Croats, Serbs, and Bosnians, fighting continued on other fronts until the NATO bombardment of Serbia in 1999. By 2009 at the latest, the role of Austrians and Austrian institutions in clearly supporting Slovenia and Croatia in their drive for independence as well as their involvement in postsocialist privatization and reinvestment opportunities became a focus of attention when the Hypo Alpe Adria Bank had to be bailed out by the Austrian tax-payers to prevent a collapse of the financial system in the Western Balkans.[7] This failed neocolonial economic adventure made tourism investment a politically hot issue in Austria. It also encouraged me to launch a research project on tourist developments before, during, and after the postsocialist transition.

In order to de-escalate the tendency to exoticize that examining a single com-munist destination might encourage, the project *Holidays after the Fall*[8] was conceived as a piece of comparative research on tourism development in two countries with very distinct interpretations of communist politics, economy, and planning practice. It investigated the planning history of hotels and resorts during the socialist period on the Croatian Adriatic and the Bulgarian Black Sea coasts.[9] But—in contrast to other works—we expanded our research to include the distinct economic and physical transformation of these projects after the fall of communism though we were aware that there were not many sources available at the time.[10] In the context of this research project I was concentrating on developments on the Croatian Adriatic coast—the territory I knew so well from my childhood—from Tito's break up with Stalin in 1948 till today.

Interestingly (and contrary to my own expectations) after years of war, disinvestment, and a long, drawn-out, and opaque privatization process, vacant hotels and resort ruins exuding melancholy still outnumbered significant new developments. The delayed introduction of investment-friendly policies, justified by high debt and complex issues of property ownership, combined with nationalism, corruption, an absence of legal certainty together with restrictive building regulations[11], can also be read as a historical happy turn of events. So, in contrast to the disastrous disfiguration of the coastlines in Spain, Bulgaria or Montenegro, Croatia's natural resources and landscape are largely intact and many of the buildings still serve as perfect 1:1 museums of modernist design ideas—obviously attracting new groups of visitors.

RUIN SAFARIS TO SOCIALIST HOTELS AND RESORTS

As part of the project I also curated and produced a traveling exhibition about the Croatian case studies. This was first shown in Graz/Austria in 2012 and in 2015 in Rijeka/Croatia.[12] To promote these exhibitions and the book I could not resist using the most striking photographs and the aesthetically most appealing ruin on the Croatian Adriatic: the resort of Haludovo on the Island of Krk. A historic promotional photograph from the height of its glamour and a current ruin-image by an Italian photographer have had wide-ranging coverage since the first exhibition and book launch—especially online.[13]

Both the Zagreb-based writer and journalist Jurica Pavičić, who used these press photos for his article[14] and Aida Vidan, a Croatian-born scholar living and teaching in the United States, who had seen the announcement online, kindly sent me a link to a YouTube video, shot in exactly the same location. In fact, the young artist responsible for it, Eve Vidan Gallagher, is Aida's daughter. At the time, she was only fifteen years old. While visiting relatives in Rijeka during summer holidays of 2013, Eve had gone to Haludovo which, despite the devastated hotel, has a very beautiful and popular beach that attracts tourists and Rijeka residents equally. She was immediately inspired to make a music clip with her best friends from Rijeka. The establishing shot of the video, surprisingly professional and directed by Filip Koludrović, shows the young singer-songwriter playing her acoustic guitar and singing while sitting on an old fridge that someone had thrown into the empty and derelict outdoor swimming pool of the hotel. A group of four equally young

Figure 14.1   Abandoned Hotel Palace at Haludovo resort on the island of Krk, Croatia.
Source: © Photo: Daniele Ansidei 2012.

actors start exploring the different spaces in and around the hotel as if they had arrived from another planet and/or the distant future.[15]

Although the young singer is not at all concerned with the historic background or the reasons for the sad contemporary state of the hotel, the questions posed mesh nicely with the specific location. More importantly, she is at least drawing attention to a site of historic interest for several reasons. Designed by the well-known Croatian architect Boris Magaš, Haludovo represented a brilliant example of the many large, strikingly designed modernist hotel complexes built in the boom years between 1968 and 1972. They were clearly intended as showcases of both a modern lifestyle and contemporary art and design, at the forefront of international standards of the time. The call for "lyrical value" in architecture through a new "monumentality" and "plasticity," together with the demand for a "synthesis of art and architecture"— first proclaimed by Giedion and Sert in 1955,[16] the masterminds behind the influential *Congrès Internationaux d'Architecture Moderne* (CIAM)—were taken very seriously in Yugoslavia.[17]

The country's pioneering role as a co-founder of the Non-Aligned Movement and its conviction that it was a ranking member of the international political avant-garde, meant it was on the look-out for a stage upon which to celebrate its radical internationalism. Major modern tourism operations were therefore conceived as cosmopolitan meeting points where the successes of Yugoslavia's third way policies could be clearly communicated to two publics—domestic and international. But instrumentalizing a hotel as a post-Second World War reconciliation project was obviously being taken to the extreme here: when the hotel was finished in 1972, the management of Brodo-komerc of Rijeka unexpectedly announced a joint venture with *Penthouse*, the US-American adult magazine,[18] to "sell Yugoslavia" to an international jet set who were to fly in via the adjacent newly built airport of Krk. At the opening ceremony—documented on film by Dejan Karaklajic and Jovan Acin,[19]—of the Penthouse Adriatic, as the casino-hotel was called at the time, Bob Guic-cone, the founder of Penthouse, presented his "pets," scantily dressed service girls imported from the United States. "Look at those cute little pets, they are our Peace Corps—the new soldiers of the Cold War," he said.[20]

Although Penthouse left the joint venture after only a few years with little media attention, the hotel remained a comparably glamorous place for seaside recreation and entertainment. After the war from 1991 to 1995, though, Yugo-slavia's erstwhile "third way" pièce de résistance would never be reopened. Today Haludovo is considered a worst-case scenario for opaque privatization in Croatia: after being used as accommodation for war refugees—like 80 percent of the hotels along the coastline—ownership changed hands several times.

Currently the majority of shares are owned by a company registered on the Isle of Man, controlled by the Armenian Ara Abramian.[21] He actually had plans for the complex drawn up, but planning permission was refused and nothing ever transpired. On the contrary, the building has since been stripped of almost all everything of any value and stands today as a crestfallen monu-ment to late modern holiday architecture and its own bizarre history.

So encountering numerous dramatic photos of the ruins in Internet forums (and not only snapshots by amateurs or ruin-selfies by tourists) comes as no surprise. There are a surprisingly large number of ambitious projects: for example, architectural photographs shot with wide angle lenses that enhance the monumental effects and affects of the late modernist structures as well as sequences of close ups shots of details of the decayed interior seemingly inspired by forensic crime-scene photographs.[22]

For a young American-Croatian girl like Eve searching for an identity, the ruin Haludovo seems a very good choice This monument of the joint venture between the United States and the outstanding political system of her grand-parents' time represents a salient piece of evidence for the contradictions that characterized both Yugoslavia's regime then and the imaginary of a liberated and liberal Croatia today. For this reason, the resort ruins of Haludovo have also been the undefeated number one attraction for participants in my own four-day guided bus-tours to *Palaces and Ruins of Socialist Hotels and Resorts* at the Northern Croatian Adriatic Coast. I originally organized it in May 2013 for the Graz of House of Architecture, the first venue of the exhibitions.[23] The

Figure 14.2 Stills from Eve Vidan Gallagher' music video: Merely Human. *Source*: Producer: Filip Koludrović 2013.

author, as travel guide, and the participants, architects, artists, and historians from Austria, used to approach the ruin from the landward side by parking near the main entrance, as if the hotel was still operating. We walked through the hallway to areas that once offered different amenities and also visited the outdoor pool that played a major role in Eve's video. We left the hotel on the seaward side, passing the American bowling alley in the basement.

Figure 14.3 A frequently photographed hotel ruin at the Croatian Adriatic coast: abandoned Hotel Palace at Haludovo resort on the island of Krk, Croatia. *Source*: © Photo: Daniele Ansidei 2012.

Although the building is closed off toward the street by patched-up barriers of wire mesh and even with brick walls on the seaward side, visitors need only follow trails on the ground to be guided to the access points. Inside, all the movable furniture has been stolen, the interior design largely destroyed, the walls covered with graffiti, staircase banisters have had their handrails ripped off and floors have been stripped of their coverings. Since doors and windows are entirely missing and all glass panels shattered, the separation between inside and outside had been largely dissolved at ground level. Nevertheless, the different functions of the spaces can be clearly identified: reception, lobby, dining room, bar, night club, bowling alley, indoor, and outdoor pools. Just as the building is suffering badly from decay and vandalism, the terraces and the many of the leisure facilities in the surrounding pine forest (for playing tennis, table tennis, boccia, or mini-golf) are being successively re-conquered by vegetation.

This situation opens up a great potential for imaginations and imaginaries: each of the devastated rooms, and re-naturalized leisure facilities is open to being charged with the memories of visitors' own holiday experiences. Passing along the thorny paths to enter this spectacular space might make many visitors think of a bewitched fairy tale castle. Others might feel that strolling around in the closed off hotel is akin to being in the evacuated "forbidden zone" of Andrei Tarkovsky's film, *Stalker* (1979), considered by many scholars of my generation to be a role model for contemporary ruin safaris.[24] Enthusiasts of modern art architecture might admire the striking construction elements representing a true synthesis of art, architecture, and landscape—or perceive the whole complex as a monumental land-art installation. And those who have been introduced into the very specific history of the hotel might start daydreaming about film sequences of spies from East and West mingling with the international jet set. These observations, especially the cinematographic associations, effects and affects experienced, were widely discussed and shared by the participants during and after the excursions.[25]

Of course, almost all participants were intensively occupied with shooting photographs of the ruin. But many of them also tried to collect physical evidence of their visit to take back home. Since almost anything of value seems to have fallen victim to vandalism and theft, none of the amateur-archaeologists needed to feel ashamed of pocketing a few of the smaller remnants. Some of the beautiful tiles from the shower and cabin walls in the hotel pool area, which seemed to have been systematically removed in some parts, were especially popular with architects. Their memorable and striking design in the form of truncated pyramids in a shade of sanitary green perfectly reveals their

Figure 14.4 Monument to Kosmaj partisan division from Second World War on top of Kosmaj mountain, near Belgrade, Serbia. *Source*: © Jan Kempenaers (School of Arts Ghent) Spomenik #3, 2006. Courtesy Breese Little Gallery London.

collectors as true connoisseurs of authentic designs and much-loved styles of the late 1960s and early 1970s.

Several people who visited the exhibitions but missed the opportunity to join the excursions asked me for how to find these places should they travel there on their own. Therefore, I offered them a Google map, a file with basic information and some helpful contact addresses. Others even organized their own guided tour, following the beaten paths.[26] Having been on one of the trips, some of the participants—like the young US-American exchange-student in Rijeka (Artibee 2015) whose Croatian friend complained that he unfortunately never had heard about these places before—were inspired to write academic articles. Others were motivated to produce their own professional art pieces: for example, the series small scale water colors and large-scale paintings by Moni K. Huber, based on collages of photographs shot during the trip[27] or the walk-through videos by Andrea Seidling.[28] I later included both works in another exhibition I curated in 2016. It focused primarily on the aspect of modernist art, design and lifestyle of these hotels which had been displayed a significant number of large-scale art pieces not unlike those in representational art museums or governmental buildings of the time[29] and commissioned from well-known contemporary artists. That same year, 2016, the ruin of Haludovo was also presented as one several modernist ruins of outstanding quality in an elaborate Croatian HRT-TV production *Betonski spavači* [Slumbering Concrete], directed by Saša Ban[30] significantly expanding the level of public attention for the topic in Croatia.

ART PRODUCTIONS AS TRAVEL GUIDES TO "LOST PLACES"

All these projects, shared and redistributed online, proved to function as true travel guides. On the other hand, the production of photo books and exhibitions about monumental late modernist architecture had already been booming for several years previously[31] and, in the context of "serious" academic architectural history, some projects had also been published.[32]

A very striking example is the photo-book by the Belgian artist Jan Kempenaers entitled *Spomenik. The End of History* 2010.[33] It is a rather thin but beautifully printed book of sixty-eight pages, offering only one page of introduction, twenty-six full page photos (the opposite pages being left entirely blank). There is a thumbnail photo index of six pages too. The photos show spectacular large-scale monuments built in Yugoslavia between about 1960 and the early 1980s which commemorate the victims of fascist aggression and mass murders during the Second World War. Furthermore, the monuments were also intended to celebrate the achievements of the partisan movement, the socialist ideology of Brotherhood and Unity and the artistic freedom Yugoslavia was so proud of.

Commissioned from some of the most famous modernist artists and architects of the time, these monuments had been characterized by rather different visual languages; they were expressive, abstract, and frequently surprisingly optimistic and included, for example, The *Monument Dedicated to Victims at the Jasenovac Concentration Camp* by Bogdan Bogdanović built in 1966, the *Monument to the Revolution* in Kozara/Mrakovica by Dušan Džamonja built between 1969 and 1972, and the *Monument to the Uprising of the People of Kordun and Banija* in Petrova Gora by Vojin Bakić completed in 1982. While these monuments were well-preserved pilgrimage sites that were promoted in travel guides and visited frequently during socialist period (especially by partisan veterans and school classes), by the time of Jan Kempenaers' phototrip in 2009 most of them were sadly neglected, many vandalized, and some even destroyed.[34]

Jan Kempenaers had to endure harsh criticism from the ex-Yugoslavian actors. Attitudes ranged from a general rejection of any foreigner having a right to interfere in the contested discourse about, and interpretation of, what they considered their "own" history—or, more accurately, *histories*—to being accused of failing to provide accurate explanations about the political and historic background. The latter is certainly true if for no other reason than the fact that the introduction to his photo-book is very short indeed. Interestingly, he had abandoned any opportunity for a more complex contextualization of the monuments in favor of a powerful reference to another artist's strategy of representation: except for the high quality printing, the strict, minimalist formal concept of his photo-book seems to conform very closely to US artist Ed Ruscha's famous and inspiring series of small scale artists books published in the 1960s. Each of these represented a limited number of different typologies of road infrastructure: for example, *Twentysix Gasoline Stations* 1963. By selecting only one photograph for each of twenty-six (!) selected monuments and only emphasizing the different

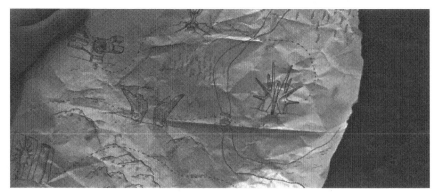

Figure 14.5   Still from Olympique's music video: The Reason I Came. *Source*: Producer: The Arcadia Agency. 2013.

Figure 14.6   Still from Olympique's music video: The Reason I Came. *Source*: Producer: The Arcadia Agency. 2013.

styles and monumentality of the central most striking sculptural elements, Jan Kempenaers also detracted them from the on-site choreography of pilgrimage whereby visitors approached the sculptures only after passing through an elaborately landscaped setting.[35]

Teaching a seminar on Art in Public Space myself where many of the students (of the Vienna University of Technology) were either born in former Yugoslavia or are second or third generation immigrants to Vienna, I felt committed to intensifying my interest in the history and legacy of post-Second World War monuments and memorials built around the same time as the hotels and resorts previously mentioned.[36] These monuments are, however, of special interest in Austria for another very serious reason: Nazi perpetrators and co-perpetrators had been discreetly re-integrated into society in Austria, our ancestors' complicity largely suppressed, and no significant antifascist monuments have ever been built in Austrian public space.

Although artists living in the successor states of former Yugoslavia had dealt with socialist monuments in their own artistic practice,[37] and brilliant analyses had been conducted and published, for example, by Milena Dragicević-Sesić (2011),[38] I decided to use Kempenaers photos to promote the works and the contested heritage. I also wanted to problematize his approach and consider the criticism he had been subjected to, especially the allegation about deriving cultural capital from the exotic aesthetics. His photos have such a strong aesthetic appeal that almost no one can resist their power and, more importantly, they are widely accessible on the Internet, extremely well interlinked with several popular web-portals and also frequently shared and redistributed via Flickr, Instagram, Pinterest, Tumblr, and other blogs.

While I was teaching in the springterm of 2014, one of my students googled and immediately and enthusiastically interrupted the seminar to inform us all that he just had found a great music clip online, shot in the monuments I had shown them just minutes before. It was a brand new video by the Austrian

Figure 14.7   Still from Olympique's music video: The Reason I Came. *Source:* Producer: The Arcadia Agency. 2013.

band, Olympique, with the title *The Reason I Came* (2014)[39] in which the lead singer stages himself as an archaeologist exploring unknown territory. He is using a hand-drawn map displaying paths to and sketches of strange objects, as if the monuments are treasures of some kind left behind by a bygone age or some alien species from outer space. The musicians admitted that they had found the "surreal and impressive locations" by accident on some Lost-Places Blog that shared abandoned ruins of all kinds, but also prominently featured Kempenaers' photos. In an interview the musicians stated that because these "surreal and mighty monuments fitted so perfectly with their song,"[40] they had started an exciting and intensive "road trip" of 2,965 km through six nations in four days to shoot the video. It was praised by pop critics as an "epic" movie about the young men's "search for identity."[41]

Interestingly, the monuments shown in the video also featured prominently in the Austrian popular-music-magazine *The Gap*. With the title "Yugo–Monuments not from our World," the article's teaser announced that "in ex-Yugoslavia there exist monuments that look like they are not from our world. Up to now only breath-taking photographs have been circulating. But we have researched the precise sites of these monuments and drawn a Google-map for you to visit them."[42]

A Slovenian student of mine seriously asked me on behalf of her colleagues to organize such a field trip for them. Others have already done the trip: one art student from the Vienna Academy of Fine Arts followed the Google Map from *The Gap* magazine and presented the travelogue as her own art work at her academy. But it seems that young people from all over the world start their road trip exploring Yugoslavia's socialist past. Just search for "*Spomenik*" [monument] in Google images and you will find endless material—including extensive visual explorations, one of them ironically named: I spy Spomeniks![43]

CONCLUDING THOUGHTS

If we would try to apply our toolkit from tourism theories, the practice of visiting lost places might seem partly related to Lennon and Foley's notion of *Dark Tourism* (2000)[44]—particularly in the case of *Spomeniks*, built on sites of mass murders during Second World War. More generally, including the hotel ruins, these visits are also close to the notion of "ruin porn" as the term is used by academics such as Leary and Mullins (2010/2012)[45] when they criticize the extremely self-centered approach of some of the young, well-off urban middle class who are driven to search for aesthetic sensations and emotional affects they feel to be lacking in everyday life.[46]

I would argue that placing buildings and monuments of sensational aesthetics in the public space and then abandoning them to dereliction without much explanation means it is unreasonable to expect to be able to entirely control visitors' on-site behavior or their visual representations and interpretations. Besides popular cultural studies have taught us that there has always been a desire for popular and undisciplined interpretation and thus for an even more pleasurable reading[47] and activity within a space. Furthermore, people "flirt with space":[48] they not only follow predetermined behavioral scripts and narrations written by others but also adapt existing scripts, stages, and stagescapes as co-writers, performatively testing their own identities and collecting souvenirs to structure the narrations they present to their peer groups at home. As Alfredo González-Ruibal has argued,[49] this seems especially inviting in spaces and places of obvious physical and ideological transformation, which are too recent and too contested to have re-established a shared hegemonic narration. The relation of lyrics and visuals in the hedonistic self-staging of the band Olympique is indeed rather arbitrary; Eve, the US-Croatian girl, brings with her the credibility of autobiographical references, while my own guided tours are clearly rendered educational at first sight. But this does not mean that I do not enjoy being at the center of the tourist experience, consciously emphasizing my Austro-centric gaze, revisiting the places of my childhood, guiding my guests into forbidden places and staging myself as an expert in front of, and in, the vacant ruins, performatively revealing forms of knowledge from different sources and, by presenting visual and material evidence in choreographed exercises of "seducation,"[50] successfully getting them to believe me.

The aspect of difference—besides the temporal transformation by dislocation—that initially drove my own interest, was based on an idealized perception of Tito's Yugoslavia (non-alignment and self-management) which I shared with many Austrians socialized in social democratic and antifascist milieus. Much more important, however, was the "exoticism" of the late modernist synthesis of art, architecture, and landscape, exemplified in these ruins of artistically inspired hotels and the mere existence of the striking anti-fascist monuments, we never had in Austria.

Visiting ruins was a compulsory part of the travel itinerary of the aristo-cratic grand tour, the educational sojourns of the bourgeoisie and, from as early as the seventeenth century when paintings of Roman landscapes with dark red skies and fragments of ruins became extremely popular all over Europe,[51] it was especially important for the travelling artist. And at least one ruin trip is on offer even on an average package tour for the sun, sand and sea experience for those in the "golden years."

As with the ruins of a bygone highly developed civilization, the mod-ernist socialist monuments of a recently eclipsed political system with its self-assured, conflicting, and ultimately broken visions seem to trigger the visitors' potential for indulging the imagination. As in other segments of tourism, strong narratives, powerful metaphors and attractive images produced during trips (on and off the beaten path) act as successful travel guides. These encourage others to start their own research trips, collect aesthetic trophies, and show them to their peer groups—also in the fields of art, science, or popular culture or the Internet—where they might well be discussed and further distributed. Surprisingly most of the comments by younger people share the frequent use of the notions of the "road trip" for as yet undetected places, entering forbidden zones, revealing hidden mysteries and excavating remnants of a different culture. This is often associated with the notion of "cosmic." This notion might easily be traced back to the spiritual and formalistic aspects of early Russian avant-garde art and architecture and to a more general enthusiasm for imagining com-munist life in space driven by the Soviet space program which was begun in the 1950s and was later an inspiration for many architects too. I doubt that all the bloggers and blog commentators know about these aspects of art history. I assume that the association is made intuitively, triggered mainly by the appeal of the alien aesthetics of the buildings and monu-ments.[52] These "cosmic" associations were also projected onto art and architecture in Yugoslavia even though it had defined itself as distinctly anti-Stalinist and anti-Soviet. It is noticeable, though, that the cosmic aspects are also cross-charged with a rather strong melancholy longing for a lost utopia here:

Whoever might have built these striking hotels and monuments seems to be perceived as a member of an extra-terrestrial species that once upon a time landed on planet Earth and left spectacular monuments, evidence of another, "third way," of life, one that sadly our species today is not yet capable of fully understanding. Is there any better argument for generating a new niche in heritage tourism?[53]

NOTES

1. Noel Salazar, *Envisioning Eden: Mobilising Imaginaries in Tourism and Beyond* (Oxford: Berghahn Books, 2012), 43.

2. Maroje Mrduljaš, "Building the Affordable Arcadia: Tourism Development on the Croatian Adriatic Coast under State Socialism," in *Holidays after the Fall: Seaside Architecture and Urbanism in Bulgaria and Croatia,* ed. Elke Beyer, Anke Hagemann, and Michael Zinganel (Berlin: Jovis, 2013), 117–207.

3. Orvar Löfgren, *On Holiday: A History of Vacationing* (Berkeley: University of California Press, 1999), 204.

4. To be honest, Yugoslavia was not the first choice right from the very beginning. As long as my brother, my cousins and I were of the age to play sandcastle building at the beach, our family traveled to the North of Italy. When we were older our Grandma—then in charge of us—preferred the Croatian Adriatic: a much safer destination (no theft, no burglary), a much more beautiful landscape, significantly better water quality, and the modern lifestyle was much more affordable.

5. E.g. the Roman amphitheater in Pula, the Byzantine and Romanesque Euphrasian basilica in Poreč, Venetian churches, palaces, and urban ensembles in coastal towns like Rovinj or hillside villages like Motovun.

6. I have to mention, first and foremost, Maroje Mrduljaš's on-going research and the work he has published to date, inter alia as part of the research project *Unfinished Modernisations*. Umetnostna Galerija Maribor, ed. *Unfinished Modernisations— Between Utopia and Pragmatism: Architecture and Urban Planning in Former Yugoslavia and the Successor States,* Exhibition catalogue (Maribor: UGM, 2012). There were also frequent reports in the online blog or magazine *pogledaj.to* [Look at it!] founded by architect Saša Randić—for example, Barbara Matejčić, "Multi-Million Investments Go Pear-Shaped." *pogledaj.to* August 1, 2010, accessed April 5, 2013, http://pogledaj.to/en/architecture/multi-million-investments-go-pear-shaped/; Barbara Matejčić, "Najbolji hrvatski hoteli su—socijalistički," *pogledaj.to,* March 2, 2015, accessed May 29, 2016, http://pogledaj.to/arhitektura/najbolji-hrvatski-hoteli-su-socijalisticki/. Saša Randić and Idis Turato had also curated an exhibition as early as 2006 for the International Architecture Biennale in Venice that was partly related to the issue. Randić and Idis Turato, *In Between: A Book on the Croatian Coast, Global Processes, and How to Live with Them,* 10th International Venice Biennale (Rijeka: K.LJ.B. 2006).

7. Austria is the number one foreign investor in Croatia. Due to the war from 1991 to 1995 and the collapse of economy almost every municipality and self-managed company in Croatia was already been heavily indebted to local banks. While the privatization process was financed with additional credit, almost all the Croatian banks were then sold to Austrian financial institutions. In addition, Valamar, one of the three largest tourist companies in Croatia today, is owned by EPIC, an Austrian enterprise.

8. *Holidays after the Fall: Seaside Architecture and Urbanism in Croatia and Bulgaria* was a research project with Elke Beyer and Anke Hagemann (see: note 2 above and 9 below). The author was wholly responsible for the exhibition of the

Croatian case studies: *Holidays after the Fall: Transformation of Socialist Holiday Resorts on the Adriatic Coast of Croatia* and the guided tours.

9. *Holidays after the Fall: Seaside Architecture and Urbanism in Bulgaria and Croatia* (Berlin: Jovis, 2013). The research project originally started at the Faculty of Architecture at Graz University of Technology where I was teaching at the Institute of Building Typology. It was primarily supported by the Cultural Department of the Province of Styria/Austria. Research partners were Elke Beyer and Anke Hagemann who conducted research on the development of the Bulgarian Black Sea Coast while I collaborated with architecture critic Maroje Mrduljaš and the journalist Norbert Mappes-Niediek.

10. In her comprehensive critical review, written a few years later, Carmen Popescu contextualizes the pioneering role of our project comparing it to other projects started around the same time which either dealt with leisure architecture too or introduced a similar comparative approach. Carmen Popescu, *A Disenchanted World? A Review of Holidays After the Fall: Seaside Architecture and Urbanism in Bulgaria and Croatia*, Architectural Histories 3 (2015): 6, accessed May 29, 2016, http://dx.doi.org/10.5334/ah.cj.

11. Norbert Mappes-Niediek, "A Thorny Thicket: The Singular Case of Workers' Self-management and Long-drawn-out Privatization in Croatian Tourism," in *Holidays after the Fall: Seaside Architecture and Urbanism in Bulgaria and Croatia,* 209–221.

12. The exhibition originally developed for the HDA Graz House of Architecture from October to December 2012, was shown in an expanded form at NGBK Neue Gesellschaft für Bildende Kunst in Berlin in August 2013, in a translated version at MMSU Museum of Modern Art Rijeka in March 2015, in a reduced form at the City Museum of Trogir in June 2015, and at AzW Vienna Centre of Architecture in November 2015.

13. See for example the popular architecture, design, and travel blog *yatzer* on May 13, 2014, accessed August 02, 2016. https://www.yatzer.com/holidays-after-the-fall.

14. Jurica Pavičić, "Sjaj i bijeda ex yu hotela na Jadranu," *Jutarnij List* March 06, 2015, accessed May 29, 2016, http://www.jutarnji.hr/kultura/art/sjaj-i-bijeda-ex-yu-hotela-na-jadranu/483685/.

15. Eve Vidan Gallagher, *Merely Human.* Director and producer: Filip Koludrović. 2013, accessed May 29, 2016, https://www.youtube.com/watch?v=oeSmstrTSqA&feature=youtu.be.

16. Jose Luis Sert, Fernand Léger, and Sigfried Giedion, "Nine Points on Monumentality," in *Architecture, You and Me,* ed. Siegfried Giedion (Cambridge, MA: Harvard University Press, 1958), 48–52. First published in Siegfried Giedion, *Architektur und Gemeinschaft* (Hamburg: Rowohlt, 1956); 40–42.

17. Many influential Yugoslav architects were members of CIAM, which held its 10th congress in Dubrovnik in 1956. Biographies of many people involved in planning and building these hotels show strong affiliations to art and many even practiced in the fields of both art and architecture. They therefore collaborated with, or at least inspired, each other: Vjenceslav Richter, Zdravko Bregovac, and Bernardo Bernardi were cofounders of the transdisciplinary avant-garde artist group EXAT 51. After collaborating on the internationally acclaimed Yugoslavian pavilion at the Expo 58 in Brussels, Richter co-founded the artist group (Nove Tendencije) in 1961 and increasingly focused on

visionary ideas for the synthesis of art and architecture (Sinturbanism 1964) which he realized in kinetic sculptures that were stimulating for many architects. Bernardi became famous for the design of furniture of buildings that were important for the representation of Yugoslavia's policy, beginning with the Expo in 58, Radničko sveučilište Moša Pijade [the workers' university] in Zagreb in 1961, international airports and many hotels. Bregovac devoted his later career exclusively to tourism architecture, translating avant-garde ideas into the pragmatics of planning. See: Vladimir Kulić, "An Avant-Garde Architecture for an Avant-Garde Socialism: Yugoslavia at EXPO '58," *Journal of Contemporary History* 47, special issue "Sites of Convergence—The USSR and Communist Eastern Europe at International Fairs Abroad and at Home" (2012): 161–184; Ljiljana Kolešnik, "New Tendencies," in *Hrvatska umjetnost: povijest i spomenici*, ed. Milan Pelc (Zagreb: Institut za povijest umjetnosti; Školska knjiga, 2010), 681–85; Armin Medosch, *New Tendencies: Art at the Threshold of the Information Revolution (1961–1978)* (Cambridge, MA: MIT Press, 2016); Eva Ceraj, "Bernardo Bernardi—The Spiritus Movens of Early Design in Croatia," *Croatian Academy of Sciences and Arts, Fine Art Archives Art Bulletin* 3, no. 63 (2013): 98–119; Ivana Nikšić-Olujić, *Zdravko Bregovac—Arhiv Arhitekta* (Zagreb: Hrvatski muzej arhitekture, 2015).

18. Penthouse was founded in 1965 by Bob Guiccone as competition for Hugh Hefener's famous Playboy magazine and was significantly more liberal in showing private parts.

19. Jovan Acin and Dejan Karaklajic: *Mi neprodajemo holivud* [We Don't Sell Hollywood], director: Milenko Stanković, Zastava Film 1973.

20. Slobodan Stanković, "La Dolce Vita—A Formula Against the Cold War," *Radio Free Europe*, Manuscript July 10, 1972, accessed April 5, 2013, http://yugoslavian.blogspot.com/2009/05/penthouse-adriatic-clubcasino-in.html.

21. For more details about the planning history and the process of privatization of Haludovo please see: Michael Zinganel, "Case Studies," in Beyer et al., ed., 2003, 264–53.

22. For the first group see, for example, the images by the Italian photographer Daniel Ansidei which I also used to promote the project; for the second see, for example, the images by the Slovenian photographer Jana Jocif, which I used in a slide show displayed on a TFT monitor in the aforementioned exhibitions, accessed July 26, 2013. http://www.flickr.com/photos/tags/haludovo/interesting/

23. The first bus-tour for Graz House of Architecture (HDA) in May 2013 was followed by tours for Vienna Centre for Architecture (AzW) in May 2014, for the Association of German Architects (BDA) Cologne in October 2014, and for the Munich University of Technology in May 2016. I also offered one-day bus-tours for Croatian audiences for Rijeka and Motel Trogir in 2015.

24. See e.g. Agata Pyzik, "Toxic Ruins: The Political & Economic Cost of 'Ruin Porn'," *AR 128, New Civic Design Realms* 2014, accessed May 29, 2016, http://www.australiandesignreview.com/features/29607-toxic-ruins-the-political-economic-cost-of-ruin. Interestingly both a collective of architects and researchers founded in Rome in the mid-1990s, called for walking the city as an aesthetic practice, and an art-based urban research project in Detroit had been named after Tarkowsky's *Stalker*. See: Francesco Careri, *Walkscapes: Walking as an Aesthetic Practice* (Barcelona: Gustavo Gili, 2003); Georgia Daskalakis, Charles Waldheim, and Jason Young, *Stalking Detroit* (Barcelona: Actar, 2001).

25. E.g. posed in a public discussion with the Viennese filmmaker Andrea Seidling on occasion of the presentation of her new film *Frontstage*—at Forum Stadtpark Graz/ Austria on March 17, 2016.

26. E.g. Antonia Dika, an architect of Croatian descent living in Vienna, who also supported me in my previous research, organized a tour for the University of Art Linz in 2015 along the entire Croatian Adriatic coast. They also visited hotels and resorts but also vacant military objects relevant to her own research. Furthermore, Motel Trogir, an art and activist group, had already re-driven the tour I organized for them in 2015. Antonia Dika, *Von Soldaten und Touristen. Verlassene Militäranlagen auf den adriatischen Inseln* [About Soldiers and Tourists: Military Sites on the Croatian Islands]. Diploma at TU Wien, 2008; Antonia Dika and Daniele Ansidei, "Pearls of the Adriatic," in *Desertmed: A Project about the Deserted Islands of the Mediterranean* (Berlin: NGBK Neue Gesellschaft für Bildende Kunst, exhibited from October 27 to December 2, 2012).

27. Moni K. Huber, *Arcadia in Decay* (Vienna: Verlag für Moderne Kunst, 2015).

28. Andrea Seidling, *Frontstage-Backspace*, Croatia/Austria, 15 min, 2015–16.

29. *Enjoying the Fruits of Yugoslavia's Third Way: Tracing for Clues in Hotels and Ruins of Late Modernity*, at Galerie Gebhart Blazek. Berber-Arts, Graz March 2016, http://tracingspaces.net/823-2/.

30. The script for the TV production was co-written by Maroje Mrduljaš, who is also the co-author of our own publication *Holidays after the Fall* (2013), accessed July 10, 2016

31. E.g. Hertha Hurnaus et al., *Eastmodern: Architecture and Design of the 1960s and 1970s in Slovakia* (Vienna: Springer 2007); Roman Bezjak, *Socialist Modernism* (Ostfildern: Hatje Cantz; Chaubin 2011); Armin Linke and Srdjan Jovanovic Weiss, *Socialist Architecture: The Vanishing Act* (Zürich: JRP Ringier and Codax, 2012); also including a book titled "Ostalgia": Simona Rota, 2013: *Ostalgia*. Catalog, Galerie Kurzala, University Cádiz, La Coruña: Fabulatorio.

32. E.g. Andreas Butter, *Neues Leben, Neues Bauen. Die Moderne in der Architektur der SBZ/DDR 1945–1951* (Berlin: Hans Schiler, 2006); David Crowley and Jane Pavitt, eds., *Cold War Modern: Design 1945–1970* (London: V&A, 2008); Vladimir Kulić, Maroje Mrduljaš, and Wolfgang Thaler, *Modernism In-between: The Mediatory Architectures of Socialist Yugoslavia* (Berlin: Jovis, 2012); Architekturzentrum Wien, eds. *Soviet Modernism 1955–1991: Unknown Stories* (Zürich: Park Books, 2012); also including a book about modernist seaside hotels and resorts at the Romanian Black Sea Coast: Alina Şerban et al., eds., *Vederi încântătoare: Urbanism şi arhitectură în turismul românesc de la Marea Neagră în anii '60-'70* [Enchanting Views: Romanian Black Sea Tourism Planning and Architecture of the 1960s and 70s] (Bucharest: Asociaţia pepluspatru, 2015).

33. Jan Kempenaers, *Spomenik: The End of History* (Amsterdam: Roma, 2010).

34. About the current status of the Monument in Petrova Gora by Vojin Bakić see e.g.: Tihomir Ponoš, "Spomenik Vojina Bakića na Petrovoj gori oronuli kostur pred raspadom," novilist.hr (29. prosinca 2013), accessed July 10, 2016. http://www.novilist.hr/Vijesti/ Hrvatska/Spomenik-Vojina-Bakica-na-Petrovoj-gori-oronuli-kostur-pred-raspadom.

35. This is the essence of several talks I had with many friends living in successor states of former Yugoslavia that do not want to be personally quoted here.

36. Since this experience I habitually re-visit at least one of these monuments whenever I travel through the territory of former Yugoslavia. I share this interest with the Croatian-born Viennese artist Marko Luli, who had already started to work on the same issue in 2002. See Marke Lulić, *Restagings* (Berlin: Revolver, 2014).

37. Bajic, Mrdjan: virtual monuments for "Yugomuseum" (1999–); Centre for Contemporary Arts, Sarajevo 2004–2006: *De/Construction of Monument*, presenting Sanja Ivekovic, *Lady Rosa of Luxembourg* and Braco Dimitrijević, *Anti-Monuments*; David Maljković, *Scene for a New Heritage,* 2004–2006; Milica Tomić, Darinka Pop-Mitić, Nebojsa Milekić, Jasmina Husanović, and Branimir Stojanović. *Monument Group,* 2007; Siniša Labrović, *Bandaging of the Wounds of Partisan Fighter in Sinj.* 2008; Luiza Margan, *Eye to Eye with Freedom,* 2014. Citizens of Rijeka was raised 22 m with a crane in order to stand eye-to-eye with the central, female partisan figure in the Monument of Liberation from 1955.

38. Milena Dragićević Šešić, "Cultural Policies, Cultural Identities and Monument Building: New Memory Policies of Balkan Countries," in *Cultural Transition in Southeastern Europe: Cultural Identity Politics in (Post)-Transitional Societies,* ed. Milohnić and Nada Švob-Đokić (Zagreb: Culturelink, 2011), 31–45, accessed on May 29, 2016, http://rci.mirovni-institut.si/Docs/ASO%202010%20Sesic.pdf.

39. Olympique, *The Reason I Came,* Producer: The Arcadia Agency, 2013, accessed May 29, 2016. https://www.youtube.com/watch?v=2Z4gcJM5bG8.

40. Tanja Schuster, "Olympisches Feuer," *The Gap,* 22.06.2014, accessed August 8, 2016. http://www.thegap.at/musikstories/artikel/olympisches-feuer/.

41. This argument was first introduced by the production company Arcadia Agency's PR campaign and afterwards copied in all media coverage, accessed May 29, 2016. http://www.vienna.at/indie-rock-band-olympique-praesentiert-erste-single-the-reason-i-came/3962527.

42. Yasmin Szaraniec, "Jugo Monumente nicht von dieser Welt," *The Gap,* August 27, 2014, accessed May 29, 2016. http://www.thegap.at/kunststories/artikel/jugo-monumente-nicht-von-dieser-welt/.

43. There is a serious problem of researching the real motivation of the projects and quoting the sources, since people usually only subscribe using nicknames to open a new blog primarily fed with images. Contacting them means adding a comment that is visible to all other subscribers, accessed August 8, 2016. http://ispyspomeniks.tumblr.com.

44. Malcolm Foley and John Lennon, *Dark Tourism: The Attraction of Death and Disaster* (London: Continuum, 2000).

45. John Patrick Leary, "Detroitism," *Guernica Magazine of Arts & Politics* (2011), accessed August 8, 2016, http://www.guernicamag.com/features/leary_1_15_11/; Peter Mullins, "The Politics and Archaeology of 'Ruin Porn,'" *Archaeology and Material Culture* (2012), accessed August 8, 2016, http://paulmullins.wordpress.com/2012/08/19/the-politics-and-archaeology-of-ruin-porn/.

46. The hypercritical discourse about "Ruin Porn" and "Ruin Safaris" developed when the City of Detroit, the symbolic figurehead of US-American mass modernization and mobility went into radical decline, became partly depopulated and had large neighborhoods vandalized. Houses were even burned down just for the fun of it. But it was also because the decay became a favorite destination for art, photo and film projects, pop music events, and psycho-geographic urban explorations.

47. John Fiske, *Reading Popular Culture* (Boston: Unwin Hyman, 1989), 34–62.

48. David Crouch and Nina Lübbren, eds., *Visual Culture and Tourism* (Oxford: Berg Publishers, 2003), 20.

49. Alfredo González-Ruibal, "Returning to Where We Have Never Been: Excavating the Ruins of Modernity," in *Ruin Memories: Materialities, Aesthetics and the Archaeology of the Recent Past*, ed. Bjørnar Olsen and Þóra Pétursdóttir (London: Routledge, 2014), 365–98.

50. Noel Salazar, *Envisioning Eden: Mobilising Imaginaries in Tourism and Beyond* (Oxford: Berghahn Books, 2012), 74.

51. Renate Trnek, *Traum vom Süden: die Niederländer malen Italien* (Vienna: Gemäldegalerie der Akademie der Bildenden Künste Wien, 2007). For those painters who could not afford to travel to Italy themselves a German workshop offered miniature models of ancient ruins for sale, to support them painting in the fashionable new style. These models are today part of the collection of Staatliche Museen Schloss Wilhelmshöhe in Kassel.

52. Like it had also coined the subtitle of one of the most popular recent photo books: *CCCP—Cosmic Communist Constructions Photographed* (Berlin: Taschen, 2011).

53. In summer 2016, Martino Stierli, the Swiss-educated art historian and new director of the Department of Architecture and Design at the Museum of Modern Art in New York, is to travel to vacant buildings and monuments of the late modernist period in former Yugoslavia, to prepare a show for the MOMA in 2017. A catalogue is also to be produced, the future's most prestigious guide for the more conservative and disciplined part of the educated class.

REFERENCES

Architekturzentrum Wien, eds. *Soviet Modernism 1955–1991: Unknown Stories.* Zürich: Park Books, 2012.

Ban, Saša. *Betonski spavači* [Slumbering Concrete]. Produced by Hulahop for HRT. Accessed May 29, 2016. http://www.hulahop.hr/en/projects/film_and_tv_production/slumbering_concrete.

Beyer, Elke, Anke Hagemann, and Michael Zinganel. *Holidays after the Fall: Seaside Architecture and Urbanism in Bulgaria and Croatia.* Berlin: Jovis, 2013.

Bezjak, Roman. *Socialist Modernism.* Ostfildern: Hatje Cantz, 2011.

Butter, Andreas. *Neues Leben, Neues Bauen. Die Moderne in der Architektur der SBZ/DDR 1945–1951.* Berlin: Hans Schiler, 2006.

Careri, Francesco. *Walkscapes: Walking as an Aesthetic Practice.* Barcelona: Gustavo Gili, 2003.

Ceraj, Eva. "Bernardo Bernardi—The Spiritus Movens of Early Design." *Croatia, Croatian Academy of Sciences and Arts, Fine Art Archives Art Bulletin* 3, no. 63 (2013): 98–119.

Chaubin, Frédéric. *CCCP—Cosmic Communist Constructions Photographed.* Berlin: Taschen, 2011.

Crouch, David, and Nina Lübbren, eds. *Visual Culture and Tourism.* Oxford: Berg Publishers, 2003.

Crowley, David, and Jane Pavitt, eds. *Cold War Modern: Design 1945–1970.* London: V&A, 2008.

Daskalakis, Georgia, Charles Waldheim, and Jason Young. *Stalking Detroit.* Barcelona: Actar, 2001.

Dika, Antonia. *Von Soldaten und Touristen. Verlassene Militäranlagen auf den adriatischen Inseln* [About Soldiers and Tourists: Military Sites on the Croatian Islands]. Diploma at TU Wien, 2008.

Dika, Antonia, and Daniele Ansidei. "Pearls of the Adriatic." In *Desertmed: A Project about the Deserted Islands of the Mediterranean.* Berlin: NGBK Neue Gesellschaft für Bildende Kunst, exhibited from October 27 to December 2, 2012.

Dragićević Šešić, Milena. "Cultural Policies, Cultural Identities and Monument Building: New Memory Policies of Balkan Countries." In *Cultural Transition in Southeastern Europe: Cultural Identity Politics in (Post)-Transitional Societies,* edited by Aldo Milohnić and Nada Švob-Ðokić. Zagreb: Culturelink, 2011: 31–45. Accessed May 29, 2016. http://rci.mirovni-institut.si/Docs/ASO%202010%20Sesic.pdf.

Fiske, John. *Reading Popular Culture.* Boston: Unwin Hyman, 1989.

Foley, Malcolm, and John Lennon. *Dark Tourism: The Attraction of Death and Disaster.* London: Continuum, 2000.

González-Ruibal, Alfredo. "Returning to Where We have Never Been: Excavating the Ruins of Modernity." In *Ruin Memories: Materialities, Aesthetics and the Archaeology of the Recent Past,* edited by Olsen Bjørnar and Póra Pétursdóttir, 365–98. London: Routledge, 2014.

Huber, Moni K. *Arcadia in Decay.* Vienna: Verlag für Moderne Kunst, 2015.

Hurnaus, Hertha et al. *Eastmodern: Architecture and Design of the 1960s and 1970s in Slovakia.* Vienna: Springer, 2007.

Jokić, Gojko. *Jugoslavija - Spomenici revolucije: turistički vodič.* Beograd: Turistička Štampa, 1986.

Karakajic, Dejan, and Jovan Acin. *Mi neprodajemo holivud.* Director: Milenko Stanković, Zastava Film, 1973.

Kempenaers, Jan. *Spomenik: The End of History.* Roma: Amsterdam, 2010.

Kolešnik, Ljiljana. "New Tendencies." In *Hrvatska umjetnost: povijest i spomenici,* edited by Milan Pelc, 681–85. Zagreb: Institut za povijest umjetnosti; Školska knjiga, 2010.

Kulić, Vladimir. "An Avant-Garde Architecture for an Avant-Garde Socialism: Yugoslavia at EXPO '58." *Journal of Contemporary History* 47. Special issue "Sites of Convergence—The USSR and Communist Eastern Europe at International Fairs Abroad and at Home." (2012): 161–84.

Kulić, Vladimir, Maroje Mrduljaš, and Wolfgang Thaler. *Modernism In-between: The Mediatory Architectures of Socialist Yugoslavia.* Berlin: Jovis, 2012.

Leary, John Patrick. "Detroitism'." *Guernica Magazine of Arts & Politics.* 2011. Accessed August 8, 2016. http://www.guernicamag.com/features/leary_1_15_11/.

Linke, Armin, and Srdjan Jovanovic. Weiss Zagreb. *Socialist Architecture: The Vanishing Act.* Zürich: JRP Ringier and Codax, 2012.

Löfgren, Orvar. *On Holiday: A History of Vacationing.* Berkeley: University of California Press, 1999.

Lulić, Marke. *Restagings.* Berlin: Revolver, 2014.

Mappes-Niediek, Norbert. "A Thorny Thicket: The Singular Case of Workers' Self-Management and Long-drawn-out Privatization in Croatian Tourism." In *Holidays after the Fall: Seaside Architecture and Urbanism in Bulgaria and Croatia,* edited by Elke Beyer, Anke Hagemann, and Michael Zinganel, 209–21. Berlin: Jovis, 2013.

Matejčić, Barbara. "Multi-Million Investments Go Pear-Shaped." *pogletaj.to* August 1, 2010. Accessed April 5, 2013. http://pogledaj.to/en/architecture/multi-million-investments-go-pear-shaped./

————. "Najbolji hrvatski hoteli su—socijalistički." *pogletaj.to.* March 2, 2015. Accessed May 29, 2016. http://pogledaj.to/arhitektura/najbolji-hrvatski-hoteli-su-socijalisticki/.

Medosch, Armin. *New Tendencies: Art at the Threshold of the Information Revolution (1961–1978).* Cambridge, MA: MIT Press, 2016.

Mrduljaš, Maroje. "Building the Affordable Arcadia: Tourism Development on the Croatian Adriatic Coast under State Socialism." In *Holidays after the Fall: Seaside Architecture and Urbanism in Bulgaria and Croatia,* edited by Elke Beyer et al., 117–207. Berlin: Jovis, 2013.

Mullins, Peter. "The Politics and Archaeology of 'Ruin Porn'." *Archaeology and Material Culture* (2012). Accessed August 8, 2016. http://paulmullins.wordpress.com/2012/08/19/the-politics-and-archaeology-of-ruin-porn/.

Nikšić-Olujić, Ivana. *Zdravko Bregovac—Arhiv Arhitekta.* Zagreb: Hrvatski muzej arhitekture, 2015.

Olympique. *The Reason I Came.* Producer: The Arcadia Agency. 2013. Accessed May 29, 2016. https://www.youtube.com/watch?v=2Z4gcJM5bG8.

Pavičić, Jurica. "Sjaj i bijeda ex yu hotela na Jadranu." *JutarnijList.* March 6, 2015. Accessed May 29, 2016. http://www.jutarnji.hr/kultura/art/sjaj-i-bijeda-ex-yu-hotela-na-jadranu/483685/.

Popescu, Carmen. "A Disenchanted World? A Review of Holidays After the Fall: Seaside Architecture and Urbanism in Bulgaria and Croatia." *Architectural Histories* 3 (2015): 1–7. Accessed on May 29, 2016. http://dx.doi.org/10.5334/ah.cj.

Pyzik, Agata. "Toxic Ruins: The Political & Economic Cost of 'Ruin Porn'." *AR 128, New Civic Design Realms* (2014). Accessed May 29, 2016. http://www.australiandesignreview.com/features/29607-toxic-ruins-the-political-economic-cost-of-ruin.

Randić, Saša, and Idis Turato. *In Between: A Book on the Croatian Coast, Global Processes, and How to Live with Them.* Rijeka: 10th International Venice Biennale, K.LJ.B, 2006.

Rota, Simona. *Ostalgia.* La Coruña: Catalog, Galerie Kurzala, University Cádiz, Fabulatorio, 2013.

Salazar, Noel. *Envisioning Eden: Mobilising Imaginaries in Tourism and Beyond.* Oxford: Berghahn Books, 2012.

Schuster, Tanja. "Olympisches Feuer." *The Gap*, June 22, 2014. Accessed August 8, 2016. http://www.thegap.at/musikstories/artikel/olympisches-feuer/.

Seidling, Andrea. *Frontstage-Backspace*, Croatia/Austria, 15 min, 2015–2016.

Şerban, Alina et al, eds. *Vederi încântătoare: Urbanism şi arhitectură în turismul românesc de la Marea Neagră în anii '60-'70* [Enchanting Views: Romanian Black Sea Tourism Planning and Architecture of the 1960s and 70s]. Bucharest: Asociaţia pepluspatru, 2015.

Sert, Jose Luis, Fernard Léger, and Sigfried Giedion. "Nine Points on Monumentality." In *Architecture, You and Me*, ed. Sigfried Giedion, 48–52. Cambridge, MA: Harvard University Press, 1958.

Stanković Slobodan. "La Dolce Vita—A Formula Against the Cold War." *Radio Free Europe*, Manuscript July 10, 1972. Accessed April 5, 2013. http://yugoslavian. blogspot.com/2009/05/penthouse-adriatic-clubcasino-in.html.

Szaraniec, Yasmin. "Jugo Monumente nicht von dieser Welt." *The Gap*, August 27, 2014. Accessed May 29, 2016. http://www.thegap.at/kunststories/artikel/jugo-monumente-nicht-von-dieser-welt/.

Trnek, Renate. *Traum vom Süden: die Niederländer malen Italien*. Vienna: Gemäldegalerie der Akademie der Bildenden Künste Wien, 2007.

Umetnostna Galerija Maribor, ed. *Unfinished Modernisations—Between Utopia and Pragmatism. Architecture and Urban Planning in Former Yugoslavia and the Successor States*, Exhibition catalogue, Maribor: UGM, 2012.

Vidan Gallagher, Eve. *Merely Human*. Director and producer: Filip Koludrović., 2013. Accessed April May 29, 2016. https://www.youtube.com/watch?v=oeSmstr TSqA&feature=youtu.be.

Chapter 15

The "Kodak Girl" on a Trip

Tourist Women from Polish Galicia in Family Photographs of 1910s–1930s

Małgorzata Radkiewicz

In this chapter, I analyze selected vernacular tourist photographs and holiday snapshots taken by middle-class women from the Polish Galicia in the 1910s–1930s. I found analytical tools for this purpose in the theoretical reflection on the development of tourism in the nineteenth and twentieth centuries, especially the two issues tackled by it. The first issue pertains to the participation and place of women in the tourist industry, the second—the links between tourism and photography, which became one of the biggest attractions of traveling for women. All of these lines, that is, mobility, tourism, and photography, can be found in the eponymous figure of this chapter— "The Kodak Girl," created by Eastman Kodak in the 1890s in order to include women among the consumers of the company's products.

I will use that commercial term as a starting point to interpret tourist photographs of the Kosiński sisters from Kraków in Poland who started to take holiday snapshots as teenagers and later on took their photo cameras (presumably more than one) to every trips no matter where and for how long.

FAMILY ALBUMS OF MODERN WOMEN

Considering tourist photographs to be a framed documentation of personal experience, I want to focus on selected images from family albums, collected at the Walery Rzewuski Museum of History of Photography [MHF] in Kraków, which accommodates, among other specimens, the Kosiński family's collection. Following the paths of technology, cultural changes, and/or gender, one can interpret tourist photographs of Zofia Kosiński and her sisters, Karola and Helena, as a register and representation of locality close to them.

The Kosińskis' collection is dominated by images of family and social life, precious because of the fact that they present everyday reality. Among the attributes of "modern" life of the first half of the twentieth century (actually, from the late 1910s to the late 1930s) above all a car appears, driven with the steady hands of both men and women. One of the portraits from the collection[1] features three Kosiński sisters in the front car seat: Zofia, Karola, and Helena.

Zofia grasps the steering wheel easily with a sure hand, which suggests this situation is not alien, or artifically arranged pose for her. The frame of the windscreen additionally emphasizes the coherence of the entire composition, illustrating the link between technology—including both photography and motorization—and a "new," modern femininity. Thus, "modernity" is, for women, coupled with mobility—not only in a physical but also mental and intellectual space. A frame featuring a woman behind a steering wheel is at the same time a symbol and a symptom of the time of technological transformations and the social-cultural dynamics connected to them. Modern women in cars seem to be always ready to leave, and, as Nóra Séllei argues in her analysis of women's travel writings, "the verb 'leaving', in itself suggests a transgressive act."[2] And that transgressive aspect of leaving is particularly important when a woman is leaving home, understood as a private space she is assigned to.

Moreover, I would argue that travel photographs taken by women, can be read as women's "narratives of departure" that, according to Janis P. Stout, present "a vision mediating between departure and discovery on the one hand

Figure 15.1   Modern women in a car: Zofia, Helena, and Karola, Kraków 1930–1935.
Source: A photograph from the collection of the Walery Rzewuski Museum of History of Photography in Kraków.

and at-homeness on the other."[3] Traces of that mediation can be found in detailed descriptions on the reverse side of the Kosińskis' travel photographs from the 1910s. In the first place, there is always information about well-known family members in the photo, introduced by names and gender roles: Mother, Father, followed by other data including time and place of travel. These descriptions express what Stout calls "yearning, not toward the settled and enclosed life of convention, but toward something fuller, some undefined compromise that would afford both home and free departure."[4]

Therefore, one can be surprised by the number of photos of women in or next to cars, and following Stout, such composition can be explained by women's "particular attention to the liminal . . . moment of departure precisely because its association with the escape from this [home] restriction and the attainment of freedom."[5] Taking photographs, modern women (un)consciously combined creativity with spatial movement, which, as in women's "narration of departure," indicates freedom and gender transcendence.

In the Kosińskis' photo albums, there are tens of similar images of cars and women—as drivers and passengers on the way either to or from holidays. On one hand, these amateur tourist photos can be regarded as a private documentation of leisure and travel experience in a series of frames. On the other hand, since they were taken by women (and eventually signed by them), each of these images can be read as evidence of a New Woman of the modern era, embodied in the figure of a "Kodak Girl."

THE FIGURE OF A "KODAK GIRL"

There is a set of advertisements from the Eastman Kodak Company of the newest cameras featuring women as clients and active users of the company's products. Yet, in 1893, the Kodak poster promoted young women as photographers, introducing them as "Kodak Girls At The World's Fair"[6] (in Chicago). The slogan: "Take a Kodak with you to the World's Fair"[7] had two goals to achieve—first, to encourage viewers, including women, to discover the world and second, to record one's experience in a series of snapshots, obviously, taken by the newest Eastman equipment.

Kodak's advertisements created needs to record as much as possible from the everyday, family activities among which tourism for leisure seemed to be the most attractive. Nancy Martha West argues that "Kodak's advertising purged domestic photography . . . by exploiting five motifs in its marketing: leisure, childhood (and specifically toys), fashion, antiques, and narrative."[8] Each of these motives played an important role in a promotion campaign for Kodak, participating in "the aestheticizing of experience."[9] Moreover, Kodak encouraged women to take portraits of relatives and friends and of themselves, allowing them to behave spontaneously and informally while posing in domestic or "leisure" settings including gardens, parks, and tourist places.

Consequently, together with promoting its technological achievements, making snapshot photography easy and simple, Kodak sanctioned a certain poetic of vitality, youth, and an active lifestyle. Moreover, images of tourist women in different means of transport, always equipped with a functional Kodak camera, created associations with a modern, independent, and mobile way of living that many viewers would love to follow. And in 1913, with a slogan "Kodak as you go," the company promoted cameras and automobiles, both used by a woman presented in a poster while stopped driving to take a photo. Once again, in Kodak's campaign, photography was combined with leisure activities such as travel and automobile touring that, of course, could be enjoyed by certain social groups with high incomes.

Obviously, such representational conventions were used to consolidate leisure as the privilege of the wealthy, however, Nancy Martha West emphasizes, Eastman Kodak's primary goal was to promote and popularize amateur photography as a simple and easy leisure activity. But the secondary goal was "to feminize it."[10]

According to West, such a women-oriented commercial strategy had two quite opposite consequences. Primarily, it created a persistent alliance between technological simplicity and femininity, reinforcing the female photographer's status ("Kodak Girl") as an amateur dependent on technological simplicity who can never achieve the status of a professional photographer.[11] Secondly, however, the figure of the "Kodak Girl," although young and sweet, embodied the modern iconic femininity: active, with an athletic body, apparently independent, with a visible sense of adventure and freedom. And Eastman profited by selling altogether its technological achievements and a modern lifestyle represented by a New Woman.[12] What is interesting is that none of the commercial images present the "Kodak Girl" within a home environment. Instead, they show women taking snapshots while traveling or vacationing and enjoying various leisure activities.

On one hand, the camera promoted by Eastman Kodak could facilitate women's entrance into a public space as active subjects who regard and document the activities of others, as well as their own. On the other hand, the advertising of photographic equipment addressed to women—as something functional and easy to use—using the figure of "The Kodak Girl," grounded the women's photographic activity in the sphere of amateur undertakings, concentrated on pleasure rather than knowledge. However, the fact that women were admitted to the zone of technology and became equipped with the latest achievements of photography must have stimulated their greater activity, since they wanted to imitate the lifestyle of "The Kodak Girl" and, similar to her, record their experiences, including tourist-like ones, in photo frames.

WOMEN TOURISTS WITH PHOTO CAMERAS

Taking the example of the family album of the Kosińskis' featuring tourist photographs, the majority of which were made by adolescent sisters (later, mature women), one can say that the camera was a link to the external world for those women. The camera was their pretext to gaze openly at everyone and everything during their trips. The camera became a kind of excuse for their prying eye. Taking photographs as a notion of recording involves many different practices and rituals in itself. However, for Mike Robinson and David Picard, the most important thing about tourist photography is that "it extends beyond ideas of collection and record and into the realms of self-making, authentication and socialization processes which are bound up with embodied doing of tourism."[13]

The photographs made by the Kosiński sisters during tourist trips with family and friends can be divided into three groups, depending on the time of their travels, different experiences of these amateur photographers, and their evolving awareness of the medium.

The oldest photographs were taken in the 1910s. These feature the excursions of the three sisters with their parents and other family members to Villach in Alps, and the Polish-Galician town Zakopane. The composition of these photographs is quite similar. They always show all of the family members in the open air, against the background of the mountains and/or pensions. All of the persons are dressed in casual clothes, suitable for mountain tourism—certainly in its recreational, not a record-seeking version. Women still wear Victorian corsets and long skirts, but also functional jackets and modest hats. Being mobile required a modernization of clothes to make it possible to move freely and cultivate vacation-time activities.

The composition of the frames is reminiscent of postcards with some modification: human figures replace a familiar panorama or building in the center. The identification of people featured in photos is easy in the case of the early the Kosińskis' trip photographs. Some photos in their album are signed at the reverse side: Mum, Dad, Helena, Karola, Zofia. Because there is often one figure missing from a photograph of the five family members, it is easy to deduct who took a picture. Actually, one of the photographs taken in Salzburg just before the First World War contains not only a usual description of people but also a note: "And Hela [Helena] is taking this picture." This emphasis on the gazing subject explains one's absence from a photo and makes a viewer realize the presence of this person in a given place with their special role—a photographer.

As Jonas Larsen explains in his essay on the "choreography and performance" of tourist photography, taking pictures while traveling is a ritual practice. As such, "photography performances are pleasurable and our holiday photos that celebrate the world's famous places, . . . and personal relationships are precious belongings."[14] Recalling the notion of the "tourist gaze" defined by John Urry, Larsen argues that "travel and gazing are modern twins, and by working together have caused an unprecedented geographical extension of the 'tourist gaze'."[15]

The capacity of the camera to capture the moment of life, the atmosphere of the place visited, the relation between places and people, but also between the photographer and her—in this case—"objects," named either on the reverse of a picture or on a page of a family album while being displayed. In that case, "photography is a practice of identity construction . . . for both photographee and photographer. The tourist has clearly power in mediating local cultures through photographs."[16]

Photographs taken by the Kosiński sisters, as well as by other "Kodak Girls," were collected and distributed in family albums, that allowed viewers to re-explore distant places once again. As Peter D. Osborne argues, the consumption of travel photography must be examined in the context of the Victorian middle-class home that provided a context in which photographs were viewed and from which "the world beyond it were imagined."[17] The viewers perspective of seeing the world was determined by the Victorian middle-class home, understood by Osborne as a set of social practices, a state of mind, and a cultural subsystem, but also as "an active and determined component in a wider system, that is a world within the world of globalizing capitalism . . . with its attendant system of communication and transportation."[18]

Tourist photographs can be analyzed as portraits of both visited places and people (family members mostly) that "were transporting the self-image of the middle class across all space . . . and across time by inscribing it into the history they themselves making."[19]

For women who just started to create their own history, photography as a tool of documentation and representation at the same time, was particularly important, although only on the domestic scale. Osborne noticed that the tradition of Victorian family albums was created by female family members, including mothers, daughters, and unmarried female relatives, collecting and subtitling images. They passionately guarded family albums, "in which the private history and moral narrative of the family paralleled the wider story of their class and nation."[20] In the case of the Kosińskis' home, women were not only guardians of family albums, but also providers of photographs taken by all three sisters.

Judging by the number of photographs by the Kosiński sisters, one can see how, at the beginning of the twentieth century, women benefited from the development of visual technology, followed by the widespread ownership of cameras, that brought "the end of a dependency upon the 'professional eye' and apparent liberation form an artistic, and acutely romantic, 'expert' framing of the world."[21]

The photographs by Zofia, Karola, and Helena from the 1920s and the 1930s are more spontaneous, more dynamic. You can see they were taken with more dexterity, permitting the photographer to catch interesting moments and events. No special arrangement or people's posing for the photo were now necessary, only a pretext sufficing—such as a car stopping on the shoulder of the road—to chronicle a tourist walk to the mountains (sometimes visible at the horizon). Additionally, these photographs indicate that the Kosiński daughters, being adults, wanted to learn new things about the world instead of just reiterating formerly blazed mountain trails, which is a fact proved by photographs from the Baltic Sea coast. What becomes noteworthy is the increasing number of photographs taken during short tourist trips to areas closer to their home, which were an opportunity for meeting friends and joint rambles or car escapades. Thus, the activities of people featured in these photographs are as important as the figures themselves. Modern, sport-training, and eagerly predisposed women prevail among these figures, being as ready as "The Kodak Girl" to drive a car, make a trek, swim, and . . . take photos.

FAR AWAY FROM HOME

In all of the Kosińskis' photographs from different periods, there is one unchanging element, namely a car as the basic means of transportation for close destinations. A photograph (from Austria) appears interesting as it shows the whole family against an airplane, which was depicted as a new achievement of technology, as well as an element of the travelers' experience.

In the foreword to the photo album with photographs of American railways, the museum curator Weston Naef argues that, in the United States, as probably nowhere else, railroads and photography advanced "so completely side by side, mutually reinforcing each other."[22] The idea is elaborated in the introduction by the author of the album Anne M. Lyden who emphasized complex connections between development of railroads and photography as vehicles for social and political change in modern society. Traveling by train, with its "framed" windows' view, was the best way to explore the physical world which photography as a visual medium recorded and defined. In her interpretation of collected American photographs of trains and railroads, Lyden says that such a kind of travel photography "has had an important bearing on how we see ourselves in this society and how our perception continues to evolve."[23]

I would argue that the same can be said about cars and women drivers who have been visible in both Kodak adverts and private photographs since the very beginning of motor technology and car industry all over the world. As Osborn argues in his analysis of photography and the development of bourgeois society, "photographs provide viewers with the means of identifying

Figure 15.2   The Kosiński family on holidays in Austria 1908–1912. *Source*: A photograph from the collection of the Walery Rzewuski Museum of History of Photography in Kraków.

themselves in and with the global system of a modern world,"[24] playing a role of "commodities, sign-commodities, prototypes of the informational and aesthetic goods which dominate our era."[25]

The connection between development of photography and developments in transport technologies reflect processes of the epoch of mobility, communication, capitalist globalization, and the construction of middle-class identity. And both photography and traveling "generally reflect processes of massification and ever-increasing circulations of knowledge about the world."[26] However, photography "became an essential pillar of modernity, not only in terms of its underlying practical technological advances, but also as the means of documenting discovery and on-going social and cultural changes."[27]

Both photography and travel were marked by "the notion of immediacy; . . . generally mirroring a 'speeding up' of social life and the closing down of distances."[28]

The photographs of the Kosiński sisters from the 1920s and 1930s feature images shot during trips, which permitted the sisters to encapsulate in a single frame both the atmosphere of a given house and its inhabitants and habitués, the photographers entertaining the ease offered them by a trip, permitting the sisters to break with the mundane routine. Therefore, their pictures shot in a garden or on a veranda, instead of photos in a parlour, reveal different principles of behavior. Even a suburban dwelling is a place to which one has to travel—the fact emphasized by the image of an automobile—thus, one has

Figure 15.3 The Kosiński family and friends in front of the "Gozdawa" House in Myślenice 21st August, 1929. *Source*: A photograph from the collection of the Walery Rzewuski Museum of History of Photography in Kraków.

to make a trip, standing for a symbolical transgression—a passage to another world.

Here, the car stands for both one's being modern—its presence in images expresses both the idea of modernity and technological development—and one's social status and privileges related to their class. At the same time, from a woman's perspective, the car is the means for gaining freedom. Therefore, Stout emphasizes that she makes the analysis of the prose of female modernists because this prose encapsulates "the experience of doubleness and looping, departing and returning," typical of "the female culture of modernism."[29]

NEW WOMEN FROM THE POLISH GALICIA

The active and "open-air" aspect of the Kosiński sisters' photographs seems to be an almost literal repetition of Eastman Kodak's advertising campaigns, as well as other companies whose commercial offer reached the Polish Galicia. Those advertisements appealed to the middle-class women, who had enough means to buy photographic equipment and materials. Moreover, the rich Kraków bourgeoisie cultivated the tradition of business trips to the commercial centers of Vienna and/or Lvov, along with tourist options—trips to resorts in the Austro-Hungarian Alps and Switzerland and/or the Polish Tatra Mountains. The number of amateur photographs taken by the Kosińskis sisters proves that they really had the benefit of both tourism and cameras, so largely advertised. It is difficult to estimate how well the sisters knew commercial advertisements using "The Kodak Girl," but, considering the broad scale of Eastman's campaign, they must have learned about the idea of a mobile woman with a camera, often in her own car, when they were purchasing their equipment.

The advertisements of photographic cameras and active leisure were promoted in Kraków and the Polish Galicia by various photographic societies, open also to women. This is proved by, for instance, the fact that the Society of Amateur Photographers in Kraków noted women participating in their photography courses in 1908. The minutes of the general assembly of this society, published in installment no. 8 of "Wiadomości Fotograficzne" ["Photographic News"] from 1908, inform that "the Society is happy to see a new team of ladies who, having participated in our beginner course, eagerly re-plant the spring-time of our Society onto a photographic paper." If amateur female photographers took snapshots of spring-time, it means that they made for the open air in the city to take pictures or, even, to make tourist trips to the countryside. Similarly, the "Wiadomości Fotograficzne" magazine includes a review of the Photographic Exhibition in Kraków in 1908, enumerating Ms. Bogdańska among the laureates, who received a letter of prize for her work. Unfortunately, neither the first name of the photographer, nor the title of her work, is given, so it is difficult to determine whether she was a graduate of photography courses for amateurs. Nevertheless, even these two small items of a press release testify to women's presence in the development of photography in Polish Galicia, mostly in big cities, such as Kraków and Lvov.

I would like to embed my interpretation of the Kosiński sisters' tourist photographs in two contexts. The first is the shift in the definition of femininity, women's modes of behavior, and even their looks, taking place at the turn of the nineteenth century, a shift that was grasped by the label "the New Woman." The term appeared as early as 1895 with the wave of modernity and urbanization; it was employed to describe the woman's identity and experience which did not fit within Victorian standards. However, it gained in significance only at the beginning of the twentieth century, when the first generation of middle-class women emerged, gaining rights to education, voting (different from country to country), and becoming active in the public space (in sports societies, social organizations, as well as feminist movements). It was for the first time in the history of manners and morality that "normal" women had access to mass entertainment (cinema), cosmetics, and bold garments—previously reserved mostly for actresses and prostitutes—as well as technology. The telephone occupied the first place among such contraptions, being followed by a car and a photographic camera, used, among other situations, during travels.

The second context for the analysis of the photographs I selected are the writings on traveling/trip-making which emphasize the fact that tourism is one of the most symbolic experiences, accessible to modern subject. Barrie Curtis and Claire Pajaczkowska write on traveling, time, and narration, concluding that "the 'trip' constitutes a lapse in the regular rhythms of mundane existence."[30] The trip is such a method for moving from place to place "where time stands still" or is reserved for "an utopian space of freedom, abundance, transparency."[31]

A way to grasp the unique character of a trip is taking photographs. This means shooting portraits of people in places that are often difficult to identify, but are linked with a concrete experience of the photographer and the photographed. Such places are impossible to reconstruct for others, especially in a domestic environment. Both the fact that one possessed a camera—popular but expensive equipment—and traveled around brought an element of exclusivity in the reality of the early twentieth century. Curtis and Pajaczkowska emphasize that tourist trips are especially linked with the reversal of a mundane order, bearing the traits of a carnival. Each trip offers "a vicarious participation in the pleasures associated with higher status, symbolically marked by exalted points of view, exclusive spaces and privileged services."[32]

Therefore, trip photographs, including those of the Kosiński sisters, feature famous resorts, villas, and restaurant interiors, along with spa gardens and parks.

On the other hand, photographs showing tourist trips indicate that each of them stimulates in every photographer an almost childish fascination with the unknown. Enthusiasm and excitation is linked, inter alia, with the double nature of this passage: a simultaneous movement in the outer and inner spaces. As Curtis and Pajaczkowska notice "this 'outer' journey of physical and spatial mobility can function as a metaphor for the 'interior' journey of the soul, the mind or consciousness."[33] What makes these journeys especially exciting is "the promise of temporal alterity and . . . of a revitalization."[34]

Furthermore, each journey as an act of leaving home could be interpreted as a repetition of one's birth—"an active a painful displacement from the safety . . . of a 'maternal' home."[35] That is why traveling becomes a mixture of fear of and fascination with unknown horizons, lands, and people. Thus, taking photos embraces the elements of gazing and cognition, as well as domesticating and placing oneself in that bravely discovered big, wide world, with a simultaneous identification of its elements. Such an aspect of taking a trip photo, which the Kosiński sisters did, is proved not only by the contents of their images but also detailed annotations made on the reverse of each photograph: date, place, names of peoples in a frame. Since the majority of the pictures feature the parents and siblings of the photographers, their world becomes double-domesticated: by the fact of taking its photograph (fitting into a frame, shooting) and by its description/giving it a name.

Taking photographs is a form of recognition and memorization that extends and intensifies the experience of unfamiliarity which constitutes the nature of travel. The photographic medium intensifies the concentration of one's mind, broadening it during traveling and extending it in sensual and temporal spheres.

Additionally, a photographic camera is used to condense one's experience of displacement in a shot, which could be an expression or a registration of something new, worth to be remembered. Amateur snapshots document the pleasure of discovering and leisure of the visitors who enjoy the privilege of unhurried sightseeing. Hence, a photo camera allows women to take "the enjoyable role of ethnographer/consumer and the positions of heightened authority which accompany the power to totalise and appropriate."[36] Looking through the lens, women assume "the role of structuralists, . . . engaged in an outsiderly process of judgement and comparison."[37]

This thesis finds its support in the case of traveling women, for whom a trip often became an opportunity to exceed the obligatory discipline and structuring order, based on binary oppositions: masculine vs. feminine, public vs. private, social vs. domestic. The repressive character of such traditional divisions often compelled women to travel, an activity that gave them the freedom of not-belonging to any category.

The ease with which they made photographs indicates that they were aware of this freedom, the traces of which can be found in the compositions and themes of shots made by "The Kodak Girls," including those from the Cracovian family, the Kosińskis.

NOTES

1. All described photographs of the Kosińskis' photos can be found in the online collection of The Walery Rzewuski Museum of History of Photography in Kraków.

2. Nóra Séllei, "Introduction: She's Leaving Home," in *She's Leaving Home: Women's Writing in English in a European Context*, ed. Nóra Séllei and June Waudby; "European Connections" ed. Peter Collier, vol. 32, 1–6 (Oxford: Peter Lang 2011), 1.

3. Janis P. Stout, *Through the Window, Out the Door: Women's Narratives of Departure from Austin and Carther to Tyler, Morrison, and Didion* (Tuscaloosa: University of Alabama Press, 1998), 11.

4. Stout, *Through the Window*, 26.

5. Ibidem, 12–13.

6. That one and other advertisements of Eastman Kodak Company, recalled here, can be found at: http://library.duke.edu/digitalcollections/eaa_K0529/, accessed March 20, 2016. http://www.kodakgirl.com/kodakgirlsframe.htm.

7. See http://library.duke.edu/digitalcollections/eaa_K0529/, accessed March 20, 2016.

8. Nancy Martha West, *Kodak and the Lens of Nostalgia* (Charlottesville: University Press of Virginia, 2000), 1–2.

9. West, *Kodak*, 2.

10. Ibidem, 40.

11. Ibidem, 53.

12. Nancy Martha West notes: "In fact the earliest ads (especially those between 1893 and roughly 1920) depict her as remarkably independent. They generally picture her outdoors, frequently on her own or in the company of another Kodak Girl, never in a company of a man. Sunburned, with a hair flying in the wind, she travels in a canoe, on a steamship, in a motorcar; she walks, rides a bicycle, plays tennis, journeys to Japan. If one of the rewards of leisure is an opportunity to enjoy personal freedom, the Kodak Girl is amply rewarded as she reveals in an ideal leisure that is beyond the reach of most American women." See: West, *Kodak*, 55–56.

13. Mike Robinson and David Picard, "Moments, Magic and Memories: Photographing Tourists, Tourist Photographs and Making Worlds," in *The Framed World: Tourism, Tourist and Photography*, ed. Mike Robinson and David Picard (Farnham, UK: Ashgate, 2009), 1.

14. Jonas Larsen, "Geographies of Tourist Photography: Choreographies and Performances," in *Geographies of Communication: The Spatial Turn in Media Studies*, ed. Jesper Falkheimer and André Jansson (Philadelphia: Coronet Books Inc., 2006), 241.

15. Ibidem, 244.

16. Ibidem, 19.

17. Peter D. Osborne, *Travelling Light: Photography, Travel and Visual Culture* (Manchester: Manchester University Press, 2000), 52.

18. Ibidem, 53.

19. Ibidem, 57.

20. Ibidem, 64–65.

21. Robinson, Picard, "Moments," 8.

22. Weston Naef, "Foreword," in *Railroad and Vision: Photography, Travel, and Perception*, ed. Anne M. Lyden, xii–xiii (Los Angeles: The J. Paul Getty Museum 2003), xii.

23. Lyden, *Railroad*, 1.

24. Osborne, *Travelling*, 56.

25. Ibidem.

26. Robinson and Picard, "Moments," 4.

27. Ibidem.

28. Ibidem, 5.

29. Stout, *Through*, 233.

30. Barry Curtis and Claire Pajaczkowska, "'Getting There': Travel, Time and Narrative," in *Traveller's Tales: Narratives of Home and Displacement*, ed. George Robertson, Melinda Mash, and Liska Tickner (London: Routledge, 1994).

31. Ibidem.

32. Ibidem.

33. Ibidem, 200.
34. Ibidem.
35. Ibidem.
36. Ibidem, 201.
37. Ibidem.

REFERENCES

Curtis, Barry, and Claire Pajaczkowska. "'Getting There:' Travel, Time and Narrative." In *Traveller's Tales: Narratives of Home and Displacement*, edited by George Robertson, Melinda Mash, and Liska Tickner. London: Routledge, 1994.

Larsen, Jonas. "Geographies of Tourist Photography: Choreographies and Performances." In *Geographies of Communication: The Spatial Turn in Media Studies*, edited by Jesper Falkheimer and André Jansson. Philadelphia: Coronet Books Incorporated, Göteborg: Nordicom, 2006.

Naef, Weston. "Foreword." In *Railroad and Vision: Photography, Travel, and Perception*, edited by Anne M. Lyden, xii–xiii. Los Angeles: The J. Paul Getty Museum, 2003.

Osborne, Peter D. *Travelling Light: Photography, Travel and Visual Culture*. Manchester: Manchester University Press, 2000.

Robinson, Mike, and David Picard. "Moments, Magic and Memories: Photographing Tourists, Tourist Photographs and Making Worlds." In *The Framed World: Tourism, Tourist and Photography*, edited by Mike Robinson and David Picard, 1–31. Farnham, UK: Ashgate, 2009.

Séllei, Nóra. "Introduction: She's Leaving Home." In *She's Leaving Home: Women's Writing in English in a European Context*, edited by Nóra Séllei and June Waudby. "European Connections," edited by Peter Collier, vol. 32, 1–6, Oxford: Peter Lang 2011.

Stout, Janis P. *Through the Window, Out the Door: Women's Narratives of Departure from Austin and Carther to Tyler, Morrison, and Didion*. Tuscaloosa: University of Alabama Press, 1998.

West, Nancy Martha. *Kodak and the Lens of Nostalgia*. Charlottesville: University Press of Virginia, 2000.

Conclusion

Bridging the Worlds: Opportunities and Challenges

Sabina Owsianowska and Magdalena Banaszkiewicz

This book presents topics discussed within anthropological studies on tourism in general, as well as the issues specific for research in Central and Eastern Europe. Anthropologists are among the authors who deal with traditional and modern forms of travel, representatives of tourism studies, as well as academics from other disciplines who are interested in the cultural and social dimension of travel. Mutual inspirations have resulted in the emergence of new theories, research methods, publications, and forms of cooperation. Nevertheless, there are still many possibilities and challenges that accompany the process of building bridges between different worlds and traditions. The importance of anthropology in tourism is highlighted by, among others, Leite and Graburn,[1] Selwyn,[2] Salazar[3] and di Giovine.[4] For a long time, tourism has not been treated seriously, however, it has recently gained widespread recognition among anthropologists as a subject for research and an instrument for achieving the goals of global ethnography.[5] What is more, the contribution of anthropology should not be underestimated, with its holistic, qualitative, and interpretative approach to research on tourism, which, considering its scale and diversified character, requires a more in-depth scientific reflection.

By identifying gaps in the gathered knowledge, one can indicate the postulated directions for further action. The following volume is also included in the (topical) thread. Based on the characteristics of the situation in Poland and other CEE countries—as included in the introduction—a number of initiatives in the field of education and research on tourism have been presented, indicating the main achievements in the area, as well as the barriers. The case studies discussed in the chapter prepared by researchers from Austria, Bulgaria, Estonia, and Poland, inform us, on one hand, about regional specificity (taking into account topics selected and/or omitted ones, preferred methods, or research perspectives) and, on the other hand, prove that anthropological research on traveling in Central and Eastern Europe touches on the same issues as in other regions, and its results contribute to knowledge on tourism both in the context of anthropology as well as the interdisciplinary approach more relevant to this phenomenon.

Aside from presenting the research output of scholars from Central and Eastern Europe, we intended to create an opportunity for exchange and cooperation between representatives of various disciplines, centers, countries, and generations. The fact that renowned anthropologists from the "center" were invited anchors the volumes in the supra-regional and global perspective (N. Graburn), while at the same time, shows the possibilities for using solutions and knowledge developed in Western countries for the needs of local tourism, cultural heritage, and education (T. Selwyn). M. Buchowski perfectly captures the specificity of the situation. The author reminds the reader of the fact that the "Iron Curtain," which divided the world for long decades after the Second World War, was erected for everyone and the consequences of this division were, and remain, visible on both sides. Suffice to mention mobility limitations, lack of access to information and obstacles in carrying out field research. However, instead of re-diagnosing the existing state of affairs, we were more interested in reflection on the extent of how much the specific experiences of researchers of tourism from Central and Eastern Europe may contribute to a better understanding of changes taking place in the modern world; primarily in terms of tourism as a complex multidimensional phenomenon and subject of research. For example, does the sensitivity gained as a result of historic dependence to empires (the Partitions, the Second World War, communism), a hybrid identity of the subordinate as well as the colonizer, allow the residents of CEE to better understand postcolonial relationships and their importance in tourism (Bachórz, Bloch)? The projects authored by two, young Polish anthropologists (Agata Bachórz[6] and Anna Horolets[7]) are a perfect example of how, by utilizing the classical terminology of postcolonial research, one can deconstruct discourses that had been functioning in the post-Soviet area for decades.

The development of studies on tourism in Central and Eastern Europe after 1989 is characterized by dilemmas and limitations familiar of Western countries: prioritizing the role of tourism in the economy and favoring projects connected with business scattering the milieu in connection with the interdisciplinary character of research, trivializing the leisure-time activity, and neglecting or underestimating the impact it has on people, culture, and environment. Simultaneously, other initiatives emerged which focused on the anthropological dimension of modern travel along with attempts to integrate the milieu (*Introduction*). Publications such as this book, as well as the monograph *Anthropology of Tourism* edited by Sabina Owsianowska and Ryszard Winiarski,[8] issued on the occasion of the fortieth anniversary of the Faculty of Tourism and Leisure of the University of Physical Education in Kraków, monographic issues of journals—*Folia Turistica*[9] or *Turystyka Kulturowa*, edited by Magdalena Banaszkiewicz and Sabina Owsianowska[10]—and also an international conference organized in 2015, are examples from recent years exclusively from Poland, though there are also meetings of anthropologists studying the issues of tourism in other countries of the former Eastern Bloc (such as the breakthrough meeting of researchers during a triple session entitled—*Tourism in (Post)socialist Eastern Europe* at the biennial meeting of European Association of Social Anthropologists which took place in Tallinn, Estonia, in 2014).

Nelson Graburn recalls the origins of anthropology of tourism and his personal engagement in the development of subdisciplines, as well as current topics requiring revision and a critical approach. Starting with the earliest topics discussed by anthropologists in the 1970s and 1980s, such as commodification and cultural change or host and guest relationships, to issues that emerged on the wave of the reflexive turn in anthropology (authenticity, subjectivity, narrative) or resulted from orienting toward gender studies in the 1990s.

The issues touched upon in the remaining chapters correspond with the list of the themes proposed by Graburn, although some topics are better represented (e.g., heritage), while others not so much (e.g., disciplinarity). They include ethnographies of various places—from Russia, through the Balkans to India (Bachórz, Bethmann, Bloch, Selwyn, Sznajder, and Kosmala)—and historical views (Banaszkiewicz, Radkiewicz); field research and discourse analysis (Bachórz, Bloch, Nieszczerzewska, Owsianowska, Wieczorkiewicz); case studies illustrating the particularity but also the universality of the topics discussed (Mikos von Rohrscheidt, Zinganel, Zowisło, Wieczorkiewicz).

It may be noted that the development of anthropological research on tourism in CEE is currently twofold: first, it is the pursuit of gathering works on the anthropology of tourism and presenting them to a wider audience, and second, for exchanging knowledge and strengthening cooperation within and outside of the region. A text authored by Tom Selwyn shows what might be the theoretical and practical effects of cooperation for tourism in post-Soviet and post-conflict destinations (Sarajevo). In detail, the author describes the consecutive stages of the project, the essence of which is a dialogical attitude, through which the mutual inspirations and experience of both parties involved—an anthropologist from Western Europe as well as residents and students—help with working out strategies for development, including symbols that are key to creating an image of tourism in the locations.

Obviously, in the case of every scientific work, this collection of texts does not exhaust the range of issues related to the anthropological perspective in tourism research. An important topic that has not been included in the preceding publication is the issue of modern technology and its influence on the experience of traveling. Although netnography is a relatively young research method, the intersections of the virtual and real worlds and their mutual interdependence arouse interest among anthropologists who see how strongly the behavioral patterns change by means of constant traveling in the virtual world.

"The future of the anthropology of tourism depends both on the development of anthropology, as well as transformations of tourism itself,"[11] as it has been rightly pointed out by Krzysztof Podemski, bringing the most important sociological and anthropological concepts of travel and tourism to Polish researchers. The above conclusion is derived not only from the fact that contemporary anthropologists have ceased to focus on the Other, strangeness, exotics, or relations between guests and hosts in terms of intercultural contact, but also that they have begun to enter new areas, describing everyday life and such forms of activities as having a barbecue on the balcony or leisure time spent on a plot or at a holiday cabin. Contemporary issues require the adaptation of the ethnographic research instrument (Kaaristo), paradigms allowing one to better describe relations between hosts and guests, tradition and modernity, the local and the global, voluntary and compulsory forms of migration, anti-tourist attitudes in cities visited by millions each year and threats to natural ecosystems.

One of the most important contemporary challenges is related to the scale of the tourism industry's impact on the natural, social, and cultural environments. The dysfunctions of mass tourism were written about as soon as the consequences of its uncontrolled expansion were realized, and since the 1970s, the critical voices have become ever louder and more numerous. The concept of sustainable development, promoted on a local, regional, and global scale is an attempt to help host communities get out of this deadlock. After several decades of efforts, it is evident that, despite solid theoretical development of the subject and the implementation of a number of best practices beneficial from the view of the host communities, there is still much to be done. Theory is not always compatible with practice, while investors' interim plans and short-term profits win when compared with postulates for finding balance between the interests of all the parties involved in the tourism system and its surroundings. Greater involvement of anthropologists in this situation could make it easier to learn about the needs of people meeting along the way to determine what steps to take, which is pointed to by Michael di Giovine.[12] While anthropologists have not been asked for consultations pertaining to tourism development issues, their advisory role has the potential to dramatically increase in the coming years.

A symptomatic phenomenon which is proof of the growing role of the anthropology of tourism is its presence as a subject in university curricula.

The subjects that familiarize students with the anthropology of tourism are primarily taught within ethnology, cultural anthropology, and cultural studies. On the other hand, in faculties specializing in teaching tourism and recreation as a subdiscipline within the framework of physical education or faculties oriented on an economic/marketing perspective, one can find more subjects related to tourism, but also taught from a humanist and social point of view.[13] In that sense, expanding educational content at an academic level with the issues of the anthropology of tourism, significantly contributes to the introduction of people to the tourism market who are more aware of their responsibility connected with their activity, as well as being conducive to creating attitudes desirable in the view of sustainable tourism. It should be noted that, it is important to maintain balance in educating different groups of interest. As Michael di Giovine stresses: "In tourism development, there is often a concerted effort to educate the locals about the benefits of embracing tourism. Respondents turned the tables, focusing on educating tourists on local culture and as well as conservation methods."[14] The necessity to pay greater attention to tourists themselves, often very negatively assessed by anthropologists for their destructive activity, and promoting positive behavioral patterns among them—is a challenge for both the anthropologists representing the academic milieu as well as for applied anthropologists. Undoubtedly, popularizing knowledge through traditional and new media or through activity in NGOs working for the development of sustainable tourism, can serve this goal. An interesting initiative attempting to implement a postulate of the broad education of tourists and representatives of the tourism industry by means of the active involvement of researchers (including mainly anthropologists), is the activity of *The Workshop for the Responsible Tourism—Post-tourist*.[15] The creators of that educational platform have set themselves the objective to explain the mechanisms governing tourism and aim to equip (potential) tourists with the awareness of global interdependencies, the causes and consequences of their behavior, as well as a self-awareness of being subject to the psychological, commercial, and ideological processes related to travel and travel narratives. As a result of such ventures, avoiding situations where visitors "who are often well-intentioned but ill-informed about cultural norms, local flora/fauna, etc., can cause a lot of damage,"[16] seems more realistic.

Involving anthropologists as observers and analysts of the processes of cultural change is the cornerstone of this discipline. With the emergence of new social-and-cultural phenomena, such as mass travel or virtual spaces, anthropologists are entering new research areas and modifying existing research methods and perspectives to be even more effective tools for description and interpretation. The art of understanding the world is the art of crossing borders and looking beyond the known horizon, while also remembering where we come from. The aim of this book was an attempt to look at the past as well as the future of the anthropology of tourism in Central and Eastern Europe. The range of issues addressed by authors can and should be widened, although the dynamics of the changes that we observed and tried to reflect on is inevitably elusive. Nevertheless, it is time to come to a stop to get the right perspective. This book represents the moment we invited you to join a conversation in which building a bridge from the past to the future is possible.

NOTES

1. Naomi Leite and Nelson Graburn, "Anthropological Interventions in Tourism Studies," in *Handbook of Tourism Studies*, ed. Mike Robinson and Tazim Jamal (London: Sage, 2009), 35–64.

2. Tom Selwyn, ed., *The Tourist Image: Myth and Mythmaking in Tourism* (Chichester: Wiley, 1996); Tom Selwyn, "Antropologia podróżowania, turystyki i pielgrzymowania," in *Antropologia turystyki/Anthropology of Tourism*, edited by Sabina Owsianowska and Ryszard Winiarski (Kraków: University of Physical Education in Kraków Press, 2017).

3. Noel Salazar, "Imagineering Otherness: Anthropological Legacies in Contemporary Tourism," *Anthropological Quarterly* 86, no. 3 (2013): 669–96.

4. Michael Di Giovine, "Anthropologists Weigh in on the Sustainability of Tourism," *Anthropology News* website, accessed August 14, 2017, doi:10.1111/AN.572.

5. Michael Di Giovine, "Tourism Research as 'Global Ethnography,'" *Anthropologies*, April 15, 2011, accessed August 14, 2017, http://www.anthropologiesproject.org/2011/04/tourism-research-as-global-ethnography.html.

6. Agata Bachórz, *Rosja w tekście i w doświadczeniu. Analiza współczesnych polskich relacji z podróży* (Kraków: Nomos, 2013).

7. Anna Horolets, *Konformizm, bunt, nostalgia. Turystyka niszowsa z Polski do krajów byłego ZSRR* (Kraków: Universitas, 2013).

8. Sabina Owsianowska and Ryszard Winiarski, eds., *Antropologia turystyki/Anthropology of Tourism* (Kraków: University of Physical Education in Kraków Press, 2017).

9. Magdalena Banaszkiewicz and Sabina Owsianowska, eds., "The Anthropology of Tourism," *Folia Turistica* 37 (2015); Magdalena Banaszkiewicz and Sabina Owsianowska, eds., "Turystyka w antropologicznej perspektywie," *Folia Turistica* 39 (2016).

10. Magdalena Banaszkiewicz and Sabina Owsianowska, eds., "Relacje między turystyką, kulturą a dziedzictwem," *Turystyka Kulturowa* 3 (2016).

11. Krzysztof Podemski, "Antropologia turystyki," in *Turystyka w naukach humanistycznych*, ed. Ryszard Winiarski (Warsaw: Wydawnictwo Naukowe PWN, 2008): 62.

12. Di Giovine, "Anthropologists Weigh."

13. Magdalena Banaszkiewicz and Sabina Owsianowska, "Antropologia a edukacja i badania w zakresie turystyki," in *Antropologia turystyki/Anthropology of Tourism*, 101–112.

14. Di Giovine, "Anthropologists Weigh."
15. Post-turysta, http://post-turysta.pl/Idea, accessed August 14, 2017.
16. Di Giovine, "Anthropologists Weigh."

REFERENCES

Bachórz, Agata. *Rosja w tekście i w doświadczeniu. Analiza współczesnych polskich relacji z podróży*. Kraków: Nomos, 2013.

Banaszkiewicz, Magdalena, and Sabina Owsianowska. "Antropologia a edukacja i badania w zakresie turystyki." In *Antropologia turystyki/Anthropology of Tourism*, edited by Sabina Owsianowska and Ryszard Winiarski. Kraków: University of Physical Education in Kraków Press, 2017, 101–112.

———, eds. "The Anthropology of Tourism." *Folia Turistica* 37 (2015).

———, eds. "Turystyka w antropologicznej perspektywie." *Folia Turistica* 39 (2016).

———, eds. "Relacje między turystyką, kulturą a dziedzictwem." *Turystyka Kulturowa* 3 (2016).

Di Giovine, Michael. "Anthropologists Weigh in on the Sustainability of Tourism." *Anthropology News* website. Accessed August 14, 2017. doi:10.1111/AN.572.

———. "Tourism Research as 'Global Ethnography'." *Anthropologies*, April 15, 2011. http://www.anthropologiesproject.org/2011/04/tourism-research-as-global-ethnography.html.

Horolets, Anna. *Konformizm, bunt, nostalgia. Turystyka niszowsa z Polski do krajów byłego ZSRR*. Kraków: Universitas, 2013.

Leite, Naomi, and Nelson Graburn. "Anthropological Interventions in Tourism Studies." In *Handbook of Tourism Studies*, edited by Mike Robinson and Tazim Jamal, 35–64. London: Sage, 2009.

Magdalena Banaszkiewicz and Sabina Owsianowska, eds. "Relacje między turystyką, kulturą a dziedzictwem." *Turystyka Kulturowa* 3 (2016).

Owsianowska, Sabina, and Ryszard Winiarski. *Antropologia turystyki/ Anthropology of Tourism*. Kraków: University of Physical Education in Kraków Press, 2017.

Podemski, Krzysztof. "Antropologia turystyki." In *Turystyka w naukach humanistycznych*, edited by Ryszard Winiarski, 48–64. Warsaw: Wydawnictwo Naukowe PWN, 2008.

Post-turysta, http://post-turysta.pl/Idea. Accessed August 14, 2017.

Salazar Noel. "Imagineering Otherness: Anthropological Legacies in Contemporary Tourism." *Anthropological Quarterly* 86, no. 3 (2013): 669–96.

Selwyn, Tom. "Antropologia podróżowania, turystyki i pielgrzymowania." In *Antropologia turystyki/Anthropology of Tourism*, edited by Sabina Owsianowska and Ryszard Winiarski. Kraków: University of Physical Education in Kraków Press, 2017.

———, ed. *The Tourist Image: Myth and Mythmaking in Tourism*. Chichester: Wiley, 1996.

Index

agency, 72, 181, 182, 184, 188, 262
alcotourism, 13, 165–67, 169–76, 177n10
alienation, 30, 31, 111–12
American Anthropological Association, 30, 36, 71, 73
Anglophone, 4–5, 12, 16n11, 27, 28, 43n54, 44n64;
Snake, 11, 36, 39n1
anthropological:
approach, 73;
center, 77;
concepts, 10, 28, 314;
dimensions, 109;
gaze, 39;
interventions, 28, 73;
investigations, 73;
journals, xii;
knowledge, 78;
methods/methodology, 74;
perspective(s), 5, 6, 39, 313;
research, 1, 6, 8, 9, 11, 12, 28, 81, 82n25, 182, 313;
scholarship, 4;
study/studies, 1, 72, 311;
subject, 71;
theories and methods, 9–10;
works, 167

anthropology of tourism, xi–xii, 5, 10, 11–12, 14, 27, 34–35, 51, 71, 72, 73, 123, 135, 167, 181, 313, 314–15, 316
Anthropology of Tourism Interest Group, 73
Aristotle, 109–10
Ash, John, 29, 177n10
Ash, Timothy G., 150, 153, 158n45
Ashworth, Gregory, 32–33, 42n38, 143, 155n3, 234n49
ATTP (anthropology of travel, tourism, and pilgrimage), 51, 52, 63–67
Austria, 113, 148–50, 158n48, 273–75, 278, 283, 286, 287n7, 288n9, 303, 311
authenticity, 30–31, 32, 73, 114, 167, 190, 200, 208, 209, 210, 219, 220, 221, 223, 224, 226, 230, 231, 264–65, 313
authorized heritage discourse, 33

Bachórz, Agata, 10, 13, 312, 313
Banaszkiewicz, Magdalena, 10, 12, 27, 35, 39, 39n3, 78, 313
Banaszkiewicz, Mikołaj, 124
barbarian, 165, 169, 172–73, 174, 176, 177n10
Bauman, Zygmunt, 9, 40n5, 43n57

319

About the Editors

Magdalena Banaszkiewicz, a cultural anthropologist, is assistant professor in the Institute of Intercultural Studies at Jagiellonian University in Kraków, lecturer at Andrzej Frycz Modrzewski Kraków University, and visiting professor at the University of Rochester (New York), University of Sophia (Bulgaria), and the European University Viadrina (Germany). The main topic of her research are dissonances connected with the commodification of socialist/communist heritage in Central and Eastern Europe. Recently, she has been exploring tourism in the Chernobyl Exclusion Zone (the research project 2016/23/D/HS3/01960 funded by the National Science Centre, Poland). Her monograph, *The Intercultural Dialogue in Tourism: The Case of Polish and Russian Relationships* was published in 2012 by Jagiellonian University Press. Since then, she has published several book chapters (i.e. in *Heritage of Death*, ed. by M. Frihammar and H. Silverman), and journal articles (*Journal of Tourism and Cultural Change* and *International Journal of Tourism Anthropology*, among others). She is also an editorial board member of "Turystyka Kulturowa" ("Cultural Tourism").

Sabina Owsianowska, PhD, is assistant professor in the Department of the Theory of Leisure and Tourism at the University of Physical Education in Kraków, Poland. She co-operates with the Institute of Intercultural Studies at Jagiellonian University; was lecturer in international projects conducted by the Czech, Slovak, and Polish universities; and visiting professor in Slovenia, Finland, and France. She focuses on anthropological aspects of tourism, cultural heritage tourism, dissonant heritage in Central and Eastern Europe, tourism promotion, semiotics, and gender issues. She is the author of several book chapters, journal articles, conference proceedings, and reviews, and her work has been published in *Folia Turistica, Journal of Tourism and Cultural*

Change, Annals of Tourism Research, Via Tourism Review, and *Turystyka Kulturowa/Cultural Tourism.* She is a member of the editorial board of the scientific journal *Folia Turistica.* In 2015, she was the main co-organizer of the International Scientific Conference "Anthropology of Tourism—Heritage and Perspectives." She is the co-editor, with R. Winiarski, of the Polish monograph *Anthropology of Tourism*, published in 2017.

About the Contributors

Agata Bachórz, PhD, is assistant professor at the Chair of Social Anthropology, University of Gdańsk. She is the author of the book *Russia in Text and in Experience: An Analysis of Contemporary Polish Travel Narratives* (2013), devoted to Polish tourists traveling to this country. She was the manager of the project, *Leisure Practices and Perception of Nature: Polish Tourists and Migrants in Iceland* (2014–2016). Her research interests include post-socialism and post-colonialism, tourism and travel, and lifestyle and food in society.

Carla Bethmann, PhD, is an anthropologist with a research focus on Central and Eastern Europe. She holds a PhD in cultural anthropology from Martin Luther University of Halle-Wittenberg (Germany). Her publications include the monograph *"Clean, Friendly, Profitable"? Tourism and the Tourism Industry in Varna, Bulgaria* (2013).

Natalia Bloch, PhD, is a cultural anthropologist and assistant professor in the Department of Ethnology and Cultural Anthropology at Adam Mickiewicz University in Poznań, Poland. She specializes in the anthropology of mobility (refugees and migration studies, anthropology of tourism) in the postcolonial context, with a special focus on the postcolonial legacy in the contemporary mobility regimes. She has conducted fieldwork in Tibetan refugee settlements as well as among host communities and migrants working in an informal tourism sector in India. She has published in, among others, the *Annals of Tourism Research* and *Critical Asian Studies*.

Michał Buchowski, anthropologist, is head of the Department of Ethnology and Cultural Anthropology at Adam Mickiewicz University in Poznań,

Poland, and the chair for Comparative Central European Study at the European University Viadrina in Frankfurt, Germany. His research interests concentrate on anthropology of post-socialist societies and neoliberalism, anthropological theories (world anthropologies), as well as migration, multiculturalism, and tolerance. A member of the Committee of Ethnological Sciences at the Polish Academy of Science, he was president of the European Association of Social Anthropologists from 2009 to 2011. He is co-editor (with H. Cervinkova and Z. Uherek) of the volume *Rethinking Ethnography in Central Europe* (2015). Recently, he has been focusing on anthropology of sport, publishing with A. Schwell, N. Szogs, and M. Kowalska, *New Ethnographies of Football in Europe: People, Passions, Politics* (2016). Currently, he conducts a study on immigrants in the Kansai Region in Japan.

Nelson Graburn was educated in natural sciences and anthropology at Cambridge, McGill, and the University of Chicago. After a postdoc with Northwestern University studying cultural change and tourist arts of the Canadian Inuit, he became professor of anthropology at the University of California in 1964, where he also served as curator of North American Ethnology at the Hearst Museum of Anthropology, and as co-chair of Canadian Studies, 1986–2009. He served as senior professor at the International Institute of Culture, Tourism and Development at London Metropolitan University, 2007–2011. He has served as co-chair of Berkeley's Tourism Studies Working Group since 2012. His recent research has focused on the study of art, tourism, museums and the expression and representation of identity with the Canadian Inuit, and in Japan and China. His main publications include *Eskimos without Igloos* (1969), *The Cultural Structure of Japanese Domestic Tourism* (1983), and 旅游人类学论文集 [*Anthropology in the Age of Tourism*] (2009) and, as editor, *Ethnic and Tourist Arts* (1976), *The Anthropology of Tourism* (1983) and, as co-editor, *Tourism Social Sciences* (with Jafar Jafari, 1981), *Multiculturalism in the New Japan* (with John Ertl, 2008), *Tourism Imaginaries through an Anthropological Lens* (with Noel Salazar, 2014), and *Tourism Imaginaries at the Disciplinary Crossroads* (with Maria Gravari-Barbas, 2016).

Maarja Kaaristo, PhD, is research associate in the Department of Marketing, Retail and Tourism at Manchester Metropolitan University, United Kingdom, and researcher in the Department of Ethnology at the University of Tartu, Estonia. Her main research interests include tourism, mobilities, waterscapes, embodiment, and history of European ethnology. Her recent publications include "Everyday Life and Water Tourism Mobilities: Mundane Aspects of Canal Travel" in *Tourism Geographies*, "Value of Silence: Mediating

Aural Environments in Estonian Rural Tourism" in *Journal of Tourism and Cultural Change*, and "Studying Home Fields: Encounters of Ethnology and Anthropology in Estonia" in *Journal of Baltic Studies*. She is the co-editor of the first Estonian socio-cultural anthropology textbook published in 2017.

Katarzyna Kosmala, PhD, is chair in culture, media, and visual arts; R&E development lead for culture and creativity at the School of Media, Culture, and Society, University of the West of Scotland; a curator; and art writer. In 2010–2011, she was a visiting research fellow at GEXcel, Institute of Thematic Gender Studies, Linköping University and Örebro University, Sweden, and visiting professor at the Getulio Vargas Foundation in Rio de Janeiro, Brazil. She researches cultural labor and discourses of creativity, identity, and community in the context of a globalizing network society, heritage and participation, art production and enterprise, and arts-run projects, as well as gender and politics of representation. Her recent publications include *Precarious Spaces: The Arts, Social and Organizational Change* (co-editor, 2016), *Sexing the Border: Gender, Art and New Media in Central and Eastern Europe* (editor, 2014), *Art Inquiry on Crossing Borders: Imaging Europe, Representing Periphery* (co-editor, 2013), and *Imagining Masculinities: Spatial and Temporal Representation and Visual Culture* (2013). She also writes regularly about video and new media art in international art journals and catalogues. She also co-curated the series *Curating Europes' Futures*.

Armin Mikos von Rohrscheidt is editor-in-chief of Polish science journal *Turystyka Kulturowa (Cultural Tourism)*. He is professor for culture management at GSW Milenium in Gniezno, Poland. He holds PhDs in philosophy, theology, and cultural sciences in the field of culture tourism. He is lecturer on various fields of study in the realm of cultural tourism. He is author of the first Polish academic monograph of its kind on tourism, *Culture Tourism: Phenomenon, Potential, Perspectives* (2008); a science monograph of themed trials, *Regional Thematic Routes: Idea, Potential, Organization* (2010); five other books, and, in addition, over sixty science publications concerning cultural tourism. Since 2008 he has been initiator of the science journal *Cultural Tourism*. He is a consultant of two European projects on military tourism. He co-owns the travel agency "KulTour.pl," a tour-operator specializing in culture touring, study, and thematic visits. He is also an active tour leader and city guide, organizing cultural excursions in Poland and Europe. He is author of the first Polish monograph on modern tour guiding (2014). His field of research is the cultural basis and the organization of respective sectors of cultural tourism: city tourism, cultural trails, thematic trails, military tourism, and city guiding.

Małgorzata Nieszczerzewska, PhD, is lecturer in the Department of Cultural Urban Studies in the Institute of Cultural Studies at Adam Mickiewicz University in Poznań, Poland. In 2007, she received her PhD in humanities on the basis of the dissertation *Narratives of Urban Imaginary*, a cultural analysis of the city space and the types of urban imaginary used by the creation of different city narratives (literature, film, city plan, and theory of the city). The book with the same title was published in 2009. Her recent areas of research include the question of urban imagination, studies on the city in literature and visual culture, and the question of ruins and abandoned places in culture. She teaches sociology of culture, animation of local cultures, history of cities, and knowledge about city cultures in the Institute of Cultural Studies.

Małgorzata Radkiewicz is assistant professor at the Institute of Audio Visual Arts at Jagiellonian University. Her research interests and publications focus on women's issues, and representation of gender in film, photography, and the arts. She published a book about women filmmakers and another about Polish cinema of the 1990s. In her book *Female Gaze: Film Theory and Practice of Women Directors and Artists* (2010), she addresses the issue of women's cinema and arts in terms of feminist theory. In her last book, *Modern Women on Cinema*, she analyzes selected film texts and reviews written by women in Poland from 1918 to 1945.

Tom Selwyn is professorial research associate in the School of Oriental and African Studies (SOAS) at the University of London and visiting professor at NHTV Breda University of Applied Sciences, Netherlands, and the University of Bethlehem, Palestine. He was awarded an Emeritus Professorial Research Fellowship by the Leverhulme Trust in 2014. He is widely published in the field of anthropology of tourism/pilgrimage with regional interests in Palestine/Israel and Bosnia-Herzegovina. His Leverhulme research is based on his direction or co-direction of four major research and development projects in Palestine and Bosnia-Herzegovina for the European Commission between 1995 and 2010 and focuses on the political economy and socio-cultural organization of tourism in Bethlehem and Sarajevo. In 2012–2015, he co-directed a research program on the future of tourism in Ethiopia for the UK's Department for International Development and British Council. He founded the MA in Anthropology of Travel, Tourism, and Pilgrimage at SOAS in 2010 and was director of studies until 2014. In 2009, he was awarded the Lucy Mair medal by the Royal Anthropological Institute, for which he was Honorary Librarian, council member for a decade, and founder of its tourism committee. His recent related publications include "Tears on the Border: The Case of Rachel's Tomb, Bethlehem, Palestine"; co-editor of *Contentious Politics of the Mediterranean: Essays in Honour of Charles Tilly*

(2011); "Shifting Borders and Dangerous Liminalities: The Case of Rye Bay" in *Liminal Landscapes: Travel, Experience and Spaces In-between* (2011); "Anthropology of Hospitality" In *The Routledge Handbook of Cultural Tourism* (2012); "The Self in the World and the World in the Self: The SOAS MA in Anthropology of Travel, Tourism, and Pilgrimage" in *Journal of Tourism Challenges and Trends* (2013); "Tourism, Sight Prevention, and Cultural Shutdown: Symbolic Violence in Fragmented Landscapes" in *Tourism and Violence* (2014). His essay on the nature of anthropology of travel, tourism, and pilgrimage will be published as an entry in the forthcoming *Encyclopedia of Anthropology* (2018).

Anna Sznajder, PhD, is a freelance researcher. She recently obtained her PhD from the School of Media, Culture, and Society at the University of the West of Scotland. Her research interests include history of lace-making in Central and Eastern Europe, women's work strategies, traditional crafts, and anthropology of ageing. She is a member of the International Bobbin and Needle Lace Organization and the Polish Ethnological Society.

Anna Wieczorkiewicz is professor at the Institute of Ethnology and Anthropology, University of Warsaw. She cooperates with the Graduate School for Social Research (Polish Academy of Sciences). Her research interests include anthropology of tourism and travel, anthropology of the body and embodiment, and anthropology of literature. During her research career, she also implemented projects during scientific internships and research grants in the United Kingdom (universities in Manchester and Leicester), Denmark (University of Copenhagen), Italy (universities in Florence and Milan), the Netherlands (School of Social Sciences in Amsterdam), Sweden (Stockholm University), and the United States (San Diego State University; Kosciuszko Foundation, New School; Fulbright Foundation). She published the books *Czarna kobieta na białym tle. Dyptyk biograficzny* [A Black Woman on a White Background: A Biographical Diptych] (2013), *Monstruarium* (2009), *Apetyt turysty. O doświadczaniu świata w podróży* [The Tourist Appetite: About the Experience the World During Travel] (2008), *Muzeum ludzkich ciał. Anatomia spojrzenia* (Museum of Human Bodies: Anathomy of the Gaze] (2000), and *Wędrowcy fikcyjnych światów. Rycerz, pielgrzym i włóczęga* [The Knight, The Pilgrim and the Rough: Travelers in Fictional Worlds] (1997). She is also the co-editor of several books on the anthropology of tourism and the body.

Michael Zinganel, PhD, graduated from Graz University of Technology, Austria, and obtained a PhD in contemporary history from the University of Vienna. In 2003 he was a research fellow at the IFK (International Centre for Cultural Studies) in Vienna. From 2001 to 2010, he worked as assistant professor at the Institute of Building Typology at the Graz University of Technology. From 2011 to 2015, he was a research adviser at the postgraduate academy of Bauhaus Dessau Foundation. In the year 2017/18 he had been guest professor at Alpe-Adria University Klagenfurt. Currently, he is teaching at Webster University and Technical University Vienna.

He works with cultural historians, writers, curators, and artists on projects about mass tourism, urban and transnational mobility, and migration: In 2010 he cofounded the research platform "Tracing Spaces." Inter alias, he co-edited, with Elke Beyer and Anke Hagemann, *Holiday after the Fall—Seaside Architecture and Urbanism in Bulgaria and Croatia* (2013). From 2014 to 2016, with Michael Hieslmair, he was head of research on the project *Stop & Go: Nodes of Transformation and Transition* and cocurated the exhibition ROAD*REGISTERS at the Academy of Fine Arts Vienna (2016). They also edited a special issue of the magazine *dérive—Zeitschrift für Stadtforschung* (No.63/ 2016). Currently, he is working on the history and transformation of a multimodal logistic terminal close to the centre of Vienna.

Maria Zowisło is a philosopher and head of the Department of Philosophy and Sociology of Tourism in the Faculty of Tourism and Leisure at the University of Physical Education in Kraków, Poland. Her main research areas are history of ideas, philosophy of culture, and philosophical anthropology. She is an author of several dozen articles, book contributions, and two books (in Polish), *Philosophy and Sport—the Horizons of Dialogue* (2001) and *Between Relic and Archetype: A Critique of the Mythological Reason* (2006). Her main publications in English are "Ecofeminism and Its Attitude towards Environmental Problems" in *Determinants of Ecological Awareness in Various Scientific Disciplines* from the Centre for Human and Environmental Studies at University of Silesia, Katowice (1992); "Jung's Concept of Individuation and the Problem of Alienation," *Analecta Husserliana*, Vol. LXVII (2000); "Existential Overcoming of Phenomenology in Hans Blumenberg's Philosophy of Life and Myth," *Analecta Husserliana*, Vol. CIII (2009); "On Virtue in the Context of Sport," *Physical Culture and Sport: Studies and Research*, Vol. XLVII (2009); and "Leisure as a Category of Philosophy, Culture and Recreation," *Physical Culture and Sport: Studies and Research*, Vol. L (2010).